D1064538

A COMPANION TO MICHAEL OAKESHOTT

A COMPANION TO

MICHAEL OAKESHOTT

EDITED BY PAUL FRANCO AND LESLIE MARSH

THE PENNSYLVANIA STATE UNIVERSITY PRESS
UNIVERSITY PARK, PENNSYLVANIA

Library of Congress Cataloging-in-Publication Data

A companion to Michael Oakeshott / edited by
Paul Franco and Leslie Marsh.
p.   cm.
Summary: "A collection of critical essays by leading
scholars on British political philosopher Michael
Oakeshott. Essays cover all aspects of Oakeshott's thought,
from his theory of knowledge and philosophies of history,
religion, art, and education to his reflections on morality,
politics, and law"—Provided by publisher.
Includes bibliographical references and index.
ISBN 978-0-271-05407-0 (cloth : alk. paper)
1. Oakeshott, Michael, 1901–1990.
I. Franco, Paul, 1956– .
II. Marsh, Leslie.

BI649.0344C66 2012
192—dc23
2012014272

The Pennsylvania State University Press is a member
of the Association of American University Presses.

It is the policy of The Pennsylvania State University
Press to use acid-free paper. Publications on uncoated
stock satisfy the minimum requirements of American
National Standard for Information Sciences—Perma-
nence of Paper for Printed Library Material,
ANSI Z39.48–1992.

This book is printed on Nature's Natural, which
contains 50% post-consumer waste.

For Shannon—LM

For Jill—PF

CONTENTS

Acknowledgments / ix
List of Abbreviations / xi

Introduction / 1
Paul Franco and Leslie Marsh

1. The Pursuit of Intimacy, or Rationalism in Love / 15
Robert Grant

PART ONE: THE CONVERSATION OF MANKIND

2. The Victim of Thought: The Idealist Inheritance / 47
David Boucher

3. Philosophy and Its Moods: Oakeshott on the Practice of Philosophy / 70
Kenneth McIntyre

4. Michael Oakeshott's Philosophy of History / 95
Geoffrey Thomas

5. Radical Temporality and the Modern Moral Imagination: Two Themes
in the Thought of Michael Oakeshott / 120
Timothy Fuller

6. The Religious Sensibility of Michael Oakeshott / 134
Elizabeth Corey

7. Whatever It Turns Out to Be: Oakeshott on Aesthetic Experience / 151
Corey Abel

8. *Un Début dans la Vie Humaine*: Michael Oakeshott on Education / 173
Paul Franco

PART TWO: POLITICAL PHILOSOPHY

9. Michael Oakeshott on the History of Political Thought / 197
Martyn Thompson

10. Oakeshott and Hobbes / 217
Noel Malcolm

11. The Fate of Rationalism in Oakeshott's Thought / 232
Kenneth Minogue

12. Oakeshott and Hayek: Situating the Mind / 248
Leslie Marsh

13. Oakeshott as Conservative / 268
Robert Devigne

14. Oakeshott on Civil Association / 290
Noël O'Sullivan

15. Oakeshott on Law / 312
Steven Gerencser

Notes on Contributors / 337
Index / 341

ACKNOWLEDGMENTS

The editors would like to thank Bowdoin College for its generosity in supporting the production of this book. We would also like to thank Rory Brinkmann for indexing the book, Shannon Selin for proofreading it, and David Hardwick for providing office support.

ABBREVIATIONS

BLPES   Archival material at the British Library of Political and Economic Science at the London School of Economics (LSE). Refer to file number (e.g., 1/1/3).

CPJ   *The Concept of a Philosophical Jurisprudence: Essays and Reviews, 1926–1951*, ed. Luke O'Sullivan (Exeter: Imprint Academic, 2007).

EM   *Experience and Its Modes* (1933; repr., Cambridge: Cambridge University Press, 1966).

HCA   *Hobbes on Civil Association* (1975; repr., Indianapolis: Liberty Fund, 2000).

LHPT   *Lectures in the History of Political Thought*, ed. Terry Nardin and Luke O'Sullivan (Exeter: Imprint Academic, 2006).

MPME   *Morality and Politics in Modern Europe: The Harvard Lectures*, ed. Shirley Letwin (New Haven: Yale University Press, 1993).

OH   *On History and Other Essays* (Oxford: Basil Blackwell, 1983).

OHC   *On Human Conduct* (Oxford: Clarendon Press, 1975).

PD   Private Diaries (private collection, various dates).

PFPS   *The Politics of Faith and the Politics of Scepticism*, ed. Timothy Fuller (New Haven: Yale University Press, 1996).

RP   *Rationalism in Politics and Other Essays*, ed. Timothy Fuller, new and exp. ed. (Indianapolis: Liberty Fund, 1990).

RPML   *Religion, Politics, and the Moral Life*, ed. Timothy Fuller (New Haven: Yale University Press, 1993).

SPD   *The Social and Political Doctrines of Contemporary Europe* (Cambridge: Cambridge University Press, 1939).

VMES   *The Vocabulary of a Modern European State: Essays and Reviews, 1952–1988*, ed. Luke O'Sullivan (Exeter: Imprint Academic, 2008).

VLL   *The Voice of Liberal Learning: Michael Oakeshott on Education*, ed. Timothy Fuller (New Haven: Yale University Press, 1989).

WIH   *What Is History? And Other Essays*, ed. Luke O'Sullivan (Exeter: Imprint Academic, 2004).

INTRODUCTION

Paul Franco and Leslie Marsh

It is now more than twenty years since Michael Oakeshott died on December 18, 1990. In that year the first book-length studies of the whole compass of his thought appeared: Paul Franco's *The Political Philosophy of Michael Oakeshott* and Robert Grant's *Oakeshott*. Since then there has been a veritable flood of scholarship, consisting of dozens of monographs and many more dozens of articles, devoted to every aspect of his thought, from his conservatism, political philosophy, and theory of history to his aesthetics, philosophy of religion, and ideas on education.[1] Given the sheer volume of this scholarship, the time is ripe to harvest some results and come to some provisional conclusions about the nature and significance of Oakeshott's multifarious philosophical contributions. This is what this volume of essays aims to do. We have asked a variety of Oakeshott scholars—some of them long-established authorities, others promising younger researchers—each to write an essay on a particular aspect of Oakeshott's thought, summarizing its main features and assessing its ultimate significance. The result, we believe, is an authoritative and synoptic guide to the wide-ranging achievements of one of the most important philosophers of the twentieth century.

Who was Oakeshott?[2] Born in Chelsfield, Kent, on December 11, 1901, he attended a progressive coeducational secondary school, St. George's, Harpenden, before going up to Gonville and Caius College, Cambridge, in 1920. At Cambridge he took the political science option of the history tripos—there was no separate political science department at this time—and in 1923 he graduated with first-class honors. In 1925 he was elected to a fellowship at Caius and shortly thereafter began teaching in the history department. His writings from this period show him to be preoccupied with two principal themes: political philosophy and theology. With respect to the former, he defended a philosophical understanding of politics against various positivistic attempts to transform political science into a natural science, either by focusing on the empirical classification of political institutions and forms of government or by treating the nature of human sociality in terms of the behavior of ants and prairie dogs.[3] With respect to theology, Oakeshott's purpose was primarily apologetic. He defended religion against the criticisms of science and history by arguing that religious experience is not to be judged by its theoretical truth but by a pragmatic criterion.[4]

In 1933 Oakeshott published his first book, *Experience and Its Modes*. It was a bold and unusually precocious book—Oakeshott was only thirty-one years old when it appeared—devoted to working out the idea of philosophy as "experience without presupposition, reservation, arrest, or modification" (*EM* 2). He developed this idea of philosophy by examining the forms of experience of science, history, and practice and showing them to be abstract and incomplete in comparison with the concrete standpoint of philosophy. That philosophy was superior to these abstract modes of experience, however, did not mean that it could dictate to them. Oakeshott argued that, within its own sphere, every mode is autonomous and immune from the authority of other forms of experience. History is independent of science and the practical attitude, and practice has nothing to learn or fear from history or science. Most important, philosophy has nothing to contribute to practical or political life. Oakeshott frankly acknowledged in the introduction to *Experience and Its Modes* that his argument was heavily indebted to the idealism of G. W. F. Hegel and F. H. Bradley, but this did not do justice to what was fresh and distinctive about it. In its engagement with twentieth-century positivism and the problem of history, Oakeshott's idealism was much closer to that of R. G. Collingwood and Benedetto Croce than to nineteenth-century British idealism.

It perhaps seems strange that Oakeshott's first book was devoted wholly to the theory of knowledge, mentioning political philosophy only once—in a footnote. But nothing was clearer in his writings from the 1920s than that such a methodological prolegomenon was necessary before the substantive issues of political philosophy could be taken up. In one such writing, he declared, a "political philosophy founded upon no metaphysical prolegomenon, or upon one fundamentally in error, is doomed to propagate not truth, but falsehood."[5] Oakeshott spent the rest of the 1930s drawing out the implications of the idea of philosophy defended in *Experience and Its Modes* for political philosophy. In the most important of his methodological writings from this period, "The Concept of a Philosophical Jurisprudence" (1938), he criticized several of the most prominent conceptions of the philosophy of law—analytic, historical, sociological, and economic—from the standpoint of his conception of philosophy as "thought and knowledge without reservation or presupposition" (*CPJ*, 170). During this time, Oakeshott also began to write on the history of political philosophy, with essays on Locke and Bentham and two lengthy reviews of books on Hobbes. To this period also belongs the book that Oakeshott co-authored with Guy Griffith, *A Guide to the Classics* (1936), which, to the disappointment of many an earnest student of political philosophy, turned out to be not about Plato and Aristotle but about the fine art of judging horseflesh and picking a Derby winner.[6]

In 1940, after the outbreak of World War II, Oakeshott enlisted in the army and served until 1945 in an intelligence unit called "Phantom," whose mission was to penetrate behind enemy lines and report on the effectiveness of artillery targeting. After the war he returned to his teaching duties at Cambridge. He was asked to edit Hobbes's *Leviathan* for Blackwell's Political Texts series, and from this came his celebrated introduction to *Leviathan* in 1946.[7] One year later Oakeshott took over the editorship of the newly founded *Cambridge Journal* and began to write a series of remarkable essays that trenchantly criticized the collectivist policies of the Attlee Labour government and the rationalist mentality that lay behind them. At its core, he argued, this rationalist mentality sought to reduce the "tangle and variety of experience to a set of principles" or ideology and to impose on the complexity of society a single overarching purpose or plan (*RP*, 6). Such a rationalist mentality inevitably gave rise to the idea of central social planning favored by the postwar Attlee government. The recent experience of war, of course, had done much to nourish the ideal of central social planning, but Oakeshott, like his famous contemporary Friedrich Hayek, rejected the popular view that society in wartime should be used as a model in peacetime.

Oakeshott's attack on rationalist politics attracted considerable attention and transformed him almost overnight from a rather obscure Cambridge don into a major public intellectual. In 1950 he was offered the prestigious chair of political science at the London School of Economics (LSE), an appointment greeted with dismay on the left. In his celebrated inaugural lecture, "Political Education," he continued his neo-Burkean critique of rationalist or ideological politics, arguing that a political ideology is merely an abridgement of a concrete political tradition and should never be taken as a self-sufficient or self-contained ground of political activity. Politics is better understood as the pursuit of the intimations of a concrete tradition of political behavior. Oakeshott summed up his skeptical understanding of politics in a memorable (and to some, nihilistic) image: "In political activity, then, men sail a boundless and bottomless sea; there is neither harbour for shelter nor floor for anchorage, neither starting-place nor appointed destination. The enterprise is to keep afloat on an even keel; the sea is both friend and enemy; and the seamanship consists in using the resources of a traditional manner of behaviour in order to make a friend of every hostile occasion" (*RP*, 60).

Much of Oakeshott's time during the 1950s was taken up with his teaching duties at the LSE, which included his legendary lectures on the history of political thought and his administrative duties as head of the government department. He did manage to write two important essays, however. The first, "On Being Conservative" (1956), disclosed a subtle shift in his thinking, reflected in his rejection of Burke as a useful guide for modern conservatism. The problem with Burke and his modern followers—Russell Kirk, for example—was that they burdened conservatism with controversial beliefs in natural law and a providential order.[8] But such metaphysical and religious beliefs, Oakeshott argued, were not necessary to defend the conservative disposition in politics. All that was needed was the recognition that in our current circumstances, marked by radical individuality and diversity, the conservative understanding of government as a limited and specific activity was more appropriate than the alternative understanding of government as the imposition of a substantive conception of the common good. One of the important implications of Oakeshott's argument in "On Being Conservative" was that, against the claims of what Andrew Sullivan has referred to as the "fundamentalist" right, there need not be a tight connection between political conservatism and cultural conservatism.[9] "It is not at all inconsistent," Oakeshott wrote, "to be conservative in respect of government and radical in respect of almost every other activity" (*RP*, 435). Robert Grant's biographical essay shows in graphic detail how Oakeshott exemplified this duality in his own life.

The other crucial essay from the 1950s was "The Voice of Poetry in the Conversation of Mankind" (1959) in *Rationalism in Politics*. In this substantial essay, Oakeshott not only provided the most complete statement of his aesthetics but also reformulated his understanding of the relationship among the various modes of experience in terms of the image of conversation. To what extent this reformulation marked a significant shift in Oakeshott's earlier idealist outlook and his conception of philosophy as presuppositionless experience is a question taken up by David Boucher and Kenneth McIntyre in their essays.

In 1962 Oakeshott gathered together many of the essays he had written between 1947 and 1961 and published them as a book under the title *Rationalism in Politics and Other Essays*. Over the next thirteen years, he published very little. Teaching and administering the government department of LSE continued to demand much of his time. In the mid-1960s he set up a popular one-year master's course on the history of political thought, which attracted a devoted following of graduate students, many of them from the United States. The approach of the seminar was novel in that it concerned itself more with historiographical issues—the nature of intellectual history and of the history of political thought—than with the long march through the canonical texts of the Western philosophical tradition. Oakeshott officially retired from his chair at the LSE in 1968, but he continued to preside over the History of Political Thought seminar until about 1980.

In 1975 Oakeshott finally published the masterpiece of political philosophy he had long contemplated, *On Human Conduct*. The central ideas of this book went all the way back to "On Being Conservative" and the writings immediately following it, "The Masses in Representative Democracy" (1957) and the 1958 Harvard lectures on *Morality and Politics in Modern Europe*. In the latter two writings especially, Oakeshott anatomized the modern European political consciousness as a divided consciousness, composed of two opposing moral dispositions and two divergent understandings of the office of government. On the one hand, there was the morality of individuality, to which corresponded a juridical understanding of government as essentially an umpire or referee. On the other, there was the morality of collectivism, formed in reaction to the morality of individuality by those unable to bear its burdens, to which corresponded an understanding of government as a manager of an enterprise, a leader, a promoter of substantive purposes, and a provider of substantive benefits.

In *On Human Conduct*, Oakeshott used the Latin expressions *societas* and *universitas* to designate these two poles of the divided European political consciousness. The former designated an understanding of the state as a non-purposive association in which members are related solely in terms of legal rules. The latter designated an understanding of the state as an enterprise association in which the members are related in terms of a common, substantive purpose, whether it be religious salvation, moral virtue, or economic productivity or redistribution. The great achievement of *On Human Conduct* was Oakeshott's philosophical account of the former mode of association, what he called "civil association," in terms of its essential postulates.

Oakeshott published three more books after *On Human Conduct*, but they consisted for the most part of earlier work. *Hobbes on Civil Association* (1975) gathered together four of Oakeshott's most important essays on Hobbes, and the title underlined Oakeshott's philosophical affinity with his great English predecessor. *On History and Other Essays* (1983) contained the "Three Essays on History" that Oakeshott had honed over the years of the History of Political Thought seminar and that represented the final fruit of his career-long preoccupation with the problem of historical knowledge. This volume also contained an important new essay on "The Rule of Law," which clarified Oakeshott's views on the relationship of law and morality. Finally, *The Voice of Liberal Learning* (1989) was a collection of Oakeshott's earlier and very eloquent essays on education. In the year after this last volume was published, Oakeshott died in the village in Dorset to which he had retired permanently after 1980.

The account of Oakeshott's life just given of course comprises only his public or official life. What about his private, intimate life? This brings us to the first essay in this volume, Robert Grant's "The Pursuit of Intimacy, or Rationalism in Love." As the title suggests, this essay is concerned with Oakeshott's love life, which he considered to be not merely peripheral but in many ways the main business of his life. It is, of course, well known that Oakeshott loved women: not only did he marry three times, but he enjoyed many, many affairs throughout his life. But Grant—who is currently working on a full-length biography of Oakeshott—takes us far beyond these well-known facts. Drawing on not only the letters and notebooks in the public archive at the LSE but also private diaries and letters as well as extensive personal interviews with Oakeshott's friends, family, and lovers, Grant shows just how central erotic love was to Oakeshott's life and how obsessively, irrationally, selfishly, and often destructively he pursued it. This Dionysiac aspect of Oakeshott's private life stands in stark contrast to the polished, Apollonian character of his writings and philosophy in general, and it will no doubt shock those who are familiar only with the latter. Nevertheless, it is no part of Grant's purpose to reduce Oakeshott's philosophy to his private life or, Nietzsche-like, to see it as a mere rationalization of his personality. Instead, he sees a more complicated dynamic at work: Oakeshott's anti-utopian politics serve as both a counterweight and a Hobbesian foundation for his erotic utopia.

The rest of the volume is divided into two parts. The first deals with Oakeshott's reflections on the various forms of human experience—philosophy, history, morality, religion, and art—what he referred to as the "conversation of mankind." The second takes up his reflections on politics and political philosophy. Because Oakeshott is best known as a political philosopher, the theme of the second part does not require elaborate justification. But Oakeshott also made important contributions to a wide variety of fields outside of political philosophy, including metaphysics, epistemology, the philosophy of history, ethics, the philosophy of religion, aesthetics, and the philosophy of education. The essays in part 1 explore these multifarious contributions and enable us to appreciate the entire range of Oakeshott's achievement.

The first two chapters deal with Oakeshott's theory of knowledge or experience in general. In "The Victim of Thought: The Idealist Inheritance," David Boucher examines the relationship of this theory of knowledge or experience to philosophical—and especially British—idealism. He makes two fundamental points about this relationship. First, he argues that although idealism was on the wane in Britain in the 1920s and 1930s, Oakeshott's brand of idealism was hardly as unfashionable as many suppose. Second, he rejects the contention that Oakeshott jettisoned or severely attenuated his idealist commitments over the course of his career, arguing instead that Oakeshott's philosophical outlook exhibits remarkable consistency over the course of fifty years. In particular, he claims that Oakeshott never abandoned his early commitment to absolute idealism or monism and that the introduction of the analogy of conversation in "The Voice of Poetry in the Conversation of Mankind" did not alter his view of philosophy. Boucher rounds off his analysis by teasing out what he takes to be the distinctive features of Oakeshott's idealism.

In "Philosophy and Its Moods: Oakeshott on the Practice of Philosophy," Kenneth McIntyre continues the discussion of Oakeshott's conception of philosophy begun by Boucher but takes a somewhat different view. Though he admits that Oakeshott's conception of philosophy as a fundamentally skeptical activity devoted to relentless interrogation of the conditions of human understanding remains unchanged throughout his career, he also maintains that there is a subtle shift in Oakeshott's conception of philosophy away from the emphasis on criticizing modal abstraction in *Experience and Its Modes* to a more pluralistic defense of the autonomy and validity of the modes of experience in "The Voice of Poetry" and *On Human Conduct*. In addition, he contends that the later Oakeshott abandons the notion of philosophy as unconditional, presuppositionless knowledge and conceives of it instead as a conditional practice that, like any other practice, rests on traditional or tacit knowledge. In this regard, he suggests that Oakeshott's later conception of philosophy has much in common with the outlook of ordinary language philosophers such as Austin, Ryle, and the post-*Tractatus* Wittgenstein.

Apart from his contributions to political philosophy, Oakeshott is perhaps best known for his contributions to the philosophy of history. Over the course of fifty years, from the important chapter on historical experience in *Experience and Its Modes* to the three essays on history in *On History*, Oakeshott applied himself to investigating the nature and presuppositions of historical knowledge. In "Michael Oakeshott's Philosophy of History," Geoffrey Thomas analyzes and assesses Oakeshott's achievement in this regard. He reduces Oakeshott's constructivist philosophy of history to four fundamental theses: first, that the past does not exist, only the present exists; second, that only experience exists; third, that the historical past is an inferential construction from experience; and fourth, that historical inquiry is autonomous and not ancillary to science or practice. He then subjects each of these theses to rigorous analysis and finds them all wanting in one respect or another. The first two theses raise large questions about the nature of time and consciousness that Thomas believes Oakeshott's idealist epistemology in *Experience and Its Modes* is unable to handle satisfactorily. With respect to the third thesis, he questions Oakeshott's coherence theory of truth and reconstructs the criterion of historical explanation in terms of what he calls "inference to the best explanation." Finally, in regard to the fourth thesis, he finds Oakeshott's attempt to exclude practical and scientific categories from historical explanation highly problematic.

The next set of essays takes up Oakeshott's conception of practical life and the attempts to overcome the permanent dissatisfaction he associates with it in poetry and religion. In "Radical Temporality and the Modern Moral Imagination," Timothy Fuller, the dean of American Oakeshottian studies, powerfully evokes Oakeshott's conception of the endlessness of practical life, which ceaselessly attempts to reconcile "what is" with "what ought to be." This constitutes the "radical temporality" referred to in the title of his essay, and Fuller goes on to elaborate the various ways in which the modern moral imagination has responded to it. The modern moral imagination, as it expresses itself in Hobbes, Locke, Hume, Smith, and Kant, is marked by a faith in human self-perfection, a faith in humanity's ability to escape the radical temporality of the human condition. Fuller argues that Oakeshott offers two alternatives to this modern politics of faith: first, a politics of skepticism that does not envisage the evanescence of human imperfection; and second, the voice of poetry, which, without denying the radical temporality of the human condition, offers a temporary release from it in contemplative delight.

The theme of the unremitting nature of practical life also appears in Elizabeth Corey's essay "The Religious Sensibility of Michael Oakeshott." Drawing on Oakeshott's two essays on the Tower of Babel to flesh out his critique of the perfectionism and obsession with achievement that vitiate modern life, Corey shows how Oakeshott conceived of religion as a corrective to these spiritual maladies. She does not conceal that Oakeshott's conception of religion, which stresses living in the present, unburdened by anxiety for worldly success or achievement, is not exactly orthodox; nevertheless, she insists that Oakeshott's work is full of authentic religious insight. Corey is particularly attracted to Oakeshott's assimilation of the religious disposition to the poetic

disposition. Both dispositions eschew the frenetic quest for worldly achievement and opt instead for delight in the present, and both offer a temporary
respite from the tyranny of practice.

Corey's discussion of the poetic character of religious experience leads
nicely into Corey Abel's essay "Whatever It Turns Out to Be: Oakeshott on
Aesthetic Experience." Focusing his analysis on the lengthy "Voice of Poetry"
essay, Abel provides a robust defense of Oakeshott's nonrepresentational
and nonpractical conception of art. Critics who suggest that Oakeshott goes
too far in severing art from truth and morality fail to grasp that Oakeshott's
fundamental philosophical concern is to identify the *differentia* of aesthetic
experience vis-à-vis other forms of experience. One of the most important differentiating features of aesthetic experience, according to Oakeshott as Abel
interprets him, is its timelessness, its denial of historicity; here Oakeshott
parts ways with the historicism of thinkers such as Gadamer and Ricoeur.
Another important differentiating feature of aesthetic experience is its playful
character versus the unavoidably worklike character of practical experience.

Paul Franco's essay on Oakeshott's philosophy of education, "*Un Début
dans la Vie Humaine*," fittingly concludes part 1 of this volume, for it is in
connection with the theme of university education that Oakeshott first introduces the image of conversation. Franco acknowledges the enormous appeal
of Oakeshott's ideal of the university as a conversation between the various
modes of understanding that make up our civilization, a conversation pursued for its own sake and not in the service of practical life or some social
purpose. Nevertheless, he questions whether Oakeshott's philosophy of education adequately addresses the problem of specialization and cultural fragmentation that exercised earlier theorists of education from Newman and
Nietzsche to Arnold and Leavis. Franco contends that Oakeshott's attempt to
hive off education from any sort of moral or practical or societal effect ultimately leads to a formalism that deprives the university of its necessary role
as a unifying cultural power.

The essays in part 2 of this volume concern themselves with Oakeshott's
political philosophy, and the first two are specifically concerned with Oakeshott's reflections on the history of political thought. What did Oakeshott
mean by the "history of political thought"? This is the question Martyn
Thompson addresses in his essay "Michael Oakeshott on the History of Political Thought." He highlights two features of Oakeshott's conception: first, that
the historical past is a construction of the historian, and therefore the meaning of any given historical text will depend on the specific question a historian
is seeking to answer; and second, that political thinking takes place on different levels, some more practical, some more theoretical, and the historian

should never confuse these levels. Taken together, these two features point to a multidimensional conception of the history of political thought that contrasts sharply with Quentin Skinner's attempt to reduce it to a history of ideologies. Thompson draws out this contrast by considering Oakeshott's and Skinner's respective interpretations of Hobbes's *Leviathan*.

Oakeshott's interpretation of Hobbes is the central subject of Noel Malcolm's essay "Oakeshott and Hobbes." Malcolm notices that there seems to be a discrepancy between Oakeshott's hostility to rationalism, on the one hand, and his admiration for Hobbes, an archetypal rationalist if ever there was one, on the other. In the first instance, Oakeshott seems to overcome this self-contradiction only by misunderstanding Hobbes and overlooking the deeply rationalist strains in his thought—for example, his antipathy to prejudice and tradition, his faith in scientific method, and his preoccupation with certainty. But Malcolm does not leave it at that. He argues that Oakeshott ultimately admired Hobbes because he saw him as an exponent of a noninstrumental conception of the state. This noninstrumentalist or nonteleological interpretation of Hobbes raises questions of its own, and Malcolm takes us through the rich debate over it in the 1930s—between Collingwood, Schmitt, Strauss, and others. In the end, though, he finds the interpretation problematic, given that Hobbes seems to see everything as instrumental to civil peace or individual self-preservation. Once again, Hobbes appears to be more of a rationalist than Oakeshott's interpretation suggests.

Oakeshott's critique of rationalism is taken up in greater depth in Kenneth Minogue's essay "The Fate of Rationalism in Oakeshott's Thought." Minogue, Oakeshott's longtime colleague at the LSE, focuses his analysis on the posthumously published manuscript *The Politics of Faith and the Politics of Scepticism*, believed to have been written somewhere around 1952. This manuscript is of particular interest because in it Oakeshott attempts to go beyond the simple condemnation of rationalism found in his earlier essays and to understand the phenomenon in a more philosophical and dispassionate manner. This leads him to interpret European politics as a salutary balance between the rationalistic politics of faith and the politics of skepticism. Minogue questions, however, whether Oakeshott succeeds in salvaging a place for faith and rationalism in our politics. In the first place, the politics of faith and the politics of skepticism are no longer in balance; the former has carried the day, and the latter has all but lost. Second, in seeking to domesticate the politics of faith as the balancer of the politics of skepticism, Oakeshott attributes to the latter some problems it does not necessarily possess. Minogue concludes that it is not altogether surprising that Oakeshott chose not to publish this work.

The theme of rationalism provides Leslie Marsh with the opportunity to compare Oakeshott with another important critic of rationalism, Friedrich Hayek, in his essay "Oakeshott and Hayek: Situating the Mind." Invoking Oakeshott's famous dismissal of Hayek in "Rationalism in Politics," Marsh makes the case that Oakeshott got Hayek plain wrong. If one understands both men to be centrally concerned with the anti-Cartesian project of socializing the mind, then a more fertile vista opens up for comparing them. Marsh approaches the topic from the perspective of the philosophy of mind and locates both Oakeshott and Hayek within the non-Cartesian wing of contemporary cognitive science known as "situated cognition." Marsh concludes his essay by showing that the commonality between Oakeshott and Hayek with respect to the theory of mind extends to their political philosophies as well, a fact that is often obscured by labeling the former thinker conservative and the latter liberal.

The topic of Oakeshott's conservatism is a contentious one, as Robert Devigne shows in his essay "Oakeshott as Conservative." Using Burke as a touchstone, Devigne demonstrates that Oakeshott's conservatism is complex and shifts over time. In his essays from the late 1940s and early 1950s, Oakeshott displays a Burkean antipathy toward rationalism and appreciation for tradition, though he also dissents from Burke on the value of philosophy and the rationality of history. Beginning in the mid-1950s, however, Oakeshott's differences with Burke become more pronounced, as he moves in a more liberal and legalistic direction. Despite this, Oakeshott's justification of the "salutary stalemate" between societas and universitas in the European political tradition seems to bring him closer to Burke's identification of the "is" and the "ought." Devigne concludes his essay by contrasting Oakeshott with the other seminal conservative thinker of the second half of the twentieth century, Leo Strauss, bringing out their very different assessments of modernity, Burke, and history.

The final two chapters in the volume deal with Oakeshott's most mature statements of his political philosophy in *On Human Conduct* and "The Rule of Law." In "Oakeshott on Civil Association," Noël O'Sullivan offers a magisterial account of Oakeshott's ideal of civil association, showing that it is addressed above all to the *moral* problem of reconciling authority with freedom in the highly pluralistic circumstances of modern Europe. Hobbes made significant progress in this normative endeavor to find a shared sense of public order, according to Oakeshott, but even he failed to provide a completely moral conception of civil association. O'Sullivan identifies several confusions about civil association in contemporary political thought: the belief that it is a mechanism for promoting spiritual renewal (Havel); the identification of it with the minimal state (Nozick), capitalism (Friedman and Hayek), democracy, liberalism, or the impossible ideal of neutrality. But he also considers some well-founded criticisms of Oakeshott's model of civil association, chief among which is the charge that it is too narrowly procedural or legalistic to have any motivating power for citizens. He concludes by examining Oakeshott's pessimism about the prospects of civil association in modern mass democracies, and in this regard he paints a very different picture of Oakeshott's later attitude toward history from the optimistic Burkean one found in Devigne's essay.

Going all the way back to his early essay "The Concept of a Philosophical Jurisprudence," Oakeshott always saw an intimate connection between political philosophy and the philosophy of law. Steven Gerencser subjects Oakeshott's philosophy of law to careful analysis in his essay "Oakeshott on Law." He argues that there is a fundamental tension between the traditionalist conception of law implicit in Oakeshott's antirationalist writings and the formalistic conception of law found in his later writings, especially "The Rule of Law." In the former, laws possess authority insofar as they reflect the customary beliefs and sentiments of a people; in the latter, they possess authority only insofar as they are the product of a formal legislative procedure. Can these opposing views be reconciled? Gerencser suggests that they can and looks to Hegel and the positivist jurist Georg Jellinek as possible models for such a reconciliation.

As is evident from the preceding summaries, the contributors to this volume, while they all agree that Oakeshott is a philosopher eminently worth studying, have widely different views about the meaning and significance of his philosophy. Such disagreement is healthy and a sign of the vitality of a thinker. It also complicates the labels—for example, "conservative" and "idealist" (to name but two)—that have sometimes prevented Oakeshott's philosophy from gaining a wider hearing. As mentioned at the outset, this volume is not meant to bring the debate about Oakeshott's philosophy to an end—his thought is too rich and multifaceted for that. Rather, the hope is that this volume can serve as a platform from which the next generation of scholars and philosophers can carry the debate forward. Oakeshott, the great philosopher of open-ended conversation, would have it no other way.

NOTES

1. Paul Franco, *The Political Philosophy of Michael Oakeshott* (New Haven: Yale University Press, 1990); Robert Grant, *Oakeshott* (London: Claridge Press, 1990). The first book devoted to Oakeshott's thought, W. H. Greenleaf's *Oakeshott's Philosophical Politics* (London: Longmans, 1966), was written prior to the appearance of Oakeshott's most important work of political philosophy, *On Human Conduct* (Oxford: Clarendon Press, 1975), as well as *On History and Other Essays* (Oxford: Basil Blackwell, 1983). A complete and constantly updated bibliography of scholarly works on Oakeshott can be found at the Michael Oakeshott Association website, http://www.michael-oakeshott-association.com/index.php/bibliography.

2. The following draws heavily on the biographical chapter in Paul Franco's *Michael Oakeshott: An Introduction* (New Haven: Yale University Press, 2004), chap. 1.

3. See Michael Oakeshott, "The Cambridge School of Political Science," 1924, in *WIH*, 45–66; "A Discussion of Some Matters Preliminary to a Study of Political Philosophy," 1925, in BLPES, 1/1/3; and "The Nature and Meaning of Sociality," 1925, in *RPML*, 46–62.

4. See Michael Oakeshott, "Religion and the Moral Life," 1927, in *RPML*, 39–45; "The Historical Element in Christianity," 1928, in *RPML*, 63–73; and "Religion and the World," 1929, in *RPML*, 27–38.

5. Oakeshott, "Discussion of Some Matters," 187–88.

6. Michael Oakeshott, "John Locke," 1932, in *CPJ*, 82–86; "The New Bentham," 1932, in *RP*, 132–50, "Thomas Hobbes," 1935, in *CPJ*, 110–21; "Dr. Leo Strauss on Hobbes," 1937, in *HCA*, 141–58; Guy Griffith and Michael Oakeshott, *A Guide to the Classics; or, How to Pick the Derby Winner* (London: Faber and Faber, 1936).

7. Michael Oakeshott, ed., introduction to *Leviathan*, by Thomas Hobbes (Oxford: Blackwell, 1946).

8. See Oakeshott's 1954 review of Kirk's *The Conservative Mind*, in *VMES*, 81–84.

9. Andrew Sullivan, *The Conservative Soul: How We Lost It, How to Get It Back* (New York: HarperCollins, 2006). Against fundamentalist conservatism, Sullivan defends an Oakeshott-inspired conservatism.

1

THE PURSUIT OF INTIMACY, OR RATIONALISM IN LOVE

Robert Grant

In what follows I refer to Michael Oakeshott by his first name, as I also do to those connected with him. This is partly to avoid the confusion of shared sur-names, though I did actually come myself to address him by his first name. My main topic will be his love life, which is not the same as his sex life, though the two are obviously connected. And perhaps both are, more dis-tantly, with his work. Michael in several places says that love was the main business of his life. If we are to take him literally, therefore, his work appears as more of a sideline or an antidote, and even he admits from time to time that he is using it to deaden his sorrows or drive away his demons.

I published a very brief biography of Michael in 1990, in my little introduc-tory book, *Oakeshott*. My chief informant had been Michael himself, whom I visited at his home in Dorset in 1987.[1] This was only for a day, but we corre-sponded thereafter. I had met him briefly about seven years earlier. But when I interviewed him he was nearly eighty-six, so it would not be surprising if his memory had occasionally erred. He told me that he had gone up to Cam-bridge in 1919, that he had graduated in 1925, and that he was elected to a fel-lowship at his college, Caius, in 1927. I wrote these unlikely sounding dates down on the spot (as I did everything else) and innocently repeated them in my book. In fact, he went up in 1920, graduated (as would have been normal) in 1923, and was made a fellow in 1925.

Other bits of misinformation were less obviously mistakes, though some may still have been. He told me he had been married twice, and that his first wife had died in the 1950s. (I already knew, from him, that he had a current

This chapter is an extended and annotated version of an address given at the biennial Michael Oakeshott Association Conference at Baylor University, Waco, Texas, November 2009. The title is a quibble on Oakeshott's famous characterization, in his 1952 inaugural lecture at the London School of Economics, of a mature politics as "the pursuit of intimations" (*RP*, 57–58, 66–69).

wife, Christel.) In fact it was three times. He had divorced his two previous wives and both had died, neither in the 1950s: the first, Joyce, in 1976, and the second, Kate, in 1964. Which of them was he airbrushing out, if he was? He had reason enough in either case, though that is not necessarily to say that he did so. He also told me that his maternal grandfather was the rector of Islington in the 1890s. In fact, two Islington churches have rectors; further-more, his grandfather, Thomas Hellicar, was not a member of the clergy at all, but a well-off Islington silk merchant.[2] According to Michael's son Simon, it was his great-grandfather Hellicar's money that enabled Michael's parents to live much more comfortably than I had previously imagined, with a sub-stantial house, a cook, a gardener, and, exotically, a Swedish lady chauffeur.[3] And that is not to mention sending their three boys to a fee-paying school (something, admittedly, considerably cheaper in real terms than now).

There is more in Michael's background of interest, and, at least to my pres-ent knowledge, it is accurate. His father, Joseph (1860–1945), had at least one distinguished forebear, the portrait painter and friend of Sir Joshua Reynolds, Daniel Dodd.[4] Despite this, Joseph's immediate family was quite poor. So, after a good grammar school education (in which he distinguished himself in French), at sixteen Joseph became a "boy clerk" in the Civil Service. This was a newly invented, fast-track position whereby clever boys, in exchange for their labor, received an apprenticeship in the "administrative" (i.e., highest) class of the bureaucracy, along with the equivalent of a university education. Joseph became a founder of the Fabian Society, a friend of George Bernard Shaw, a principal clerk (divisional head) in the Inland Revenue at Somerset House, the author of Fabian pamphlets, and eventually a founder and governor of the London School of Economics, where, after his death, his son Michael was to be Professor of Political Science.[5] According to a widespread, long-standing rumor, Oakeshott Avenue, in Holly Lodge Estate, Highgate, North London, is named after him.[6] In old age he looked (and was) benignly Elgarian.

Joseph, so his grandson Simon has told me, was not "officer class," unlike his wife, Frances Maude (1869–1964). She was a suffragette, a Christian (where he was agnostic), and somewhat domineering. During the Great War she was commandant of a small military hospital. Although, according to Michael's second wife, Kate, Joseph was a "dear old man" (and his mem-oirs bear her out), there was always tension in the house. The boys tended to side with their mother, but—apart from the dutiful, military Brian, the eldest—rather neglected her in her old age. She was undemonstrative, ran a tight ship, and excited respect rather than affection. She and Joseph, how-ever, were kind and solicitous to Michael's and his younger brother Stephen's abandoned wives. Michael married thrice; Stephen twice; Brian, like his par-ents, only once.

Like Brian, who was head boy, Michael and Stephen were sent to a new "progressive" coeducational school, St. George's, Harpenden.[7] Here both met their future first wives, the sisters Joyce and Barbara Fricker.[8] Joyce was a year older than Michael; they had known each other since before their teens and had always been close, but did not marry until 1927. St. George's was so liberal, and the supervision additionally so lax during the Great War (owing to the dearth of staff), that a certain amount of sexual hanky-panky went on among the pupils. Hand holding was allowed, but kissing emphatically not. How the one was supposed to be prevented from turning into the other, and that from graduating to full sexual intercourse, given a suitable time and place, is a mystery. Accordingly, such things happened. Some pupils later blamed their subsequent marriage breakdowns on this de facto license.[9]

But the school also had a pious ethos, and Michael and Joyce were both fervent Christians, of a touchingly innocent, Franciscan cast. Michael composed religious stories and fables, which Joyce copied into an exercise book; later, but still before their marriage, they collaborated on a little devotional anthology, the unattributed texts being culled from all over by Michael, and the whole calligraphed, illustrated, and illuminated by Joyce, in a sometimes medievalizing, sometimes Kate Greenaway–ish style. She was an artist of considerable talent and, after St. George's, had trained at the Slade School of Fine Art in London. The title of this anthology is "Scala Precis," a ladder (or staircase) of prayer. Joyce's cover page depicts a stylized peak of rock against a background of white clouds and blue sky. It is ascended by a steep, winding path and crowned by a clump of trees and a lawn. Here four children, a goat, and a couple of rabbits are joyously scampering about, with another child about to join them. Adults and youths of various ages are making their way up, some assisted by sticks or staves, and some still at the very bottom.

The conceit is familiar, that of the spiritual life as an uphill journey. But the summit, the terminus of the quest, is peopled by children happily at play, whereas the four figures at the bottom, just beginning their toilsome pilgrimage, are two of them elderly, while two are using walking sticks (including a young-looking man with a Dick Whittington bundle, showing that he has left home and is not turning back). One carries a scythe, suggesting either the Grim Reaper or the utilitarian world of subsistence-driven labor, or both. It seems that the children's world at the summit transcends these mortal concerns. The people on the whole get younger as they climb, meaning perhaps either that children are naturally closest to God, Wordsworth-fashion, or alternatively that, though we age physically, as we develop spiritually we *become* more childlike.

The whole work is a naive celebration of innocence, verging on the sentimental, but its simplicity is undeniably affecting. Tears feature in many excerpts; they signify repentance, and they are wet, washing the soul clean and restoring it to its pristine purity. There is also an insistence on the absolute value of selflessness, much at odds with some of Michael's later opinions and (it must be said) behavior. Here is an incomplete list of sources: the Bible (naturally, including the Book of Isaiah, the Epistle to the Ephesians, and the Epistle of Saint James), Wordsworth's translations of Michelangelo, Evelyn Underhill, the medieval mystic Ruysbroeck, a fable of Ruskin's, George Eliot, William James's *The Varieties of Religious Experience*, the contemporary religious writer "Michael Fairless" (Margaret Fairless Barber), the 1920 Lambeth Conference, Tennyson (spectacularly misquoted), Masefield, the Victorian hymnodist Frederick Faber, F. W. H. Myers's *St Paul*, Villari's *Life of Savonarola*, Plato's *Symposium*, Turgenev's *Poems in Prose* (twice), Péguy's *Mystery of the Holy Innocents*, *The Winter's Tale*, Sri Ramakrishna, and the Norwegian novelist Johan Bojer (author of *The Great Hunger*, 1916).[10]

As well as illuminating each page's initial capital, Joyce designed an endpaper illustrating the collection's various themes and anecdotes, each represented by a vignette enclosed in a lozenge-shaped pane. There is a striking central pane, four times larger than the others, in which, in a clearing beside a brook, under a flowering cherry tree, a barefoot boy in tunic and shorts is kneeling, his face in his hands. Lying on the ground before him are a small ecclesiastical cross and an open book. Two fawns browse innocently nearby, and a young girl tends a flower on the path leading away from the clearing. The reference to the text is unclear and may not be narrowly specific. Furthermore, is the boy weeping, or praying, or both? Perhaps to do the one is implicitly, if wordlessly, to do the other.

What seems remarkable is that this earnest little work was produced by two grown-up young people in their twenties. Simon has told me that they were very likely virgins when they married. At all events, something went wrong almost immediately. I do not say that it was sexual, but it certainly had a sexual dimension. Within three years or so, Joyce was delightedly pregnant with Simon, but Michael was urging her to have an abortion (then illegal).[11] According to Simon, Michael had discovered that he liked sex, she that she didn't, though she later had an affair with Michael's openly polygynous colleague Joseph Needham, the biologist and (subsequently) sinologist, who in 1966 beat him to the mastership of Caius College. During these fraught years Joyce lost her faith entirely; Michael retained his, though in a very attenuated, secularized, and mystical fashion.[12]

One entry in "Scala Precis" suggests the then not uncommon route that Michael may have taken, which was to identify love with belief. The extract consists of some lines by the Princeton theologian Henry van Dyke, the epigraph (by himself) to his Christmas fable "The Story of the Other Wise Man" (1896). The Other Wise Man never makes it to the Epiphany, being delayed and impoverished by charitable works on the way, but finally encounters the Savior at his crucifixion:

> Who seeks for heaven alone to save his soul
> May keep the path but will not reach the goal;
> While he who walks in love may wander far;
> Yet God will bring him where the blessèd are.[13]

The sentiment is very Oakeshottian. It is antisalvationary, in that strict religious observance (or even belief) avails nothing, since "salvation" cannot be pursued or purchased, while an unspecified "love," however deviant ("wander far"), may itself be, or conduce to, a kind of salvation.

Michael's notebooks at the London School of Economics largely record his reading, but for the critical years 1928 to 1934 he kept a parallel set, which are still in private hands.[14] These are mostly about erotic love, in the classic tradition of Shelley, Hazlitt, Stendhal, Amiel, and the rest (many of whom are quoted). One really interesting—not to say perverse—entry suggests that love (or at least a certain kind of love), like death, is an escape from individuality: "Love is a foretaste of death. In the moment of love one loses the burden of consciousness, and tastes beforehand the pleasures of extinction, and when it is over the taste of individual existence is bitter."

If this were so, as it well may be for some lovers, it would follow that since the partner must similarly be existentially annihilated in the act of love, it hardly matters who that partner is. And the resurfacing, in the lover's consciousness, of the partner as an individual, would equally, like the lover's own individuality, taste bitter.[15] From this—a thought perhaps worth bearing in mind throughout what follows—one might conceivably construct a defense of anonymous, orgiastic, or crazily promiscuous sex, à la Foucault (or indeed Sade), whose goal, explicitly, is extinction.[16]

A constant archetype or ideal, to which Michael returns obsessively, is La Belle Dame Sans Merci (the title, of course, of a poem by Keats). La Belle Dame (alias "LBD") is traced through a succession of young women of Michael's acquaintance, and even in strangers. "Following her—" he writes, "shops, theatres, trains, open doors, windows, passing cars, glimpses here and there." And—he adds disconcertingly—"following her in children." He asks why this ideal should invariably take a female shape: "Besides the appeal of sex," he writes, "the feeling that here is the true life of the 'otherworld' [sic], free from the cares and anxieties, fears and inhibitions of life as I have known it and transformed into its perfect self." One catches here a whiff of the later Michael on the "poetic" as an escape from the material and quotidian. Accordingly, LBD appears also in literature and art, so that the fictive and the actual become yet more blurred. She appears even in music, which is not representational. "Most nearly met her there," he notes cryptically: "See the ideal more clearly."

Her mercilessness, like the rest of her, is effectively Michael's invention, though it is also true that as a cultural stereotype (one, however, that he chose to appropriate) she comes ready-equipped with it. He knew that LBD was a fantasy, but, unaccountably, still pursued her. "What we love," he writes, "is a projection of ourselves, an ideal, something we imagine, and then attach to somebody, and persuade ourselves that we have discovered and not made it." As Michael himself clearly saw, such a love inevitably fails, as love object after love object (with the emphasis on the word *object*), having her own life to live, must disappoint the lover, who must either force her to conform to his ideal, or himself move on. Nearly all of this syndrome can be found in Shelley (notably in his poem "Epipsychidion"), whom Michael frequently cites.[17] (He also quotes Saint Augustine's famous phrase about being in love with loving, which Shelley used as the epigraph to "Alastor.") It is curious that two decades later, in "Rationalism in Politics" (the essay), he entirely rejects Shelley's *political* idealism, along with that of Shelley's father-in-law Godwin (*RP*, 7, 10, 31; cf. 436). But, until his old age, he did not abandon his similar erotic notions (and even then not entirely).

His marriage to Joyce was doomed from the start, though they had been friends since childhood. In 1928, after barely a year—and shockingly—he writes, "Joyce—gained but lost. To know is to lose." That apothegm, by the way, comes from D. H. Lawrence, described in Michael's *Experience and Its Modes* as a champion of "the integrity and separateness of the self" (*EM*, 271). Here is Lawrence, in *Fantasia of the Unconscious* (1922): "To know, is to lose. When I have a finished mental concept of a beloved, or a friend, then the love and the friendship is dead. It falls to the level of an acquaintance. As soon as I have a finished mental conception, a full idea even of myself, then dynamically I am dead. To know is to die."[18]

Several of these expressions recur verbatim in Michael's diaries. It seems to have escaped both him and Lawrence that it may not be the beloved's fault that she is reduced to a "finished mental concept," such as Strindberg thought the characters of the "bourgeois" stage were.[19] The fault may rather be the lover's, whose fantasy-object from the outset is just such a "finished mental concept," which he then clamps over any likely passing candidate. If you again spot a political analogy and detect Michael's rationalist prowling in the shadows, I suspect you are not wrong. For the political visionary, the superficial love object is not a person, but the entire human race ("Man, oh, not men!" in Shelley's phrase); but the underlying one, just like the romantic lover's, is himself.

Let me now introduce a major player, whom I was lucky to know for a couple of years until her recent death at the age of ninety-six. This was Céline Jenkins, née Haegler, who was ten years younger than Michael and a Girton College undergraduate from 1929 until 1932. Like Michael, she too had been "progressively" educated, at St. Christopher School, Letchworth, and indeed it was there, accompanying a friend who was also a parent, that Michael had first seen her, at the school sports day. At Cambridge Céline was a frequent visitor and overnight guest of the Oakeshotts. She became engaged to a graduate student in classics, Romilly Jenkins (later a distinguished Byzantinist), and, with considerable courage given the penalties they would then have faced if detected, spent nights with him.

Knowing this, yet true to form, Michael fell in love with her and languished in virtual silence for three years, devoting pages upon pages to his freaks and fancies concerning her (she is, for example, quasi-homophonically, Selene the moon goddess, sometimes abbreviated to a capital sigma, Σ). She was not unique, however, since, albeit in more "sublunary" mode—all this is in his private diaries from 1928—his devotion already extended simultaneously to Molly, Gemma, Effie, Winifred, Sancha, Ruth, Odette, Bea, and Cynthia, whoever they were, and to Jean Beecher, another artist schoolfellow, the daughter of his father-in-law's business partner. He wrote a poem to Jean's breasts, somewhat uninventively titled "To Jean's Breasts," though the addressees, had they been able to read, would doubtless have been happy enough to receive it.[20] As befits his conception of love, these girls' real-life differences (which must have existed) sink under the ideal role in which Michael has cast them all.

Not so Céline, even to him. She became a firm and loyal friend to Joyce and, without any real inkling (at least at first) of Michael's feelings for her, fought Joyce's corner stoutly and resisted Michael's indirect persuasions, by giving her books and the like, to share his tastes and values, which were becoming more and more Lawrencean and egocentric. (He quotes Nietzsche a lot around this time.)

A true magpie historian, Michael kept every scrap of correspondence he ever received, even long-paid tradesmen's bills,[21] but there is not so much as a Christmas card from these other girls, except Jean (of blessed mammary). Did they even know of his infatuation (after all, Céline didn't)? We do not know what Joyce thought about them. She was by all accounts a truly admirable and, even though Michael's rejection hurt her deeply, an astonishingly self-sufficient person. The first sizable collection of letters at the British Library of Political and Economic Science, running to about four hundred pages, is from Céline, and its first fully legible postmark is December 2, 1929 (she was negligent, in her youth, about dating letters, and most of hers lack envelopes and thus postmarks). She married after graduating in 1932 and left with Romilly for the British School at Athens, returning to Cambridge with him in the mid-1930s and keeping up a regular correspondence with Michael until the war. Thereafter their exchanges were increasingly sporadic but lasted until his death.

I think he admired and valued her resistance, perhaps regarding it as a challenge, perhaps also forgetting that it must be unrelated to his feelings for her, since, if he ever declared himself fully, it was only once she was as good as married, in other words, totally out of reach (at least at this novice stage of his amatory career). Even in her nineties her culture, intelligence, and wit were undimmed, and her letters show that those qualities were well developed before she was twenty. If Michael had been infatuated by her alone, and not, like Cherubino, by the entire female sex besides, his feelings for her might have been wholly understandable.

She was tough-minded, and tough on him, too. Doubtless aware of Michael's interest in Turgenev and also (one supposes) of that writer's hopeless erotic languishings in real life, she not unjustly describes Turgenev's typical protagonist as "a young man who bursts into hot inexplicable tears on every page" (BLPES, 10/1/14, probably end of June 1930). And here she is, a mere eighteen-year-old, on Virginia Woolf's *Jacob's Room*, which Michael had lent her: "She says everything beautifully but I am beginning to wonder if she has anything to say. Saying nothing rather well is inclined to be the curse of the age" (postmarked December 18, 1929). Sir Ronald Fraser, a senior civil servant, who in his own old age (the 1970s) became a guru of the New Age, wrote a proto–magic realist novel in the 1920s, called *The Flying Draper*. "I was bored by it," wrote Céline in the same letter, "and thought it badly and unconvincingly written and third hand, [and] just couldn't imagine why it had taken your fancy."

The reason it had, I think (and I have read it), was that, though grounded in the mundane—the world of H. G. Wells's Kipps, a draper's apprentice—it also opened on to Michael's metaphysical "otherworld." Unlike Fraser's hero, drapers do not regularly discover in themselves a capacity for levitation. But Michael was the least materialist, or materialistic, of men. He always believed in the "otherworld" and also that, like Kant's realm of freedom, it was at once cotemporal, perhaps even cospatial, with the physical world, yet still, like a parallel universe, totally distinct. There is something of this in Saint Augustine, who Michael told me was his intellectual hero ("my great man") and also in the seventeenth-century mystic Traherne, whom Michael cites in "The Voice of Poetry" (*RP*, 523).[22] The point (as I took it) was that "salvation," if only we can attune ourselves to it, is accessible here and now, rather than a future reward or a quid pro quo for anything. You might say that is good news for sinners.[23]

A favorite Fraser novel of Michael's was *Rose Anstey* (1930), about a self-willed young woman (like Sue in *Jude the Obscure*, only worse) who sacrifices many innocent people to her caprices, ensnares a decent middle-aged man into marriage, then deserts him for a glamorous aviator, with whom she half-intentionally dies on a Lindbergh-style transatlantic flight.[24] Though historically and ideologically interesting, as a novel it is wearisome, mannered, and generally preposterous. But Michael gave it to Céline and copied many extracts from it into his diary. On first skimming it, "it is . . . most extremely like you," she writes and adds that "his philosophy of life must be rejected, tho' you I know would agree with it wholeheartedly" (BLPES, 10/1/14, "Sunday 7th" [presumably September 1930]). Later, with remarkable frankness, she writes,

> You *do* give yourself away in the books you recommend. I understand why Powys [Llewelyn Powys, whom Michael knew] appeals to you, he expounds a philosophy very similar to Frazer's [*sic*] . . . and try as I will I cannot agree with it. . . . How *can* one trip along one's way quite regardless of everyone else? It never brings one lasting happiness as far as I have found, both Chris [the semiautobiographical hero of Powys's *Apples Be Ripe*, also 1930] and Rose Anstey are colossal [*sic*] egoists but because they were both exceedingly attractive individuals they are allowed to ride rough-shod over all else. . . . Do you suppose you would be any the happier, your personality any the richer, had you completed relations with, say, the same half-dozen women you have wanted to, turned your hand to the same half-dozen new modes of life that may have come your way? I don't think so, but I know you do. (BLPES, 10/1/14)[25]

She evidently knew that most of his grand passions had gone unconsummated. In an earlier letter she says that his conception of love was hers when she was fourteen.[26] She told me that she didn't find him attractive sexually; but she added that he might have preferred women who were not attracted to him because it left more scope for fantasy. His love life at this time she described to me with sardonic, indeed withering, finality, as being "more *in posse* than *in esse*." (And Simon too, more kindly, has said of his father that "the emotion of being in love might often have been enough.")

Céline also told me that she felt a great warmth for Joyce, which colored her view of Michael. Quite early on, she writes at the end of a letter: "Give my best love to Joyce, will you? I wonder if you realise how lucky you are in having a wife like Joyce, she is worth a thousand of practically everyone you meet; but this you will say is impertinence, and I quite agree" (BLPES, 10/1/14).[27]

She must have seen that things were not well. Here she is later, when Joyce is pregnant: "I dare not congratulate you on the hope of being a father, you are obviously repulsed by the idea . . . but I can imagine a little of how Joyce feels, and that she is happier than she has ever been in her life. I don't suppose one can get more pleasure out of anything than one would from bearing a child to the man one loved. . . . I suppose what you really object to is the responsibility, but that is probably worse in prospect than in fact."[28]

If Joyce had endured this far she was a saint, because a year or two earlier he had been writing in his diary as follows and can hardly have dissembled for long: "As I sat listening to her singing—this song which I used to love and now hate—the whole burden of my past came upon me with such insistence that I cried out. How, how to get rid of it, how shall I gain a contemporary life, how shall I throw off what ties me to what is no longer me?" And he now writes, "Seeing before me the vistas of life with no love—the life lived always with one whom I do not love, and with her child." (Notice he does not say, with *my* child.) "All the devastating details of that life. A posthumous life. And the contrast between it and the life of love—the grace and vitality of it. It is not hatred—simply, No Love" (PD, 1930).

"How shall I throw off what ties me to what is no longer me?" Well, most of us prefer altruism (at least in a sense), to be tied to what is *not* ourself. Egoism, to be tied to oneself, everything to be subsumed in and subservient to oneself, is probably a worse servitude than being tied to another.[29] But, "to be in love," Michael writes, "is heaven itself—to be loved is hell, or at least insufferable boredom" (PD, 1932). I do not wish to moralize, but there does seem to be something unpleasant here, as there also is about his repeated Nietzschean fulminations against gratitude, because it recognizes an obligation to something other than oneself, and obligations constrain one's "freedom." And yet the late W. H. ("Jack") Greenleaf, quite rightly on the evidence, could draw attention three decades later to Michael's "deep and genuine patriotism."[30] Maybe duties to people and to one's country are different. Or maybe we just change. After all, he had changed once already, from a pious young believer in Christian selflessness. There is nothing in the nature of things to say that one cannot change again, or change back to what one was.

At all events, Michael left his wife and child and returned to college. Simon was four and recalls asking Joyce whether it was he, Simon, who had driven his father away.[31] Michael kept some toys in his college rooms, and Simon came to play once a week, on Sundays. And it is true that Michael saw to Simon's later education (at Marlborough) and either paid for it or saw that it was paid for. But Simon—a psychiatrist—told me that it took him thirty-five years in therapy to recover from Michael's desertion and from grief on his mother's behalf. Joyce, however, seems to have been resilient, and she had the support of Michael's parents. What they thought about it all, and what (if anything) they said to Michael, I have yet to discover.

Michael's feelings for Céline had been nothing if not obsessional. Let us go back a couple of years, to an incident at the time of her graduation in 1932, shortly before she married and left for Athens. The episode is absurd but worth recounting. Céline had, she told me, a Cambridge friend, Shanti Dhavan, a tennis champion and future president of the Cambridge Union (the first Indian to hold that office), who years later, after Indian independence, became high commissioner in London and eventually (1969–71) governor of West Bengal. Shanti was in love with her, but she was engaged to Romilly and did not reciprocate, at least not in kind. However, Michael lent her his and Joyce's house (presumably they were away) to accommodate herself and her mother during May Week for the usual end-of-year festivities. While there, she allowed Shanti to visit, though evidently without having asked the Oakeshotts' permission. Like Céline's school, her mother espoused the doctrines of Mme. Blavatsky—"all that mystical rubbish," as Céline robustly characterized it to me—and was consequently keen on Indians, as incarnations of Oriental Wisdom.[32] (She had already collected a few on this trip.) This was surely excuse enough for inviting Shanti, if one were needed (and why should it be?).

I raised this whole business with her on account of an extraordinary, pages-long letter in the archive (BLPES, 10/1/14, dated May 31, 1932), written by Michael, accusing her of having "killed" him by this (unspecified) act of betrayal. (Remember, Michael had never fully "come out" to her. Moreover, he knew perfectly well that she loved and was engaged to Romilly.) The letter is neatly written, with no corrections, and there exist previous, plentifully overscribbled drafts in his notebooks. (Also loose in the file is a further letter, a foul copy dated June 14 and even lengthier, repeating, expanding upon and justifying the burden of the earlier.) Having largely forgotten its blistering rhetoric, I read the earlier aloud to Céline, but, as I read on, I did so with mounting horror at what I had started and could not now leave off.

She was shocked, I could tell, and I apologized for having forced her to relive the experience. But I had mistaken the source of her disquiet, which was that she was hearing the letter for the first time.[33] It had never been sent, which explains why it was filed along with her letters to him. (There is no mention of it in her letters.) At any rate, she did not recall having received it, and such were its contents that she could scarcely have forgotten it if she had, especially since she remembered all the attendant circumstances.[34] On finding out what Céline had done, Michael must have remonstrated with her in person (and, if doing so was to have made any sense, must have confessed at least some of his feelings), because there is a bleak little farewell message from her in the archive. But things must also have been patched up fairly soon (and Michael have either cooled down, or moved on), since within a couple of months she was cheerfully sending him an invitation from Athens, and, after the Jenkinses' return from Greece in 1934, she, Romilly, his fellow classicist Guy Griffith, and Michael ("all passion spent," as she wrote to me) would regularly make up a party for evenings and outings (not least to New-market races), a jolly foursome that lasted until the war dispersed it.

The Shanti episode is revealing in several ways. The first question, which is what in part had so shocked Céline, is how Michael could have had, or per-suaded himself that he had, such overmasteringly powerful emotions, com-mitted them to paper (doubtless further stoking them in the process), and then not communicated them to her, at least not in their full-blown epistolary form. Could they really have been sincere, or might it all have been some kind of conscious or half-conscious stratagem of which he eventually thought bet-ter? Is there not something faintly sinister about his ability to dissemble, not just his immediate sense of betrayal but, during them, his years of infatuation too? Would a woman not be made uneasy at the thought that she might long have featured as a pliable fantasy object in somebody else's imagination, and thus that her true relations with him had been quite different from what she had taken them to be?

Then again, nearly all Michael's letters are neat and legible, as is this, which was clearly destined to be sent (why else make a fair copy?) but, as it seems, never actually was. Although few letters from him survive, those he sent cannot have been many fewer than the huge number he received, on the latter's internal evidence. Even assuming (what is unlikely) that he never took more than a couple of drafts, and though he was quick in composition,[35] I still see no denying the possibility that he spent hours every day in social and (especially) amatory correspondence. If love was indeed the central business of his life, then this would not be surprising. What is surprising is how he ever got any work done, until one reflects that, as suggested earlier, his work evidently functioned as a necessary anodyne.[36]

Again, his "love" seems to have been remarkably self-centered, which only confirms his own diagnosis of its origins and operation. To direct such bitter reproaches at someone largely ignorant of the role she had been playing in his fantasy for three years, and therefore guiltless of any "betrayal," argues a considerable detachment from reality on his part. But then, his idea of love—as of poetry, if in a different way—was precisely, and frankly, that it does indeed involve a detachment from reality.[37]

Given the contradictions with which it is riven, it could hardly not have done so. The private notebooks of 1928–34 illustrate these contradictions, one is inclined to say ad nauseam, until one reflects that none of this was meant for anyone's consumption except Michael's, and that a man may surely be allowed to bore (or nauseate) himself if he so wishes. But a more or less coherent sequence apparently composed sometime from July 1931 onward, after Céline had gone away until October, exposes them in a conveniently small and quotable compass. This sequence is preceded by some draft letters to Céline, which presumably, like the "betrayal" ones of 1932, were never completed or sent. These indicate an intention to call the relationship off on the grounds of its intolerability; to him, that is, for she seems to have been blithely content with things as they seemed to her to be. What made them intolerable to him was the impossibility of their developing into a sexual relationship, which as he surely rightly foresaw, would have been disastrous, had it been possible.

Somewhat unusually for him at this period, an element of moral scruple seems also to have entered into his calculations, or so he tells himself. Either he has already discussed their relationship with her, or he intends to do so, and has decided unilaterally that they should part; also (which is both excusable and understandable) he has been less than candid with her about the true nature of his feelings. He may not even have told her of his decision. At all events, she has gone. (This is roughly a year before the Shanti pantomime.)

He now reflects: "All my life there has been this distrust of intimacy—at home, parents, brothers, friends. No frankness, openness. But all inside, seething and alone. I have always been alone. And when most alone I have wanted intimacy; when I have most distrusted it I have desired it. No freedom; only death and frustration." There is surely adolescent self-pity here, not to say considerable, even quasi-deliberate, self-deception, and a certain theatrical posturing, if only before a mirror. (Remember, this man is thirty: Hamlet's age, which is not altogether reassuring.) The emotion has a forced, factitious quality. It is as though Michael had just discovered that he ought to be feeling *Angst*, and had accordingly decided to sign up for some, although, by his own earlier testimonies, he has been reasonably happy until now. He goes on:

> Marriage: the attempt to free myself from the foreign world in which I lived and which I hated. But that too has failed. I am now as much a

prisoner as ever. . . . How difficult it is to live with other people—and how impossible not to. Intimacy, intimacy—and all I get is acquaintance. And when I press for intimacy;—the world goes to pieces. If it is refused I am lost; if it is given, it turns to dust and ashes. Intimacy is impossible? Then why do we crave it? Is life a radical contradiction? Oneness, oneness; & always plurality. To be alone and yet intimate with another. To find one's aloneness with another.

A vulgar response to these thoughts, interesting though they are, might be, "Stop it, you're breaking my heart." Also, a marriage finally crowning a devoted friendship unbroken since late childhood can scarcely be called either a bid for freedom or an escape from anything. "Chocolate-boxy" or not, it is what it is, and nothing else; most men or women finding themselves so situated would scarcely be able to believe their happiness, or their luck.

Finally: "Once it seemed as if life would offer what I asked of it—with Céline; but now that appearance of satisfaction has gone. Even this 'shaddow [sic] of stability' is gone. I want stability and I want freedom. Intimacy and aloneness. A world & freedom. And these, it seems, can never be had together. Satisfied love?—but can love be satisfied[?] Love is ever unsatisfied." He began by complaining of his aloneness and now says he wants it after all, under the guise of "freedom." Whether the contradictions of which he speaks are really intrinsic to life, or to love, or are merely idiopathic, peculiar to himself, they are clearly there. Maybe what Michael called love was by its very nature "ever unsatisfied"; but Joyce's entirely "normal" love for him, which was neither slavish nor demanding, was perfectly satisfied, or would have been, if he had only accepted it at its true, high worth. The only thing wrong with it was that it was greater than he deserved.

These reflections are immediately followed, in the private notebook, by some strutting, unbelievably preposterous nonsense about Céline, from whom Michael has had a "letter of parting": "She must return, because she is mine. And even if she does not return, she is mine for ever. I am master of her dead, if not alive. R[omilly] may have her body, but I have her mind and soul." (Nothing like hedging your bets.) "I shall go to her," he continues loftily, "no longer as a servant, no longer to give myself to her, to abandon myself to her, but as a master. I am her home. And when I go to her again it will be to ask when she is coming to me. I can wait: wait for her to awake." (Dream on, one might say, for it is not she who sleeps, but you.) The next entry, another self-consolation, reads, "A woman doesn't like being made love to except against her will." One surely need not be a feminist to find this statement disquieting.

The time has surely come to take leave of all this (and there is plenty more), if the reader is not also to take leave of his or her patience. So, here is one final extract almost immediately following from the last, to be read with irony or not, according to taste:

> I want a relationship without a name. Something profound, danger-
> ous, risky, incomplete and yet satisfying. . . . Something experimental.
> Something in which there is no routine. I want a lover, someone with
> whom love—this unnamed relationship—can grow and blossom. . . .
> My life has been spent in seeking her; indeed, I believe the purpose
> of life is to seek her, & the satisfaction of life to find her. . . . She gives
> me no peace; each year, each month I must set out again to find her.
> And if I did not identify this search with life itself, the number of my
> disappointments would long ago have made me hopeless. But, as with
> all lovers, I must have her or I die. For to be without her is not to be
> born, and to lose her is to die. For not until I have found her shall I have
> found myself.

Some will revel in this welter of paradox; the more sober or jaded may ask just how something "incomplete" can simultaneously be "satisfying," or how "a relationship without a name" can suddenly qualify for the label "love," which is nothing if not a name; but none can deny that the writer of those lines, as was claimed at the very beginning of this essay, is putting "love," as he understands it, at the center of his existence and is prepared to sacrifice both himself and others to it.[38]

As already noted, Céline didn't find Michael sexually attractive, and she told me also that she never so much as kissed him. On the other hand, she said, he did introduce her to nude bathing, an activity she was presumably absolutely free to decline, and which later, in 1955, got him into trouble with the law (see BLPES, 11/3; and his letters in August and November of that year to Eric and Marie Dowling, 15/2/2).[39] Michael set great store by sex, but he was not so much a sex maniac as a love junkie. Like many young men, espe-cially then, he had sampled casual sex in a brothel but pronounced it "sor-did."[40] "One should reserve . . . sexual intercourse with one's lover for those occasions when it is utterly impossible to resist," he wrote in the private note-books; "[I must] henceforth reserve myself for La Belle Dame Sans Merci—who can never come. Perversion, yes! but who is not perverted? Where is the normal sexual life?"

Wherever it was, he nevertheless wrote that "a sexless life is a living death" and avoided one, with notable and increasing success. For many years he had a lover of last resort in the painter Elisabeth (Beth) Vellacott (1905–2002), a friend of Joyce's. Another backstop (to judge by her letters) was Barbara Johnston, daughter of the London Underground typeface designer Edward Johnston and sister to Priscilla, who was married to Max Gill, designer of the first Underground map and brother of the (now) notorious Eric.[41] Later, in the army, Michael acquired the most unlovely nickname of Dipstick, but I doubt if it was earned in the customary manner, namely, through frequenting prostitutes. La Belle Dame Sans Merci would surely have cut little ice in the officers' mess. I should think it most likely that Michael spoke of compliant young women back home and sought out others where he was. A memoirist, I forget who, recalls his pursuit of "pretty Dutch girls" in Holland, and Sir Peregrine Worsthorne, who served under him, has testified to Michael's success in this area.[42]

It was Beth Vellacott who on a gypsy-caravanning holiday in Dorset introduced him to his future second wife, Kate Burton.[43] (It seems this bohemian excursion, as was only right and proper, involved some unplanned bed swapping.) I cannot dilate on Kate's tragedy here. If it were less monotonously and horribly predictable, it might deserve a volume to itself. Indeed, it as good as occupies several volumes already. Taken out of their boxes, her twenty years' worth of letters (BLPES, 9/3) would make a pile five feet high. It is a masochistic researcher who contemplates them with anything but despair, especially once he has read a few.

Born in 1911, Kate was the same age as Céline, and six years Beth's junior. She had married one Ian Cox, who worked for the BBC in Manchester and whose treatment of her was so unpleasant that she fled to London with their small son and lived in Islington in poverty with a load of arty bohemians. (It is not clear whether she did so particularly to be near Michael, whom she had met before moving south.) But she knew everybody who was anybody and has interesting things to say about them: the Bloomsberries, the Cornfords, the neo-Pagans (including her on-and-off flatmate, Brynhild Olivier), the documentary filmmaker Humphrey Jennings, the painter Jean Varda (who had danced with Nijinsky), the modernist architect Ernö Goldfinger and his wife the grocery heiress Ursula Blackwell, and many more, including the Johnstons and Gills (already mentioned), together with Desmond ("Sage") Bernal, Ralph Parker, and other fashionable communists.[44] She was a brilliant woman, a scholar of Newnham with a well-deserved double First in English, but of a needy and neurotic disposition, if excusably so in her circumstances.

Céline, Romilly, and his fellow classicist Guy Griffith—with whom Michael wrote his book about horse racing—didn't much care for Kate, finding her (in Céline's expression) "brittle," and Guy said right from the start of the relationship, which was seriously under way by 1936, that it would never last, as it didn't.[45] Kate's interminable letters to Michael begin in that year and alternate, often in the one letter, between the gushing, the gossipy, the trivial, the amusing, the seriously intelligent and critical, the beseeching, and the downright abject and piteous. They married at the end of 1938 and lived together in Shelford (outside Cambridge) until 1940, when Michael enlisted, so the wags said, to escape Kate. Obviously, no correspondence exists for this short period. Her letters, sometimes as many as three a day, resume in 1940. To judge by their contents, Michael must have replied fairly regularly, though his output can scarcely have matched hers.[46] Until he was deployed to Holland after D-Day, he returned from his army duties for weekends three or four times a year, often (so it seems on other evidence) taking in Beth Vellacott's bed en route. Once demobilized he moved back into his college room, leaving Kate with her son Christopher in Shelford. Their large cottage was called West End; in her letters to him thereafter she calls it Wits' End.

To Kate's great grief, having previously promised her a child, he had refused to have one with her and never took any interest in his stepson.[47] I spoke to her late daughter-in-law, Cecelia Cox, and she assured me that nothing of Michael survived in Kate's life apart from his surname, and not a single letter. Kate spoke little of her sufferings, though there are photographs which speak volumes. She had given supervision in literature at Newnham but retrained as a psychiatric social worker, was very good at it, and was loved and respected by her colleagues. Being married to her might have been trying for anyone, but the fact is that Michael broke her heart, not out of deliberate cruelty, but through sheer, prolonged emotional starvation. As Simon put it to me, when faced with a hopeless situation, what he did was simply walk away. (And indeed, what else could he have done? The thing is not to get into it in the first place.) Kate died in her sleep, it was thought of a stroke, in 1964, aged only fifty-three. Some friends put together a little posthumous tribute and had it professionally printed. It mentions neither husband.

There are many other people I could discuss, but elsewhere. As is well known, Michael led a very active love life in the 1940s and 1950s (and even later), having affairs, usually overlapping, with—only among others, note— Iris Murdoch (twice), Jenifer (Mrs. H. L. A.) Hart, Mary Walsh (with whom he had an illegitimate son, Sebastian, before deserting them both), Barbara Hoyle (wife of the cosmologist Fred Hoyle), his son Simon's girlfriend Bobbie Kirk, and Rosemary Wormald, wife of the Peterhouse historian Brian Wormald, who was entangled at the time with the notorious Catherine Walston, Graham Greene's mistress. This for the most part was a mere sexual merry-go-round (or perhaps *danse macabre*), with some exceptions. Almost unbelievably, Michael seems seldom to have been sleeping with fewer than three women at once.[48]

Here we come up against two conflicting bodies of evidence. Professor John Charvet, whom Michael appointed to the London School of Economics in 1965, says his affairs were discreet. The late Dr. Anne Bohm, however, who ran the graduate school, told me they were not. "He never tried to hide it," she said, "he was proud of it all." "Proud," she went on, "that he'd seduced all his students' wives: it was all part of life." She did not know about his failure to secure the mastership of Caius, but her triumphant response, when I told her, verged on contempt: "Hah! So they didn't want him seducing their wives." (This was probably true, though his successful rival Joseph Needham's sex life was almost as notorious.) And yet almost the first thing she had told me was that "everybody loved him."

This is not credible, taken literally. There will have been many—for example, his married male students, by her own account—who had no cause at all to love Michael, and it is surprising that he apparently pursued his relentless career of seduction with his cuticle intact. In any other profession or period somebody, surely, would have "called him out" or, as in "Sapper" or Dornford Yates, "thrashed him on the steps of his club." There are no threatening letters from aggrieved husbands, or if there were, Michael (uniquely) did not keep them. The nude bathing incident of 1955 was provoked by the return to Australia of his research student Eric Dowling and his wife Marie, with whom Michael (inevitably) purported to be in love, though whether there was an actual affair is doubtful. At all events, Michael was apparently so overwhelmed by their (or rather her) departure that—Turgenev-style, and true to type—he burst into tears at Victoria Station, refused to adjourn to the pub with colleagues also at the send-off, rushed home, packed his car hastily, and drove off to Dorset for a week's camping to recover, and it was during this week that the offense (indecent exposure) was inadvertently committed.[49]

I mention this episode, not so much for its unintentionally comic character as for its implicit confutation of Dr. Bohm's popularity thesis. Although Dowling's correspondence with Michael is genial enough, I have it from Michael's pupil Professor Conal Condren that Dowling did not love Michael at all, for good reason as it seems, and never had a good word to say about him.

There is still the question of how public Michael's affairs were. The Bohm-Charvet discrepancy is probably explicable. By the time of Professor Charvet's appointment Michael was into his third marriage and his mid-sixties, when even he might be expected to have calmed down (a bit). But he presented different faces to different people and was compelled to do so by his chosen

manner of life. Professor Charvet must have known Michael's amatory reputation but could still truthfully have said that he himself had never seen
evidence of it. So very many people, including him, have said to me—independently of one another and often in these exact words—that Michael "kept
his life in separate compartments," that it must be true, and there are also
good reasons why. There is no other way of juggling several mistresses simultaneously, for a start. It would have been perfectly possible for Dr. Bohm and
Professor Charvet to be admitted individually only to this or that compart-
ment, and never both to the same one.

There is plenty more evidence of the same kind, and it does not always
concern his amatory adventures. Clearly Michael adapted himself to his company, only more elastically than most, and in such a way as virtually to frag-
ment (or multiply) his identity, each persona inhabiting one of many separate,
mutually insulated "worlds" and varying accordingly.[50] Perhaps promiscuity,
whether sexual or social, was as near as he could get to that obliteration of the
self he had hankered after as a young man.

I come now to Michael's last grand passions. One, in the late 1950s, was
Patricia Gale (Mrs. George Gale, later Mrs. Maurice Cowling), and I do not yet
have the whole story. Pat was half Michael's age. After a brief capitulation, so
she told me, and even while he was living for months on end with the Gales
in Staines or (disastrously) vacationing with them in Rome and elsewhere,
she kept him as much at arm's length as she could, despite his anguished
pleadings and all-night, all-weather vigils. These were well-honed techniques
that had seldom failed him before; as to the latter, I am not alone in having
wondered whether he had copied it from James Joyce's story, "The Dead."

He had also used these same persuaders on the other grand passion of
his middle age, June Hooper (later Plaat). June (b. 1925) was his number one
mistress for three or four years from 1949. Like Céline, only at Newnham,
she was another brilliant, tough-minded undergraduate, who he used to say
was the only woman he ever really loved.[51] She told me, however, in the very
same words as Pat Gale, "Oh yes, I loved him, but I was never in love with
him." June left not only all Michael's letters to her but a manuscript memoir
concerning him too. She read out bits to me as she was writing it. It is only a
first draft, a six-page codicil to a book-sized manuscript memoir of her family,
and she died suddenly, in 2005, before she could revise it.[52] Only after her
death (which I felt as a real loss, as I did Céline's) did it come my way. There
is so much of interest in it, and also in what June told me, that I cannot go
into the full story here.

But a few random points in temporary conclusion may not come amiss.
June told me how, when Iris Murdoch first made a play for Michael on his

arrival at Oxford in 1949, he claimed virtuously to have refused her advances, saying that he was already "plighted to another" (i.e., herself). I knew this tale already from someone else and said so. "He was such a frightful liar," June replied. "I expect he comforted her afterwards." (He did. June did not know at the time that Michael was already sleeping with Jenifer Hart, but Jenifer and Iris knew about June and, it seems, about each other. This asymmetrical arrangement was not unusual. Presumably the novices had to be broken in gently.)

Second, at the urging of their shared Newnham tutor—the literary scholar Enid Welsford, who knew she was involved with Michael—June went to see the desolate Kate and was so appalled by what she saw, and by what Kate warned her to expect, that she called off the affair.[53] "But," June told me, "Michael did one of his Romeo acts, and I succumbed."[54] She told Noël O'Sullivan (though not me) a near-incredible story about Michael's visit to her parents in Kirkcudbright, seeking their approval to marry her. However, his constant uxorious fondling of her in front of them, which June evidently did nothing to discourage (doubtless because it was early days, and she was still besotted), led her mother to say, after being closeted alone with him, "If he tries to marry you, I shall kill him."[55] As June frequently asked me, about other aspects of his behavior, "What on earth can he have thought he was doing? Did he even *know* what he was doing?" There are certainly moments, recorded by both him and others, and this one particularly, when one can only conclude that he didn't.

Last, at the other extreme of unrealism, there was Michael's medievalizing romanticism. June said, and wrote, that he saw himself as—indeed, while the fit lasted, actually *was*—a Petrarchan lover or a lovelorn troubadour. (Noël O'Sullivan independently described him to me as a would-be troubadour; we both knew, of course, that he wasn't always.) The girl in the narrative, June wrote in her memoir, was the Sleeping Beauty, Greensleeves, the Rose in a walled garden, not a real garden but a tapestry one, in which he, Michael, was intent on keeping her. But once the Rose had been plucked, and the Sleeping Beauty had awoken, looked around and laid claim to her own life, the spell was broken. Michael, June said, was a "ruthless Romantic." "How," she wrote to me (mostly with Kate in mind, though with Joyce and Simon too), "could he not know the desolation and misery he was causing? How could he bear the knowledge?" And this is from her memoir: "Despite his great intelligence . . . there was a curious blankness somewhere at the centre of his being of which he knew nothing, and which it was therefore axiomatic no one else could know."

Having written those arresting—even compelling—words, she crossed them out. How much credence then should we give them? (As much as a thought? Or an unsent letter?) Did she think better of them? Or did she think of something better, but never got to write it down? Many critics have said much the same about the elusiveness of Michael's philosophy, which of course is not to say they are right.[56] Perry Worsthorne, who actually knew Michael much better than most, said to me that "nobody really knew him" and asked, "Was he simply indifferent to people?"

June felt she could never get to the bottom of him, if indeed there was one. "I longed to know what it felt like to be Michael," says her memoir, "what he thought about when he wasn't writing or teaching, but he guarded these chambers like Bluebeard's room." She got "fed up with being a nymph" (in the same sense, doubtless, as Michael was a classic nympholept) and went back to Scotland:

> He was desolated by my escape . . . & wrote me a great many letters which I didn't much like because they were too full of lingerings on my physical charms—breasts, legs, hair—which made me uneasy and irritable. . . . Looking back, I'm surprised by his lack of ingenuity. . . . Why didn't he guess I was far more likely to be won . . . by appreciation of me-as-me rather than by my body, and that even one or two apples from his cornucopia of intellectual riches would hold me much more securely than pages about my breasts and legs? Our blind spots are curious.[57]

They are indeed. I would bet a small sum, however, that two decades earlier he never sent Jean Beecher that tribute to her breasts.

It is time, if only provisionally, to take stock. Much that I have said will have shocked you, painfully, if you knew and loved Michael but suspected none of it, or from surprise, if you knew only his work. The tensions, contradictions, bizarreries, and irrationalities of his personal life are scarcely reflected at all in his work's characteristically polished, Apollonian surface. But his romantic-erotic-*libertin*-Dionysiac side (hereafter, if inadequately, "Dionysiac" for short) is now wide open to view, undeniable and disturbing, and a biographer cannot ignore it, especially when Michael himself explicitly stresses its centrality to his life and purposes. (It is perfectly possible to say that, though the work is by definition part of the life, the life is not, or not directly, part of the work.)

This Dionysiac side of him has struck even nonintimates. There was an outré, reckless, even "dangerous" quality, wholly at odds with his Olympian writerly persona, to his private thinking (and reading), especially as expressed in late-night conversations with John Gray or others at the Carlyle Club.[58] Professor Gray surprised me, since I had not yet seen the notebooks, by speaking of Michael's consuming interest in mysticism, be it sex mysticism, English nature mysticism,[59] or the full-blown Russian theological variety (Dostoyevsky, Shestov, Rozanov, Berdyaev, and others). Michael was drawn, said Gray, to "extreme" thinkers in the Nietzsche and Kierkegaard mold. Such enthusiasms are a far cry from his "normal" pantheon of statesmanly pragmatists such as "Trimmer" Halifax and the third Marquis of Salisbury, and from his simultaneous piety toward sober traditional institutions such as Parliament, the army and the universities. Astonishingly, Michael seems to have believed, or at least been interested, in astrology sufficiently to have his horoscope professionally cast (BLPES, 13/3) and to have tried also to persuade his friend and companion-about-town Shirley Letwin to share his interest.[60]

We may ask whether it makes sense, Nietzsche-fashion, to reduce his thought to his life, that is, to see it as a justification or rationalization of the life he either chose, or was impelled, to live: in short, to reduce it ultimately to temperament, constitution, or the like (or indeed, Marx-fashion, to socio-economic factors).[61] The pitfalls are obvious: any such explanation must be open to the same reduction and thus similarly invalidate itself. In fact, why seek an "explanation" at all? Why not just say that his (or anyone's) thought is a straightforward, unproblematic *expression* of his life? After all, it is part of it, and such a contextual account of ideology, as the "precipitate" of a concrete historical situation, is characteristic of Michael's own thinking. On the other hand, should we not say that the life is (in part) the consequence of the thought, since life is action, and action is the product of thought?

At one point Michael notes that "what I write here is merely a kind of justification of my temperament," adding, "I write it to persuade myself." (Of what, exactly?) But since he also describes his temperament as "quietist and indolent," it is presumably not the radical Dionysiac antinomianism of the private notebooks that he is referring to (the context provides no help), but the familiar conservative, Apollonian, antiactivist Oakeshott (BLPES, 2/1/10, 77, 1928). In another passage from the same public notebook, however, we get a glimpse of Michael's alternative Dionysiac credo (elaborated more fully in the private notebooks) and a most revealing suggestion as to its nature and origin:

> How many causes have I not adhered to in the belief that here was something enchanting, dangerous, living, and something in which one could find oneself. In the flush of youth I believed in socialism, because I thought it would be thrilling. I did not hate injustice; I merely wanted to escape from an existence without a purpose. Now I believe in love—& for the same reason. And by love I mean the adventure of a relationship

which knows no bounds. Love is the greatest "cause." It is so m
fuller & more satisfying than any other that it deserves to be in its (
entirely different category. But love is also the most dangerous—un
you are content to be a mere Casanova. (BLPES, 2/1/10, 90, 1928)

Well, we know that much of the time, especially in the 1950s, he was so c
tent. But he here sees erotic love ("a relationship which knows no bounc
as the same kind of "thrilling" utopian project as the socialism he has c
grown, and as supplanting it, because, though similarly redemptive (prom
ing "escape from an existence without a purpose"), it is "so much fuller a
more satisfying." In short, Michael's Dionysiac yearnings and goals, and 1
romantic libertinism in which he sought to realize them, at no matter wl
cost, amount to a kind of Rationalism in Love. By extension, his private no
books and associated literary enthusiasms (Powys, Lawrence, Fraser, and o
ers) then constitute its ideology, manifesto, or "scriptural" component.

As we have seen, this project was both incoherent and destructive, par
because, though irrational, it was rationalist in Michael's sense and th
apt to collide with reality, and partly because, as Céline objected, it was pr
foundly selfish.[62] One might also call it, to adapt his accusation against rati
nalist politics, "the erotics of inexperience" (an inexperience if anything on
underscored by the frequency of his sexual conquests, since he seems to hav
learned, and to have expected to learn, nothing from them). But there is n
reason to regard Michael's Dionysiac side as necessarily more "fundamei
tal" than the Apollonian persona and the cluster of associated values, whic
predominate in his published writings. There is no call, in short, to accus
Michael of "hypocrisy" because in his private life Dionysus was (possibly
more often in the driver's seat than Apollo. In his public, official life—in fact
in almost any sphere, public or private, in which sex was not involved—h
lived out his Apollonian values as regularly as he flouted them in the sexua
sphere, as can be seen from his life-long friendships, his care for and gener
osity to his pupils, and his love of, and loyalty to, not only his own country,
culture, and civilization, but others too.[63] (Michael said that a man should
have two countries; his other was France.) His eventual third marriage, to the
twenty-seven-year-old Christel Schneider in 1965, was different from the others, and successful; he told me and many others that it was a kind of restitu-
tion, though not of course to her personally.[64] Would one therefore call him a
traitor to Dionysus, hypocritical in short, for not being as selfish in everything
as the project demanded?

Both sides of his nature were real, though each, seen from the other's
standpoint, was illusory. But it was Dionysus who failed the objective reality

test, and erotic matters feature not at all, even negatively, in Michael's Apollonian writings, which is just why people are surprised and even shocked when they learn about his private life. It is a totally different world from the one they associated with him. And yet, the two worlds are connected, if only functionally. Could it be that Michael's anti-utopian politics were, first, a counterweight to his erotic utopia, but also, secondarily, a foundation for it, through the Hobbesian security and consequent freedom of action they guarantee? The Dionysiac project is unsustainable in the long run, but it is even less sustainable when not pursued against a background of Apollonian order. We need not be paid-up Freudians to see the parallel between the two sides of Michael Oakeshott, with their equivocal relations, and Freud's pleasure and reality principles, of which the second acts both as a constraint on the first, and by doing so, as its safeguard. As for "free" love, even if all the contracting parties had met their responsibilities and endured their miseries (as they didn't), it was certainly not free for those totally outside the contract, such as Michael's sons, who picked up much of the tab.

But for all that, Michael's work stands or falls on its own terms (it stands) and by its own merits (which are considerable). That much of his life was at odds with it doesn't invalidate the work at all. Evelyn Waugh, to take an extreme example, was a most disagreeable and unpleasant man, as Michael wasn't, and himself admitted as much, but his novels make perfectly plain that he knew what goodness and decency were, and prized them, though they were beyond his reach. And, by some patient and long-suffering friends, he too was loved.

NOTES

1. Robert Grant, *Oakeshott*, Thinkers of Our Time (London: Claridge Press, 1990), 11–23. I gave a brief account of this meeting in the Oakeshott memorial number of the *Cambridge Review*: Grant, "Inside the Hedge: Oakeshott's Early Life and Work," *Cambridge Review* 112 (1991): 106–9.

2. To simplify considerably, in the Church of England a rector is "grander" than a vicar.

3. Though Michael's mother had money, their house actually belonged to her brother, also named Thomas Hellicar.

4. Dodd is reputed, in family circles, to have designed Portland Place, something usually attributed to the Adam brothers, but I have found no suggestion of this in the *Dictionary of National Biography* or elsewhere.

5. Michael told me that his father's world was straight out of Trollope's *Three Clerks*. Joseph's account of the Civil Service, in his scattered manuscript notes and memoirs, is more like Joyce's *Dubliners*. He notes the frequency in his profession of two things in particular, alcoholism and suicide. He comes across as a man of wholly unself-righteous honesty, decency, and integrity, with compassion and understanding toward his weaker brethren. His papers are also full of wryly amusing anecdotes and reminiscences, which he has evidently been at some pains to collect.

6. Oakeshott Avenue, Holly Lodge Estate, Highgate, London N6. To view, type Oakeshott Avenue N6 into Google's search box and click on "Images" and "Maps." "Holly Lodge Estate," *Wikipedia*, last modified March 23, 2010, http://en.wikipedia.org/wiki/Holly_Lodge_Estate. Simon Oakeshott doubts the truth of the rumor.

7. The editorial title, "Inside the Hedge" (see note 1), is based on my quotations from Michael's memoir of his school days; see H. W. Howe, ed., *A Portrait of the Founders* (Harpenden: St. George's School, 1967), 14–18. Michael described the school as "surrounded by a thick, firm hedge," inside which was "a world of beckoning activities and interests." The headmaster, the Reverend Cecil Grant, was at once a man of undogmatic piety, with pre-Raphaelite tastes, and a serious amateur philosopher, who introduced his sixth-form pupils to Hegel. A socialist, he was also a friend of the educationist Maria Montessori ("the Dottoressa," as he called her) who twice visited St. George's. Michael kept up with Grant until his death in 1946.

8. There is an attractive photograph of both girls in the school lacrosse team, undated but most likely from about 1915–16.

9. Information in part from Simon, but see also Howe, *Portrait of the Founders*, 8–9.

10. "More things are wrought by prayer / Than this world dreams of. Wherefore let thy voice / Rise like a mountain [*sic*] for me night and day." How anyone could possibly, even in memory, misread "fountain" as "mountain" is beyond me. (See Tennyson, "Morte d'Arthur," lines 247–49, and see note 21, on Michael's poetical efforts.) A character in Bojer's novel, during a famine, sows his own last few grains of barley by night in his enemy's field, "that God might exist" (an episode quoted and illustrated in "Scala Precis"). In an illuminating essay the literary editor of the *Chicago Evening Post* suggests many resemblances between Bojer's and (as they developed later) Michael's views of life:

> What saves Bojer's novels from being didactic and, therefore, misleading is his adherence to the great truth that there is no such thing as a science of ethics, but that there is such a thing as an art of conduct. You cannot make general rules of conduct, for every case has its not to be duplicated features. . . . In all four of these novels we see men trying this, that and the other patent medicine of conduct. . . . The typical Bojer novel may be said to exhibit a modern soul tortured with moral ideas, as Rolland said of Tolstoy, . . . but always blundering towards an adjustment with the world, . . . not finding a chart as our ethical teachers would assure us is possible, but finding that there is no chart and that we must keep on blundering until, by trial and error, we make our own adjustment. . . . Bojer shows us the futility of charts and the great perils of self-deception. We keep our souls by eternal vigilance and by feeding them upon the bread of the moment.

Llewellyn Jones, introduction to *Johan Bojer: The Man and His Works*, by Carl Gad (New York: Moffat, Yard, 1920), 19–21.

11. Years later Joyce told Simon that Michael's first words on hearing her news were "Can't you get rid of it?" Almost unbelievable, perhaps, but alas, not entirely. Latterly, however, Michael was vehemently opposed to abortion (information from Professor Kenneth Minogue). Perhaps, as in other matters, he felt he had something to expiate.

12. He told Céline Jenkins (see main text, to follow) that God was "only an idea," but since, as an idealist, he held that everything equally was "only an idea," this tells us little, as does the fact that (as he told me) he always attended chapel when revisiting Caius, of which he was an honorary life fellow. In his later years, however, visiting an ecclesiastical ruin with his pupil David Manning of Durham University, he asked Dr. Manning (who told me this story) to leave him alone briefly so that he could pray.

13. Henry van Dyke, *The Story of the Other Wise Man* (New York: Harper and Brothers, 1896).

14. For this reason I give no detailed references, only Michael's own general dates.

15. Compare Michael's diary entry: "We fall in love with a friend; we lie with her, & wake to find beside us a stranger" (PD, 1932). Do we? Or does it depend on what kind of people "we" are?

16. It is true, in a sense, that the sexual act involves a renunciation of individuality. But it does not follow that annihilation of self and other is either the result or desired. As even Michael sometimes concedes, in a grown-up relationship both, in identifying themselves with the loved other, become a kind of third, joint, super-individual. See Donne's "The Ecstasy" or, indeed,

without the sexual component (which Donne discounts as "dull sublunary" love), see Montaigne on his friendship with Étienne de la Boëtie (*Essays*, I, 27).

17. This syndrome is also a repeated theme in Thomas Hardy, moving center stage in his *The Well-Beloved*, which no less an admirer of Hardy than D. H. Lawrence (himself admired by Michael) called "sheer rubbish, fatuity." Michael, as letters from various people show, would often send Hardy's novels to his friends as presents.

18. D. H. Lawrence, *Fantasia of the Unconscious* (New York: Seltzer, 1922), 91.

19. See the preface in August Strindberg, *Miss Julie* (1888), trans. Michael Meyer (London: Methuen, 1967). One might have thought, however, that implicitly to commend, as Michael does, "the integrity and separateness of the self" was effectively to attribute to it something like the character of "a finished mental concept."

20. Michael wrote a fair amount of verse, some of it published in Cambridge magazines. It is not, on the whole, good, though when in pseudomedieval or "Jacobethan" lyric mode it sometimes reads well enough (the model here being largely James Joyce's *Chamber Music*). In particular it seems to have a deficient sense of rhythm. It seems curious that a notable prose stylist should be an inept versifier, though there is always the earlier, and much worse, example of Michael's hero Hobbes, whose poetry is well up to *Stuffed Owl* standard, namely, atrocious.

21. Oddly, for one both so bohemian and so indifferent to (and generous with) money, he was minutely scrupulous about account keeping. (Presumably if you don't look after your money you don't then have it to give away.) He was similarly scrupulous, both in the army and as a don, in performing his administrative duties, though doubtless the motivation there was somewhat different.

22. Augustine also furnished the motto, "Love, and do what thou wilt," for Rabelais's Abbey of Thelema, celebrated by Michael as a nursery of spontaneous virtue (*OHC*, 78). But the same motto was later adopted (with predictable ease) to dignify the libertine projects of Sir Francis Dashwood, of Hellfire Club fame, and the occultist Aleister Crowley, who gave the name Thelema (meaning "Will") to the "religion" he founded.

23. It certainly was for the Brethren of the Free Spirit, since, already being one with God, they could not sin. This medieval so-called heresy descended to the Ranters of seventeenth-century England, to William Blake, and even (so the late Sir Frank Kermode claimed) to D. H. Lawrence. In his copy of Norman Cohn's *The Pursuit of the Millennium*, Michael has marked the following passages in the appendix by and about the Ranters: "If a man were strongly moved by the spirit to commit adultery &c and on praying against it again and again it continued . . . he should do it"; "we can commit any sin, for we esteem not any thing to be unclean . . . we are pure, say they, and so all things are pure to us, adultery, fornication etc. we are not defiled"; "they say that for one man to be tyed to one woman, or one woman to one man, is a fruit of [Adam's] curse; but, they say, we are freed from the curse; therefore it is our liberty to make use of whom we please."

24. Ronald Fraser, *Rose Anstey* (London: Cape, 1930).

25. This letter was sent sometime in early October 1930, from Somerville Lodge, 53 Elsworthy Road, Hampstead, and headed "Tuesday." By Llewelyn Powys's request, Michael read aloud book 4 of Hobbes's *Leviathan* to him on his deathbed in Switzerland in 1939 (information from Professor John Gray). He knew, and admired, all three Powys brothers. Powys's title, it may not be irrelevant to note, is taken from a bawdy West Country rhyme: "Apples be ripe / And nuts be brown; / Petticoats up / And trousers down."

26. Céline wrote to him, "Do you *really* fall in love with the consumate [*sic*] ease that you lead one to suppose? Children aged 14 are very inflamable [*sic*] & at that age I found love a very solemn business which ended rather badly" (BLPES, 10/1/14, sent from Hampstead, headed "Saturday," and probably dating from September 1930).

27. BLPES, 10/1/14, undated, no envelope, but headed "Wednesday," sent from 53 Elsworthy Road, Hampstead, and situated in file between cards postmarked December 1929 and May 1930.

28. Ibid., dated only "Saturday 20th." The most likely month is September 1930—the only other possible month is December 1930—September 20 was almost exactly six months before Simon's birth.

29. See the master/slave parable in G. W. F. Hegel, *Phenomenology of Spirit*, trans. A. V. Miller (Oxford: Clarendon Press, 1977), secs. 178–96.

30. W. H. Greenleaf, *Oakeshott's Philosophical Politics* (London: Longmans, 1966), 84. See also note 64.

31. A pupil of Michael's, Professor Martyn Thompson of Tulane University, remarked to me, "He liked children, so long as they were other people's." Others have made similar comments.

32. The theosophists eventually abandoned St. Christopher School, Letchworth, and it was taken over by Quakers (information from Céline).

33. She wrote to me afterward that "the trip down Memory Lane was a painful one and gave me some wakeful hours." "I never realised," she went on, "that Michael was experiencing feelings as intense as those expressed in that letter of May 1932. Being hopelessly in love I thought of as being part of the persona he liked to project, 'l'homme maudit.'. . . I still cannot pin down any incident that could have triggered such an explosion of jealousy. Perhaps he sensed that he never attracted me physically which Shanti did. Jealousy is the most destructive of all the emotions and the one I should place first and not ninth of the Ten Commandments" (June 27, 2004).

34. There is a draft note from him, headed merely "Friday" and therefore apparently (though not certainly) written three days after the June 14 draft letter (Tuesday), saying he hopes she has burned "that letter" (which one?) "long ago" (how long ago could it be?) because it contained "so many outrageous things." But this too was among his papers, not hers, and so presumably was never sent either. There is a real unsolved mystery in all this, of course. If Michael never sent the May 31 letter (and he seems otherwise not to have kept fair copies of letters he did send), why should he bother with writing, or at least beginning to write, the June 14 letter? And yet, as I read the May 31 letter to her, everything indicated that Céline was telling the truth in saying she had never received it (and she was a truthful person). There seem to be two possibilities: first, that she had repressed the memory of having received it, and therefore really thought she hadn't done so. But if so, why would she remember all the circumstances? Wouldn't one repress those memories too? The second is that Michael was playing out a fantastic imaginary game with himself, in which he wrote possibly two fictional (and unsent) sequels to a letter he either knew he had never sent in the first place or convinced himself he actually had sent when he hadn't. Neither is impossible, given that he was clearly almost out of his mind at the time.

35. He told me that his brilliant and penetrating review of E. H. Carr, "Mr Carr's First Volume" (*CPJ*, 10, 325–33), was written in a single evening.

36. Regarding his troubled affair with Rosemary Wormald (see main text, to follow), he wrote, "I suppose I shall take refuge in work" (BLPES, 15/2/2, to Marie Dowling, April 5, 1957), and similarly, referring to his final loss of Pat Gale (ditto), that "The Voice of Poetry" had been "written to exorcise the worst kind of misery" (to Eric Dowling, October 24, 1959). These are not the only examples. The paucity of his published work compared with the considerable amount he actually wrote (as evidenced by the sheer size of the BLPES archive) may also be significant. He says in various places that he writes mainly for himself, which could mean, mainly *to escape* himself, and possibly, as I shall argue later, to do so by constructing an alternative "Apollonian" self in his writings.

37. His idea of love also testifies to considerable confusion. He says he is jealous, though not of Romilly, because he knows she loves him (what kind of reason is that?); he also says he doesn't care if she has slept with Shanti, since that is "not my business." So of what exactly was he jealous, except of the attention she allegedly gave to Shanti, who loved her, but whom she did not love in return? In any case, one would have thought jealousy and "free love" (in which Michael evidently now believed) were incompatible, even if the jealousy was not specifically sexual.

38. There is no small element in it of what Denis de Rougemont later called "Tristanism," in *L'amour et l'occident* (Paris: Plon 1939), a book that excited Michael's interest when it appeared. Michael noted in 1928, "Absolute carelessness of reputation, etc.: new standard of what is important. Cp. Proust, *A l'ombre des jeunes filles en fleur.*" And again: "Love & the complete indifference to others which comes with it. The others disappear: we abandon ourselves completely, reputation, position, ambitions, everything to love." But he added, to his credit, "Perhaps to abandon, to forget the person, who loves us but whom we do not love" [Joyce, i.e.] "will mean her death—she will sink back into a kind of dumb despair, the feeling of failure and inferiority will sweep over her and drown her soul. And yet, when love is elsewhere, what are we to do [?]" (PD, 1928). Further on he noted, "Tristram & Isold [*sic*]—the identification of the beloved with the whole world"

(1930). What this means, in practice, is that the beloved actually eclipses and annihilates the entire "real" (shared, objective) world.

39. As Céline tactfully put it, he never "became excited." (Would one?) But of course his taste for nude bathing may have had no immediate sexual motive, simply being part, rather, of the "progressive" Edwardian ethos. He may have been introduced to it in Germany in the 1920s, by the back-to-nature Wandervögel movement. There is much in traditional nudism to suggest that, so far from being erotically driven, it is actually puritanical in tendency, being an attempt, mithridatically as it were, to immunize oneself against ("irrational") sexual desire by outfacing its normal visual stimuli. Michael's brush with the law was neither the first time, nor the first time in that place. He and Mary Walsh (the mother, later, of his second son, Sebastian) had been reported to the police the previous year for skinny-dipping on the same stretch of the Dorset coast, near Chesil Beach. They were on a visit to the writer Alyse Gregory, Llewelyn Powys's widow, who lived nearby (information from Mary Wong, formerly Walsh).

40. Note this, however: "If I went with a prostitute I should want to bring her flowers" (PD, 1932).

41. These letters (BLPES, 10/1/13) are attributed in the catalog to "B. A. J.," which is how she signs herself when not plain "Barbara." The name "B. Johnston" appears only on the back of one envelope (postmarked August 25, 1941), which is clearly how it has come to be overlooked. But that this can only be the Barbara Johnston identified here is everywhere confirmed by the letters' contents (e.g., she has a sister Priscilla, who is married to Max, etc.).

42. *Tricks of Memory* (London: Weidenfeld and Nicolson, 1993), 71; personal information from the author.

43. Kate often refers in her letters to Dorset and gypsy caravans as a *locus amoenus*, or lost romantic idyll. Though seldom fully at ease with ordinary working-class people, Michael was keen on gypsies and read and recommended to his friends books about them (e.g., Konrad Bercovici's *Between Earth and Sky*, 1925). His army friend Sir John Jacob Astor bought a gypsy caravan, "in which he and Oakeshott would tour the countryside of Berkshire and Gloucestershire, establishing a close rapport with gipsies" (Astor's obituary, *Daily Telegraph*, September 13, 2000). According to Simon, one of Michael's daydreams was to live like the painter Augustus John in 1909, with two "wives" and various ragged children (presumably not Michael's own) in a pair of gypsy caravans parked on Grantchester Meadows. Rupert Brooke, who was then living in Grantchester, told J. M. Keynes that John, who was ostensibly there to paint the classical scholar Jane Harrison, spent most days getting drunk and picking fights with the locals in Cambridge pubs. See Keynes to Duncan Grant, July 25, 1909, quoted in Michael Holroyd, *Augustus John* (London: Chatto and Windus, 1996), 286.

44. Brynhild ("Bryn") Olivier was sister to Noël Olivier, Rupert Brooke's girlfriend. See Paul Delany, *The Neo-Pagans: Friendship and Love in the Rupert Brooke Circle* (London: Macmillan, 1987). For those who are interested, this book contains a great deal about nude bathing and the like (see note 39). It also recounts the arrival of Augustus John at Grantchester (65). So does Brooke's letter to Noël of July 25, though it is silent concerning John's alcoholic escapades. See Pippa Harris, ed., *Song of Love: The Letters of Rupert Brooke and Noël Olivier, 1909–1915* (London: Bloomsbury, 1991), 14.

45. For all that, and by Kate's own account, Guy and his wife Marjorie were exceedingly kind to and solicitous of her during Michael's wartime absences. "Brittle" suggests a certain hardness, which Kate did not have. "Fragile" or even "frail" is more like it, at least to one who has read her letters. But she was not incapable of standing up for herself. In a letter of February 23, 1942, she says of Barbara Johnston, who is asking to come and stay, that she, Kate, "could never belong to or understand that world of grown-up intimate passionate sensual promiscuous people. . . . It seems as if one is bound to be hurt while these people are about." She had written to Michael earlier that "just seeing Barbara's [hand]writing brings me always face to face with something I can't understand, I mean that Barbara & you seems to be something strange and inimical to the life I thought was you and me, the life I thought I'd chosen" (BLPES, 9/3/25; November 15, 1940, 9/3/16). Needy though Kate undoubtedly was, it is hard not to sympathize with her here, or to deny, either, that her intuition was spot-on.

46. Kate mentions that she is spending five pounds a year on postage. At the prevailing rates, that amounts to 480 letters, an average of more than one a day.

47. Most of Kate's letters on the topic date from September 1941 (BLPES, 9/3/21). But perhaps the bleakest representative extract comes after a conjugal visit, from a woman in defeat but still desperate to distraction for a child with the man she loves: "I belong to you happily—yes, I am a good girl, I have the curse" (9/3/22, November 8–9, 1941). She describes herself on September 1, 1941, as a "glutton for happiness." Even Michael might be forgiven if he found that and similar effusions off-putting.

48. According to Simon, Michael didn't like loneliness or gaps and probably always needed at least one lover "in reserve" for whenever the main relationship of the moment should fail. (Space forbids comment.)

49. Michael had to appear in court, where he was given a conditional discharge and bound over to keep the peace. The case, inevitably, got into the popular press. Everybody, including his friends, was vastly amused except Michael, who, oddly for someone so bohemian, called it the longest day of his life.

50. An irresistible parallel with Michael's modal theory (*EM*, throughout; *RP*, 157–61, 488–516, etc.) suggests itself, and I have drawn attention to it elsewhere. But whether it is more than a curious morphological coincidence is a question that must be deferred.

51. June told me she met Michael in her freshman year, 1946, aged nineteen (when she was actually twenty-one, according to the Newnham College Register) and gave me the impression that their affair lasted six or seven years, but their letters show that they met in her final year, 1949, and parted for good in 1953. She met Freddie Plaat, of Penguin Books, that year and married him the next. Despite her keen intelligence and intellect, her degree results were mediocre (though still considerably better than W. H. Auden's or Evelyn Waugh's). Like many admirable students of the old school, she evidently knew that there was more to life, and to university, than exams (though Michael must have been a distraction from them).

52. I fancy the codicil's belated composition was prompted by my first visit to her in 2003 and that the family memoir, to which she appended it, already existed. I never dared ask her whether she had kept Michael's letters, let alone whether I might see them—she could be quite fierce and was deeply displeased to learn (from me) that her letters to Michael were publicly accessible, since no one had asked her permission—but they came into my hands after her death.

53. Kate was "ravaged," "shattered," "hag-ridden," June said. "I had never seen a human being so utterly *corroded* by suffering." "Don't tangle yourself up with Michael," said Kate, "he will chew you up and spit you out, just as he did me."

54. This particular "Romeo act" involved the stock nocturnal vigil outside her window (a technique, so Kate told June, which he had also used on her) and turning up outside the school where she was teaching, then visibly waiting all day for her to emerge. "He had his beseeching face on," June told me. She also told me that with time and age she had found herself getting more "judgmental" (her word) about Michael's behavior.

55. It seems that with age he found it increasingly hard to keep his hands to himself. One much-circulated story has it that a certain young woman, now a public figure of some note, when dining with the elderly Michael in company had constantly to stop him from pawing her under the table. The story is untrue, but only as regards the victim. The real one, so the woman's husband has told me, was not his wife but a previous girlfriend. Michael might posthumously be grateful for having lived before the full horrors of modern journalism. The "indecent exposure" episode was bad enough, but today's tabloids would not scruple to brand him a "stalker" and a "sex pest."

56. Even if the critics were right, few would regard E. M. Forster's somewhat similar judgment on Joseph Conrad, that "the secret casket of his genius contains a vapour rather than a jewel," as a seriously damaging criticism. After all, Michael's doctrine, like Conrad's, is that there *is* no doctrine; in other words, that there are no jewels, and we had better content ourselves with the least unfragrant of whatever vapors have chanced to waft our way.

57. June complained to me that he would never introduce her to his high-powered intellectual friends and half admitted that it was partly these connections that had first attracted her to him.

Her successor Mary Walsh told me something similar regarding herself. Oddly, neither troubled (or was encouraged) to familiarize herself with Michael's work, and June first read (and disliked) the essay "Rationalism in Politics" when I sent her a copy.

58. The Carlyle Club is an Oxford political philosophy society, named after the historians R. W. and A. J. Carlyle, not after Thomas of that ilk. After one such meeting in the 1980s Isaiah Berlin (who admittedly did not love him, which is another story) wrote that Michael seemed "slightly deranged." Elsewhere, Noël O'Sullivan has told me, Michael expressed admiration for Alain-Fournier (*Le Grand Meaulnes*), Ortega y Gasset (*On Love*), Isak Dinesen (Karen Blixen), Camus's *Caligula*, and, more exotically still, for French or French-influenced decadents such as Nerval, Villiers de l'Isle-Adam, Huysmans, and "Baron Corvo," especially Corvo's *Desire and Pursuit of the Whole*. Most of those in the latter group feature in Mario Praz's study of morbid eroticism, *The Romantic Agony* (1933), an entire section of which, on the femme fatale, is headed "La Belle Dame Sans Merci."

59. Compare Michael's interest in things Chinese. He recommended Émile Hovelaque's *La Chine* to Kate; it draws a parallel between Chinese nature pantheism and Wordsworth's. And of course there were the Wandervögel, and the influence on them of, for example, Ludwig Klages's essay "Man and Earth," all of which would seem very "eco" today.

60. The late Shirley Letwin, his executrix and the dedicatee of *On Human Conduct*, is universally supposed to have been his mistress, but a glance at the relevant correspondence in the British Library of Political and Economic Science will show just how inappropriate this label is. She appears to have succumbed, once, to his customary invitation to join him in a sexual "adventure" (*sic*) but immediately (and honorably) to have called the affair off out of loyalty to her husband. Their relations seem thereafter to have subsided into a Platonic friendship that offered many and differing benefits to both parties.

61. This is a probably a false dichotomy, since to follow an impulse is inevitably to choose to do so.

62. I asked Céline if she thought he was selfish. "Yes," she replied. "But aren't we all?" Unlike June, she had perhaps become less "judgmental" with the years. She wrote to me that Joyce, who had more cause for resentment than almost anyone, was never "judgmental" (again, as with June, Céline's word).

63. His patriotism (in part a family inheritance) was so innocent and unthinking that he quite literally could not believe that the "Cambridge spies" were guilty. After all, were they not (like himself) educated, civilized gentlemen? He was convinced it must "all have been got up by MI5" (information from John Gray). One would love to hear George Orwell's thoughts on the matter.

64. Christel has told me that she never expected fidelity, which is just as well.

PART ONE

THE CONVERSATION OF MANKIND

2

THE VICTIM OF THOUGHT: THE IDEALIST INHERITANCE

David Boucher

Philosophical knowledge is knowledge which carries with it the evidence of its own completeness. The philosopher is simply the victim of thought.

—Michael Oakeshott, *Experience and Its Modes*

Michael Oakeshott's indebtedness to philosophical idealism has been touched on by many commentators as incidental to their main concerns, and his relative silence after World War II compared with his defiant proclamations of loyalty before it gave rise to suspicions that he was no longer as committed to its tenets as he once was or that if there were remnants of idealism to be detected in the later work they were almost unrecognizable.[1] This is not a view unanimously shared. There may be many reasons why Oakeshott ceased to wear his idealist credentials on his sleeve, but the fact that he had abandoned them was not one. He seems to have had a certain sensitivity to the criticisms of him as a philosopher of the day before yesterday. On the presentation of his *Festschrift*, Oakeshott made light of the honor, expressing surprise given that he had read somewhere: "Oakeshott, yes, an interesting survival; out of date before he was born; you can't take him seriously. Not the sort of thing to make one exactly glow with pride. True enough, though; and I thought that perhaps I really would be able to get over this vast expanse of sand intact leaving a foot-print" (BLPES, 1/3, various speeches).

After World War II the sorts of metaphysical and epistemological considerations that permeated *Experience and Its Modes* were touched on but not systematically addressed in his later writings. Some modifications in the vocabulary were necessary to accommodate developments in his thought and incorporate them into the larger point of view, but they were added in essays that deliberately left "much to the reader, often saying too little for fear of saying too much" (*OHC*, vii). Commentators such as W. H. Greenleaf, Wendell John Coats Jr., and Efraim Podoksik acknowledge the changes in vocabulary and nuance but insist on a basic consistency in his philosophy. Podoksik, for instance, contends that Oakeshott's philosophical framework and the nature of his engagements were "consistent throughout his writings, although he modified his views on some points."[2]

When Oakeshott developed his philosophical ideas, idealism, while not ascendant, could still boast a powerful intellectual presence. Most of the important thinkers in British idealism were still actively contributing to philosophical and practical controversies, with the exception of T. H. Green (1836–1882), David George Ritchie (1853–1903), R. L. Nettleship (1846–1902), and Edward Caird (1835–1908), who had all died. Oakeshott evaded the influence of the strident Cambridge realism and was seduced instead by the towering figure of J. M. E. McTaggart (1866–1925) and the less well-known William Ritchie Sorley (1855–1935). In Scotland Henry Jones (1852–1922), the heir to Edward Caird (1835–1908), and Andrew Seth Pringle-Pattison (1856–1931), the joint editor with R. B. Haldane (1856–1928) of *Essays in Philosophical Criticism*, were formidable forces.[3] At Oxford J. A. Smith (1863–1939), Harold Joachim (1868–1938), R. G. Collingwood (1889–1942), and the indomitable F. H. Bradley (1846–1924) kept the idealist flag flying. Bernard Bosanquet (1848–1923) had left St. Andrews in 1908 but remained one of the most influential figures in British philosophy until he died. Both Bosanquet and Bradley were leading figures in British philosophy and both in different ways contributed to the shaping of modern analytic philosophy. John Henry Muirhead (1855–1940) remained a venerated figure. Overseas Josiah Royce (1855–1916), John Watson (1847–1939), William Mitchell (1861–1962), and Brand Blanshard (1892–1987) continued to keep idealism in the public gaze.

It was not, then, such a "strangely bold thing" for Oakeshott to declare his allegiance to idealism in 1933, and to F. H. Bradley in particular.[4] The second edition of Bradley's *Ethical Studies* was published in 1927, and shortly after *Experience and Its Modes*, Bradley's *Collected Essays* appeared and W. D. Lamont published the *Introduction to Green's Moral Philosophy*.[5] W. R. Boyce Gibson and Bernard Bosanquet were at the forefront of pioneering continental ideas in Britain, and whereas analytic philosophy eventually came to dominate British philosophy, we should not be anachronistic in underestimating the competition of ideas during the 1920s and 1930s.[6] Indeed there was an audience out there for idealism, albeit diminishing, and the answers Oakeshott gave to many of the metaphysical and philosophical problems he addressed were directed not at the realists, but to the diversity of idealists, both absolute and personalist.

Nor should we overestimate the extent to which the likes of G. E. Moore delivered the killer punch. Moore's "Refutation of Idealism" did not have as its target contemporary idealists. The main target of Moore and his followers was Berkeley's subjective idealism, and in particular Moore wanted to refute the view that knowing makes no difference to what is known. We can have direct knowledge of the external world, Moore contended, and be absolutely certain of common-sense propositions, such as holding one's hand in front of oneself and proclaiming that this is a hand. Any object is "precisely what it would be if we were not aware" of it.[7]

Berkeley contended that there can be nothing but spirits, active on the one hand and passive sensible objects on the other, and that objects do not exist except as perceived by the active spirit.[8] Berkeley described himself as an immaterialist and his doctrine is opposed to materialism, whereas the opposite of idealism is realism. It is in fact very doubtful whether Berkeley wished to deny the realist contention that we are directly aware of objects that continue to exist unchanged even when we cease directly to perceive them.

Regardless of whether Moore was right about Berkeley, idealist contemporaries were certainly not so naive as to believe that nothing existed except mind. Jones, for example, anticipated Moore's criticism when he argued that no self-respecting idealist would deny the distinction between thought and reality: "It is inconsistent with the possibility of knowledge that it should *be* the reality it represents."[9] Bosanquet took Moore head on and accused him of misunderstanding idealism. He asserted that as far as he was concerned a chair is a chair and what the upholsterer or anyone else in a drawing room has to say about it is descriptively true. But there may be other questions the upholsterer has never asked, such as those of the physicist. What the physicist says does not deny or contradict the chair maker any more than an economist's understanding of a coin contradicts a metallurgist's.[10]

Implied in this criticism is one of the principal tenets of the absolute idealists, namely, that there are modes or forms of experience, each of which has some integrity in the understanding of the world it conveys. The term *modes of experience* is used by Bosanquet, but all the absolute idealists subscribe to the idea, even though they differ on such issues as their relationship to one another and to the whole.[11]

Idealists and realists were not as antagonistic toward each other as is commonly thought. Harold Joachim, for example, submitted the second chapter of The Nature of Truth to his "friend Bertrand Russell" before the book was published.[12] R. G. Collingwood was a respected figure internationally and a very close friend and godfather to the son of the realist E. F. Carritt. Even the younger generation of philosophers opposed to idealism admired Collingwood's work. A. J. Ayer, against whom Collingwood directed much of *An Essay on Metaphysics* in an attack on logical positivism, admired his older colleague. Ayer maintained that his esteem for Collingwood came in the 1930s. He admired the style of all of Collingwood's books but was particularly impressed by the application of his theory of absolute presuppositions in *The Idea of Nature*.[13] Ayer devoted a chapter to Collingwood in his *Philosophy in the Twentieth Century*, alongside Bertrand Russell, G. E. Moore, Hilary Putnam, and W. V. O. Quine.[14]

Gilbert Ryle, Ayer's tutor and Collingwood's successor to the Waynflete chair of metaphysical philosophy, published *The Concept of Mind* in 1949. Both Ryle and the British idealists were anti-Cartesian. Ryle wanted to deny the mind and body dualism, which was the received orthodoxy. Ryle called it "the ghost in the machine." Like Oakeshott, Ryle maintained that it is a category error to conjoin or disjoin statements about mental and physical processes as if they are of the same logical type or as if they are species of a genus called experience. The mind cannot be separated from its "overt acts and utterances."[15] Ryle was more than generous in attributing to his idealist predecessor a significant role in exorcising the ghost in the machine.[16]

The publication of Oakeshott's *Experience and Its Modes* in 1933 was in the same year that Collingwood published his *An Essay on Philosophical Method*. Almost every commentator points to the affinity between Collingwood's *Speculum Mentis* and Oakeshott's *Experience and Its Modes* but misses the affinity with *An Essay on Philosophical Method*.[17] To a large extent Collingwood's essay on philosophical method is a defense and justification of the method he employed in *Speculum Mentis*, with special emphasis on establishing the differentiae of the philosophical concept in contrast with that of the scientific. Oakeshott's *Experience and Its Modes* combines at once the exemplification and justification of philosophical method. It is an explication of the idea of unconditional knowledge, demonstrated through interrogating the conditionality of abstract arrests in experience, where the unconditional is an unachievable ideal toward which the philosopher is en route.

CAMBRIDGE IDEALIST INSPIRATION

What did Cambridge have to offer Oakeshott by way of idealist inspiration? Sorley was one of the forerunners of idealism in contributing to what was essentially the idealist manifesto, *Essays in Philosophical Criticism*.[18] Sorley's contribution was titled "The Historical Method," in which he identified the parameters of the range of questions to which the method was appropriate and the limits beyond which it had nothing to offer. This, of course, was a subject that was to preoccupy Oakeshott throughout his life. It has also gone unnoticed that the title of one of Oakeshott's famous early essays, "Religion and the Moral Life," is the title of one of the chapters in Sorley's *The Moral Life*.[19] In it he argues that religion provides the unity for the diverse expressions of morality: temperance, courage, wisdom, justice, and benevolence. Oakeshott's own treatment, while consistent in its conclusion with Sorley, owed more to Bradley. The view that religion is somehow the completion of morality seemed to Oakeshott preferable to the alternatives, which posited no relation between the two or their complete identity (*RPML*, 45).

Sorley was largely preoccupied with the debates of the latter part of the nineteenth century, particularly with the relationship between evolution and ethics, and the ethics of naturalism in general.[20] In 1926, however, he delivered the Herbert Spencer Lecture at Oxford, with the subject of "Tradition." In it we find Sorley identifying many of the features that Oakeshott was later to elaborate in his critique of rationalism in politics. The question that Sorley posed, for instance, is the same that Oakeshott set himself in one of his most famous essays (*RP*, 6–43) and the emphasis on tradition is one to which the younger man also subscribed. Sorley contended, "The question is therefore forced upon us whether the individual can thus cut himself off from tradition, as Descartes and many others have sought to do, and whether, if he can, the result is altogether to the good. What, we may ask, are the true place and function of tradition in human life and thought?"[21]

As a student of history Oakeshott had little formal training in philosophy at Cambridge. He attended McTaggart's Introduction to the Study of Philosophy and took the political thought option in both parts of the tripos. McTaggart's lectures were directed at students who were not studying philosophy and introduced some of the main ideas. No reading was prescribed and no prior knowledge assumed. McTaggart was a personal idealist and a critic of absolute idealism, immersing himself in metaphysical problems.[22] Andrew Seth Pringle-Pattison's *Hegelianism and Personality* voiced concerns developed by the personalists.[23] McTaggart was in sympathy with placing the individual at the center of inquiry. The whole has to be understood from the standpoint of the experiencing individual. In believing that everything that exists is spiritual he declared himself an ontological idealist but qualified this commitment by declaring that the content of spirit must fall within a self, with no part falling within more than one self.[24] It is only for the individual consciousness that judgments about whether something is good, bad, or worthy ultimately have meaning. Value does not consist in relations among individuals, nor in the whole they comprise, but instead in being one of the terms of the relation itself. If one person loves another, value or goodness does not reside in the relation, but in being one of the related terms.[25] Following Rudolph Eucken, W. R. Boyce Gibson contended that the central idea of absolute idealism, that the real is rational, is upheld by personal idealism, but "from the point of view of the personal experient."[26]

McTaggart differs from fellow personalists such as Pringle-Pattison and Rashdall in that he had very little sympathy for religion. His personalism, like that of Pringle-Pattison, inclined him to meticulous study and criticism of Hegel, who, in McTaggart's view, had better than any philosopher before or after penetrated more deeply into the nature of reality. Hegel was mistaken, however, in taking philosophy to be the highest expression of the absolute. McTaggart conceded that philosophy may be the highest level of human knowledge but not of reality. Reality for McTaggart is not one undifferentiated spiritual whole but a community of finite spirits. Ultimate reality is spiritual, consisting of individual minds and their contents. For him this entailed the exclusion of space, time, and material objects. Behind the appearance of such things, inevitably misperceptions, are minds and parts of the contents of minds. Oakeshott differs on this point. For him philosophy is the ultimate experience, without reservation or arrest.

In Pringle-Pattison's view, absolute idealism is dangerously close to consigning the finite individual to insignificance. This criticism is particularly pertinent to Bradley, to whom Oakeshott expresses his debt in *Experience and Its Modes*. Bradley's radical skepticism is at its most unrelenting in his treatment of the finite individual and personality. The individual "only exists through an intellectual construction."[27] Only that which is noncontradictory, consistent, and self-subsistent is real. This character is possessed only by reality as a whole, the absolute. It is beyond our comprehension in discursive thought. The individual self is not real but merely an appearance of reality. The finite individual, or self, exhibits a greater degree of reality only insofar as it contains within itself more of the "total Universe," that is, insofar as it becomes transmuted and self-consistent, in other words, to the extent that the self becomes less distinct from other selves.[28] The implication is that the individual is more real as part of a community and less abstract than the idea of an isolated individual. Individualism, the idea that only the individual is real, is a "mere fancy." A person is a person only insofar as that person is "what others are." A person is simply not "real" outside of a community. Self-realization is the realization of something beyond the self "and so must be called a universal life."[29]

The question of finite individuality is at the heart of both absolute and personal idealism and was central to McTaggart's philosophical explorations. This is the problem that Oakeshott addresses throughout *Experience and Its Modes*. He does not ask what is real in a mode of experience. Instead, he asks what in each is an "individual" or a thing. Take the historical mode, for example. The historical individual is an abstraction. It is an arbitrary designation not even circumscribed by birth and death. These starting and ending points do not exhaust the relations in which an individual stands to the world. That which went before, the significant antecedents, and that which follows add coherence to the designation. It is in the practical mode, however, that we cling with tenacity to the idea of the autonomous self. In practical life, as in other modes, the thing, or the individual, is designated and presupposed, not defined. Completeness is not the criterion of designation of the individual, but instead the individual is designated by what is separate and self-contained. The practical self, the person, is the creation of practical thought and is presupposed in all action. The postulate or presupposition of the self is self-determination, which entails freedom, which itself requires no demonstration, because it by definition belongs to the practical self. To reject the principle of self-determination, and the consequent implication of freedom, is to deny the world of practice and its foundational postulate, namely, the "separateness and uniqueness" of the individual. The individual in practical life is just as much an abstraction, an arrest or modification of experience, as the individual, or thing, presupposed in all the other modes (*EM*, 268–74). It is these views that most strongly differentiate Oakeshott from McTaggart's personal idealism and betray his affinity with Bradley's absolutism.

THE IDEALIST CONCEPTION OF PHILOSOPHY

The starting point for an idealist conception of philosophy is the assumption of unity or monism. It does not begin, as Descartes did, with a dualism between the mind and its objects, explaining knowledge in terms of the mind's conformity to reality. In addition, it rejects the dualism of Kant, in which the mind cannot know things in themselves, only as they are perceived by mind. The idealists admired Kant's starting point, namely, that the mind does not conform to its objects but instead reality conforms to mind through the imposition of certain a priori categories such as space and time. This was Kant's Copernican revolution, but he failed to see the logical absurdity of claiming that we cannot know things as they are in themselves.[30] Furthermore, the idealists rejected Berkeley's subjective idealism, in which reality is mind dependent and which implies that nothing exists independently of mind. Jones argues, for example, that Berkeleian idealism "as a theory of the subjective in pursuit of the objective, is as false as Materialism which starts from a mere object and looks for a subject."[31]

The point the idealists wanted to make, and often not without obfuscation and obscurity, was that the world is unintelligible without mind and that there is mutual inclusivity. This mutual inclusivity can only be understood, however, by rejecting the question of epistemology that arises when we assume a duality between the mind and its objects. If we begin by assuming that experience is an undifferentiated whole, then the question becomes one of ontology, that is, how out of this unity do we explain the multiplicity of modes of understanding, such as history, poetry, natural science, religion, and so on. When thinking is taken to be the process by which Spirit or God realizes itself, the subjective and objective are not separated by ideas but instead are the differentiations of the one comprehensive unity.[32]

Hegel's importance for the British idealist, then, is that he dispenses with the problem of epistemology and provides a metaphysic that is also a logic of the process and development of mind. For Caird, agreeing with Hegel, the highest aim of philosophy "is to reinterpret experience, in the light of a unity which is presupposed in it, but which cannot be made conscious or explicit until the relation of experience to the thinking self is seen—the unity of all things with each other and with the mind that knows them."[33] For him the purpose of philosophy is to reconcile what the modern world has divided and fragmented as a result of two competing tendencies. They were subjective idealism, which had "infected" British philosophy since Berkeley, and realism and naturalism, being equally as one-sided in abjuring the subjective and conceiving everything as a mechanical system.

The implication of starting with the principle of unity is that wherever a dualism is found it must be transcended in a synthesis that includes the best of both sides. Almost invariably when the British idealist addresses a substantive problem we are presented with two sides, a subjective and objective, the contradiction between which is resolved in a synthesis.[34] Oakeshott is no exception. The most prominent exemplification is in his characterization of the history of political philosophy. In the introduction to his edition of Hobbes's Leviathan, he argued that there are three traditions of political philosophy, which stand in a dialectical relationship to one another. They are the antithetical traditions of Reason and Nature, and Will and Artifice, the shortcomings of which are overcome in the synthesis of Rational Will (HCA, 7–8).[35]

In a review of Leo Strauss's interpretation of Hobbes, Oakeshott had previously used this triadic conception to expose both the deficiency and achievement of Hobbes. For Oakeshott Hobbes's significance is that he began his inquiries with the human will rather than law, which almost every political philosopher since has followed. What was missing, however, from the whole Epicurean tradition to which Hobbes belonged was an adequate theory of volition. The solution that enabled the problem to be overcome consisted in the union of a reconfigured theory of natural law with the Epicurean theory of Hobbes. The union is exemplified in such phrases as Rousseau's "General Will," Hegel's "Rational Will," or Bosanquet's "Real Will" (*HCA*, 147–48).[36]

In listening to McTaggart's lectures Oakeshott would have learned that metaphysics is the "systematic study of the ultimate nature of Reality." Metaphysics was critical of its own assumptions and critical of the validity of scientific conceptions of reality, without denying that despite their conditionality they may nevertheless be compelling.[37] In *Appearance and Reality*, Bradley understood metaphysics in exactly this way. McTaggart differed from Oakeshott and Bradley in believing that answers to philosophical questions make a difference to what is known. In this respect, he clearly opposed, as Collingwood was to do, the logical positivists. McTaggart unapologetically spent the latter part of his life addressing metaphysical questions on the justification that the answers were potentially of profound practical importance. He contended that a good deal of human happiness or misery depends on answers to metaphysical questions such as whether the world is good or evil, whether God exists, whether human action is determined or free, and whether we are immortal.

Idealists and neo-idealists understand philosophy to be experience self-critical of itself. The starting point is not ignorance from which we progress to knowledge. Instead, it is the endeavor to understand better something that is already understood (*CPJ*, 171; cf. *OHC*, vii). Dilthey nicely encapsulates the idea when he says, "in order to understand, one must have already understood."[38] Bosanquet elaborates and suggests that philosophy cannot tell us anything that we do not already know. Instead, it tells us the significance of what we know.[39] Oakeshott formulates this philosophical principle in the following terms: "there is no such thing as a transition from mere ignorance to complete knowledge: the process is always one of coming to know more fully and more clearly what is in some sense already known" (*CPJ*, 171).

Realists portray philosophical analysis similarly but differ in the manner of their execution. The critic of idealism L. Susan Stebbing wrote a hostile review of *Experience and Its Modes* and practiced a method common to the Cambridge School. She contended in 1932 that metaphysical analysis is "discovering *what it is precisely* which we already in some sense knew."[40] The similarity in phraseology should not deceive us. The method of Cambridge realists was decompositional, while for Oakeshott and other idealists it was regressive. The Cambridge realists take something as given and break it down into its components and structure. G. E. Moore's common-sense philosophy is an example of this method. The idealists, however, use regressive analysis, concerned more with the postulates, principles, and presuppositions on which, or from which, conclusions are generated. It is a method whose roots reach back to ancient Greek geometry. *Experience and Its Modes*, unsurprisingly, rejects the decompositional method of analysis prevalent in the Cambridge of its day and exemplifies regressive analysis.

Philosophy for the idealists, because they begin with the principle of unity, necessarily entails being aware of the assumptions that underpin the differentiations into which this unity has fragmented. Take McTaggart, for example, who maintained that metaphysics rests on certain assumptions, but unlike the natural sciences it does not make them uncritically.[41] Although Oakeshott and Bosanquet differ considerably in their conclusions, they nevertheless shared the same conception of philosophy and expressed it in the same vocabulary. Bosanquet asked himself what a philosophical inquiry implies. His answer was that everyone knows that a flower is a different thing when understood by the botanist, chemist, or artist, and philosophy cannot hope to compete with these specialists in their own terms. Instead, the philosopher takes the flower, interrogates it, and determines its place and significance in the totality of experience: "And this we call studying it, as it is, and for its own sake, without reservation or presupposition."[42] Oakeshott's view is identical: "Philosophical experience, I take to be experience without presupposition, reservation, arrest or modification" (*EM*, 2).

Every aspect of experience, then, is an invitation to relate it to a wider context in which it becomes more intelligible. The context itself belongs to a wider whole that endows it with meaning. Bosanquet suggested that understanding something for its own sake did not mean understanding it in isolation. Philosophy had to "reveal its true position and relations with reference to all else that man can do and can know."[43] In this light, Oakeshott's characterization of political philosophy appears less eccentric than it first appears. If politics is the subject matter, the task of philosophy is to "establish the connections, in principle and in detail, directly or mediately, between politics and eternity" (*HCA*, 5).

Furthermore, Oakeshott is typically idealist in subscribing to its conception of logic. When Harold Joachim published *The Nature of Truth* in 1906 and referred to "current logic," there was no mistaking to what he was referring. It was the philosophical study of thought and knowledge associated with Bradley and Bosanquet, the legacy of Hegel handed down through Lotze and

Sigwart. By 1933 the idea of "current logic" had become much more ambiguous. It was then seen not so much as a branch of philosophy, but more as a science of symbols and forms severed from what was symbolized or formed. This was evident in symbolic or formalistic logic and those aspects of logical positivism that went under the name of the theory of logical analysis. Oakeshott, like Bradley, Bosanquet, and Joachim, took logic to be the philosophical study of thought and knowledge, and this necessarily entailed interrogating the modes, or arrests, in what Joachim called the "timeless and complete actuality."[44]

How, then, does idealism deal with the competing claims to truth that each of the modes of experience generates? As we have seen, there is no world independent of our conceptions of it, no independent "it" awaiting interpretation. Interpretation and what is interpreted are inseparable. In this respect idealists reject the correspondence theory of truth, which posits an independent reality to which minds must conform. The criterion of truth is the accuracy with which we describe that reality. Statements are discrete propositions about the world that can be tested against the reality they describe. For the idealists the various modes or universes of discourse fall below ultimate reality or truth, but within their own domain they are able to demarcate what makes sense and what does not. The logic is still a propositional logic, but not of discrete statements. A proposition brings a whole world of ideas to bear on its veracity. The truth it exhibits depends not on its correspondence to an external reality but on noncontradiction and coherence. One fact or statement has no truth value without its relation to a whole range of facts and propositions that affirm it.

Joachim understands this as a cohering unity of ideas, which he calls a "significant whole," in which all its "constituent elements reciprocally determine one another's being as contributory features in a single concrete meaning." Truths are, for G. R. G. Mure, the property of judgments in that they are implicated in a coherent unity of judgments.[45] The criterion of truth, then, is internal to a system, and there cannot be anything outside it that acts as the arbiter of fact and not fact. Oakeshott subscribes to this theory and contends that "coherence is the sole criterion: it requires neither modification nor supplement, and is operative always and everywhere" (EM, 37).

Truth is the union of coherence and comprehensiveness. A mode, or significant whole, is the "arbiter of fact."[46] This does not mean that anything we conceive that is consistent is true. Bradley contends that something is true within a system when its opposite is inconceivable.[47] For Oakeshott it is what the evidence obliges us to believe. Joachim explains how this works. For him a "significant whole" is one whose constitutive elements are reciprocally involved and determine one another's being as contributory to a particular meaning. The cohering elements reciprocally adjust and control one another. This is why a centaur is inconceivable because its constituent elements resist entering into reciprocal adjustment.[48] Conceivability means for Joachim systematic coherence that is the determining feature of a significant whole, or what Oakeshott calls a mode of experience or world of ideas or imaginings. For Oakeshott coherence is at once the test and definition of truth (*EM*, 34–37).

DID OAKESHOTT ABANDON HIS ABSOLUTE IDEALISM?

It has been suggested by many that Oakeshott moved a considerable way from his early idealism in his later works after World War II. It is true that he did not wear his credentials so prominently on his sleeve, but I contend that in its fundamentals Oakeshott remained an absolute idealist.[49] "The Voice of Poetry in the Conversation of Mankind" for many commentators constitutes the point at which Oakeshott most explicitly renounces much of what he had held about modality, monism, and philosophy. Terry Nardin suggests that in the later writings of Oakeshott much of what he had argued in *Experience and Its Modes* is reconsidered. He contends that these "writings are certainly less systematic and certainly less 'Idealist' . . . and 'the Absolute' vanishes entirely."[50]

Steven Gerencser argues that Oakeshott ceased to be an absolute idealist and became a skeptical idealist. The young Oakeshott allowed absolute idealism to dominate his tendency to skepticism. After 1945 the skeptical Oakeshott subdued and almost consigned to oblivion the absolutist Oakeshott. Gerencser states his point boldly: "The signal work that clearly reveals this change is Oakeshott's 'The Voice of Poetry in the Conversation of Mankind': this essay shows Oakeshott to have abandoned many of the commitments of philosophical idealism by the mid-fifties." This claim is based on the contention that although there are elements of skepticism in the early Oakeshott, they are exhibited only in relation to the modes. Philosophy, on the other hand, claims "final certainty" and upholds "a universal claim to truth."[51] If Oakeshott held these views attributed to him, we would have to concede that a revolution occurred in his thought by the time he introduced poetry as one of the autonomous modes.

Oakeshott, however, never subscribed to the view that philosophy is about final certainty. Indeed, he argued in *Experience and Its Modes* that philosophy has nothing to do with the search for universal knowledge: "It is only in the childhood of thought, when knowledge appears undifferentiated and each fresh piece of information seems significant just because it is fresh, that universal knowledge can appear to satisfy the philosophic passion" (*EM* 2). Even the philosopher offers us provisional knowledge. Oakeshott purported to offer us not absolute knowledge but instead "a general point of view, neither complete nor final" (8). This is why it is a misnomer to characterize Oakeshott as having a "system."[52]

The distinction between absolute idealism and skeptical idealism is in fact a false dichotomy out of sympathy with idealism's rejection of dualisms. Skepticism is in fact perfectly consistent with absolute idealism. Bradley is the archskeptic, yet at the same time the most systematic and powerful exponent of absolute idealism. For him the absolute is always just beyond our grasp. Coming to know it immediately adds something to it and hence alters its character. The perfect self-consistency of the absolute is a criterion, not a body of knowledge. It is what enables us to interrogate the veracity of the claims to truth offered by the modes. Nothing is absolutely unknowable, and nothing is perfectly knowable. Understanding, as I have already suggested, is the coming to know better something already understood. The veracity of what is achieved in understanding is dependent on the degree of coherence achieved. Knowledge and truth are always present in however small a degree; just as they can never be completely absent, they are never finally achieved. Philosophy is not in the business of measuring the precise degree of inadequacy, but instead, from the point of view of the whole, to recognize what is asserted as an arrest and an abstraction: "What is achieved in Experience is an absolutely coherent world of experience, not in the sense that it is ever actually achieved, but in the more important sense that it is the criterion of whatever satisfaction is achieved" (*EM*, 35).

Gerencser is mistaken in thinking that this conception of philosophy is absent from *On Human Conduct*.[53] It is in fact presupposed in Oakeshott's characterization of theorizing: "The engagement of understanding is, then, a continuous, self moved, critical enterprise of theorising. Its principle is: Never ask the end. . . . The notion of an unconditional or definitive understanding may hover in the background, but it has no part in the adventure" (*OHC*, 2–3). What this means is that the absolute can never be to the fore, but it is always, as it was in *Experience and Its Modes*, there as the ultimate criterion of conditionality.

The view that Oakeshott's conception of understanding underwent a radical transformation is unsustainable. As we saw, understanding always entails relating something to its context. Understanding a statement made by a historian entails relating it to the postulates of what it is to be engaged in the activity of being a historian, which itself has to be related to its place in the whole world of experience. Coherence is always the criterion by which their adequacy is measured.

Simultaneous with reiterating this conception of understanding in *On Human Conduct*, Oakeshott revised the essays in *Hobbes on Civil Association*. Many passages were changed, but it is significant that he did not change those in which he expressed his view of understanding. His view is exemplified in the following passage: "Even if we accept the standards and valuations of our civilization, it will be only by putting an arbitrary closure on reflection that we can prevent the consideration of the meaning of the general terms in which those standards are expressed; good and evil, right and wrong, justice and injustice. And, turning, we shall catch sight of all that we have learned reflected in the *speculum universitatis*" (*HCA*, 5).

Further evidence to sustain my interpretation of the consistency of Oakeshott's commitment to idealism is the collection of essays he published in 1983. They were revised and presented year after year at the History of Political Thought seminar, in which Oakeshott participated long after his retirement, at the London School of Economics. Throughout the period when he talked of platforms of conditional understanding in *On Human Conduct*, he did not abandon the modal understanding that he had espoused in *Experience and Its Modes*. The three essays on history are in fact a continuation of the exploration he undertook in *Experience and Its Modes* and "The Activity of Being an Historian," namely, to explore the modal conditionality of the different claims to knowledge. History for him is an autonomous mode of understanding that generates conclusions consistent with its distinct postulates. It is logically incapable of confirming or denying statements made in the other modes or of saying anything of relevance about them (*OH*, 2).

The undertaking he embarked on in *On History and Other Essays* was to determine the postulates of history and not to examine the truth of historical statements. He was concerned to identify the conditions in terms of which they may be recognized as conclusions. Oakeshott did not go on to relate history to the concrete totality of experience, because in the essays in *On History* his task is more narrowly circumscribed, as it had been, for example, in 1936 in a lecture on history and the social sciences.[54] He did, however, just two years after this, return to what he took to be the ultimate philosophical endeavor. It is, in principle, the attempt to relate a subject to the concrete totality of experience, because this constitutes the complete context incapable of being turned by criticism into a text itself requiring a context (*CPJ*, 154–83). In sum, then, the philosopher may take on more limited undertakings, such as an exploration of the postulates of any conditional form of understanding, but such an exercise is only a respite from the "ideal character" of philosophical inquiry, which in principle relates everything to the universe as whole.

THE CONVERSATIONAL CHARACTER OF PHILOSOPHY

When Oakeshott elevated poetry to the status of an autonomous world of ideas equivalent to history, science, and practice, he also sought to give a greater degree of clarity to the relationship that persists among them and of each to philosophy (RP, 488–554). Previously, the modes were implicitly characterized as mutually indifferent to one another, related only as arrests in the concrete totality of experience, that is, philosophy. Each had marked its boundary with an unwelcoming sign: trespassers will be shot. Each makes propositions about the world, but none can persuade others of their merits.

The utterances of the poetic imagination are clearly not propositional. We do not ask if they are right or wrong; we merely delight in the images they conjure. To portray a less eristic relationship between the modes without compromising their integrity, nor their relation to the whole, while at the same time accommodating the nonpropositional character of the poetic world of ideas, Oakeshott suggested that the most appropriate analogy was that of a conversation.[55]

In Gerencser's view this constitutes a significant change in Oakeshott's understanding of philosophy. Philosophy, he claims, is now a mere voice among other voices. What this means is that Oakeshott has abandoned "absolute idealism, with its particular conception of philosophical experience and its rigid proscription against the interaction of philosophy and other forms of experience and their expression."[56]

Absolute idealism does not depend on positing autonomous modes of experience, or on suggesting that the intrusion of one into another is to commit a category error. But Gerencser is mistaken in thinking that the move to the vocabulary of conversation entails abandoning this view. For Grant and Franco the image of a conversational relationship in which each voice is valued is clearly a move away from monism and embraces pluralism, and in so doing transforms Oakeshott's conception of philosophy. Franco contends, "In 'The Voice of Poetry,' the monism of Experience and Its Modes is abandoned and replaced by the pluralism implied in the image of conversation."[57]

The assumption here is that the different modes in Experience and Its Modes were not valued for themselves and that when Oakeshott called them abstractions it was in a pejorative sense. Each, however, was an achievement, in attaining a degree of coherence capable of generating conclusions consistent with its postulates. Each is deficient only in relation to the whole, that is, philosophy itself, experience without reservation, presupposition, or arrest. In other words, each mode, world of ideas, world of imaginings, idiom of discourse, and so on is conditional, incomplete in itself, unable to maintain what it asserts when subject to philosophical scrutiny.

Despite the fact that it is not always as explicitly stated, this remained Oakeshott's position throughout his work with only slight changes of emphasis. What he says about the philosopher engaged in unconditional understanding in *On Human Conduct* is in fact a rationalization of what he exemplified in *Experience and Its Modes*. He contends that the "unconditional engagement of understanding must be arrested and inquiry must remain focused upon a *this* if its identity is to become intelligible in terms of its postulates" (*OHC*, 11). As we saw, the idea of unconditional knowledge always hovers in the background. The *this* that philosophy inquired into in the earlier work was history, science, and practice, understood in terms of their postulates, with the addition of poetry in "The Voice of Poetry." Each, in the vocabulary of *On Human Conduct*, is a platform of conditional understanding having its own idiomatic voice.[58]

What I have suggested, then, is that the modes were always valued as conditional knowledge, or understanding. But even if Oakeshott did not initially value the modes, and later came to do so, why would that constitute a move away from monism or absolutism to pluralism? Both Bosanquet and Bradley remained absolutists while at the same time respecting the integrity of the knowledge the modes generated. Bradley contended that the methods of natural science must be respected, on the assumption that scientists know their own business, and that if natural science rejects every form of explanation except the mechanical that is of no concern to the metaphysician. Natural science has no right to extend itself beyond its boundaries, but within them "every sane man will consider it sacred."[59]

The introduction of the idea of a conversation is not a significant change of emphasis. It is a new analogy better able to characterize the kind of relationship he had in mind that persists between the modes and with philosophy. The image of a conversation is the answer to the question of how the different modes, or worlds of imaginings, are related to one another. It does not necessarily characterize the relationship that holds within a mode. A conversation is not an inquiry, nor is it an argument (*WIH*, 187). The participants "are not concerned to inform, to persuade, or to refute one another, and therefore the cogency of their utterances does not depend upon their all speaking in the same idiom; they may differ without disagreeing" (*RP*, 489). Philosophy is a conversation in which the eristic relation of argument and confrontation is replaced by a dialectical relation. It was Plato's achievement that he united for all time the relation between philosophy and conversation (*WIH*, 194). Philosophy as an activity is itself conversational, but it is not itself a "voice" in the conversation between what Oakeshott had previously referred to as arrests in experience. Philosophy has a voice, but it is very different from the others. Gerencser agrees that philosophy is a voice that springs from the conversation and is parasitic on the other voices in its exploration of the quality and style of each in relation to the others (*RP*, 491).[60]

Some of the voices, such as the practical and scientific, have a tendency to allow what is said to become loosely attached or even to break away from its manner of utterance. This gives the voice the appearance of a body of conclusions, which has become eristic, having discarded its conversational manner of utterance (*RP*, 492–93). The adeptness of philosophy is facilitated because "there is no body of philosophical 'knowledge' to become detached from the activity of philosophizing" (493).

What is the view of philosophy that emerges from Oakeshott's introduction of the analogy of conversation and to what extent is it consistent with the views that he had always held? There are three prominent elements characteristic of philosophy. First, it is not eristic, nor does it attempt to persuade. Second, it is parasitic on the other voices. And, third, it is not a body of knowledge.

On the first point Oakeshott was consistent throughout his life. Philosophy, he contended in his first book, does not consist in "persuading others, but in making our own minds clear." "It is," he argued, "something we may engage in without putting ourselves in competition. It is something independent of the futile attempt to convince or persuade" (*EM*, 3, 7).

On the second point, the issue is not whether Oakeshott moved away from absolute idealism to skeptical idealism, the contention Gerencser makes, but whether he remained faithful to monism, the point that Franco denies, that is, the principle of unity and the commitment to understanding its fragmentations in terms of their postulates. He always remained faithful to the view that experience, or what is going on, is one undifferentiated whole and that our attempts to understand it involve making identifications in terms of postulates. This is the view he defended in both *Experience and Its Modes* and *On Human Conduct*. The questioning of the postulates on which the differentiations in experience rest is philosophical activity, and consequently this activity is parasitical on the modes or platforms of conditional understanding.

On the third point, that philosophy is not a body of knowledge, there is no suggestion in *Experience and Its Modes* that Oakeshott held a different view. There was no question, Oakeshott contended, of presenting the reader with a system of universal truths. Instead he purported to offer a point of view necessarily provisional in its conclusions. Philosophy had no special or exclusive source of knowledge, "it was merely experience become critical of itself" (*EM*, 82). Philosophy is differentiated from the modes not because it offers absolute certainty as opposed to lesser degrees of truth; instead it is the determination to investigate every presupposition it encounters, in other words, to be permanently en route. It is a manner of thinking rather than a body of knowledge.[61]

CONCLUSION: THE DISTINCTIVE FEATURES OF OAKESHOTT'S ABSOLUTISM

What, one may ask, is distinctive about Oakeshott's idealism that makes him worth reading? First, with R. G. Collingwood, Oakeshott makes the single most important contribution to establishing the autonomy and integrity of history as a mode of understanding independent of, and impervious to, intrusions from natural science. Oakeshott rejected the idea of a speculative philosophy of history and dissociated himself from the activity of retrospectively identifying movements and patterns in history, which so clearly characterized Hegel and his followers. Jones, for example, faithfully reproduced Hegel's philosophy of history in his *Idealism as a Practical Creed*.[62] History for him was the unfolding of freedom in the world, beginning in Asian despotism when only one was free, the despot; in the Greco-Roman world some are free, namely, citizens; and in the modern Germanic world all are free.

Oakeshott instead followed Dilthey in rejecting this aspect of absolute idealism. The meaning that we find in history is not imposed on it by constructing a metanarrative, but instead is to be inferred from the evidence. The philosophy of history was for Oakeshott, taking his inspiration from F. H. Bradley, the examination of the conditionality of the historical mode of experience, or world of ideas, to identify what differentiates the activity of being a historian from any other. What many have found puzzling and even difficult to comprehend is Oakeshott's contention that not every attitude to the past is historical. This historical past is characterized by its disinterestedness. It is a dead past and the historian "creates" history by constructing events on the basis of contingently related evidence.[63] The past is merely a category in terms of which we organize present evidence. There is a practical past, the attitude to which is not one of disinterest and in terms of which we relate the evidence to our current concerns. There is nothing wrong with such an attitude; it simply needs to be distinguished from the historical past. The practical past encompasses "emblematic" characterizations and "legends," which may inspire a people at times of adversity. A history book may do many things, but it will not be history unless it constructs its narrative on historical postulates. A historian may find the historical manner of thinking difficult to sustain and lapse from time to time into other ways of thinking that bear no logical relation to history. As Oakeshott contended in a notebook, "To write history is so difficult that most historians are forced to make concessions to the technique of legend" (BLPES, 2/1/16).

Second, the relationship among the modes of experience and their relation to the whole makes Oakeshott's position quite distinctive among the idealists. Each of the modes is an arrest in experience as a whole and unsatisfactory in that each fails to achieve complete coherence from the standpoint of the whole. In other words, the modes are unable to sustain the claims to truth that they make when their postulates are subjected to the dissolving scrutiny of philosophy, which is experience as whole, without "presupposition, reservation, arrest or modification." That is, it is "merely experience sought and followed entirely for its own sake" (*EM*, 2, 82). The task of philosophy is to consider each of the modes purely from the standpoint of its ability to offer us what is satisfactory in experience (83). It is not the task of philosophy to rank the modes in relation to one another; there is no criterion by which it can be done because each is unsatisfactory in its own way, and none has anything to offer the others in terms of insights or conclusions. To impose the conclusions of one mode into another is simply to commit a category error. The modes, worlds of ideas, or platforms of conditional understanding are in relation to one another completely autonomous, but in relation to experience as a whole they are all conditional arrests. The eloquence and tenacity with which Oakeshott put forward these views distinguish him as one of the leading philosophical idealists.

Third, Oakeshott succeeded to a greater degree than Hegel in maintaining the position that philosophers have nothing to contribute to the activities whose postulates they interrogate. The implication is that the practical mode of experience rests on distinct postulates that, if intrusive on the other modes or into philosophy itself, would commit a category mistake. It is no business of the modes or of philosophy to make recommendations about how the other forms of experience should conduct themselves. There is, then, in Oakeshott a separation between theory and practice, which makes him more consistent with Hegel, and to some extent with Bradley and McTaggart, than with any of the other British idealists who thought the role of philosophy was not only to explain the world but also to change it. They were deeply committed to solving the social ills consequent on the industrial revolution and urbanization.

In this respect they were what Oakeshott pejoratively called *philosophes*, or theoreticians, and he included among their company Locke and Bentham. In taking this stance, Oakeshott paradoxically allied himself with the critics of idealism, such as Russell, Moore, Wittgenstein, Cook Wilson, Ayer, and later Weldon and Austin.

Fourth, Oakeshott maintained a radical autonomy of the modes that no other idealist, not even Bradley, tried to sustain. In assuming unity the idealists were obliged to explain how this unity became differentiated into the different modes or forms of experience. Unlike most of the idealists, including Hegel, Oakeshott did not see an inner logic giving rise to successive forms of experience, each taking into itself what was positive in those below. The idea of degrees of truth, most closely associated with Bradley, implies a hierarchy of forms, which Oakeshott rejected. Oakeshott did not provide us with an ontology of the genesis of his modes of experience. He took them as given and interrogated their postulates to expose their conditionality. There were for him no limits to the modes, but only four have arisen coherent enough to generate conclusions consistent with themselves, despite the conditionality of the truths they offer. Oakeshott contended, "Activities emerge naïvely, like games that children invent for themselves. . . . [Our ancestors] set our feet on the paths that have led to these now narrowly specified activities" (*RP*, 151). It is futile to search for the origins of the modes because "all that can be discerned are the slowly mediated changes, the shuffling and reshuffling, the flow and ebb of tides of inspiration, which issue finally in a shape identifiably new" (17–18).

What has been suggested, then, is that Oakeshott's adoption of idealism was not in itself as radical or as brave a move as may appear from the present vantage point. There was an audience for what he was saying in 1933. He was typically idealist in assuming the starting point of unity and in exploring the differentiations to which the fragmentation of unity gave rise. He also subscribed to idealist logic, which is the philosophical study of thought and knowledge, entailing the postulates that underpin the modes, or arrests, in experience. It has further been suggested that Oakeshott always remained an absolute idealist, or monist, and that the introduction of the analogy of conversation did not alter his view of philosophy.

NOTES

1. Some such view is expressed in a number of important studies of Oakeshott. See, for example, Robert Grant, *Oakeshott* (London: Claridge Press, 1990), 65–70; Steven Gerencser, *The Skeptic's Oakeshott* (London: Macmillan, 2000), esp. 33–51; Terry Nardin, *The Philosophy of*

Michael Oakeshott (University Park: Penn State University Press, 2001), 44–45; and Paul Franco, *Michael Oakeshott: An Introduction* (New Haven: Yale University Press, 2004), 125.

2. W. H. Greenleaf, *Oakeshott's Philosophical Politics* (London: Longmans, 1966), 32; Wendell John Coats Jr., *Oakeshott and His Contemporaries* (Selinsgrove: Susquehanna University Press, 2000), 49; Efraim Podoksik, *In Defence of Modernity: Vision and Philosophy in Michael Oakeshott* (Exeter: Imprint Academic, 2003), 39.

3. Andrew Seth Pringle-Pattison and R. B. Haldane, eds., *Essays in Philosophical Criticism* (London: Longmans, Green, 1883).

4. Franco, *Michael Oakeshott*, 24.

5. F. H. Bradley, *Ethical Studies*, 2nd rev. ed. (Oxford: Oxford University Press, 1927); Bradley, *Collected Essays*, 2 vols. (Oxford: Oxford University Press, 1935); W. D. Lamont, *Introduction to Green's Moral Philosophy* (London: Allen and Unwin, 1934).

6. W. R. Boyce Gibson, *Rudolph Eucken's Philosophy of Life* (London: Adam and Black, 1907); Bernard Bosanquet, *The Meeting of Extremes in Modern Philosophy* (London: Macmillan, 1924).

7. G. E. Moore, "Refutation of Idealism," reprinted in *Philosophical Studies* (London: Routledge, 1922), 29.

8. George Berkeley, *Treatise Concerning the Principles of Human Knowledge* (Indianapolis: Merrill, 1970), secs. 22, 23.

9. Henry Jones, *A Critical Account of the Philosophy of Lotze: The Doctrine of Thought* (Glasgow: Maclehose, 1895), 273.

10. Bosanquet, *Meeting of Extremes*, 5.

11. Bernard Bosanquet, "Life and Philosophy," in *Contemporary British Philosophy*, ed. J. H. Muirhead (London: Allen and Unwin, 1924), 60.

12. Harold Joachim, *The Nature of Truth*, ed. R. G. Collingwood, 2nd ed. (Oxford: Oxford University Press, 1939), 3.

13. A. J. Ayer, *Part of My Life* (London: Collins, 1977), 78–79; R. G. Collingwood, *An Essay on Metaphysics* (Oxford: Oxford University Press, 1938); Collingwood, *The Idea of Nature*, ed. T. M. Knox (Oxford: Oxford University Press, 1945).

14. A. J. Ayer, *Philosophy in the Twentieth Century* (London: Allen and Unwin, 1984).

15. Gilbert Ryle, *The Concept of Mind* (1949; repr., Harmondsworth: Penguin, 1970), 17, 23–24, 26.

16. Gilbert Ryle, "Philosophical Arguments," inaugural lecture (Oxford: Clarendon Press, 1945), 4; cf. Allan Donagan, *The Later Philosophy of R. G. Collingwood* (Oxford: Clarendon Press, 1962), 292, and Richard Sclafani, "Wollheim on Collingwood," *Philosophy* 51 (1976): 358. Oakeshott reviewed Ryle's *The Concept of Mind* in 1950 and described it as being in the "highest class" and having something about it of the "philosophical classic" (*CPJ*, 318).

17. See, for example, Podoksik, *In Defence of Modernity*, 10–16; R. G. Collingwood, *An Essay on Philosophical Method* (Oxford: Oxford University Press, 1933); Oakeshott, *EM*; and R. G. Collingwood, *Speculum Mentis* (Oxford: Oxford University Press, 1924). Writing to Collingwood on May 18, 1938, and congratulating him on having performed a miracle in offering sense at last in the philosophy of art, Oakeshott remarks that he has not forgotten that he promised to send something for Collingwood to consider for Oxford University (in the private collection of Teresa Smith, Collingwood's daughter). In the preface to *OHC*, Oakeshott remarks that the themes of the book have been with him almost as long as he can remember. One may assume that it is the book that Oakeshott promised Collingwood in 1938!

18. Sorley wrote to Oakeshott on October 24, 1925, to congratulate him on election to a fellowship at Gonville and Caius, Cambridge: "I had the privilege of reading your dissertation and am convinced that you have both the insight and the power for producing a work of genuine value on political philosophy" (BLPES, 6/1).

19. W. R. Sorley, "The Historical Method," in Pringle-Pattison and Haldane, *Philosophical Criticism*, 125; Sorley, *The Moral Life* (Cambridge: Cambridge University Press, 1911), 126–40.

20. See, for example, W. R. Sorley, *On the Ethics of Naturalism* (Edinburgh: Blackwood, 1885), and *Recent Tendencies in Ethics* (Edinburgh: Blackwell, 1904).

21. W. R. Sorley, *Tradition*, Herbert Spencer Lecture delivered at Oxford, May 19, 1926 (Oxford: Clarendon Press, 1926), 15.

22. J. M. E. McTaggart, "Introduction to the Study of Philosophy," in *Philosophical Studies*, ed. Stanley Victor Keeling (1934; repr., New York: Books for Libraries, 1966), 183–209; Personal idealists exhibited a good deal of internal variety, more so than among the absolute idealists. The most prominent personal or subjective idealists were Andrew Seth Pringle-Pattison, Hastings Rashdall, Henry Sturt, W. R. Boyce Gibson, the American Brand Blanshard, and the idiosyncratic J. M. E. McTaggart, Oakeshott's teacher.

23. Pringle-Pattison, for example, objected to absolute idealism's "unification of consciousness in a single Self"; *Hegelianism and Personality* (Edinburgh: Blackwood, 1888), 215.

24. J. M. E. McTaggart, "An Ontological Idealism," in Keeling, *Philosophical Studies*, 273.

25. J. M. E. McTaggart, "The Individualism of Value," in Keeling, *Philosophical Studies*, 97–109. Also cited in Coats, *Oakeshott and His Contemporaries*, 108, from the copy found among Oakeshott's unpublished papers.

26. W. R. Boyce Gibson, "A Peace Policy for Idealists," *Hibbert Journal* (1906–7): 409.

27. Andrew Seth Pringle-Pattison, *The Idea of God in the Light of Recent Philosophy* (Oxford: Clarendon Press, 1920), 266. See also William Sweet, "'Absolute Idealism' and Finite Individuality," *Indian Philosophical Quarterly* 24 (1997): 431–62; and F. H. Bradley, *Appearance and Reality*, 2nd ed. (Oxford: Oxford University Press, 1897), 464–65.

28. F. H. Bradley, *The Principles of Logic*, 2nd ed., with commentary and terminal essays (Oxford: Clarendon Press, 1932), 656; cf. Sweet, "Absolute Idealism," 434–35.

29. Bradley, *Ethical Studies*, 166–67, 173.

30. Henry Jones, *The Philosophy of Martineau* (London: Macmillan, 1905), 6–7. See also Henry Jones, *Philosophy of Lotze* (Glasgow: Maclehose, 1895), 371.

31. Henry Jones, "Idealism and Epistemology," in *The Scottish Idealists: Selected Philosophical Writings*, ed. David Boucher (Exeter: Imprint Academic, 2004), 139.

32. Edward Caird, *Hegel* (Edinburgh: Blackwood, 1903), 55.

33. Edward Caird, "Metaphysic," in *Essays on Literature and Philosophy*, vol. 2 (Glasgow: Maclehose, 1892), 442.

34. For an exemplification, see William Mitchell, "Moral Obligation," in Boucher, *Scottish Idealists*, 141–58.

35. For an extended discussion of these traditions, see David Boucher, "W. H. Greenleaf and the Triadic Conception of the History of Political Thought," *Idealistic Studies: An International Philosophical Journal* 16 (1986): 237–52; and David Boucher, "Oakeshott and the History of Political Thought," *Collingwood and British Idealism Studies* 13, no. 2 (2007): 69–101.

36. For an excellent discussion of Oakeshott's relation to Hobbes, see Ian Tragenza, *Michael Oakeshott on Hobbes* (Exeter: Imprint Academic, 2003).

37. McTaggart, "Introduction," 183, 184.

38. Wilhelm Dilthey, quoted in William Kluback, *Wilhelm Dilthey's Philosophy of History* (New York: Columbia University Press, 1956), 27.

39. Bernard Bosanquet, *The Essentials of Logic* (London: Macmillan, 1903), 166.

40. L. Susan Stebbing, "The Method of Analysis in Metaphysics," *Proceedings of the Aristotelian Society* 33 (1932–33): 93.

41. McTaggart, "Introduction," 184.

42. Bernard Bosanquet, *The Philosophical Theory of the State* (London: Macmillan, 1899), 2.

43. Ibid.

44. Joachim, *Nature of Truth*, vii, 176.

45. Ibid., 66; G. R. G. Mure, "Benedetto Croce and Oxford," *Philosophical Quarterly* 4 (1954): 329.

46. F. H. Bradley, *Essays on Truth and Reality* (Oxford: Oxford University Press, 1914), 218.

47. Bradley, *Appearance and Reality*, 476.

48. Joachim, *Nature of Truth*, 68.

49. See also David Boucher, "The Idealism of Michael Oakeshott," *Collingwood Studies* 8 (2001): 75–100.

50. Nardin, *Philosophy of Michael Oakeshott*, 44–45.

51. Gerencser, *Skeptic's Oakeshott*, 3, 6.

52. See, for example, Stuart Isaacs, "Philosophical System," chap. 3 in *The Politics and Philosophy of Michael Oakeshott* (London: Routledge, 2006).

53. See also Coats, *Oakeshott and His Contemporaries*, 48.

54. Michael Oakeshott, "History and the Social Sciences" (*CPJ*, 129–34).

55. At the same time he changed the vocabulary from "modes of experience" to "worlds of imaginings." "Experience" had signified too passive a relation to the acquisition of knowledge, and talking of imaginings enabled him to incorporate both propositions and nonpropositional statements into the larger picture. See Greenleaf, *Oakeshott's Philosophical Politics*, 32.

56. Gerencser, *Skeptic's Oakeshott*, 35.

57. Franco, *Michael Oakeshott*, 125.

58. I have suggested elsewhere that the distinction between practices and processes, the former exhibiting human intelligence, while the latter does not, leading to two categorically distinct "orders of inquiry," within each of which there are different idioms, some of which are reducible to one another, constituted an interesting development. It does not, however, undermine the underlying consistency of his thought, which he reiterated in *On History and Other Essays*. See "Overlap and Autonomy: The Different Worlds of Collingwood and Oakeshott," *Storia, Antropologia, e Scienze del Linguaggio* 4 (1989): 69–89; and "Human Conduct, History, and Social Science in the Works of R. G. Collingwood and Michael Oakeshott," *New Literary History* 24 (1993): 697–717.

59. Bradley, *Appearance and Reality*, 440; cf. Bosanquet, "Life and Philosophy," 60.

60. Gerencser, *Skeptic's Oakeshott*, 37

61. Maurice Cranston, "Michael Oakeshott's Politics," *Encounter*, January 1987, 83; and "Remembrances of Michael Oakeshott," *Political Theory* 19 (1991): 324.

62. Henry Jones, *Idealism as a Practical Creed* (Glasgow: Maclehose, 1909).

63. For a fuller discussion, see David Boucher, "The Creation of the Past: British Idealism and Michael Oakeshott's Philosophy of History," *History and Theory* 22 (1984): 193–214.

3

PHILOSOPHY AND ITS MOODS: OAKESHOTT ON THE PRACTICE OF PHILOSOPHY

Kenneth McIntyre

Among nonacademic intellectuals and political theorists, Michael Oakeshott is known primarily as a conservative political thinker who produced a series of essays in the 1950s critical of "rationalist" or "ideological" politics.[1] Others who have read more deeply in Oakeshott's corpus are aware of his contributions to the philosophy of history and of his considerable achievement as a philosopher of practical and political life.[2] Although there has been a significant increase in the attention paid to Oakeshott's contributions to the theoretical understanding of history and politics, Oakeshott's understanding of the character of philosophical activity has remained relatively neglected.[3] This neglect is unfortunate because Oakeshott was one of the few political philosophers of the twentieth century who also provided a more-or-less systematic theoretical context to his political philosophy.[4] Thus, an examination of his understanding of the character and activity of philosophizing is a necessary part of any treatment of his more generally known ideas about the logic of historical explanation, the nature of poetic experience, or the character of practical life and the place of politics within that life.

In this chapter, I examine Oakeshott's understanding of the character of philosophical activity. Oakeshott's thoughts on the subject are scattered throughout his essays, but his most extensive and concentrated reflections on philosophy are found in three works: *Experience and Its Modes*, "The Voice of Poetry in the Conversation of Mankind," and the first essay of *On Human Conduct*. His treatment of the activity of philosophizing in these three different pieces manifests a remarkable degree of continuity in terms of the kinds of questions and concerns which animate his inquiry and in terms of the proper disposition of the philosopher. Oakeshott understands philosophical activity as informed by an unconditional commitment to the interrogation of the conditions of understanding and thus maintains that the disposition of the philosopher is fundamentally skeptical toward the world as it normally appears. Philosophy is understood as a kind of mood that draws us away from the various practices in which we normally engage in order to question the logic of those practices. Thus, there is a distinction between the activity of philosophizing, which is expressive of a disposition toward appearances, and the particular conclusions of philosophers, which, as such, represent a further invitation to reflect on their specific conditions and on conditionality itself.

In terms of his own philosophical conclusions, Oakeshott's work manifests a consistent commitment to conceiving various practices or modes of understanding, such as history, science, and art, as quasi-sufficient, autonomous, and independent worlds logically unrelated to one another and in viewing philosophy as a nonnormative, second-order, explanatory activity in relation to the modes. But his essays also reveal significant terminological changes related to Oakeshott's various attempts to stress different aspects of the character of modality, and they strongly suggest substantial equivocation on Oakeshott's part concerning the criterion of a successful or coherent set of philosophical conclusions.

Thus, though his vision of philosophy as a disposition to investigate the conditions of intelligibility remains relatively unchanged throughout his long life, the conclusions that Oakeshott sets down as the result of his inquiries often reveal subtle and interesting adjustments of perspective and sometimes disclose serious tensions both between and within his various iterations of the nature of philosophy. To scrutinize more carefully both the continuities and discontinuities in Oakeshott's treatment of philosophy, it is useful to examine his work chronologically instead of thematically. Thus, I approach Oakeshott's work through the three primary elaborations of his understanding of philosophy manifested in *Experience and Its Modes*, "The Voice of Poetry in the Conversation of Mankind," and *On Human Conduct*. Such an inquiry offers support to one of Oakeshott's own descriptions of the coherence of his work. He writes that his essays "do not compose a settled doctrine, [instead] they disclose a consistent style or disposition of thought" (*RP*, xii).

Furthermore, I attempt to place his work in the milieu of several philosophical conversations taking place during his career. Like most of his contemporaries, Oakeshott rarely mentions his interlocutors by name, thus leaving the task of placing Oakeshott's philosophy in its proper intellectual context largely up to the interpreter. But despite his reserve, Oakeshott's essays on philosophical activity are often redolent of the most intriguing insights of his contemporaries. His insistence on the unity of philosophy and its character as a mood of unconditional inquiry with a criterion of absolute coherence places his work within the tradition of philosophical idealists such as Bradley, Croce, and Collingwood and also links his work with the hermeneutic tradition represented by Gadamer. Oakeshott's defense of the autonomy and variety of modally different ways of conceiving the world and his elucidation of a traditionalist epistemology connect his work with that of ordinary language philosophers such as Austin and Ryle and the post-*Tractatus* Wittgenstein and with philosophers of science such as Polanyi and Hayek.

Oakeshott is concerned, first and foremost, with defending the integrity and autonomy of philosophy against the attempts of those such as Moore, Russell, and the logical positivists to subsume it under the authority of science and also against the arguments of those such as Heidegger and the American pragmatists suggesting that philosophy should be subordinated to the primordial claims of practical life. Indeed, Oakeshott's most notable contribution to philosophy consists not only of his defense of its autonomy but also of his delineation, elaboration, and celebration of the irreducible variety of modern human experience and of his insistence on the character of philosophical inquiry as an unconditional engagement to investigate the conditionality of that experience.

EXPERIENCE AND ITS MODES

Experience and Its Modes, published in 1933, was Michael Oakeshott's first major publication and is one of only two books that he published during his lifetime. The rest of his work consists of essays and collections of essays, and, in fact, Oakeshott even suggests that his second book, *On Human Conduct*, can be read as three separate essays.[5] In *Experience and Its Modes*, Oakeshott offers his most extended and systematic statement about the character of philosophical activity. The book is written explicitly within the tradition of philosophical idealism, and though Oakeshott rarely mentions either his allies or his adversaries by name, he admits that "the works from which I am conscious of having learnt most are Hegel's *Phänomenologie des Geistes* and Bradley's *Appearance and Reality*" (*EM*, 6).[6] Oakeshott never publicly repudiates or renounces his understanding of his work as primarily idealist, despite the changes in terminology and emphasis that occur in his various works on philosophy.[7]

The reception of the work was marked by the divisions that defined British philosophy at the time. The idealism of Green, Bradley, and Bosanquet, which had dominated British philosophy in the late nineteenth century, had been eclipsed by the realism of Moore, Prichard, and Cook Wilson and the logicism of Russell.[8] Thus, Oakeshott's publication was either ignored or viewed critically as a restatement of a moribund philosophy.[9] Nonetheless, Oakeshott's themes in *Experience and Its Modes* inform all of his subsequent work on the character of philosophy. His three most significant conclusions are first, that philosophy can be understood both as an activity informed by a certain kind of skeptical disposition and as a particular set of conclusions reached by an identifiable philosopher; second, that philosophy can be distinguished from other ways of understanding the world by a logical criterion defining what counts as an adequate understanding; and, third, that philosophy necessarily includes the investigation, elucidation, and critique of the claims of other ways of understanding the world.

Even though *Experience and Its Modes* is his most comprehensive treatment of the character of philosophy, Oakeshott spends only about one-third of the book dealing specifically with questions concerning philosophical activity, and, of this, much is devoted to an exposition of the philosophical temperament. According to Oakeshott, philosophical activity is a manifestation of "a mood, a turn of mind," or disposition toward the received conclusions that the world gives to us (356). This mood is fundamentally skeptical and interrogative and, at the same time, introspective. He insists that "philosophy should be regarded as the determination to be satisfied only with a completely coherent world of experience. For it is not merely its actual achievement which differentiates philosophical from abstract experience, it is its explicit purpose" (357). As an activity, it can be distinguished from any particular conclusions reached at the end of the activity. Such conclusions are not to be understood philosophically as the pronouncements of a magus but instead as invitations to further inquiry. Indeed, Oakeshott insists that, considered as an activity, "philosophy consists, not in persuading others, but in making our own minds clear" (3).[10] The conclusions associated with any particular philosopher's activity of philosophizing are, therefore, less compelling than the philosopher's arguments, and the arguments are best understood as exemplifications of the philosophical temperament rather than as attempts at rhetorical manipulation.

Oakeshott's insistence on the dispositional skepticism of philosophical activity leads to his rejection of both the importance of authority in philosophy and the relevance of philosophy to practical life. He writes that philosophy "recognizes neither 'authorities' nor 'established doctrines,'" because such institutions present themselves as conclusions to be interrogated rather than as dogma to be accepted and deployed (*EM*, 347). Philosophy as an activity requires neither the reverence of the postulant nor the

deference of the exegete. Ironically, ignorance, in its literal sense, is irrelevant to philosophical activity, because, for the philosopher, the conclusions
of other philosophers are invitations to further reflection.[11] But the impetus
toward a philosophical disposition need not arise because of an engagement
with a philosophical tradition but can emerge from almost any encounter
with the given world. The interrogation of the conditions of various given
worlds of understanding, like the questioning of the arguments and conclusions of other philosophers, renders both the activity and conclusions
of philosophy irrelevant to the successful navigation of such given worlds.
Oakeshott insists that "philosophy is without any direct bearing upon the
practical conduct of life, and . . . it has certainly never offered its true followers anything which could be mistaken for a gospel" (1).[12] Indeed, philosophy
is an escape from the normal requirements of getting and spending, and it
requires a severe discipline to remain committed to such a useless (i.e., nonutilitarian) activity.

This discipline is supplied and the philosophical disposition sustained by
a criterion by which other forms of life and other explanations of the forms
of life can be judged. In *Experience and Its Modes*, Oakeshott claims that
"philosophical experience is . . . experience without reservation or arrest,
without presupposition or postulate, without limit or category; it is experience which is critical throughout and unencumbered with the extraneous
purposes which introduce partiality and abstraction into experience" (*EM*,
347). Philosophy thus understood is not practical, historical, or scientific
but the adjudicator of the character and adequacy of practicality, historical
explanation, and scientific explanation. Unlike other forms of activity and
understanding, philosophical activity begins with a determination of its own
self-reflective and autonomous norms of judgment. Philosophy is, first, an
exploration of its own character, which issues in a vision of itself that is at
one and the same time a provisional conclusion and an invitation to further
reflection. Oakeshott claims that *Experience and Its Modes* is an exploration
of the idea of philosophy as experience without arrest, presupposition, or
modification.

Thus, the tasks that Oakeshott understands to be central to the activity of
philosophizing are, first, an exploration and self-definition of a criterion or set
of criteria, which then inform judgments about the adequacy of our understanding of the world; and, second, a critical investigation of what Oakeshott
calls arrests or modes of experience, which do not meet the criterion of adequacy. He writes that "I consider it . . . the main business of philosophy . . . to
determine its own character. . . . It must [also] fall within the task of philosophy to consider the character of every world of experience which offers itself"
(*EM*, 83). Oakeshott focuses on the first of these tasks only in *Experience and*

Its Modes and rarely revisits the task of philosophical self-definition again, concentrating his theoretical work instead almost solely on the latter task of investigating the modes of experience. One of the difficulties associated with the activity of philosophy as self-definition is that it resembles a situation in which a carpenter is engaged at inventing or altering his tools while at the same time occupied in the practice of carpentry, a situation Oakeshott subsequently describes as an impossibility.

Nonetheless, in *Experience and Its Modes*, Oakeshott proceeds from philosophical self-definition to the examination of less satisfactory forms of understanding. He conceives of philosophy as experience or judgment that has become self-conscious and critical of itself, and he attempts to demonstrate philosophical experience's independence from and superiority to the claims of practical, historical, or scientific experience. Philosophical experience, unlike other types of experience, is "experience without presupposition, arrest, or modification . . . , [which] carries with it the evidence of its own completeness" (*EM*, 2). Oakeshott begins with this purely stipulative assertion, while also, ironically, appropriating the term *experience* from the empiricist and logicist opponents of idealism. Of course, Oakeshott is not using the term in the same way. Instead of referring specifically to the immediate impingement of external stimulation on the senses or to sensa themselves, Oakeshott argues that experience is a concrete whole that cannot be separated into its components. He writes that "what is at first given in experience is single and significant, a One and not a Many" (20). Thus, human beings begin with a world of experience, or, in other words, they are "thrown" into a world of meanings and are therefore never completely ignorant.[13]

The general character of this experience of the world is thought or judgment, not in isolation, but of a world that is always already given to us. There are no independent "building blocks" or bare data on which to build. Instead, human understanding consists of getting to know in a more satisfactory way what one already knows in a confused or inadequate way. As Oakeshott suggests, "there is nothing immediate or 'natural' in contrast to what is mediate or sophisticated; there are only degrees of sophistication . . . [and] the process in experience is the continuous modification and extension of this datum [i.e., the given], which is given everywhere in order to be changed and never merely to be preserved" (*EM*, 20).[14] The movement from a given to an achieved world brings about a more unified and coherent world, and this newly achieved world is always immanent in the given world, but does not in any sense rest on the older given world. Understanding always consists of the transformation of a given, less-than-coherent world into a more satisfactory one, and this conception of human understanding remains a consistent theme of Oakeshott's work on philosophy throughout his career.

But Oakeshott rejects the notion that his account of understanding entails the metaphysical claim that a completely coherent world of ideas exists or will come to exist. In rejecting this conclusion, he distinguishes himself from other idealists such as Hegel and Bradley. He claims that "what is achieved in experience is an absolutely coherent world of ideas, not in the sense that it is ever actually achieved, but in the more important sense that it is the criterion of whatever satisfaction is achieved. Absolute coherence as the end in experience is implicit in the character of experience because, where partial coherence is achieved and found to be momentarily satisfactory, the criterion is always coherence itself, that is, absolute coherence" (*EM*, 35). Thus, Oakeshott suggests that coherence, like presuppositionless and unconditional experience, is a logical criterion of philosophical activity instead of the telos, or expected result of such activity. This mitigates the absolutism of his idealism and places his thought more in line with that of Croce and Collingwood, both of whom understood their idealism in provisional rather than absolute terms.[15]

Nonetheless, the manner in which Oakeshott expresses this criterion or end of philosophical experience raises certain difficulties that seem inherent in the tradition of idealism, broadly considered. His description of the completely coherent world of philosophical experience is formalistic and devoid of substantive content, and, in this, it opts for perhaps the lesser of two evils available to idealist metaphysics. As idealist philosophers approach the absolute, they either end in the formalism of criteria and conditions, like Kant, or in the ambiguous mysticism of quasi-theological speculation, like Hegel, and neither delivers on the promise of a single, concrete, complete, and coherent world of experience.

But, as mentioned, Oakeshott rarely revisits metaphysical questions about the ultimate or absolute end of experience, and his treatment of questions concerning truth and coherence become more closely tied to his examination of the specific practices that constitute modern life. The way that Oakeshott treats these specific practices, or modes of experience, is one of the most notable aspects of his understanding of philosophy. For Oakeshott the second task of the philosopher, after the self-definition of the activity of philosophy itself, consists of the investigation, elaboration, and critique of these various arrests in experience.

This activity forms by far the largest portion of Oakeshott's own philosophical practice and, in *Experience and Its Modes*, occupies two-thirds of the text.[16] His examination of the character of modality produces four central conclusions: first, the activity of philosophizing and the activity that occurs within the presuppositions of a mode of experience are radically discontinuous;

second, the modes themselves are only incompletely coherent and constitute not an aspect of experience but the totality of experience from an abstract point of view; third, because the various modes are constituted by their own specific presuppositions, the understanding to be achieved within each mode is irrelevant to the understanding of any other mode; and, finally, the understanding achieved within each mode has nothing to contribute to philosophy, and philosophy contributes nothing to the internal achievements of modal understanding.

For Oakeshott in *Experience and Its Modes*, the idea of absolute unconditionality is the criterion of satisfactory philosophical reflection, and thus anything that falls short of that kind of unconditionality is the result of not fulfilling the implicit task of philosophy. But he recognizes that a majority of experience does not approach this sort of unconditionality, and he even admits that philosophical conclusions themselves, insofar as they invite inquiry into their conditionality, are never quite unconditional either. Oakeshott suggests that the concrete understanding of the whole of experience is usually arrested, and when the criterion of philosophical satisfaction is ignored, an abstract world of ideas emerges at the point of arrest. Oakeshott refers to these abstract worlds as modes of experience because of their character as modifications of the concrete whole.[17] He writes that "a mode of experience is experience with reservation . . . shackled by partiality and presupposition" (*EM*, 74). The various presuppositions that constitute a particular mode of experience cannot be questioned while operating or functioning within the mode itself. For example, physicians presuppose a particular conception of causation when dealing with patients. If they were to question whether it were true that symptoms always have causes, they would not thereby become bad physicians but would cease to be acting as physicians at all. The postulates that constitute these various modes of experience act as absolute presuppositions, defining the logic of understanding and explanation possible within the mode while also acting as de facto limitations on the kind of questions appropriate to the mode and serving as emblems of modal partiality.[18]

Furthermore, modes of experience are not constituent parts of the whole of reality but the whole considered from a limited viewpoint. As such, the modes are defined not by a subject matter or methodology but by their specific presuppositions. As Oakeshott notes, "from one standpoint, such a world of ideas is free and self-contained" (*EM*, 75). That is, if one accepts the presuppositions of any particular mode of experience, the mode itself appears to be more or less coherent and satisfactory. Despite the radical discontinuity between the criterion of philosophical satisfaction and the arrests of modal experience, Oakeshott defends the internal sufficiency of modal experience and, in so doing, develops one of the central features of his philosophical work: the celebration of the diverse ways that modern human beings have come to enjoy and experience the world. He writes that "each abstract world of ideas, insofar as it is coherent is, then, true so far as it goes, true if its postulates are accepted, true if its reservations are admitted" (77). Nonetheless, in *Experience and Its Modes*, Oakeshott insists that the modes themselves are philosophically unsatisfactory, and, insofar as that is the case, none of them are necessary from the point of view of the criterion of satisfaction. In fact, except for the world of practice, they are all recent developments in the human encounter with the world and could conceivably disappear or be replaced by other modes.

Because they are unnecessary, Oakeshott believes that a genetic account of the modes is irrelevant to a philosophical understanding of them.[19] Nonetheless, he insists that an account of the relationship among the modes themselves and between the modes and philosophy is necessary to avoid intellectual confusion. For Oakeshott, unlike other idealists, each mode of experience is completely independent of the other modes because of the distinctive presuppositions associated with the mode.[20] He claims that "between these worlds . . . there can be neither dispute nor agreement; they are wholly irrelevant to one another" (*EM*, 327).

The various modes exist as a result of a set of specific presuppositions or postulates that constitute the conditions of the mode itself. The modes do not share the same presuppositions, so it is impossible to move in argument from one mode to another without resulting in what Oakeshott calls "the most subtle and insidious of all forms of error—irrelevance" (*EM*, 76). The *ignoratio elenchi*, or category mistake, is central to Oakeshott's critique of modern attempts to reduce history, art, or practice to science; for any attempt on the part of one mode to regulate or judge other modes is both inappropriate and philosophically unjustifiable.

Oakeshott observes that "what, from the standpoint of one world, is fact, from the standpoint of another is nothing at all" (327).[21] For example, historians, when investigating the past, presuppose a past inherently different from the present and thus irrelevant to the concerns of, say, a politician or a moralist whose past is constituted primarily by questions of its usefulness and, as such, dissolved into the present. The politician doesn't use historical "facts" to support an argument but conceives of the past as a storehouse of ready-made symbols and arguments whose relevance is solely based upon their utility. Or, to offer another example, artists understand metaphor as intrinsically meaningful, whereas, in the world of practice or science, metaphors are useless unless they can be treated more or less as a form of literal symbolic

language. The scientist is not merely appropriating a fixed and finished arti-
fact created by a poet but instead transforming it into something understandable as an answer to questions about precision, stability, or measurability.
Oakeshott's insistence on the complete autonomy of these various modes of
understanding is one of the characteristic features of his philosophical work
and remains a consistent feature of his theoretical investigations throughout
his life.

Finally, just as the modes of experience have nothing to contribute to one
another, they are irrelevant to philosophy. The criterion of philosophical adequacy is unconditional understanding and, since the modes are constituted
by specific conditions (i.e., the acceptance of their presuppositions), they are
inherently conditional and inadequate. Philosophy is not merely the result
of the accretion of each mode's particular kind of partiality but "is the complete world which every abstract world implies and from which it derives its
significance" (EM, 80). Philosophy, understood as unconditional or presuppositionless understanding, is logically prior to any particular partiality, and
such a partiality contributes nothing to such an understanding. A philosophical understanding of the modes abolishes them, not empirically but logically,
by demonstrating their conditionality. Insofar as this is the case, however, it
means that not only do the modes of experience have nothing to add to satisfactory philosophical experience but also that philosophy contributes nothing
to the various modes. He writes that "History, Science, and Practice, as such,
and each within its own world, are beyond the relevant interference of philosophic thought" (332).[22] Thus, the second kind of philosophical activity results
not in a methodology or normative theory of science, history, or practice, but
in an elucidation of the logic of each world consisting of an examination of
the presuppositions of each world.[23] The activity is both explanatory and critical, but it is also expressive of the disposition of the philosopher not to be
satisfied with particularity, abstraction, or conditionality. In this conception,
philosophy is more closely identified with an attitude or commitment than
with a final result, and this philosophical mood animates all of Oakeshott's
work.

"THE VOICE OF POETRY IN THE CONVERSATION OF MANKIND"

Oakeshott's next iteration of the character of philosophy appears in "The
Voice of Poetry in the Conversation of Mankind," an essay published more
than twenty-five years after Experience and Its Modes.[24] The continuities of the
essay with Oakeshott's earlier work are evident, and they strongly suggest

that Oakeshott's reconsideration does not entail a significant rejection of his earlier position. But there also appear changes in terminology and emphasis that suggest both that Oakeshott's purposes in the essay differ from his purposes in his earlier work and, more important, that there has been a subtle shift in Oakeshott's understanding of the activity of philosophy.

As mentioned earlier, Oakeshott does not revisit the sort of metaphysical questions about the nature of universality, of concreteness, and of reality that animate the first part of *Experience and Its Modes*.[25] Instead, he focuses primarily on the relationship between the various modes, and his primary purpose is to elucidate the character of the poetic mode and defend its autonomy in relation to the worlds of practice and science. Indeed, beginning with "The Voice of Poetry" and continuing to the end of Oakeshott's career, the primary function of philosophy moves from the definition of itself as an activity and the critique of modal abstraction to the elaboration and defense of the autonomy of the various ways that human beings understand their world. This conception of philosophy retains the notion that the criterion of philosophical achievement is unconditional understanding while also conceding that philosophy is primarily a second-order activity that consists of exploring the logic of the various practices characteristic of the modern world instead of attempting to reduce these practices to a single, universal, ruling practice.

The altered situation of philosophy in "The Voice of Poetry" reflects, in part, Oakeshott's essays in the late 1940s on rationalism and traditionalist epistemology.[26] These essays and "The Voice of Poetry" manifest the influence of both the philosophy of science of Michael Polanyi and the linguistic philosophy of Gilbert Ryle, J. L. Austin, and Ludwig Wittgenstein.[27] Oakeshott's essays are not, in themselves, reconsiderations of the nature of philosophy, but manifestations of such reconsiderations. But while providing important insights into epistemological questions, they also introduce certain tensions within Oakeshott's work on philosophical activity. The primary problem rests in Oakeshott's insistence on the embeddedness of human consciousness and his emphasis on the centrality of practical knowledge on the one hand and his notion that philosophical explanation is necessarily unconditional or complete on the other. This tension persists throughout his work and is only partially mitigated by Oakeshott's own recognition of the distinction between philosophy as an activity and philosophy as a set of conclusions.

The most important conclusion to be taken from "Rationalism in Politics" and "Rational Conduct" is that rationality is a characteristic immanent within practices and varies accordingly and not an independent or universal quality of a separable human faculty called reason or mind. Therefore, questions about the rationality of ideas or actions are necessarily questions of contextual knowledge and connoisseurship, or of "knowing how" instead of "knowing that."[28] Oakeshott distinguishes between technical knowledge, which is "susceptible of precise formulation," and practical knowledge, which "exists only in use, is not reflective and . . . cannot be formulated in rules" (RP, 12).[29] This practical, or tacit, knowledge consists in knowing how to engage in particular practices such as cooking, playing baseball, conducting a scientific experiment, or writing a poem.

The character of rationality related to each of these practices is specific to the practice itself and does not involve a prior cognitive operation, such as composing a recipe for Peking duck, constructing a method or a plan for hitting a baseball, composing a hypothesis about the relation between force and energy, or creating a model of an ideal poem, before then engaging each respective activity. Instead, Oakeshott claims that "it is the activity itself which defines the questions as well as the manner in which they are answered. . . . Activity . . . is something that comes first, and is something into which each [person] gradually finds his way: at no time is he wholly ignorant of it; there is no identifiable beginning" (RP, 117–18).

As in *Experience and Its Modes*, Oakeshott claims that human beings always and everywhere inhabit a world of meanings, and rationality consists of acting and thinking in such a way that we move from a given world of meaning to a more satisfactory one. Actions always take place within specific worlds, and it is the character of these worlds or practices that give meaning to the actions. As Oakeshott observes, "all specific activity springs up within an already existing idiom of activity. . . . We begin with what we *know* . . . and if we knew nothing we could never begin" (121). Thus, knowledge consists in getting to know something better that we already know, but imprecisely or inadequately in some way. This dialectical conception of knowledge is consistent with Oakeshott's early work.

But two problems arise in these essays that ought to inform the interpretation of the receding centrality of philosophical self-definition in Oakeshott's later work. First, Oakeshott characterizes all knowledge, including philosophical knowledge, as consisting in large part of a kind of practical or tacit knowledge not reducible to rules. In fact, it seems that the communication of practical knowledge is possible only through showing and not saying.[30] But this very ineffability renders the notion of a completely communicable explanation or understanding of the world of concrete experience impossible. It is not merely that the criterion of unconditional presuppositionless understanding can be approached only in a fleeting or ephemeral way but that the criterion itself is necessarily incomplete, because it is an abstraction from any truly concrete philosophical activity. Like any human practice, philosophical activity involves practical knowledge, which is not amenable to any sort of reduction to a set of criteriological statements.

Furthermore, because philosophy is a practice like other human practices, it involves "knowing how" to do things philosophically. Unlike other practices, a central part of the practice of philosophy consists of reflection on the practice itself. Nonetheless, the fact that questions about rationality and knowledge are inherently questions about the conditions under which knowledge claims are made suggests that all knowledge is inherently conditional. If this is so, then there can be no possibility of unconditional, presuppositionless knowledge, and philosophical activity must be understood not as an attempt to grasp the world in its completeness and universality but instead as the endeavor to make the practice of philosophy more coherent by examining the immanent conditionality of the world of experience.

This notion of philosophy as a second-order activity consisting of the examination of the logic of other worlds of experience informs Oakeshott's work "The Voice of Poetry in the Conversation of Mankind." Oakeshott's primary purpose in the essay is to offer a philosophy of aesthetic experience, something he had neglected in *Experience and Its Modes*.[31] This purpose accounts for at least one of the terminological changes in the essay. Oakeshott refers to the modes of experience as modes of imagining, a term more fitting for considering a world that many identify with imagination. For our purposes, however, the more important changes concern Oakeshott's approach to the activity of philosophy. Oakeshott does not revise his notion of the dispositional character of philosophical activity but, instead, extends the notion to include the mode of poetic experience. For Oakeshott "there is no *vita contemplativa*; there are only moments of contemplative activity abstracted and rescued from the flow of curiosity and contrivance. Poetry [like philosophy] is a sort of truancy, a dream within the dream of life" (*RP*, 541). This is true not only of poetry and philosophy, however. Neither historical inquiry nor scientific explanation is necessary for the continuation of human life, either, and both can be considered, like philosophy and poetry, to be momentary escapes from the "deadliness of doing."

In terms of the two tasks of philosophy, self-definition and the exploration of the general character of modality, the first has receded and been almost completely replaced by the second. In "The Voice of Poetry," Oakeshott offers only an exiguous account of the activity of philosophy, which he relates to understanding the various modes of imagining. Human activity generally consists of the recognition, construction, and manipulation of images. These images are not conclusions drawn from the immediate experience of bare data but always appear within the context of a conditional world of meaningful understandings. Oakeshott writes that "images . . . correspond to a specific mode of imagining which may be discerned . . . by ascertaining what sort of questions are relevant to be asked about its images . . . [and, thus] an image is never isolated and alone; it belongs to [a] world or field of images" (*RP*, 497). These modes of imaginings are the same ones that Oakeshott examines in *Experience and Its Modes* (practice, science, and history), with the addition of the mode of poetic or artistic imagining, the elaboration of which is the ultimate purpose of the essay. Thus, philosophical activity consists in part of reflecting on the character of human imagination.

But since human imagining takes place only within the various modes of imaginings that constitute the conditions of the appearance of images, the primary activity of philosophy involves the exploration both of the conditions constituting these modes of experience and imagining and of their relation to one another. Oakeshott writes that "philosophy [is] the impulse to study the quality and style of each voice [or mode], and to reflect upon the relationship of one voice to another" (*RP*, 491). Philosophy elucidates the presuppositions or postulates that constitute the modes of imagining, but the critical stance of philosophy toward the conditional, abstract, or arrested modality of experience has become a secondary consideration. Philosophy is still concerned with discerning the place of the various modes of experience "on the map of human activity."[32] But it is less clear where the location of philosophy is on such a map, especially when understood in terms of the criterion of unconditional or presuppositionless experience. Indeed, Oakeshott admits that "I do not myself know where to place an experience released altogether from modality" (513). Thus, the tension between the criterion of unconditionality and the inherent conditionality of all experience becomes apparent, and the question of the possibility of unconditional understanding becomes overtly problematic.[33] For Oakeshott this tension resolves itself in his distinction between the activity of philosophy, which is an investigation of the conditions of experience in which every condition is susceptible to questioning, and the conclusions of any particular philosopher, which can be understood as resting on conditions that invite further inquiry.

As a second-order explanation of modality, philosophy retreats from the preeminently critical treatment of modality and instead examines and preserves the diversity of human experience. The relationship between the modes of imagining that Oakeshott describes in "The Voice of Poetry" is largely unchanged from that depicted in *Experience and Its Modes*. He writes that "each mode begins and ends only with itself. . . . The images of one universe of discourse are not available (even as raw materials) to a different mode of imagining" (*RP*, 514). That is to say, the modes are autonomous and the facts, arguments, conclusions, images, and ideas of one are completely irrelevant to another. But Oakeshott introduces a new metaphor to illustrate the relations between the modes:

> The diverse idioms of utterance which make up current human intercourse have some meeting-place . . . and . . . the image of this meeting-place is not an inquiry or an argument, but a conversation. In a conversation, the participants are not engaged in an inquiry or a debate; there is not "truth" to be discovered, no proposition to be proved, no conclusion sought. . . . There is no symposiarch or arbiter . . . and voices which speak in conversation do not compose a hierarchy. . . . In it different universes of discourse meet, acknowledge each other and enjoy an oblique relationship which neither requires nor forecasts their being assimilated to one another. (489–90)

A conversation, unlike an argument, necessarily consists of various diverse voices engaged in an activity intrinsically valuable. The modes of experience or imagining are here conceived as languages, each with its own characteristic grammar and vocabulary not reducible to a common ideal manner of speech. Philosophy, as the examination and elucidation of these various languages, is "a parasitic activity; it springs from the conversation, because this is what the philosopher reflects upon, but it makes no specific contribution to it" (489).[34]

At the same time and somewhat paradoxically, Oakeshott suggests that philosophy is a model of conversability, which he defines as the capacity to take part in the conversation without attempting to transform it into an argument or sermon. He suggests that "the voice of philosophy . . . is unusually conversable [because t]here is no body of philosophical 'knowledge' to become detached from the activity of philosophizing" (RP, 492).[35] Conversability is connected, not with the capacity of a language or mode to proselytize successfully, but with a manner of speaking or thinking about the world of experience. As Oakeshott notes, "each voice is at once a manner of speaking and a determinate utterance. As a manner of speaking, each is wholly conversable. But the defect to which some of the voices are liable is a loosening (even a detachment) of what is said from the manner of utterance, and when this takes place the voice appears as a body of conclusions reached (dogmata), and thus, becoming eristic, loses its conversability" (493).

Oakeshott argues that art, like philosophy, is preeminently conversable because its conclusions (e.g., paintings, poems, symphonies) are less detachable from the activity of art and thus less susceptible to the conversion of such conclusions into creedal statements. Science, practice, and, to a lesser extent, history are all more amenable to such a conversion and thus regularly appear to offer themselves as the whole of experience instead of merely one manner of experiencing. For example, consider the great difficulty of deriving any set of dogmatic conclusions from, on the one hand, Wittgenstein's consideration of the rabbit/duck drawing or Austin's discussion of "pretending" and, on the other, Rothko's color bar paintings, Henry Moore's sculptures, Pound's cantos. Compare the perplexity confronted in these situations with the ease with which E. O. Wilson detaches the conclusions of sociobiology from its scientific context and attempts to apply them to human activity or with which Rawls abstracts certain political conclusions from the practices of Western social democracies and attempts to apply them to every possible variation of political life.

Oakeshott's distinctive way of characterizing the relations between the modes of imagining also reveals a final function that philosophy serves. In focusing on the character of the modes and their relations, philosophical activity can play a prophylactic role. In relation to the poetic world, Oakeshott observes that "philosophic reflection may perhaps hinder the critic from asking irrelevant questions and from thinking and speaking about poems in an inappropriate manner, and this . . . is something not to be despised" (*RP*, 495). Thus, despite being relegated to a parasitic activity, philosophy can at least have the secondary effect of clearing away some of the misconceptions or confusions that accompany our normal thinking about our particular modal practices. Philosophy can be understood as therapeutic insofar as it rids us of infelicitous, inappropriate, and irrelevant manners of making our way through the various worlds of experience.

ON HUMAN CONDUCT

Oakeshott's final statement about the nature of philosophical activity appears fifteen years after "The Voice of Poetry" in the first essay of *On Human Conduct*. Like "The Voice of Poetry," *On Human Conduct* focuses on the exploration and elucidation of one mode of experience (practice) and does not constitute a systematic reexamination of the activity of philosophizing.[36] These various restatements of Oakeshott's position on the character of philosophy can be partially explained by pointing to Oakeshott's argument in *Experience and Its Modes* that to fully understand any particular practice or world of experience, that practice or world must be placed within the context of the whole of experience, which involves explaining the relationship between any particular practice or world and the philosophical explanation of the whole of experience.[37]

But there are obvious terminological changes in Oakeshott's various essays on philosophy that suggest subtle alterations of his views, and the discontinuity in terminology between Oakeshott's earlier work and *On Human Conduct* is quite striking. Instead of the term *philosophy*, Oakeshott speaks of theorizing and theorems, and instead of *modes of experience* or *imagining*, he writes of platforms of conditional understanding. These changes do not, in themselves, necessarily involve a repudiation of his earlier account of philosophical activity. Indeed, Oakeshott's understanding of philosophy in *On Human Conduct* is consistent with the account given in "The Voice of Poetry." Philosophy is a disposition that leads to two distinct activities. First, it involves a commitment to explore the general character of the conditionality or modality of human understanding. The task of philosophical self-definition has changed from the search for an absolute criterion of judgment to reflection on the inherently conditional character of human experience. Second, philosophy serves to elucidate the presuppositions of specific modes or platforms of conditional understanding. The relationship between these modes or platforms also appears to be consistent with his earlier work, as the platforms are autonomous and irrelevant to one another. Thus, despite the radical changes in terminology, Oakeshott's conception of the activity of philosophy in *On Human Conduct* remains largely unchanged from his prior statement of it in the 1950s.

As in "The Voice of Poetry," Oakeshott insists that philosophy is a second-order activity consisting, first, in the consideration of the general character of human understanding and, second, in the investigation of the presuppositions or postulates of various specific ways of understanding the world. He writes that "philosophical reflection is recognized here as the adventure of one who seeks to understand in other terms what he already understands and in which the understanding sought (itself unavoidably conditional) is a disclosure of the conditions of the understanding enjoyed and not a substitute for it. . . . [Philosophy] may enlighten but it does not instruct" (*OHC*, vii). For Oakeshott philosophical understanding is of a different conditional quality than common understanding because it is concerned with the conditions that constitute common understanding and is thus inherently nonnormative.

Unlike in *Experience and Its Modes*, however, Oakeshott emphasizes the necessary conditionality of even philosophical understanding, and there is no mention in *On Human Conduct* of a criterion of unconditional or presuppositionless experience. Instead, Oakeshott emphasizes the distinction between the activity of philosophizing, which is an unconditional engagement, and the conclusions of such an activity, which are themselves susceptible to further investigation and elucidation.[38] He writes that "the engagement of understanding is not unconditional on account of the absence of conditions, or in virtue of a supposed terminus in an unconditional theorem; what constitutes its unconditionality is the continuous recognition of the conditionality of conditions . . . [and thus] the irony of all theorizing is its propensity to generate, not an understanding, but a not-yet-understood" (11). The philosopher is not engaged in the attempt to reach an understanding of the world that is in itself unconditional or presuppositionless but is instead unconditionally committed to understanding the general conditionality of all understanding or experience. The philosopher, or theorist, maintains an attitude of sceptical dissatisfaction with understanding because it always rests on conditions that can be further explored. The results of such in an engagement in philosophical reflection (i.e., theories or philosophies) are inherently provisional, or, as Oakeshott puts it, they "are interim triumphs of temerity over scruple" (11). And, of course, they lose their concrete character when they are detached from the activity that produced them and transformed into sets of doctrines or dogmas.

The activity of philosophizing always begins with something already understood, which invites the theorist to interrogate its conditions. As in his earlier works, Oakeshott maintains that understanding always and everywhere takes place within an already given world of meaning and that it consists of getting to know something better and in a different way than one already knows it. He writes that "we inexorably inhabit a world of intelligibles," and understanding consists of making that world even more intelligible (*OHC*, 1). This world of intelligibles is composed of "facts" constituted by a set of presuppositions or conditions that make their appearance possible and that Oakeshott describes as a platform of understanding. Like modes of experience and imagining, these platforms of understanding are conditional identities, and the philosopher seeks to understand them in terms of their postulates, or conditions.[39] Oakeshott claims that "in identifying the component conditions of this conditionality and in making these postulates the terms of his understanding [the philosopher] comes to occupy a new platform of conditional understanding" (9). The philosopher is not in fact engaged in an unconditioned activity, but, insofar as the result of the activity is an elucidation of the conditions or presuppositions of a particular platform of understanding, the conclusions of the philosopher are irrelevant to the practices associated with that particular platform or mode. Thus, although the disposition of the philosopher toward the engagement to question the conditions of any particular world of experience must remain unconditional, the philosopher must inevitably "drop anchor" on a platform of conditional understanding to "catch theoretical fish" (11).

In *On Human Conduct*, Oakeshott is fishing for an elucidation of the world of human beliefs, institutions, and practices. Therefore, the question that informs his inquiry concerns the differentia between activities that are exhibitions of intelligence and those that are not. Oakeshott's answer is to make a categorical distinction between platforms of understanding that presuppose a world composed of intelligent practices and platforms of understanding that presuppose a world composed of nonintelligent processes.[40] This categorical distinction informs the recognition of any particular identity, and categorically distinct identities, such as a boxing match and tidal flux, cannot be reduced to their opposite category. This distinction between practice and process constitutes two different platforms of understanding but does not involve any claims about mind/body distinctions. Oakeshott suggests that "mind . . . is the intelligent activity in which a man may understand and explain processes which cannot understand and explain themselves," while body is viewed as a process to be understood by mind (*VLL*, 3).

Furthermore, the categorical identification of any particular thing in the world also predicates an idiom of inquiry, such as ethics or jurisprudence in the case of intelligent practices or biology or chemistry in the case of nonintelligent processes. These idiomatic platforms of conditional understanding are also constituted by their postulates, and Oakeshott insists that "each is autonomous . . . and . . . capable of its own conditional perfection" (*OHC*, 17). The elucidation of the postulates of these idiomatic platforms of understanding is recognizable as the second task of philosophy for Oakeshott, and it is not to be confused with the creation of either a methodology or a set of normative axioms for the various idiomatic practices. The philosopher's concerns are distinct from the practitioner's and cannot serve as a substitute for them because the philosopher's concerns are of a different conditional character. Once again, Oakeshott maintains that the arguments, ideas, facts, and values that appear within the various idiomatic platforms of understanding are irrelevant to one another and that philosophical understanding is irrelevant to the practices involved in such idioms.

Oakeshott's notion that there are both categorical and idiomatic distinctions between the platforms or modes of understanding appears to reduce, to some extent, the actual independence of the modes from one another by suggesting that idiomatic platforms are less distinct than categorical ones. The term *idiom* reflects Oakeshott's notion that the different modes or platforms of understanding resemble distinct languages, but it doesn't seem to be as strong as the term *categorical*.[41] On the other hand, an idiomatic expression is an expression that cannot be literally translated from one language to another and thus serves Oakeshott's purposes quite well. The distinction between the use of *categorical* and *idiomatic* appears to be deployed primarily to criticize reductionist attempts to arrive at a purely scientific explanation of human conduct. Although Oakeshott adamantly rejects the idea, the distinction also lends itself to the notion that there is some bare datum that could be identified in terms of intelligence or lack thereof. That is, though it might make sense to claim that one can view human action either in terms of intelligent practices such as intending, believing, and arguing or in terms of nonintelligent processes such as digesting, perspiring, or aspirating, it does not appear as credible to consider anything else in this way. There appear to be things (e.g., tides, mineral deposits, forests, solar systems) inherently or naturally nonintelligent and not susceptible to consideration under the idiomatic modes of understanding associated with practices. Thus, the "facts" about the tide or the stars or the animal world are not wholly constituted by the categorical distinction but seem to be prior to such considerations and, in fact, require that they be considered in terms of processes.

It might reasonably be asked whether Oakeshott thought that he was making a significant alteration in his conception of the character of modality and the relations of the modes to one another. The answer is that it appears quite unlikely that he believed himself to be doing so. In 1975, the same year that *On Human Conduct* was published, Oakeshott delivered an address titled "A Place of Learning," in which he referred to the character of history, practice, literature, and science as modally distinct languages, suggesting that, at this time, he continued to view the distinctiveness of the modes as absolute (*VLL*, 23, 28). Furthermore, in *On History*, published in 1983, Oakeshott again reverted to the language of modality, asserting that "a mode of understanding . . . is . . . an autonomous manner of understanding, specifiable in terms of exact conditions, which is logically incapable of denying or confirming the conclusions of any other mode of understanding . . . [and] a mixture of modes . . . spells total inconsequence" (*OH*, 3, 26). Thus, though there certainly appears to be some ambiguity in Oakeshott's presentation of the character of and relations between the modes or platforms of understanding in *On Human Conduct*, it does not seem to be the result of an intentional change in his conception of the general character of conditionality and the independence of the various forms of human experience. Oakeshott remained committed to defending the autonomy of these forms against reductionism of any sort.

CONCLUSION

Although it is unlikely that he will soon be considered by academic philosophers to be a figure whose significance is on par with Heidegger or Wittgenstein, Oakeshott's understanding of the activity of philosophizing remains a compelling one. Oakeshott chose his adversaries well and his choice of themes also served to link him with several of the most important critical developments vis-à-vis the dominant traditions of philosophy in the past century. Oakeshott's primary targets were, on the one hand, those philosophers, such as the Cambridge realists and the logical positivists, who attempted to subsume the distinctive character of philosophical inquiry under the category of scientific method and, on the other, those, such as the existentialists and pragmatists, who attempted to do the same under the concept of practice. His consistent defense of the intellectual validity of the plurality of human experience and his insistence on the traditional character of knowledge place his work in conversation with that of linguistic philosophers such as Austin and Ryle and the later Wittgenstein, hermeneutic philosophers such as Gadamer, and philosophers of science such as Polanyi and Hayek. Furthermore, though his understanding of the place and character of philosophical self-definition changes from the explicit absolute idealism of its initial statement in *Experience and Its Modes* to a more reticent provisional kind of idealism in "The Voice of Poetry" and *On Human Conduct*, Oakeshott maintains a consistent emphasis both on the skeptical disposition inherent in the engagement of philosophizing and on the nonnormative character of philosophy. Finally, one of the central values of Oakeshott's essays on philosophy lies in their manifestation of his own philosophical disposition. Oakeshott's work is valuable not because it displays correct conclusions or dogmas but instead because it exhibits the practice of a truly engaged mind attempting to make the map of human experience just a bit more coherent.

NOTES

1. See, for example, Perry Anderson, "The Intransigent Right at the End of the Century," *London Review of Books* 14 (1992): 7–11.

2. See, for example, Paul Franco, *The Political Philosophy of Michael Oakeshott* (New Haven: Yale University Press, 1990); and Luke O'Sullivan, *Oakeshott on History* (Exeter: Imprint Academic, 2003).

3. The most complete treatment of Oakeshott's philosophy can be found in Terry Nardin, *The Philosophy of Michael Oakeshott* (University Park: Penn State University Press, 2001). But among those who focus on Oakeshott's political philosophy, both W. H. Greenleaf and Paul Franco emphasize the centrality of Oakeshott's conception of the nature of philosophy to his theoretical treatment of politics. Franco writes that "at the heart of Oakeshott's political philosophy lies a

doctrine about the nature of philosophy." *Political Philosophy*, 13; and W. H. Greenleaf, *Oakeshott's Philosophical Politics* (London: Longmans, 1966).

4. For example, Oakeshott's concern with the broader theoretical context of any philosophy of politics can be usefully compared with the lack thereof in the work of John Rawls, which, despite spending a great many pages explaining modern economic theory, relied for its philosophical context on the recognition that it emerged from within the set of conclusions associated with analytic philosophy.

5. Oakeshott writes that *On Human Conduct* "is composed of three connected essays, [and] each has its own concern" (*OHC*, vii).

6. Oakeshott also notes that his understanding of philosophy "derives all that is valuable . . . from its affinity to what is known by the somewhat ambiguous name of Idealism" (*EM*, 6).

7. For an account of Oakeshott's idealism, see David Boucher's essay in this volume. See also Greenleaf, *Oakeshott's Philosophical Politics*.

8. Oakeshott acknowledges this situation in the introduction, writing that idealism is considered by most to be "decadent, if not already dead" (*EM*, 6). Later in the decade, in 1938, Rudolf Metz declares that idealism in Britain "has almost entirely receded into history." Rudolf Metz, *A Hundred Years of British Philosophy*, ed. J. H. Muirhead, trans. J. W. Harvey, T. E. Jessop, and Henry Stuart (London: Allen and Unwin, 1938), 258.

9. In her review of the book, L. Susan Stebbing suggests that "those who have not been convinced by Bradley are not likely to be converted by Mr. Oakeshott." "Review of *Experience and Its Modes*," *Mind* 43 (1934): 405. It is not surprising that the book was received in this fashion, since Oakeshott actually describes the work as a "restatement of [idealism's] first principles" (*EM*, 7).

10. Oakeshott's views on philosophy as a means of clarifying one's own thoughts were not eccentric among his contemporaries. Gilbert Ryle writes of his work in *The Concept of Mind* that "I am trying to get some disorders out of my own system. Only secondarily do I hope to help other theorists to recognize our malady and to benefit from my medicine." *The Concept of Mind* (1949; repr., Chicago: University of Chicago Press, 1984), 9. In a similar fashion Ludwig Wittgenstein notes that "working in philosophy . . . is really more a working on oneself." *Culture and Value* (Chicago: University of Chicago Press, 1980).

11. Wittgenstein reportedly said that "as little philosophy as I have read, I have certainly not read too little, *rather too much*. I see that whenever I read a philosophical book: it doesn't improve my thoughts at all, it makes them worse." Quoted in Ray Monk, *Ludwig Wittgenstein: The Duty of Genius* (New York: Penguin Books, 1990), 496. John Aubrey writes of Hobbes that "he was wont to say that if he had read as much as other men, he should have knowne no more than other men." *Brief Lives*, ed. Richard Barber (Suffolk: Boydell Press, 1982), 157.

12. Oakeshott also notes that "philosophy is born an outcast, useless to men of business and troublesome to men of pleasure" (*EM*, 355). G. W. F. Hegel also rejects the relevance of philosophical conclusions to practical activity, writing that "when philosophy paints its grey in grey, then has a shape of life grown old. By philosophy's grey in grey it cannot be rejuvenated but only understood." *The Philosophy of Right*, trans. T. M. Knox (Oxford: Oxford University Press, 1967), 13.

13. Hans-Georg Gadamer makes a similar argument, maintaining that "the interpreter's own horizon is decisive, yet not as a personal standpoint that he maintains . . . , but more as an opinion and a possibility that one brings into play and puts at risk." *Truth and Method*, trans. Joel Weinsheimer and Donald G. Marshall, 2nd rev. ed. (New York: Continuum, 1989), 388.

14. R. G. Collingwood writes that "in a philosophical inquiry what we are trying to do is not to discover something of which until now we have been totally ignorant, but to know something better which in some sense we knew already." *An Essay on Philosophical Method* (Bristol, UK: Thoemes Press, 1995), 11.

15. Benedetto Croce writes that "I had to criticize [Hegel's] idea of a final system from the idea, which I wish had been his, of a provisional dynamic system constantly developing and of provisional and dynamic systematization." *My Philosophy*, trans. E. F. Carritt (London: Allen and Unwin, 1949), 20.

16. In fact, Oakeshott suggests that his examination of the character of philosophical activity is "a preface to the main business I have undertaken" (*EM*, 81). I leave the consideration of Oakeshott's treatment of the various specific modes of experience (e.g., practice, science, history,

poetry/art) to one side in this essay and focus instead on his treatment of modality in general. For his examination of the logic of each mode, see the specific essays concerned with them in this volume.

17. Oakeshott uses a variety of terms to describe these arrests, including "modes of experience," "voices in a conversation," "worlds of imaginings," "idioms of discourse," and "platforms of conditional understanding." He appears to alter these terms to emphasize different aspects of these worlds of experience, but it also seems that the terms are interchangeable to Oakeshott. For example, he uses "platforms of conditional understanding" in *On Human Conduct* but produces during the same period essays in which he continues to use the term "modes" to describe these various worlds (*OHC*, 1–31, and *VLL*, 28).

18. For a discussion of the character of absolute presuppositions, see R. G. Collingwood, *An Essay on Metaphysics*, ed. Rex Martin, rev. ed. (Oxford: Clarendon Press, 1998), 21–77.

19. Collingwood criticizes Oakeshott for not offering a genetic account of the modes of experience. He writes that "if philosophy is concrete experience . . . it cannot separate the *what* from the *why*." R. G. Collingwood, *The Principles of History and Other Writings in the Philosophy of History* (Oxford: Clarendon Press, 1999), 156. It does seem somewhat odd that Oakeshott claims that, since the modes are abstract, they are philosophically irrelevant, yet he spends the great majority of both *Experience and Its Modes* and the rest of his scholarly work on explaining the character of the various modes, and not on philosophy itself.

20. For a contrasting view, see G. W. F. Hegel, *The Phenomenology of Spirit*, trans. A. V. Miller (Oxford: Oxford University Press, 1979), or R. G. Collingwood's *Speculum Mentis* (Oxford: Clarendon Press, 1924). For a comparison of Collingwood and Oakeshott on this issue, see also David Boucher, "Overlap and Autonomy: The Different Worlds of Collingwood and Oakeshott," *Storia, Antropologia, e Scienze del Linguaggio* 4 (1989): 69–89.

21. Gilbert Ryle argues that a category mistake is at the heart of the wrongheaded conception of the mind/body problem, which he calls the doctrine of the "Ghost in the Machine." Ryle's work had a significant influence on Oakeshott's later work on rationalism. *Concept of Mind*, 15–18.

22. For a critique of Oakeshott's argument that philosophy is irrelevant to the various modes of experience, see Dale Hall and Tariq Modood, "Oakeshott and the Impossibility of Philosophical Politics," *Political Studies* 30 (1982): 157–76. See also John Liddington, "Hall and Modood on Oakeshott," *Political Studies* 30 (1982): 184–89.

23. Collingwood, rejecting Hegel's claim that philosophy is irrelevant to practice, suggests that any adequate understanding of the logic of an activity will necessarily have an effect on that activity. He writes that "when people become conscious of the principles upon which they have been thinking or acting they become conscious of something which in these thoughts and actions they have been trying . . . to do: namely to work out in detail the logical implications of those principles." *The Idea of Nature* (Oxford: Clarendon Press, 1945), 2. Oakeshott's later essays on the relation between philosophy and practice reflect, at least partially, a recognition of the salience of Collingwood's argument.

24. Michael Oakeshott, "The Voice of Poetry in the Conversation of Mankind," in *Rationalism in Politics and Other Essays*, exp. ed. (Indianapolis: Liberty Press, 1991), 488–541. Oakeshott discusses the character of philosophy in an essay from the late 1930s titled "The Concept of a Philosophical Jurisprudence," but his treatment of the subject in the essay does not differ substantially from his treatment in *Experience and Its Modes*. For example, Oakeshott claims that "philosophical thought and knowledge is simply thought and knowledge without reservation or presupposition" (*CPJ*, 170).

25. Oakeshott suggests that he wants to avoid questions concerning the general character of the "categories of 'truth' and 'reality'" (*RP*, 514). It is also likely the case that Oakeshott does not revisit these questions because he does not believe that the answers that he arrived at in *Experience and Its Modes* are in need of serious revision.

26. The two most important of these essays are "Rationalism in Politics" and "Rational Conduct" (*RP*, 5–42, 99–131).

27. The most important philosophical development in Britain during the period between 1930 and 1960 was the emergence of linguistic philosophy as an alternative to the naive realism and scientism of the analytic school. At the same time, developments in the philosophy of science,

specifically Michael Polanyi's arguments about the character of tacit knowledge, also undermined the positivist epistemology that had supplanted philosophical idealism as the prominent tradition in Anglophone philosophy. The skepticism of Ryle and Wittgenstein about the universal relevance of scientific methodology and the alternative account of scientific knowledge offered by Polanyi appealed to Oakeshott's own skepticism about the natural sciences. For an examination of the connection between these various thinkers, see Mark Mitchell, *Michael Polanyi: The Art of Knowing* (Wilmington: ISI Books, 2006), 141–44; J.C. Nyíri, "Wittgenstein's Later Work in Relation to Conservatism," *Wittgenstein and His Times*, ed. Barry McGuinness (Oxford: Basil Blackwell, 1982), 61–64; W.H. Greenleaf, "Idealism, Modern Philosophy, and Politics," *Politics and Experience: Essays Presented to Professor Michael Oakeshott on the Occasion of His Retirement*, ed. Preston King and B.C. Parekh (Cambridge: Cambridge University Press, 1968), 93–124; and Leslie Marsh, "Ryle and Oakeshott on the Know-How/Know-That Distinction," in *The Meanings of Michael Oakeshott's Conservatism*, ed. Corey Abel (Exeter: Imprint Academic, 2010).

28. Gilbert Ryle argues that "knowing how to apply maxims cannot be reduced to, or derived from, the acceptance of those or any other maxims. . . . We learn *how* by practice, schooled indeed by criticism and example, but often quite unaided by any lessons in . . . theory." *Concept of Mind*, 31, 41. Oakeshott writes a very positive review of Ryle's book, noting that "this is a piece of philosophical writing in the highest class . . . [which] has something of the vitality and the power of standing on its own feet which belong to the philosophical classic" (*CPJ*, 318).

29. Michael Polanyi writes that "by acquiring a skill, whether muscular or intellectual, we achieve an understanding which we cannot put into words." *Personal Knowledge: Towards a Post-Critical Philosophy* (Chicago: University of Chicago Press, 1962), 89. Oakeshott writes a generally favorable review of *Personal Knowledge* but suggests that "there are many Hegelian echoes [in the book], and its argument might have been improved if these echoes were made more explicit" (*VMES*, 151).

30. Oakeshott claims that "practical knowledge can neither be taught nor learned, but only imparted and acquired" (*RP*, 15). Ryle says that "learning *how* or improving in ability is not like learning *that* or acquiring information. Truths can be imparted, procedures can only be inculcated." *Concept of Mind*, 59.

31. Oakeshott describes "The Voice of Poetry," not as a complete reconsideration of his earlier work, but as "a belated retraction of a foolish sentence in *Experience and Its Modes*" (*RP*, xii). He is referring to his inclusion of poetry within practical experience. He writes a similar essay reexamining the mode of historical explanation titled "The Activity of Being an Historian" at the same time that he writes "The Voice of Poetry" (*RP*, 151–83).

32. Oakeshott writes that "the consideration of poetry becomes philosophical when poetic imagining is shown to have, not a necessary place, but a specific place in the manifold of human activities" (*RP*, 494).

33. Steven Gerencser suggests that this tension is evidence that Oakeshott has rejected his earlier idealism for some form of skepticism. See *The Skeptic's Oakeshott* (New York: St. Martin's Press, 2000), 33–51. For a critique of Gerencser, see Kenneth B. McIntyre, *The Limits of Political Theory: Oakeshott's Philosophy of Civil Association* (Exeter: Imprint Academic, 2004), 34–39.

34. In Wittgenstein's terms, "philosophy may in no way interfere with the actual use of language; it can in the end only describe it. For it cannot give it any foundation either. It leaves everything as it is." Or, as Austin puts it, philosophy is "an operation which leaves us . . . just where we began." Ludwig Wittgenstein, *Philosophical Investigations*, 3rd ed., trans. G.E.M. Anscombe (Oxford: Blackwell, 2001), 42; and G.J.L. Austin, *Sense and Sensibilia*, ed. G.J. Warnock (Oxford: Oxford University Press, 1962), 5.

35. Louis O. Mink discusses the "detachability" of conclusions from various types of inquiry in his essays on the logic of historical explanation. He notes that, in history, "conclusions are *exhibited* rather than *demonstrated*," and thus such conclusions cannot be detached from the arguments made to support them. *Historical Understanding* (Ithaca: Cornell University Press, 1987), 79.

36. Oakeshott writes that if a thinker "is concerned to theorize moral conduct or civil association he must forswear metaphysics" (*OHC*, 25).

37. See Oakeshott's discussion of the place of ethics within the world of philosophical explanation (*EM*, 331–46).

38. Oakeshott's primary purpose in substituting the terms *theorizing* and *theorem* for the term *philosophy* is to distinguish between the activity and the conclusions of the philosopher (*OHC*, 3n1).

39. Oakeshott writes that "a platform of conditional understanding is constituted by its conditions which, from different points of view, may be recognized as assumptions or as postulates" (*OHC*, 8).

40. This categorical distinction bears some resemblance to that posited by Wilhelm Dilthey in defending a distinctive method of understanding the human sciences, and Oakeshott points to Dilthey as one of the primary influences on his understanding of practical activity (*VMES*, 16). Wilhelm Dilthey, *Introduction to the Human Sciences: An Attempt to Lay a Foundation for the Study of Society and History*, trans. Ramon Betanzos (Detroit: Wayne State University Press, 1988), 76–148.

41. The idioms relevant to practices include history, aesthetics, ethics, and jurisprudence. The last two are identified by Oakeshott as pseudophilosophical concepts (*OHC*, 16, 17; *EM*, 331–46).

4

MICHAEL OAKESHOTT'S PHILOSOPHY OF HISTORY

Geoffrey Thomas

"Determinatio negatio est," says Spinoza: to specify the nature of anything is also illuminatingly to say what it is *not*.[1] This remark, whatever its general force, applies exactly to Michael Oakeshott's philosophy of history. Oakeshott is a polemicist, a prince of skeptics, throughout his writings on the nature of history. To be sure, his position can be characterized positively: he is a constructionist. He holds that the historical past is an inferential construction from present experience. So, clearly enough, here's the first negative: Oakeshott rejects any idea of the reality of the past. The past does not exist; if it did, the historian would not need to construct it inferentially or in any other way. It would just be *there*, open to investigation.

The nonreality of the past is a major negative theme. Another of Oakeshott's principal themes, that of the autonomy of history, also carries heavy negative implications. Oakeshott has a strong sense of the autonomy of history. Historical inquiry has its own internal impetus. It defines its own problems, poses its own questions, and has sole authority in regard to its methods. Its practitioners also decide who is a good or competent historian. Oakeshott's insistence on autonomy is not accompanied by very much if anything of a methodology of history as a specific craft of inquiry. But it does carry some punchy negatives. One of these is a rejection of scientific categories from historical explanation. More precisely, Oakeshott will have nothing to do with causal explanation in history. The notion of cause is a mistaken intrusion—an outside interference—from the scientific realm. Nor is science the only source of irrelevant categories. The realm of practice sends its saboteurs into historical inquiry, and the price of history is eternal vigilance against them. Practice obtrudes its unwelcome attentions in three ways: one, by seeking to use history as a repository of practical wisdom, as a guide through analogies and parallels to the current world; two, by moral judgment on historical phenomena; and three, by false teleology, projecting ends, goals, processes as inherent in the course of historical events.

It is hardly too much to say that Oakeshott's positive theory of history is a coda to the rehearsal of these errors: the errors of assuming the reality of the past, applying the category of causation to historical inquiry, and allowing the intrusion of practical considerations into the work of the historian. In his own terms Oakeshott is concerned with the "philosophy of history" in the sense of an inquiry "about the nature of historical truth and the validity of historical knowledge" (*WIH*, 203). He is not occupied with the methodology of historical research (e.g., how to decide whether there are too many or two few word dividers on a putative Ugarit tablet) or with speculative delineations of great historical patterns such as we find in Saint Augustine's *The City of God*, in Hegel's *Lectures on the Philosophy of World History*, or in Oswald Spengler's *The Decline of the West*.[2]

TEXTS AND CONTINUITY

"What did he say?" "Did it change?" "Where were his views expressed?" I take these natural questions in order. What Oakeshott said about history—his canonical philosophical view about the nature of historical inquiry—can be summed up in four theses: (1) the past does not exist, only the present; (2) only experience exists; (3) the historical past is an inferential construction from experience; (4) historical inquiry is autonomous, not a part of or ancillary to either science or practice. These theses are a framework; the framework will be filled in later. But is there simply "a" framework, a fixed set of theses? Or did these theses emerge from earlier, less clearly defined or more tentative ideas, and did Oakeshott ever significantly qualify them? Thus we raise the developmental issue.

Since Oakeshott's writings on history extend from the 1920s to the 1980s, the developmental issue presses quite sharply. So, simply put: how much continuity is there between the 1920s writings published in *What Is History?*, *Experience and Its Modes*, "The Activity of Being an Historian," the reflections relevant to historical inquiry in *On Human Conduct*, and the three essays included in *On History?* Opinion is divided. My own view is that the four theses did not spring full-fledged from Oakeshott's mind sometime in the 1920s. But if we exclude the *scripta minora* of the 1920s writings, all Oakeshott's work from *Experience and Its Modes* onward states or implies or is consistent with, and none of it contradicts, the theses.

There are minor elaborations, retractions, and reformulations across texts. The idea of a "mode"—hence of history as a mode of experience—so salient in *Experience and Its Modes* undergoes some slight attenuation of meaning in *On History*.[3] Also new language appears en route; historical inquiry becomes a "voice" in a conversation (*RP*, 488). Regardless, the four theses remain throughout the essence of Oakeshott's philosophy of history. This is my view and I am not dogmatic about it. But it *is* my view and I will work with it.

ONLY THE PRESENT EXISTS

To begin with the first thesis: Oakeshott upholds a version of presentism, the view, as usually stated, that only the present exists. But precisely what version? Before we tackle that, it is noteworthy that Oakeshott plainly accepts the reality of time despite Bradley's dismissal of time as an incoherent concept in chapters 4 and 14 of *Appearance and Reality* and J. M. E. McTaggart's lastingly influential denial of the reality of time.[4]

But why mention these figures? To take them in turn, Bradley is clearly the philosophical mind behind the second chapter of *Experience and Its Modes*, which contains the book's main discussion of epistemology and metaphysics. To this extent L. Susan Stebbing's remark is correct that "those who have not been convinced by Bradley are not likely to be converted by Mr. Oakeshott," though there is much in Bradley that is not in Oakeshott (crucially the ultimate inadequacy of the discursive intellect) and much in Oakeshott that is not in Bradley (crucially the modes).[5] Perhaps Oakeshott accepted Bradley's acknowledgment that time is real as appearance even if appearances are ultimately incoherent. But if we immerse ourselves in Bradleian exegesis we will never resurface. Next, McTaggart is relevant because Oakeshott attended McTaggart's introductory philosophical lectures as an undergraduate. McTaggart's profound assault on the reality of time exerted no impact on Oakeshott, at least as evidenced by the text of *Experience and Its Modes*. This is curious— or not: time is the ultimate conundrum, and Oakeshott may have felt that the reality of time is more probable than any arguments against it.

If time is real, perhaps only as appearance, why should only present time be real? To begin, we can redefine presentism as the view that only present things exists. To say that only the present exists is to invite the idea that the present, or indeed time itself, is a kind of substance—itself a thing—and this in turn revives unhelpfully some major disputes in the history of science. So we'll talk from now on about present things (objects, events, states of affairs, properties, relations). If I were to define the set of all the things that exist, I would appear on the list, you would too, but the Boston Tea Party and Barack Obama's great-great-grandson would not. Moreover, since if we hold that only present things exist, we are unlikely to regard this as a matter of mere chance about present things; our position is probably best stated as "necessarily it is always the case that only present things exist," in other words, "necessarily there are no nonpresent things." For convenience I will omit "necessarily" as understood.

A clarification before we proceed: the presentist needs to tell us how the extension of the present is to be construed. Is the present an instant, a point without extension, that is, without successive parts? Or is the idea rather that the present is not exactly a point but is like one? Lieb explains this as "the idea of a present that is extended *far enough* for something to occur in it, though the occurrence is present *all at once*."[6] This is, of course, William James's notion of the "specious present." I am uncertain of the logical coherence of the specious present, since at any instant within it something will be strictly past and something will be strictly future, that is, not present (cf. *OH*, 7–14). But the specious present is intrinsic to common sense, and the presentist may use it with that unphilosophical proviso.

Two objections to the view that only present things exist need to be considered. The first rests on a tenseless theory of time. On such a theory "only present things exist" analyzes out as "only present things existed, exist, or will exist." There are philosophical motivations for such a theory but the tenseless approach looks wrong for historical inquiry; the Soviet Union existed but is not a present thing.

This leads directly to the second objection, one based on the special relativity theory. No equations are to follow, but we can take from special relativity theory the denial that there is absolute (space-time frame independent) simultaneity. This is a problem for presentism because on the presentist approach, since only present things exist, equally (assuming plurality) only things simultaneous with one another exist. But there is no such simultaneity, tout court; simultaneity must be indexed to a frame of reference.[7] Now, a ready move is to say that we can surrender absolute simultaneity for simultaneity relative to a frame of reference. Since there are different frames of reference, none of which are privileged, however, simultaneity remains as elusive as ever. I think the most feasible response to this is the practical one that, as Quine puts it, we do not need to take differences between frames of reference into account "in our daily rounds."[8] Oakeshott's views, if any, on special relativity are unknown; I accept the Quinean compromise on his behalf.

I ascribe presentism to Oakeshott on the dual ground that he holds (1) that only experience exists, a topic to be dealt with immediately, and (2) that "experience is present through and through" (*EM*, 110). In any event, since Oakeshott plainly does not believe that the past exists (hence his constructionism) and betrays no sense that the future exists, only the present remains.

ONLY EXPERIENCE EXISTS

Now for the second thesis. Oakeshott holds not just that only the present exists or that only present things exist. He claims that only experience exists (*EM*, 17, 50, 54, 56), so present things can exist only as part of present experience. What are we to make of this? What is "experience"? This is a hard question for anyone, and it cannot be said that we get much from Oakeshott by way of a formal answer. But it is pretty clear that by "experience" Oakeshott refers to consciousness and that he recognizes three aspects of consciousness. How much more he might mean by "experience" I make no comment on, but he means at least these three aspects. Consciousness has a sensuous, phenomenal, or qualitative aspect of the sort exemplified by pain. This is the "what it is like" aspect of consciousness: "I have a stabbing, throbbing, smarting, stinging . . . pain"—a sensation. There is also the representational aspect of consciousness: "I see a book on the desk," or more simply, "There is a book on the desk." The third aspect of consciousness is the desiderative; we have not only sensations and representations but also wants and preferences, which can motivate to action. Such preferences can reflect or embody perceived well-being, selfish or altruistic desires, moral judgments of evaluation ("The New Deal was an exercise in social justice"), obligation ("George W. Bush should have made proper plans for the postwar social reconstruction of Iraq"), and more besides. This is a list, not a complete enumeration, nor are its items mutually exclusive.

Oakeshott would insist on one point about all three aspects of consciousness, namely, that they have conceptual content. A sensation, a perception, or a want or preference is "had" under a description, and a description presupposes a conceptual scheme. To realize that one has a pain, one must know what it is like to have an unpleasant or distressing localized sensation. To perceive a book on a desk, one must know about the nature and functions of books and desks among human artifacts; to see the book as red, one must be aware of color contrasts. One cannot just sense, perceive, or desire without some conceptual specification. In *Experience and Its Modes*, Oakeshott lays stress on the conceptual content of consciousness, and many have seen this as a salient instance of his "idealism."[9] It is no such thing; anyone who recognizes "the theory-ladenness of observation" and "the myth of the given" will equally endorse the conceptual content of consciousness, and nobody has ever suggested that these writers are idealists.[10]

But Oakeshott's "idealism" might appear evident in his view that only experience exists. The idea would be that for an idealist all that exists is either consciousness or a product of consciousness, and the claim that only experience—consciousness—exists looks like just such an idea. It depends, of course, on the precise sense in which Oakeshott intends the claim that only experience exists.

My inclination is to say that it cannot be strictly true that only experience exists; experience needs an "experiencer," a subject of consciousness to which experience(s) can be ascribed. Hume's attempt in *A Treatise of Human Nature* to dispense with such a subject ended in failure, and I doubt the likely success of any other attempt.[11] To suppose that this subject is fictitious, in the sense that it is itself only an experience, is simply to reinstate the problem one level up: what is it that has *this* experience? An alternative approach is to accept that experience needs a subject of experience but to deny that anything short of the whole of reality, the Absolute, can fulfill this role, since no subject short of the Absolute is self-dependent. There are shades of this approach in Oakeshott, and clear evidence of it in his nineteenth-century forebears, F. H. Bradley and Bernard Bosanquet. Even Bradley and Bosanquet accept the reality at some level of the finite individual as a subject of experience, however. Let's assume that Oakeshott's claim that only present experience exists goes along with an equal recognition of subjects of experience.

It is likely that in claiming that only experience exists Oakeshott follows Bradley: "We perceive, on reflection, that to be real, or even barely to exist, must be to fall within sentience. Sentient experience, in short, is reality, and what is not this is not real. We may say, in other words, that there is no being or fact outside of that which is commonly called psychical existence. Feeling, thought, and volition (any groups under which we class psychical phenomena) are all the material of existence. And there is no other material, actual or even possible."[12] Now we may note that Bradley here first restricts experience to "sentient" but then extends his claim to "psychical" experience, that is, what is or can be experienced by a mind—or, as I should prefer to say, to what falls within the scope of consciousness. It is clear that psychical experience can in principle include more than sense experience. How can we exclude in advance, for example, telepathy or extrasensory perception? But even without such dubious denizens of consciousness, just what can Bradley mean when he says that "there is no being or fact outside of that which is commonly called psychical existence"?

Timothy Sprigge makes a brave attempt to explain Bradley's view and to render it plausible. In Sprigge's account, it makes no sense to refer to something as existing, or as capable of existence, unless one can conceive of it as having certain experiences or of ourselves as having certain experiences. The number 7 exists: a claim that makes no sense unless we can calculate, for example, $4 + 3 = 7$. The unseen interior of a house exists: a claim that makes no sense unless we can conceive of someone's or something's perceiving it. My friend exists: a claim that makes no sense unless I have certain thoughts about him, and he has his own world of consciousness.[13]

Much might be said about this; the least that can be said is that it equates, or conflates (depending on one's point of view), the epistemological and the metaphysical. There is a priori no connection between the conditions on which a claim makes sense and the conditions on which something does or can exist. Bradley's *Appearance and Reality* may or may not secure such a connection, but I cannot see that Sprigge's exposition does so or that Oakeshott's arguments in *Experience and Its Modes* weld such a connection. This last point holds good, even if Oakeshott is not following Bradley as interpreted earlier. All that the claim that only present experience exists delivers, so far as I can make out from Oakeshott's and Bradley's actual arguments, is a restatement of Kant's assertion in *The Critique of Pure Reason*, that "thoughts without content are empty, intuitions without concepts are blind." In other words, to talk of X when nothing could conceivably amount to an experience of X, and to talk of experiencing X when no conceptual specification of X is conceivable, are deep forms of nonsense—exposed devastatingly in the "Transcendental Dialectic."[14]

An acceptable reading of the claim that only experience exists is that, by the Kantian test, things do not exist *for us* if nothing could conceivably count as our experiencing them. With this I go along. If we add that the past and future are unreal, then we reach the view that only present experience exists. If we further add that the things we experience are all experienced as having conceptual content, and that this makes them (by a distinctly tenuous logic) a part of our experience, then present things—shoes and ships and sealing wax, cabbages and kings—can exist only as part of present experience. It is a position I am happier to ascribe to Oakeshott than myself to defend. There remains the different but related question whether, if all experience is present experience, it isn't just *my* present experience. But there isn't the space to examine the matter here, nor do I think we would learn much from Oakeshott about it.

THE HISTORICAL PAST IS AN INFERENTIAL CONSTRUCTION FROM EXPERIENCE

In *Experience and Its Modes* Oakeshott has a particular take on experience, namely, that it is "modal." He does not intend "modal" in the Kantian sense of relating to judgments of actuality, possibility, and necessity. Nor is he influenced in his use of this terminology by the Spinozan modes, which are particular ways in which the attributes of extension and thought (and infinitely many other, to us unknown, attributes) are expressed. (This lump of sugar is a mode of extension.) Rather they are types or kinds of experience, distinguished in ways that Oakeshott explains. The three major modes are history, science, and practice.[15]

How are the modes differentiated? In the historical mode, experience is regarded *sub specie praeteritorum*, that is, as being past: *praeterita* are things that have gone before. In the scientific mode, experience is taken *sub specie quantitatis*, that is, as having magnitude or number; and in the practical mode, experience is seen *sub specie voluntatis*—as satisfying or failing to satisfy our wants and preferences or as subject to judgments of evaluation and obligation.

The historian is concerned with objects and events simply qua past; the scientist, with objects and events as exhibiting quantitative relationships; and the practical agent regards them in terms of wants, preferences, aversions, praise, or condemnation. "Practice" covers Aristotelian praxis and poiesis: a doing or acting with or on other persons and a fashioning or making. That's a workable notion, and Oakeshott's characterization of science will also broadly pass muster. It is at least typical of science to quantify where it is able to do so: "The speed of light in air is 3.00×10^8 m/s"; "The de Broglie wavelength λ is given by h/p where h is Planck's constant and p is the momentum of the particle"; "The mass number is the total number of protons and neutrons in the nucleus of an atom." Quantification is not sufficient for scientific status. Is astrology a science merely because it deals in quantitative predictions? Doesn't a science need to be quantitative and falsifiable or subject to whatever constraints non-Popperians prefer? And is quantification necessary? We know that humans differ from chimpanzees in roughly only 1.6 percent of their DNA, but this small difference accounts for great qualitative differences between their minds and ours. To say that these qualitative differences are really quantitative is to assume physicalism, and the credibility of physicalism is debatable and not purely a scientific issue. But we should not make heavy weather of this. I don't think Oakeshott's quantitative angle on science, which I have discussed because he emphasizes it, is really what concerns him when, as we'll see, he resists the "intrusion" of science into history. It is the causal, necessitarian, and nomological aspects of science that chiefly exercise him.

We should not think of the modes in terms of a logical geography of experience, with history or historical inquiry covering one area, science or scientific inquiry another, and practical life a third, like different countries on a map (cf. *EM*, 71). Science, history, and practice are different angles on the whole of experience. Here is a solid sphere, something experienced: a three-dimensional closed surface, of which every point is equidistant from another point, its center; it is made of silver, the element with atomic number 47. This is a scientific description, indefinitely extendable but of a recognizable kind. Here is the same sphere: it can be used as a ball in a game or as a missile for breaking a window. This is a practical description, indefinitely extendable across the different uses to which the sphere can be put. Here is the familiar sphere yet again: it can be dated to a New York silversmith who made it in 1833. This is a historical description.

Oakeshott does not claim to offer a complete enumeration of the modes, and his ideas about what the particular modes cover and include is not uncontroversial. In *Experience and Its Modes* he subsumes aesthetic experience under the mode of practice, because as pleasurable it serves our wants and preferences. This inclusion of the aesthetic within the practical was retracted when he later referred to a "foolish sentence" in *Experience and Its Modes*, in which he had excluded the aesthetic—poetry—as a mode in its own right (*RP*, xi). Religion is also subsumed under practice: religion "cares nothing for what lies beyond the world of practice; if it looks to 'another' world, it is for the purpose of determining what shall be our conduct in 'this' world" (*EM*, 294). W. G. de Burgh cogently defended a rival view of religion as a way of life in which praxis is throughout subordinated to *theoria*.[16]

The modes are, in Oakeshott's account, mutually exclusive; any attempt to transfer the categories of one to another involves *ignoratio elenchi*. This is, I think, one part of his debt to Aristotle—"I am not ashamed to say that I learned most . . . from Aristotle, Hegel, and Dilthey" (*VMES*, 183)—who insists on different categories, and no mixing, for different activities and inquiries.[17] Moreover, each mode regards itself—that is, its practitioners see it—as fully satisfactory in its own terms. A comprehensive and coherent account of the world of experience can be given by a scientist, a historian, or an agent engaged in practical activity, from their respective angles of vision. In other words and less metaphorically, science, practice, and history are self-contained universes of discourse. Each is capable of making full sense of its subject matter within the limits of its own conceptual categories.

Oakeshott considers this a false view of the matter. Science, practice, and history are all incapable of the task. Philosophy exposes their inadequacies, and it is a fair conclusion that philosophy achieves a degree of comprehensiveness and coherence that history, science, and practice lack. This is where *Experience and Its Modes* leaves matters.

Experience and Its Modes is pervaded by modal language. The modes are the principal structure within which Oakeshott discusses history, science, and practice. My own view is that the interest of his views on history does not depend on the modal apparatus, and this for two reasons. In the first place, I do not think that Oakeshott offers a sufficiently detailed and sophisticated analysis of the concept of a mode to vindicate its structural role. Second, his distinctive views—that the past does not exist, that only experience exists, that the historical past is an inferential construction from present experience, that historical inquiry is impartial, neutral, and autonomous, and that causation has no part to play in historical explanation—can be set out and appraised without reference to the modes. In fact, I have already discussed the claims that the past does not exist and that only present experience exists without invoking the modes, and the strategy will work for the other claims.

THE HISTORICAL PAST IS A LOGICAL CONSTRUCTION FROM PRESENT EXPERIENCE

Oakeshott is often credited with, which means discredited for, holding a coherence theory of truth. He certainly rejects a major rival, the correspondence theory (*EM*, 108). The pragmatic theory, the other main possibility of which Oakeshott is likely to have been aware, accords a primacy to practice that he could scarcely endorse since it means a domination of one mode over others. It might appear, therefore, that by default Oakeshott accepts a coherence theory. The language of "coherence" figures extensively in *Experience and Its Modes*.

Now, nobody has been able to state a coherence theory of truth in satisfactory form, despite the best efforts of a range of theorists from Harold Joachim to Nicholas Rescher. I have a suggestion: Oakeshott needs and espouses a coherence theory of belief. In *Experience and Its Modes* Oakeshott was an epistemologist, not primarily a metaphysician. Truth belongs to metaphysics. Oakeshott's mantra is "what the evidence obliges us to believe" (*EM*, 108; cf. 110), an epistemological matter. Oakeshott, as I read him, wants to create a historical past that is a coherent—or as I prefer to say, "rational"—set of beliefs based on present experience.

Rational is a term to use with extreme circumspection, and indeed humble excuse, in setting out Oakeshott's views. Oakeshott is exactly inimical to rational conduct in the specific sense of action that embodies (or seeks to embody) rationalism. Polemical attacks of great brilliance on rationalism appear in *Rationalism in Politics* and elsewhere. But *rationalism* is a term of art for Oakeshott and rationality of belief of the kind mentioned earlier requires nothing special, nothing (in the minimal sense assumed here) that does violence to Oakeshott's critique of rationalism. Oakeshott is opposed to reason in the sense in which Descartes most often uses *intuitus*, or intuition, and speaks of *lux rationis*, the light of reason. The thought here is of self-evident and incorrigible beliefs—in the form of *clarae et distinctae ideae*, "clear and distinct ideas"—vouchsafed through the use of reason independently of experience though not of God. The possibility of such beliefs is classically annihilated by Kant in "Transcendental Dialectic."[18]

When I refer to *rational belief*, however, I have no such sense of reason and rational in mind. I mean by *rational* what the term means in ordinary language. A belief is rational if it is logical in the sense of not involving non-sense, self-contradiction, or reliance on invalid forms of inference (the fallacy, say, of affirming the consequent); of not being ad hoc, an add-on that doesn't integrate with anything else one believes; and, more positively, of being based on relevant considerations and sufficient evidence and of being self-critical in ways that leave it open to revision. An ad hoc belief would not be based on sufficient evidence, nor would a belief based on irrelevant considerations, so there is some cross-connection between these criteria. I prefer the term *rationality* because I am reasonably clear about what the criteria mean, and I think they are the desiderata that Oakeshott would apply. To put the point another way: the evidence would never oblige us to form nonsensical, self-contradictory, or ad hoc beliefs relying on fallacious forms of inference, based on irrelevant considerations or insufficient evidence.

Nor is it clear what else coherence would require. Then let's think. One possibility is circular: belief A derives its justification from belief B, which derives its justification from belief C, which derives its justification from belief D, which (to keep the circle small) derives its justification from belief A. Whether or not derivation is to be understood in terms of entailment (e.g., "A & ¬ B" is a self-contradiction), it is hard to see how this process of circular justification could increase whatever justification A had in the first place. If A does not have any independent warrant, its derivation from a set of beliefs that terminates back at A itself leaves A unwarranted. A theory of rational belief is precisely a theory of warranted belief, however. We can use rationality as a working definition of coherence in the absence of anything better, if indeed anything better is needed. To reassure: no connection with Oakeshott's bête noire of rationalism is, of course, implied.

But can one have a theory of belief, a fortiori a theory of coherent or rational belief, without a theory of truth? Belief aims at truth. Still, on the one hand, it is possible to believe rationally without a belief's being true. On the evidence available to him it was rational for Saint Thomas Aquinas to believe in the geocentric theory; the actual falsity of the theory is nothing to the point.

On the other hand, while the concept of belief involves the concept of truth, I question whether a theory of truth has to be brought on stage. After all, we can say that a deductively valid argument is truth preserving, that its conclusion cannot be false if its premises are true, without taking a view on (say) Tarski's semantic theory of truth. In other words, we can use the concept of truth by virtue of its connection with concepts that we have mastered—I have just given deductive validity as a case in point—without the kind of definitional commitments that come with a theory of truth.

Why does Oakeshott need the historical past to be an inferential construction from anything? For all that has been said about the lack of a need for a theory of truth, isn't such a theory ready to hand? Doesn't the correspondence theory serve the historian's turn? No, actually: it is clear that Oakeshott cannot consistently use a correspondence theory of truth, at least as typified in the work of Moore, Russell, and the Wittgenstein of the *Tractatus*. On such a theory, a sentence, statement, proposition, belief, or judgment (whatever one's choice of truth bearer) is true if and only if it corresponds to the facts or to certain states of affairs—truth makers. I am not quite sure what a fact, if it is not simply what a true sentence, or any of the rest, states, and this characterization is unhelpfully circular. States of affairs appear more promising. If I say "Jupiter is the largest planet in our solar system," this is true if and only if that is how things really are: that is, if there is an actual state of affairs in which Jupiter is the largest planet. Exactly how a structural relationship of correspondence could obtain between a sentence (say) and a state of affairs is hard to make out. Wittgenstein's picture theory plainly does not work. Russell, Moore, and other correspondence theorists have never settled the question convincingly.

But Oakeshott's objection to the correspondence theory for the truth of historical sentences, statements, propositions, or judgments cuts deeper than this. In the case of the past, there is nothing for any of these items to correspond with. Since past things do not exist, they cannot constitute states of affairs, and so in the domain of historical discourse the correspondence theory is bereft of truth makers.

The historian is concerned—or, not necessarily the same thing, the historian who follows Oakeshott's prescriptions is concerned—with the historical past. This is another term of art in Oakeshott's writings. Oakeshott talks of historical events and historical objects, and some of his instances might occasion surprise. "Consider: what we have before us is a building, a piece of furniture, a coin, a picture, a passage in a book, a legal document, an inscription on stone, a current manner of behavior or a memory. Each of these is a present event" (*RP*, 161). Now, events are such things as movements and alterations, states, processes, omissions, and conditions, and none of the items in

Oakeshott's list looks plausibly like any of these. One might more naturally identify the items as *objects*. Oakeshott does use the language of objects: "An historical inquiry emerges in a concern with a present comprised of objects recognized not merely to have survived, but as themselves survivals . . . as things in respect of their being vestigial" (*OH*, 46–47). What are we to make of this terminological kerfuffle?

Not much, I think: Oakeshott's meaning is reasonably clear. As the building, piece of furniture, coin, and the rest enter into our experience, so they are events. Our experience has undergone an alteration in respect of perceiving them. And as historians, out to construct a historical past, we regard ourselves as perceiving vestigial objects; we contemplate the building as a survival, residue, vestige of what no longer exists: as "circumstantial evidence for constructing a past which has not survived" (*OH*, 80). Oakeshott is not interested in the classification of evidence, as an archaeologist may distinguish between artifacts and ecofacts: humanly made or modified objects and environmental remains that provide clues to human activities. Nor, of course, since it would mark an unwarranted intrusion of the scientific into the historical, is he interested in a calculus of probabilities about evidence of the sort offered by Bayesianism. Then where do we go from here? In a phrase Oakeshott does not use, we infer to the best explanation of whatever evidence we are concerned with. What beliefs, if accepted, would best explain the evidence?

The logical form of inference to the best explanation (IBE) is:

1. Q is the case
2. P is presupposed by the best explanation of Q
3. Therefore, P is the case

Here is a coin bearing the image of King Charles I of England (Q). We assume that there was such an English king; we assume that currency was issued in his name; we assume that the coin was legitimately manufactured as part of that currency; we assume that its chemical composition gave it the durability to survive several centuries. On the basis of these and other beliefs, which we presuppose, we infer that we are confronted with a vestige of Carolinian currency (P). This is a good explanation, one that satisfies the criteria of rational belief, and it is better than the next-best explanation, that is, that the coin is a forgery. Inference to the best explanation is neither deductively valid nor necessarily correct. Perhaps the coin is a forgery after all.

If the historical past is an inferential construction from experience, it does not follow that the historical past is a logical construction out of experience in the sense that the historian's statements can be analyzed without remainder into statements about the relevant evidence. To say that we infer P as the best explanation of Q is not to say that the set of statements composing P can be analyzed without remainder into the set of statements composing Q. Inference to the best explanation is not a form of logical atomism or of any other kind of reductionism.

Point taken, it may be replied, but IBE gives, if used as in this example, too static a picture of what the historian aims to deliver. The historical past is a realm of change. The historian does not try to explain merely vestiges, as in the coin example, but from such vestiges whole sequences of events such as the course of a battle, the carrying out of projects, and the enactment of programs. Oakeshott observes,

> Change in history carries with it its own explanation; the course of events is one, so far integrated, so far filled in and complete, that no external cause or reason is looked for or required in order to account for any particular event. The historian, in short, is like the novelist whose characters (for example) are presented in such detail and with such coherence that additional explanations of their actions is superfluous. . . . [The historical past is] a world of events intrinsically related to one another in which no *lacuna* is tolerated. (*EM*, 141, 143)

The history/fiction analogy invites a mild degree of scrutiny. It is true that if, say, in *Middlemarch* we ask by what roads and with how many horses Mr. Casaubon traveled to the Vatican, there is no answer. But the question does not arise for the reader; we can make complete sense of the story without asking this question. To ask it is to press an irrelevancy. Yet I wonder how far even the most detailed historical narrative achieves or can achieve what I may term this irrelevancy of the missing detail?

If, however, the requirement is simply to make adequate sense of the evidence, where "adequate" presumably bears some relation to professional standards, IBE satisfies just this demand. A good, let alone the best, explanation could hardly be one that exhibits lacunae. Where a lacuna begins, good explanation ends. I should make clear my strategy here: to argue that since IBE fulfills the requirements of Oakeshottian coherentist explanation, therefore the two are identical, would be a simple fallacy. My suggestion is rather that Oakeshott's account of the nature of coherentist explanation, in *Experience and Its Modes* and later in *On History* with its imagery of the "dry wall" (*OH*, 94), is too indeterminate to work with and that IBE represents an account of historical explanation that fulfills the purposes that coherentist explanation is meant to serve and that Oakeshott could without inconsistency accept. If Oakeshott's coherentist explanation *can* be explained without this kind of reconstruction, the outcome would be of great interest.

IBE does not deal in necessary connections. Its conclusions lack deductive validity and in this sense are not necessary. This fits with Oakeshott's claim that historical explanation does not recognize necessary events (*OH*, 74). As well, IBE does not invoke fortuity, another of Oakeshott's proscribed categories: "historical understanding has no place for fortuitous relationships" (71). Qua "chance" no event can be explained. "The airplane door flew open by chance." This is uninformative unless we say something like (Q) "The door lock was weak, the door appeared to be firmly closed, the flight attendant only cursorily checked the door before takeoff," and then (P) "The airplane door flew open."

Oakeshott's favored term for historical explanations is that they are *contingent*. A historical explanation merely posits a "significant relationship" between *explanans* (what does the explaining) and *explanandum* (what needs to be explained)—between Q and P. I take "significant" as meaning "intelligible." In the example earlier, the airplane door flying open was an intelligible event, given the antecedents. We look in vain, I think, for more any more precise specification of significance from Oakeshott. The most likely source of help is to invoke a notion of practical rationality to match that rationality of belief sketched earlier. We can use the ideas of instrumental rationality—of acting on means toward ends—and of rule following, to mention only two standard possibilities, to make an action intelligible. (The reference to acting on means toward ends—A φd in order to ψ—is to be separated from any rational choice implications of maximizing expected utility, and acting on a rule may be a matter of "individual subscriptions to a multiplicity of practices" [*OHC*, 100].)

Two further points may be noted. In the first place, each of the supporting beliefs in our explanation is subject, or may be, to the same process of inference to the best explanation. We assume that there was an English king, Charles I. We believe this on the basis of other vestiges of which the best explanation is that there was such a king. Second, the historical past has a propositional character. A historical explanation has the logical form: on the available evidence, it is rational to believe that P (e.g., there was a seventeenth-century English king, Charles I, in whose name currency was issued). The historical past is a set of propositions about the past that it is rational to believe.

This is my construction of "what the evidence obliges us to believe." But that phrase still needs scrutiny. I advance three considerations, of which the first is that what the evidence obliges us to believe, or what it is rational to believe on the available evidence, has a broad variety of logical forms. It may be rational to believe a conjunction (a & b), a disjunction (a v b), a possibility (◊p), or even that there are insufficient grounds to form any belief (e.g., about the identity of Jack the Ripper). Matters may be even worse. Hugh Trevor-Roper wrote in *Hermit of Peking*, his biography of the sinologist and fantasist Sir Edmund Backhouse, of "the uncertainty of the boundary between fact and fiction" with which the evidence of Backhouse's memoirs left him. "The iridescent centre of the web is too obviously a work of art, deliberately spun. But where exactly does the web of fantasy meet the solid thorns of fact? Through this mysterious Backhousian twilight it is difficult to distinguish the gossamer from the twig. Sometimes a shaft of external light enables us to do so at some particular point; but without such external aid we can never be sure."[19] If only we knew *what* the evidence obliges us to believe!

The second consideration concerns the degree of epistemological warrant. The evidence may oblige us to believe that something is barely possible, quite likely, highly probable, beyond reasonable doubt, virtually certain, and indefinitely many things in between. For example, the evidence may not oblige us to believe that a certain event occurred but only that a nonnegligible probability attaches to its occurrence. In ancient Greek history the evidence may oblige us to believe that there is only a slight probability that the Peace of Kallias occurred but a strong probability that, if it occurred, it did so in 449 B.C.E. On the other hand, we may be virtually certain that the Plague and the death of Pericles happened at Athens in 429 B.C.E. Equally, the evidence may oblige us to believe that we do not know and have no safe grounds for conjecture on how far the early dialogues of Plato represent the views of the historical Socrates.

Finally, we must take note of the "us" in "what the evidence obliges us to believe." Who are *we*? Given the widespread and intractable nature of certain historical controversies, there may on occasion be a reluctance to go beyond "what the evidence obliges *me* to believe." We needn't reduce the matter to Rorty's "what our peers will, *ceteris paribus*, let us get away with saying," but there is a sense in Oakeshott of a community of historians engaged in the project of constructing the historical past and in appraising one another's constructions by a shared set of standards.[20]

HISTORICAL INQUIRY IS AUTONOMOUS

Historical inquiry is "an autonomous manner of understanding, specifiable in terms of exact conditions" (*OH*, 2). The autonomy of historical inquiry is for Oakeshott largely a matter of its exemption from categories imposed on it by science and practice. I take practice first. This is the realm in which things are assessed as satisfying or failing to satisfy our wants and preferences or as subject to judgments of evaluation and obligation.

In Oakeshott's view historical inquiry delivers no guidance in respect of our wants and preferences about the contemporary world. It is not a repository of parallels or analogies. History is not "philosophy teaching by examples."[21] It also delivers no judgments of evaluation or obligation, and it discloses no teleology, no inevitable trends or natural or normal courses of development that reveal a historical past congruent with our wants, preferences, and evaluations. "The Activity of Being an Historian" provides a list of historical statements that violates Oakeshott's construction of the autonomy of historical inquiry:

1. "The summer of 1920 was the finest in my experience."
2. "He died too soon."
3. "King John was a bad King."
4. "The death of William the Conqueror was accidental."
5. "It would have been better if the French Revolution had never taken place."
6. "He dissipated his resources in a series of useless wars."
7. "The Pope's intervention changed the course of events."
8. "The evolution of Parliament."
9. "The development of industrial society in Great Britain."
10. "The Factory Acts of the early nineteenth century culminated in the Welfare State of the twentieth century."
11. "The loss of markets for British goods on the Continent was the most serious consequence of the Napoleonic Wars."
12. "The effect of the Boer war was to make clear the necessity for radical reform in the British Army."
13. "The next day the Liberator addressed a large meeting in Dublin." (*RP*, 162–63)

This is a mixed list. Let us see what might be wrong with it. Statement 1 is plainly evaluative. History makes no evaluations. Statement 2 assumes a practical goal in terms of which a death was untimely. The historian may record but does not, qua historian, share or endorse any practical goals. Statement 3 is a moral judgment or at least an evaluative judgment of some kind. It is alien to historical inquiry. Statement 4 assumes a natural or normal course of events that was in some way violated by an accident, something unintended and unforeseen. But for the historian there is simply the course of events. The point will bear elaboration. Oakeshott is not denying anything so obvious, so well attested by experience, as that agents' behavior can be deliberate, accidental, ignorant, and the rest. What an agent does, or what happens to an agent, in the historical past can be accidental, but in the historian's narrative it is not an accidental fact but the fact that there was an accident, and that fact fits into a connected sequence of events. Statements 5 and 6 are evaluative judgments. Statement 7 is to be treated in the same way as statement 4. From the viewpoint of practical agents, the pope's intervention may have altered the course of anticipated events, but for the historian the intervention was simply one event among others. Statement 8, not really a statement but a phrase, reveals a teleological view that a pattern of events can be discerned: that here was an institution that developed in distinct stages through which it gained entrenchment and power. Quite what is wrong with this?

Oakeshott offers elucidation in *On History*: "a teleological process is recognisable as a passage of change in virtue of the differences which compose it being understood as exemplary stages which succeed one another in a uniform order and in which an initial condition, identified in terms of its kind, reaches an exemplary *terminus* already known to be potential in it" (103). In this sense, of course, there was no evolution of Parliament. Oakeshott makes another point: "a teleology is an ideal process of change which, protected by the terms of its abstraction, is incapable either of diverging from its course or of failing to reach its destination" (*OH*, 104). Oakeshott is right, of course, that the gradual entrenchment of Parliament, its increasing independence of the monarch, the relative importance of the House of Commons, and various other factors we might include in "the evolution of Parliament" proceeded with nothing like the comparative necessity with which an acorn develops into an oak tree.

Statement 9 is on the surface less objectionable. But I think Oakeshott's idea here is mainly that the historian can create a historical past only in which certain events might in hindsight have this description given to them. When, for instance, Hargreaves invented the spinning jenny in 1765, and Arkwright patented his machine for spinning by rollers in 1769, and Compton produced his "mule" in 1779, none of these innovations were a part of "the development of industrial society in Great Britain." It is only when these events had been associated in narrative with a whole host of other innovations that the term *development of industrial society* became remotely applicable. No historian could infer, simply from evidence about it, that the invention of the spinning jenny was a part of the development of anything. No historian could look for "the development of industrial society" as a first-order inquiry.

Statement 10 makes teleological assumptions and leaves unexplained why the welfare state of the twentieth century represented "the" endpoint of the Factory Act legislation. A "culmination" is a climax or conclusion. The statement also appears to include evaluative elements. Statements 11 and 12 are clearly practical and evaluative; "serious consequences" are measured by an evaluative standard, and only somebody solicitous about the efficiency of the British Army would regard its radical reform as a matter of more than indifference. "The Liberator" in statement 13 is Daniel O'Connell (1775–1847), and the title is plainly a laudatory and hence evaluative description.

In his exclusion of the practical from the domain of historical inquiry, Oakeshott shows some affiliation with Weber's idea of *Wertfrei* inquiry. But Weber accepted that an inquirer's values will play some part in his or her choice of subject matter. It is hard to see how this is to be avoided, though a proper response on Oakeshott's behalf may be that the values involved are cognitive or intellectual. These are not, or are not obviously, what he wants to exclude when he bolts the door against the intrusion of practice into historical inquiry.

A more serious point perhaps concerns the value-freedom of the language the historian uses. There is, outside econometric history, no special historical vocabulary. The historian uses ordinary language, and ordinary language is value saturated. When we say, for instance, that "Hargreaves invented the spinning jenny in 1765," some kudos attaches to "invented." Invention is an achievement. Much more might be said, but space presses and I simply raise the issue.

So much for the false role of practice in historical inquiry. Whence the ban on science? The main problem concerns causation, necessity, and covering laws—universal generalizations that a particular casual relationship instantiates. Oakeshott displays his attitude clearly in the following passage:

> The general character of the scientist's concern with the world appears in his notion of "cause" and "effect." When the practical man recognizes an event as a "cause" he recognizes it as a *sign* that some other event may be expected to follow; and the ground of his recognition is his experience of the world in relation to himself. For the scientist, on the other hand, "cause" is a much more precise and more restricted notion; and "cause" in his sense is so difficult to determine that it lacks practical usefulness. It is the necessary and sufficient conditions of a hypothetical situation. "Cause" and "effect," that is, denote general and necessary relations and not merely a relation which it has proved practically useful to observe. (*RP*, 159–60)

I have three comments about this passage. In the first place, we can safely read "the necessary and sufficient conditions of a hypothetical situation" as involving the assumption of a covering law: "If and only if A then B." Second, it is far from clear that causal explanations in science require both necessary and sufficient conditions. Suppose I say, "If P then Q"; I state a causally sufficient condition. The occurrence of P is causally sufficient for the occurrence of Q, but it may not be necessary: the occurrence of R might have been equally sufficient. Third, the existence of a covering law may be little more than a tenuous metaphysical assumption in scientific explanation. Consider the following from Elizabeth Anscombe:

> Now it's not difficult to show it prima facie wrong to associate the notion of cause with necessity or universality in this way. For, it being much easier to trace effects back to causes with certainty than to predict effects from causes, we often know a cause without knowing whether there is an exceptionless generalisation of the kind envisaged, or whether there is a necessity.
>
> For example, we have found certain diseases to be contagious. If, then, I have had one and only one contact with someone suffering from such a disease, and I get it myself, we suppose I got it from him. But what if, having had the contact, I ask a doctor whether I will get the disease? He will usually only be able to say, "I don't know—maybe you will, maybe not."
>
> But, it is said, knowledge of causes here is partial; doctors seldom even know any of the conditions under which one invariably gets a disease, let alone all the sets of conditions. This comment betrays the assumption that there is such a thing to know. Suppose there is: still, the question whether there is or not does not have to be settled before we can know what we mean by speaking of the contact as cause of my getting the disease.[22]

Two further considerations are relevant to Oakeshott's anticausal bias. One of these is the famous "reasons versus causes" debates that exercised Anglo-American philosophy in the 1950s and 1960s. Oakeshott, we should recall, favorably reviewed Gilbert Ryle's 1949 *The Concept of Mind* (*CPJ*, 317–18). Very roughly, Ryle is sharply opposed to "category mistakes" (cf. *ignoratio elenchi*). Here is a brief quote that conveys the flavor of Ryle's approach: "In short, then, the doctrine of volitions is a causal hypothesis, adopted because it was wrongly supposed that the question, 'What makes a bodily movement voluntary?' was a causal question. This supposition is, in fact, only a special twist of the general hypothesis that the question, 'How are mental-conduct concepts applicable to human behaviour?' is a question about the causation of that behaviour."[23]

The anticausal camp took matters further with a so-called logical connection argument that reinforced Ryle's stance from another angle. The argument holds that causes must be independent of their effects in the sense that the statement of a cause involves no reference to its effect. If I say "the cat's jumping on the table caused the vase to break," there is no logical connection between (the statement of) the event of the cat's jumping on the table and that of the vase's breaking. Neither presupposes nor implies the other. But, it was claimed, reason explanations do not enjoy this logical independence. "X φd because he wanted to φ," which we can take as an example of a reason explanation, contains the common element "φ," and so reason and action are not logically independent; hence reasons cannot be causes. The debate cannot be resolved here. My own view, following Davidson, is that reason explanations are causal explanations.[24]

Some will see the cloven hoof of empiricist atomism here, and indeed the logical connection argument derives from Hume ("there is no object which implies the existence of any other").[25] But Oakeshott is very far indeed from the kind of idealist holism that we find in Bosanquet and qualifiedly in Bradley, in which the aim—or desideratum—is a comprehensive and coherent system of propositions that explains the whole of reality and in which any part of the system serves as ground or consequent for any other. He gestures toward such a system in *Experience and Its Modes*—"since [knowledge] is a system" (41)—but leaves its nature unspecified. The doctrine of modes, resistant to mutual assimilation, cuts plainly across the idea of any such system. Even if, on final reflection, the modes are indefensible "arrests" in experience (32, 79), Oakeshott has nothing better to offer along the lines of systematicity except for a vague indication of the supersession of modes under a full philosophical analysis of experience.

Whatever the case, Oakeshott's statement, for example, that "psychological mechanisms cannot be the motives of actions" (*OHC*, 22) puts him on the reasons-as-noncauses side of the divide in a debate of which we know that he was at least partially aware. To tie up a loose end, one element of his debt to Dilthey, and also Hegel, acknowledged earlier, is the sense that reasons or motives are socially and historically specific.

The second consideration centers on the nature of the historical past. This past is an inferential construction from experience. As inferential it is propositional, and there can be no causal relations between propositions. So when we say that "Caesar crossed the Rubicon, because he wanted to test the loyalty of his soldiers," there can be no causal relation between the crossing and the desire to test his soldiers. There is simply a proposition inferred as the best explanation of the evidence.

The autonomy of history may exclude practical and scientific categories from historical inquiry, but it does not guarantee internal coherence within such inquiry. Historians disagree, not over everything all the time but significantly about, for example, the origins of the Pennsylvania experiment (1681), the reasons for the fall of Quebec (1759), the nature of the three-fifths compromise (1787), the motivations behind the Monroe doctrine (1823), the relationship between the explosion of the *Maine* and the outbreak of the Spanish-American War (1898), the origins of World War I, the reasons for Hitler's conquest of power in 1933, the nature of Stalin's "cult of personality," the rationale of the United Kingdom's agreement with France and Israel to attack Egypt in 1956, the factors behind the Republican dominance in U.S. politics in the 1950s, the reasons for "the collapse of communism," the sources of radical Islam. (I leave the reader to decide whether Oakeshott himself would have regarded all or any of these topics as proper to historical inquiry.) All that Oakeshott's idea of the activity of being a historian requires is that there are professional standards for deciding on the quality of an explanation. On deciding, that is, on the truth of the explanans and on its explanatory power and, of course, on whether there *is* an explanandum.

REVIEW

Oakeshott does not claim to delineate historical practice. He does not engage in a strictly second-order inquiry into the nature of history that takes historical inquiry wholly as it stands. "What I am offering is a view of history from the outside. It is a view of history, not from the standpoint of the historian, but as it appears to one whose interests lie to one side of that of the historian" (*EM*, 86). Though he plainly has his preferences among historians— F. W. Maitland (*RP*, 173), Sir Ronald Syme (*OHC*, 100), Herbert Butterfield (*WIH*, 219–23), and others receive honorific mention—nevertheless he seldom and sparingly uses them to illustrate the writing of autonomous history, and one wonders if he regarded any of them as flawless exemplars of "the activity of being an historian." Yet historians (who else?) must have some say in defining the standards for adequate explanation, even if they observe Oakeshott's extrusion of science and practice. It would smack of rationalism for Oakeshott to assume that simply by reading his texts one could learn the craft of historical inquiry. Importantly, historical inquiry fails the test of comprehensiveness. Science, history, and practice are different angles on the whole of experience, but Oakeshott denies the claims of any of these modes to live up to this requirement. Only experience exists, but the historian

> is accustomed to think of the past as a complete and virgin world stretching out behind the present, fixed, finished and independent, awaiting only discovery. The past is something immune from change. And this view encourages the historian; he thinks that if he slips, the past does not fall. In short, the past *for* history is "what really happened"; and until the historian has reached back to and elucidated that, he considers himself to have performed his task incompletely. . . . Nevertheless, this view of the past cannot, I think, be maintained unmodified. It is what the historian is accustomed to believe, and it is difficult to see how he could go on did he not believe his task to be the resurrection of what once had been alive. . . . But the view suffers from a fatal defect: it implies that history is not experience. And consequently it must be set on one side as a misconceived view of the character of the past *of* or *in* history. (*EM*, 106–7)

As a charge against historical inquiry, this depends on Oakeshott's view that only experience exists and indeed that the past is unreal. With its eminently challengeable presuppositions, this view is hardly a knock-down critique. My overall sense of Oakeshott's theory of history is that it offers a constructionism logically independent of the dubious and frankly unworked out epistemological background from which it emerges, particularly in *Experience and Its Modes*. I also think that an adequate constructionist theory of history needs to be far more specific about the logic of evidence and better versed in contemporary notions of necessity, causality, and covering laws than Oakeshott anywhere reveals.[26]

NOTES

1. Benedictus de Spinoza, "Epistola 50," *Benedicti de Spinoza Opera*, vol. 2, ed. Carl H. Bruder (Leipzig, Germany: Tauchnitz, 1844), 299.

2. Saint Augustine, *The City of God*, trans. H. Bettensen (Harmondsworth: Penguin, 1972); G. W. F. Hegel, *Lectures on the Philosophy of World History*, trans. H. B. Nisbet (Cambridge: Cambridge University Press, 1975); Oswald Spengler, *The Decline of the West*, 2 vols. (London: Allen and Unwin, 1918–1922).

3. Luke O'Sullivan, *Oakeshott on History* (Exeter: Imprint Academic, 2003), 221–22.

4. F. H. Bradley, *Appearance and Reality* (London: Swan Sonnenschein, 1893), 35–43, 205–22; J. M. E. McTaggart, "The Unreality of Time," *Mind* 18 (1908): 457–84.

5. L. Susan Stebbing, review of *Experience and Its Modes*, *Mind* 43 (1934): 405.

6. Irwin. C. Lieb, *Past, Present, and Future* (Urbana: University of Illinois Press, 1991), 55.

7. "Putnam's Thesis," in *A Future for Presentism*, ed. C. Bourne (Oxford: Oxford University Press, 2006), 160. Bourne's text contains a useful discussion of presentism, to which I am indebted.

8. W. V. O. Quine, *Quiddities* (Cambridge, MA: Belknap University Press, 1987), 199.

9. Simon Blackburn, "Is Epistemology Incoherent?," in *The Philosophy of F. H. Bradley*, ed. A. Manser and G. Stock (Oxford: Oxford University Press, 1984), 155.

10. Norwood R. Hanson, *Patterns of Discovery* (Cambridge: Cambridge University Press, 1958); Wilfrid Sellars, *Epistemic Justification* (Ithaca: Cornell University Press, 1989).

11. David Hume, *A Treatise of Human Nature*, ed. L. A. Selby-Bigge, rev. P. H. Nidditch 2nd ed. (Oxford: Clarendon Press, 1978), 252, app.

12. Bradley, *Appearance and Reality*, 144.

13. Timothy Sprigge, *Theories of Existence* (Harmondsworth: Penguin, 1984), 62–63.

14. Immanuel Kant, *Critique of Pure Reason*, trans. P. Guyer and A. Wood (Cambridge: Cambridge University Press, 2008), A51, 193–94, 384–589.

15. I ought perhaps to explain my view of Oakeshott's indebtedness or otherwise to Hegel and R. G. Collingwood, names often mentioned in connection with *EM*. Hegel's *Phenomenology of Spirit* (1807), is equally the story of kinds of experience, some of them purely notional, such as bare sensation, of which the inadequacies are exposed. But in the *Phenomenology* there is a pattern or pathway of progressively less inadequate types (or understandings) of experience, culminating in philosophy as alone wholly adequate to the workings of Absolute Spirit. *EM* is not quite like this. There is not a graded shedding of inadequacies running smoothly from sensation, perception, self-consciousness, reason and science, ethics and culture, through religion to the final deliverance of "absolute knowing."

Collingwood's *Speculum Mentis* was published in 1924. Like *EM* it covers types or kinds of experience, but the types are not wholly the same. Collingwood examines art, religion, science, history, and philosophy. Whether Oakeshott had read *Speculum Mentis* when he wrote *EM* is a vexed question. Oakeshott denied that he had, though as Podoksik points out, Collingwood's exact phrase and opening sentence, "all thought exists for the sake of action," occurs in a different context in *EM*, 317. Collingwood, *Speculum Mentis* (Oxford: Clarendon Press, 1924), 15; Efraim Podoksik, *In Defence of Modernity: Vision and Philosophy in Michael Oakeshott* (Exeter: Imprint Academic, 2003), 13. This may be just coincidence, but the philosophical projects of *Speculum Mentis* and *EM* are significantly different. To begin, Collingwood refers to "the map of knowledge"; it is the book's subtitle. Oakeshott thinks, by contrast, not of discrete segments of experience but of the whole of experience differently regarded. More than that, Collingwood regrets the disintegration of intellectual life in which art, religion, science, history, and philosophy diverge with mutual indifference or hostility. Oakeshott could contemplate no such reintegration as Collingwood wants. The categorical differences between history, science, and practice wholly preclude it. The reader is referred further to Podoksik's excellent discussion.

16. W. G. de Burgh, *The Relations of Morality to Religion* (London: Milford, 1935), 16.

17. Aristotle, *Nicomachean Ethics*, trans. T. Irwin (Indianapolis: Hackett, 1985), bk. 1, chaps. 3 and 6.

18. René Descartes, *Meditationes de prima philosophia*, ed. A. Buchenau. (Leipzig: Druch, 1913), med. 2, sec. 28; med. 4, sec. 3; S. Gaukroger, *The Blackwell Guide to Descartes' Meditations* (Oxford: Blackwell, 2006), 25, 180; Kant, *Critique of Pure Reason*, 384–589.

19. Hugh R. Trevor-Roper, *Hermit of Peking* (London: Eland, 1976), 322–23.

20. Richard Rorty, *Philosophy and the Mirror of Nature* (Princeton: Princeton University Press, 1979), 176.

21. Henry St.-J. Bolingbroke, *Letters on the Study and Use of History* (London: Cadell, 1779), 14.

22. G. E. M. Anscombe, *Metaphysics and the Philosophy of Mind* (Cambridge: Cambridge University Press, 1981), 135–36.

23. Gilbert Ryle, *The Concept of Mind* (London: Hutchinson, 1949), 67.

24. Donald Davidson, *Actions and Events* (Oxford: Oxford University Press, 1991), ch. 3.

25. Hume, *Treatise of Human Nature*, 86.

26. The following texts all deal interestingly and some excellently with Oakeshott's philosophy of history: R. G. Collingwood, *The Idea of History*, ed. J. Van der Dussen, rev. ed. (Oxford: Oxford University Press, 1993); William H. Dray, "Michael Oakeshott's Theory of History," in *Politics and Experience: Essays Presented to Professor Michael Oakeshott on the Occasion of His Retirement*, ed. Preston King and B. C. Parekh (Cambridge: Cambridge University Press, 1968); Paul Franco, *The Political Philosophy of Michael Oakeshott* (New Haven: Yale University Press, 1990); Jack W. Meiland, *Skepticism and Historical Knowledge* (New York: Random House, 1965); O'Sullivan, *Oakeshott on History*; William H. Walsh, *An Introduction to the Philosophy of History* (Hutchinson: London, 1967); Walsh, "The Practical and the Historical Past," in King and Parekh, *Politics and Experience*.

5

RADICAL TEMPORALITY AND THE MODERN MORAL IMAGINATION: TWO THEMES IN THE THOUGHT OF MICHAEL OAKESHOTT

Timothy Fuller

My intention is to reflect on two themes that run through the whole of Oakeshott's thought: first, the radical temporality of the human condition and, second, the character of modernity's response to radical temporality. The first is, for Oakeshott, universal in experience to all times and places; the second is peculiar to a development in the modern West that, Oakeshott suggests, began to come into sight about five centuries ago and persists into the present and that manifests our particular experience of, and response as he understands it to, the universal condition of radical temporality. The second theme emerges as Oakeshott's exploration of the distinctively modern response to the universal condition. My approach here prepares the way to expound a "philosophy of politics," which Oakeshott has described as "an explanation or view of political life and activity from the standpoint of the totality of experience" (*RPML*, 126).

My reflections are based on considering the whole of his work, published and unpublished, but among those writings especially important are the following: *Experience and Its Modes* (1933); "The Concept of a Philosophical Jurisprudence" (1938); *The Politics of Faith and the Politics of Scepticism* (1950–52); the essays in *Rationalism in Politics* (1962); his various writings on Hobbes (especially the original 1946 introduction to the Blackwell edition of *Leviathan*); *On Human Conduct* (1975); and the essays in *Religion, Politics, and the Moral Life* (1993). In short, I am attempting, following his lead, to put into other words what I already understand Oakeshott to be saying. I begin with radical temporality.

ON RADICAL TEMPORALITY AND HUMAN CONDUCT

In our day the word *change* is much used, often more or less arbitrarily associated with progress and improvement, even though, in itself, the word can equally carry the connotation of loss or decline. In current parlance little thought of any depth is given to the significance of this word or to its prominence in contemporary discourse. No doubt this is because its usage is largely associated with various public policy proposals laden with ideological implications, far removed from philosophical reflection.

Inherent to human existence, change is a defining feature of practical life and, dramatically, of politics. Oakeshott understands the human being to be "for itself," trying to make more coherent what seems incoherent, trying to cure dissatisfaction in quest of what is imagined will bring satisfaction (*VLL*, 19). We are free beings, according to Oakeshott, because we must determine for ourselves what we understand ourselves to be. This is the ordeal of consciousness; we are incomplete beings searching for completion. This is the human condition.

In short, the practical life is constituted in efforts to alter our existence as we currently understand it or to ward off alterations that threaten what we at present take to be satisfactory. Initiating change or defending against change are both alterations and, as they are ever present, have no point of termination. We may talk of programs or plans for change, but we do not require programs or plans for us to be immersed in the experience of change, which proceeds regardless of programs or plans. The conduct of life is inseparable from the experience of change, and every attempt to get beyond the felt necessity of change is an effort to get beyond the life that we have been given.

Since this radical temporality is a universal condition of human existence, all human actions belong to the realm of change, including actions that aim to bring changes to conclusive closure. We talk of what is practical or impractical, but these terms are themselves immersed in the medium of change about which we are trying to get our bearings. What is practical or impractical is a matter that can never be finally settled, because human conduct can never be finally settled except perhaps in death. "Practice is activity, the activity inseparable from the conduct of life and from the necessity of which no living man can relieve himself" (*EM*, 257). "Change we can believe in" is an argument within this endlessness, as is the proposition to be "suspicious of all change." We need hardly profess belief in change, although much rhetorical energy is spent in such professions; indeed, we have no choice but to accept it. Believing that this or that particular change is the change to end all changes requires suspension of disbelief of a certain kind.

There is a discrepancy between the way things seem to be and what we would like to be the case. If we want to preserve a state of affairs we must characterize what it is we wish to save. To characterize it is already on the road to an abstraction that is not identical to the state of affairs we started out to save. We save, so to speak, a version of that state of affairs. There will thus always be a residual something that is not saved, and an incipient dissatisfaction with what we believe we have saved, leading to further adjustments to "get it right" this time, and the next time that is sure to follow. This is a world that may justly be called mortal: everything in it is coming to an end in the course of a beginning of something else. It is, as Hobbes would say, a restless search for power after power unto death. But, in the meantime, at each moment there is an experience of mortality, as endings and beginnings intrude on each other in a ceaseless flow of actions, with little deaths prompted by our will to make the world more coherent than for us it is.

It is natural that we should have ideas about how change has proceeded up to this point and ideas about where change seems to be taking us. But where change seems to be going is a matter of intimations extrapolated from what we already know in experience. There is no break between past and future, although it is common for us to impose conceptual breaks on the flow of our experience. We do have plans, programs, and theories, which we construct out of this flow, and they do have effects on how we interpret the past and also on how we will go forward, but they cannot be developed independently of the contingent conditions in which we pursue them or, as we like to say, "put them into practice." The point is, they were never outside of practice, whatever that could possibly mean.

Nevertheless, there is a tendency to imagine ideal worlds that are taken to exist independently and that we wish to bring into the currently unsatisfactory world to transform it. This too is natural to us and is implied in our desire to transcend the ordeal of change, and as well because we quite understandably want to assuage the pains of conscious existence. Such ideal worlds may be helpful in clarifying our self-understanding and purposes to ourselves, but the reality in which we are immersed, and which we experience as transcending the momentary and evanescent, is never captured by the images of it that we make for ourselves, even if we fall in love with those images, as we frequently do.

The appeal of the "to be" that is "not yet" depends on forgetting or downplaying the mortal flow within which the "to be" must be born and to which it forever owes a debt. Human action generates the thought of two realms of experience, but the two are one world conceived in different aspects. The mediation of them through action can reach only some degree of satisfaction because the two already inhabit one realm from the outset, and every mediation is within the one world of experience. Were this not so, it is hard to see what mediation, as an act of human willing, could possibly mean. And certainly no mediation to end all mediation is available to us. It is rather as if we must both acknowledge the character of our existence and yet deny it at the same time. We are moved in recognizing that what is the case now may not be the case tomorrow and was not the case yesterday, and yet we are also moved by the thought that we can bring this situation under our control. We engage to do what cannot be done, but this very condition drives us on to try to do it.

There are those who hope to make a virtue out of this necessity by appealing to the consequences of alternative courses of action, for example, the pragmatists and the utilitarians. But here too the consequences are integral to the flow of experience. What we take to be the consequences will be what we abstract from the mortal flow of endings and beginnings to designate as relevant outcomes by which to judge success or failure. We may initiate actions but we do not control the unfolding that follows from those actions. In short, the appeal to "what works" cannot resolve the endlessness of practical life. We know in any case that whether something works is itself a matter of argument. We should admit that we cannot know in advance the success of the ideas we put forth, for they are dependent on what is "not yet" and thus their validation remains to be seen. Even substantial agreements on outcomes, when we get them, are unstable and subject to revision, although some come to seem to us inevitable and irrevocable. We will forever be hostage to developments of which we cannot, at present, know, albeit we must proceed as if we knew what we need to know. One might call this the "delayed eschaton" of modern progressivism. Moreover, the appeal of this lies in the implicit thought that a time will come when there will be no further consequences of concern to us—the time when consequences, which were always driving forces before, are no longer consequential, and thus no longer mutating criteria of what we take to be true. Against this faith the endlessness of practical life reasserts itself, and we still do not know what a fully satisfactory world might be.

The attempted escape from the endlessness of practical life is only the promise of ultimate rescue at some distant point when what we think we want now will come to pass in such a way that we will be glad to have it. As Hegel reminds us, however, much human effort is spent in undoing the results of our past successes. In this situation we have the experience of freedom but seek a condition beyond freedom. The unavoidable question of what our freedom is for dramatizes the predicament we are considering. The ordeal of freedom is that we must deal with the question of purpose, direction, or redemption. We participate in defining what purpose, direction, or redemption means, even as we want these to have independent validity in themselves. We understand ourselves to be deciding for ourselves how we ought to be, but how do we deal with the absence of a voice to proclaim, "Well done thou good and faithful servant"?

How we ought to be is embedded in what we have been and imagine ourselves to be coming to be. Does this "ought to be" belong to one as an individual? That is, do we individuals merely place value on matters that interest us or that we find desirable? Is the "ought to be" emergent in a social matrix shaping what we take to be our individuality? We suffer tension between self-assertion and self-forgetting, between separation and adjustment, and if we engage to mediate this tension by seeking the life we wish to live, this too is the inescapable onwardness of our existence. Mutability and thus mortality bespeak "the central fact of practical existence; death is the central fact of life. I do not, of course, mean merely human mortality, the fact that we must one day cease to be; I mean the far more devastating mortality of every element of practical existence, the mortality of pleasures and pains, desires, achievements, emotions and affections. Mortality is the presiding character in practical experience. . . . Practice is never the mere assertion of the present; it is essentially action, the alteration of 'what is' so as to make it agree with 'what ought to be'" (*EM*, 273–74).

As Montaigne would tell us, the unacknowledged goal of life is death. That is, we move forward through time both by necessity and by design. We go on to new things as if we want to speed toward death, when we are actually trying to run away from it. In this sense every day is equally natural and equally on the path of time. To be anxious for the future is usually to be anxious for a future other than the one we will with certainty experience. Habits help to dampen these anxieties, bringing an unstudied propensity toward balance against lurching from one thing to another. But judgment and assertion cannot be circumvented, nor can we avoid revision of judgments and assertions. Habits, however, allow the eye of judgment a little rest. Custom mediates these tensions. To depart from habit and custom involves the belief, as in modern rationalism, that we can get to the end of the road more efficiently, without hesitations and qualms. By "divers paths" we come to the same end.

If we say that certain ideas are necessary, or that "their time has come," and thereby appeal to finality, we do not thereby extricate ourselves from the endlessness of practical life. Goals to be sought because they "ought to be" are already intimated in the current state of affairs. But because these are intimations and not necessary implications, there are dissenting voices and alternative views. Attempts to silence the dissents only confirm their practical reality. Indeed, the dissenting voice may be, and often is, within ourselves. If the goals were necessary implications of the current state of affairs, perhaps they would unfold more naturally and easily. All of these are productions of the human mind, which show the open-endedness of the human imagination. Behind the rational plan lurks Fortuna. If we thought that discussion is more important than winning or losing, we would perhaps make peace with our mutability. But we seldom do this. Politics is unforgiving in this respect, prompting us to overcome the limitations we cannot avoid.

We must, then, live in radical temporality, but we do not have to live for it. We can come to terms with it by acknowledging it and learning to expect no more of it than it gives. "To philosophize is to learn how to die." But traditional philosophy is drawn to a transcendent dimension of which we would say not that "it ought to be" but that "it is" and does not require to be "put into practice." The temporal/mortal existence gives rise to the thought of its negation or its completion in the eternal/immortal. But unless we experience this through living fully in the present moment we will at best have a momentary sense of release from our ineluctable time-boundedness. The philosopher is the "victim of thought" (*EM*, 3) dwelling in the tension between the quest for the whole and the spectacle of irrationality, prejudice, and contingency:

> We hope one day for what we fear the next. What gave us pleasure yesterday causes only pain to-day. We desire what does not bring us satisfaction. We love what we hate, and hate what we love. Neither our desires nor our hopes nor any other mood in practical experience can be persuaded to compose a consistent whole; the random, unguided element is on the surface for all to see. . . . Our particular attempts to convert "what is here and now" into "what ought to be" are governed by no general rules. Nobody not forced to do so by some moral or spiritual tyranny—tyranny of education or command—conducts his life according to a set of absolute principles, unmodified by the common-sense, intuition or insight which interprets such principles. . . . We shall find nowhere a completely integrated world of practical experience. (300)

The philosopher—the victim of thought—in attempting to live in but not for the world of radical temporality discovers the unforgiving nature of practical life, offended as it is by the reminder that it cannot fulfill itself, that its part is to pursue what it must ultimately fail to procure. We know it as the combination of romantic quest with calculating struggle for power.

The presupposition of practical experience is that "what is here and now" and "what ought to be" are discrepant. And practice is not the reconciliation of these worlds as worlds, but the reconciliation of particular instances of this discrepancy. To reconcile these worlds generally and absolutely would involve the abolition of discrepancy, the denial of what is presupposed throughout. . . . Permanent dissatisfaction . . . is inherent in practical experience. . . . The modification or change of reality is a meaningless conception. . . . Practice purports to throw reality into the future, into something new and to be made, only to discover that this is also a contradiction of the character of experience. . . . Change is the concept or category under which reality is known in the world of practical existence. What is not transient is, for that reason, not real for practical experience. (*EM*, 346)

And "the principle of transience lies . . . beyond the reach of practical activity itself. . . . Consequently, the world achieved in practical experience does not differ from the given world. . . . Practical truth is not ultimate truth" (308). To be dead to the world of practice, of change, as Socrates says, is the beginning of philosophy. And, as Oakeshott says, "freedom from extraneous purpose and irrelevant interest is the sign of all seriously undertaken thought" (311).

THE MODERN MORAL IMAGINATION RESPONDS
TO RADICAL TEMPORALITY

By "moral imagination" I mean, along lines suggested by Charles Taylor, "the ways people imagine their social existence, how they fit together with others, how things go on between them and their fellows, the expectations that are normally met, and the deeper normative notions and images that underlie these expectations . . . shared by large groups of people . . . that makes possible common practices and a widely shared sense of legitimacy."[1] Or as Oakeshott says, "Again, all moral judgment whatever may take the form of a reference of a situation to a rule of action, good always appearing as 'what is my duty,' but this is no reason for rejecting the view that, in the last analysis, moral judgment is the reference of a situation to an end, or the view that moral judgment is a judgment with regard to the coherence of life involved in living and acting in a particular way" (*RPML*, 136).

More specifically, I focus here on the modern moral imagination as it informs modern thinking on human relations. I want to start by considering Hobbes (on whom Oakeshott wrote more systematically than on any other political philosopher) and in particular the following observation in Hobbes's introduction to *Leviathan*:

> But there is another saying not of late understood, by which [human beings] might learn truly to read one another, if they would take the pains; and that is *nosce teipsum, read thy self* . . . to teach us that for the similitude of the thoughts and passions of one man to the thoughts and passions of another, whosoever looketh into himself and considereth what he doth, when he does *think, opine, reason, hope,* &c, and upon what grounds, he shall thereby read and know, what are the thoughts and passions of all other men upon the like occasions. . . . He that is to govern a whole nation must read in himself, not this or that particular man, but mankind, which though it be hard to do, harder than to learn any language or science, yet when I shall have set down my own reading orderly and perspicuously, the pains left another will be only to consider if he also find not the same in himself.[2]

This sets a direction for the modern moral imagination down to the present day. Let us notice all that Hobbes is saying to us: (1) the thoughts and passions are basically similar from one person to the next; (2) by introspection into one's own inner self one can imagine the basic pattern of reasoning and passion common to human beings and thus can infer how others are likely to respond in similar circumstances; (3) at the level of governing a nation this knowledge is essential because the task of governing extends far beyond our close personal relations—indeed, governing requires a certain kind of impersonal or depersonalized relationship to all subjects of a commonwealth; (4) at the same time, since there is no fundamental difference in these patterns between rulers and subjects, there is basic similarity in capacity for insight among all human beings; (5) what distinguishes one human being from another is the relative ability to grasp the basic structure of human conduct accurately by bracketing one's idiosyncrasies, foibles, and particular goals; and (6) the office one holds does not distinguish one's basic humanity from that of others. Hobbes claims that in *Leviathan* he has worked out in detail what this basic human similitude is, and the test of his argument is for the reader to consider whether he has expounded the fundamental character of human relations "scientifically," that is, in detachment from merely personal preferences and goals.

Hobbes is, in other words, elaborating the prototype of the modern moral imagination that emphasizes not mere self-interestedness—the aspect of Hobbes's thought most commonly noticed—but also the capacity to enter into the views of others by inference from the universal basic structure of thought and emotion. We thus eventually arrive at enlightened or rational self-interest: the conscious and disciplined pursuit of our interests by which we take account of our inevitable implication in the unavoidable presence of others similarly self-interested and capable of disciplining their pursuits in the same way.

Reflection on our experience leads us to conclude that our desire to set ourselves apart from, or above, others will be frustrated if we do not learn to behave in a "moral way." The moral way is the disciplined way of self-restraint of enlightened self-interest, which individuals acquire through reflection on the lessons of experience. We can acquire the practice of self-regulation. We find it possible to imagine the inner life of others according to the basic similarity of one person to another in the common human condition. It is in learning how to discipline our self-interestedness that we demonstrate "moral imagination." We recognize something about ourselves in others. As Oakeshott says, following Hobbes, "moral activity may be said to be the observation of a balance of accommodation between the demands of desiring selves each recognized by the others to be an end and not a mere slave of somebody else's desires" (RP, 502).

Hobbes sets the stage for further development of the modern moral imagination. Subsequently, John Locke, Adam Smith, and David Hume, for instance, emphasize the instinct of sympathy, the capacity for pity at the sight of others' pain. The moral imagination allows us to identify ourselves with others even though each of us must be a "for itself," always remaining individuals who are "for ourselves" (see VLL, 19). The combination of self-interestedness with sympathy defines the modern moral imagination. Out of it we imagine and can systematically describe a spontaneous civil association of innumerable voluntary transactions governed by a procedural rule of law that, as it turns out, permits the growth of wealth and the projection of an ideal of infinitely expanding prosperity. Consider also Immanuel Kant's project to achieve perpetual peace through the expansion of the commercial-republican order to all the world. The movement from Hobbes to Kant and beyond brings to sight two great moral aspirations of modernity: perpetual peace and ever-expanding prosperity.

What appears to many readers to be Hobbes's pessimism about the human condition is nearly the opposite of the truth. Hobbes thought he had outlined the basic science of human conduct that, to the extent we learn it, makes it possible for us to transform human relations along the lines further developed in the movement from Locke to Smith and Hume to Kant, to John Stuart Mill, and beyond. These later writers work out the basis for confidence that the spontaneous order enabled by enlightened self-interest is not reliant for its stability on massive coercive power in central governments. Rather, it promises a more enduring stability than that maintainable by coercion, and it expresses the faith of classic modern liberal thought. These are fundamental assumptions of modernity. What does an Oakeshottian philosophical appraisal of these assumptions reveal? Let us consider Kant's expression of these assumptions as a means to this appraisal.

Kant's essay—"An Old Question Raised Again: Is the Human Race Constantly Progressing?"—advocates a "predictive history," a philosophy of the future, a kind of prophetic history. This is possible only if we commit ourselves in advance to goals that certify the dignity and enlightenment of humanity. That is, we must adopt ideals for the future worthy in themselves and then act toward the future under their inspiration. Given the sorry record of human history how can we believe in, or summon the energy to work for, these ideals? Kant's answer is that nothing less is worthy of a being who wishes to achieve true dignity and happiness. Here the modern moral imagination projects a moral transformation in the human condition. We must imagine our perfection and then gather the resources to pursue that imagined perfection. We must strive for what Kant calls "moralized politics" as opposed to "political morality."

Kant means by "political morality" the expedient calculation of self-interest we associate with Machiavelli. By "moralized politics" Kant means transforming enlightened self-interest to include the goal of a perfected human condition. This goal builds into enlightened self-interest the motive of transforming self-interest, no matter how rationally it may be pursued, into that higher virtue to which enlightened self-interest in the past seemed to be a barrier. This is to say that human beings have the capacity to construct their own vision of perfection and then find ways to make the vision a visible reality in human relations. We incorporate the ideal end-state into our self-interest. The science of conduct in Hobbes is to be perfected in the moral idealism of Kant.

Kant fully understands that the plausibility of the path to perfection is hindered by the record of past history. But if human beings are genuinely free in the sense that they make their ideals for themselves, they can thereby inspire themselves to strive unceasingly to make the ideals actual. We must become the cause of our own advance to completed enlightenment. To do this we must achieve a cosmopolitan point of view in which we regard humanity as a whole and not only in local identity. This is to extend Hobbes's original insight for the possibility of a permanently stable commonwealth—the internal cosmopolitanism of the citizens or subjects of the state—to the possibility of a universal commonwealth composed of republics who see the similitude of the thoughts and desires of one another.

The emergence of this ideal in Kant's time, which he thought was incarnated in the great revolutions of the seventeenth and eighteenth centuries, is for him the sign of progress because the new ideals of peace and prosperity are coming to be accepted as self-evident to modern people. Their validity does not lie initially in their plausibility but in their intrinsic appeal to beings who seeks dignity and affirmation in their own terms. There is a latent moral disposition in the human race that at this moment in history is coming triumphally to sight. Perpetual peace will replace perpetual conflict. Living in hope for the heavenly kingdom will be transposed into a project to use self-interest to transform ourselves into an existence beyond self-interest. This is the apex of the modern moral imagination. Kant sees himself at a revelatory moment in which the moral disposition of the human race begins to reveal itself fully, to be formulated as a project for the future that, he thinks, cannot disappear. Contingent events cannot derail the moral direction, history cannot sweep away the ideal:

> The human race has always been in progress toward the better and will continue to be so henceforth. To him who does not consider what happens in just some one nation but who has regard to the whole scope of all the peoples on earth who will gradually come to participate in progress, this reveals the prospect of an immeasurable time—provided at least that there does not, by some chance, occur a second epoch of natural evolution which will push aside the human race for other creatures.

As the sense of duty to what ought to happen expands, it "will also extend to nations in their external relations toward one another up to the realization of the cosmopolitan society," increasingly resistant to the "mockery of the politician who would willingly take the hope of man as the dreaming of a distraught mind." And offensive war, "which constantly retards this advancement," will be renounced altogether.[3]

If the modern moral imagination is preoccupied with the ideals of peace and prosperity, bolstered by free market economy and the confidence science and technology impart, that imagination is nevertheless attended by a haunting question: is it possible that we could advance materially and decline spiritually? From the first appearance of the modern moral imagination there has been an accompanying, dissenting theme. "Modernity" constitutes itself in the dialectic of what Oakeshott calls the "politics of faith" with the "politics of skepticism." This is the internal dialectic of the modern moral imagination.

The politics of skepticism is the modern renewal of the residual legacy of the classic/Christian heritage of Western civilization, which, in refusing to subscribe to Kant's (and those following him such as Marx) predictive history of the future, remembers and contemplates both the past record of the corruption induced by the acquisition of power and also Hobbes's admonition that "covenants without the sword are but words." As Oakeshott puts it,

> In the politics of faith, the activity of governing is understood to be in the service of the perfection of mankind. . . . Human perfection is sought precisely because it is not present . . . [and] is to be achieved by human effort, and confidence in the evanescence of imperfection springs here from the faith in human power and not from trust in divine providence. . . . Man is redeemable in history . . . [and] the chief agent of the improvement, which is to culminate in perfection, is government. (*PFPS*, 23–24)

Moreover,

> One of the characteristic assumptions, then, of the politics of faith is that human power is sufficient, or may become sufficient, to procure salvation. A second assumption is that the word "perfection" (and its synonyms) denotes a single, comprehensive condition of human circumstances. . . . Consequently, this style of politics requires a double confidence: the conviction that the necessary power is available or can be generated, and the conviction that, even if we do not know exactly what constitutes perfection, at least we know the road that leads to it. (26)

By contrast, the politics of skepticism expresses "prudent diffidence" in recognizing politics as a "necessary evil" and "expects human conflict . . . seeing no way of abolishing it without abolishing much else at the same time . . . to be sparing of the quantity of power invested in government" (33).

Modernity constitutes itself both in rejecting the classic/Christian heritage and in acknowledging that heritage only insofar as it is made the preamble to our present and yet also in its failure to rid itself of this heritage that irritatingly reminds us that the ideal picture of our future opposes the actual structure of reality as we have always experienced it. In the terms of this chapter, the modern imagination's response to radical temporality is haunted by the fear that its response is inadequate and hostage to the actual future that may befall us. Modernity knows itself to be responding to a powerful critique that it cannot embrace but that it cannot shake off and forget either. Like all escha-tological speculations it suffers indefinite postponement.

One can go on to suggest that the modern moral imagination exempli-fies a profound dialectical tension between the philosophy of the future and the classic/Christian inheritance. What we call the "postmodern" bespeaks a condition of declining confidence in the claims of enlightenment embodied in philosophies of the future. This uncertainty is accompanied by aggres-sive bewilderment about alternative ways of imagining ourselves. The loss of confidence in utopian politics understandably issues in the feeling that we have lost the meaning of life because we have put so much faith in politics as the locus of meaning. The modern departure from the Platonic/Aristotelian/biblical understanding—that politics is an instrument in the service of that which transcends the mundane—makes us resistant to a return or leaves us with the sense that there is no path of return. Nor can we cure this disease by projecting yet new and different imagined futures, insofar as the enlighten-ment project has lost its innocence in its own crisis of faith.

Among his responses to this, Oakeshott offers openness to the "voice of poetry in the conversation of mankind." The voice of poetry is an alternative to, but not a substitute or replacement for, the scientific/technological/pro-gressive voice. The voice of poetry is also not a political voice. For Oakeshott the poetic voice is a different way—within the modern context—of imagining our world. He does not intend it as an alternative to the historical reality in which we must think and act, but as the way to find experiences of delight that captivate us but do not urge us to look beyond this world to an alternative world. It is to seek the poetic in the interstices of the quotidian. Poetic images in our contemplation of them

> provoke neither speculation nor inquiry about the occasion or condi-tions of their appearing but only delight in their having appeared. They have no antecedents or consequents; they are not recognized as causes or conditions or signs of some other image to follow, or as the products or effects of one that went before; they are not instances of a kind, nor are they means to an end; they are neither "useful" nor "useless." . . . Moreover, the image in contemplation is neither pleasurable nor pain-ful; and it does not attract to itself either moral approval or disapproval. Pleasure and pain, approval and disapproval are characteristics of images of desire and aversion, but the partner of desire and aversion is incapable of being the partner of contemplation. (*RP*, 510)

We note that this establishes Oakeshott's dialectical, or perhaps one should say his conversational, response to the preoccupation with historical existence in favor of an experience where the anxieties of seeking perfection and perpetuating imperfection do not intrude. It falls short of the pull of the eternal, but it does not necessarily exclude it since that, for Oakeshott, is a matter for individuals to consider. He offers the poetic voice as a gentle way to acknowledge the terrors of the radical temporality of the human condition, at least in offering release for a time from the interminable modern project to perfect ourselves in the realm of perpetual peace and infinite prosperity. The project is interminable, because there can be no guarantee against falling back into war (which may seem obvious in a way) nor insulation from the failure of material wealth to assuage spiritual longing (for which empirical evidence abounds). Oakeshott allows for a glimpse of the transcendent in the transitory release into the contemplative experience of the poetic voice. He is stoic, but he points to a more comprehensive moral imagination that, while it need not abandon modern accomplishments, would recognize their subordinate and inevitably incomplete character. It is his Socratic turn, disclosing his philosophical imagination by questioning the assumptions of the modern moral imagination in the universal context of the radical temporality that is the human condition.

NOTES

1. Charles Taylor, *Modern Social Imaginaries* (Durham: Duke University Press, 2003), 23.

2. Thomas Hobbes, *Leviathan*, ed. Michael Oakeshott (Oxford: Blackwell, 1946), 5–6.

3. Immanuel Kant, "An Old Question Raised Again: Is the Human Race Constantly Progressing?," in *Kant on History*, ed. Lewis White Beck (New York: Macmillan/Library of Liberal Arts, 1963), 147–48, 151.

6

THE RELIGIOUS SENSIBILITY OF MICHAEL OAKESHOTT

Elizabeth Corey

I have often thought that one of the best introductions to the philosophy of Michael Oakeshott is a children's book by Arnold Lobel. *Grasshopper on the Road* describes the journey of a remarkably even-tempered grasshopper who meets various other insects on his way down a pleasant country lane. Each of these insects displays some modern pathology. Grasshopper first encounters the members of the "I Love Morning" club, who raise placards extolling the virtues of morning while shouting such slogans as "Morning Is Best" and "Hooray for Morning." Grasshopper is welcomed into the club when he reveals that he, too, loves morning. But when he remarks that he also loves afternoon and evening, the other insects turn on him in disgust and order him out of their ranks. A bit later, he meets "The Sweeper," a housefly who has noticed a speck of dust on her rug. Her effort to sweep it away has made her aware of the dust that has collected on the floor next to the rug, and also on her front stoop and sidewalk. She realizes, in despair, that there is also a great deal of dust on the road in front of her house. It is here, as she attempts to sweep clean a gravel road, that she meets Grasshopper. The book is full of subtle political commentary of this sort. It playfully lampoons the vanity of attempts to control the world, the desire of people to find purpose in life by joining a movement, and the general human inability to enjoy life as it happens. It is a wonderfully Oakeshottian book.[1]

Grasshopper is a poetic image, a book for children. But it serves as an emblem of Oakeshott's thought in a number of ways, not least because of its curious mixture of moral admonition and poetic delight. Oakeshott's writing displays both of these qualities. On the one hand he warned against political ideology and moral dogmatism in his more polemical essays such as "Rationalism in Politics." On the other hand he often employed religious and poetic images to point toward an alternate mode of existence in the world. In such images Oakeshott evokes a way of living that can at times escape the moral and practical concerns with which human beings are almost always preoccupied. This "religious" or "poetic" dimension of Oakeshott's thought is fascinating to trace from his youth onward. Early on he explicitly called it the religious life, while later he tended to call it a poetic disposition. But however he labeled it, Oakeshott continually returned to this theme of an alternative way of orienting oneself in the world, and it stands at the center of his work. In other words, the two sides of Oakeshott's writing, the practical/moral and the religious/poetic, are related in a certain way. His practical essays, which aimed always at placing some limits on our hopes and ambitions (especially in politics), can be understood as written in the service of a religious or poetic ideal. Oakeshott particularly wanted readers to see that politics is limited in the satisfactions it can offer, and he illuminated a range of experiences that proved more complete in themselves.

In the paragraphs that follow, I consider a religious image that Oakeshott employed to illuminate the corruptions of modern political and social life: the myth of the Tower of Babel. I then turn to an examination of one of Oakeshott's central concepts, the mode of practice, and consider what Oakeshott thought were its possibilities as well as its unavoidable limits. For despite the fact that he thought much of importance might be achieved in the practical world, Oakeshott ultimately found it insufficient as a way of explaining the entirety of human experience. Thus I end with a discussion of his view of poetry, a view that seems to have permeated every aspect of his thought. It is a poetic view of life, a sensitivity to all that might fall under the aspect of the aesthetic, that Oakeshott saw as giving human experience both poignancy and meaning.

THE TOWER OF BABEL

As a young man Oakeshott was quite interested in religious questions, although this preoccupation seemed to recede over the course of his career. In a number of early essays, published posthumously as *Religion, Politics, and the Moral Life*, Oakeshott took up issues such as the relationship of religion and morality, the importance of history for Christian belief, and the kind of person who might properly be called religious. Throughout the 1920s he published a number of book reviews on religious topics and was especially concerned with the relationship of religion to theology—or, in his view, the utter incongruity of the two. In *Experience and Its Modes* there is also a substantial consideration of religion as part of the mode of practice. But after

1933 Oakeshott wrote little else that mentioned religion. He provided only a tantalizingly short treatment of it in his 1975 magnum opus, *On Human Conduct*. It is therefore not unreasonable to conclude that Oakeshott's interests simply changed. He was, perhaps, religious in youth but lost that religion as he grew older, preferring to examine more concrete topics such as history, politics, and law.

But such an interpretation fails to take account of one of Oakeshott's most central insights, an insight not grounded in some partisan position but in a profound sense that most people had religion wrong. An often overlooked remark in "Rationalism in Politics" confirms this. "If we except religion," wrote Oakeshott, "the greatest apparent victories of Rationalism have been in politics" (*RP*, 8). And though he did not explicitly tell his readers what rationalism in religion meant, one can imagine what his answer might have been. Under the pressure of a long-delayed Second Coming, Oakeshott explained elsewhere, the lives of ordinary Christians were transformed from simple love of neighbor and faith in Christ into a moral ideology expressed in abstract propositions and creeds. And therefore religion became something not to be pursued simply and intuitively as a way of living but as adequate and complete subscription to moral rules. It had become a constant Pelagian striving to live up to an unattainable ideal. And thus the intermittent beauty, poetry, and spontaneity of daily life were suppressed in the hope of someday—a day that lay always in the future—attaining eternal life. This was most adequately expressed, Oakeshott thought, in the image of the Tower of Babel. He wrote two separate essays on the subject, neither of which is explicitly religious in character. But both, in different ways, express an essentially religious view of human experience.

An idea implicit in the Tower of Babel myth, as Oakeshott recounted it, is that human beings are constantly threatened by two different impulses. On the one hand, we are (to use a patently modern word) "insecure." We compare ourselves to others, we want what others possess, we doubt our abilities, and we constantly seek some firm, moral standard by which to measure our conduct. We are aware of the possibility of failure and would much prefer guaranteed success. And yet at the same time we are also full of pride, which Oakeshott once explained to his students as "thinking of yourself as, and behaving as if, you were other than in fact you are. It is trying to occupy a place in the *ordo universi* other than that which properly belongs to you" (*LHPT*, 330). When we see a problem we often attempt immediately to fix it, since we are inclined to think of human ability as limitless.

Poised between these two extremes of insecurity and pride, human beings continually build "towers of Babel" as ways of alleviating anxiety and engaging in so-called important affairs. The modern world is awash in such projects, which consist of national and international initiatives and movements of all kinds. Tower building can also take place within individual souls whenever people subscribe dogmatically to an ideology or orient their life toward a purportedly vital worldly end.

Oakeshott first expressed the problem of Babel in an essay from 1948, in which he set out two contrasting types of morality. The first type, customary or habitual, is learned continually from childhood and cannot be avoided. It is a stable form of morality in which conduct simply issues from someone who has naturally learned how to act. The other form of morality, which Oakeshott called a "morality of ideals," is "the reflective application of a moral criterion" (*RP*, 472). To engage in this a person ought to be something of a philosopher, for action is not intuitive but must constantly be referred to a predetermined rule or ideal. The chosen rule or ideal, moreover, has the tendency to become an idol. "Every moral ideal is potentially an obsession," Oakeshott lamented. "The pursuit of moral ideals is an idolatry in which particular objects are recognized as 'gods'" (476). His analysis explains the contemporary worship of such goods as "equality," "social justice," or "tradition." Any of these pursued exclusively is bound to overlook other perhaps equally important goods that ought to receive attention. To attempt the complete achievement of any of these on earth was, in Oakeshott's view, to construct a tower of Babel.[2]

In his later Tower of Babel essay, written in 1979, Oakeshott poked fun at modern ideological projects by retelling the myth for a modern audience. Here Babel is a place "full of the bustle of getting and spending" (*OH*, 191). In esteeming freedom, choice, and acquisition, it is a strikingly accurate image of the contemporary western city. Nimrod, the city's ruler, proposes that the entire community join in a building project to reach heaven. Babel's inhabitants would then be able to launch an assault on a God who had not given them the goods they deserved. The bulk of the essay consists in a humorous but incisive critique of all-consuming projects imposed on or agreed to by societies. And of course the story ends in death and destruction, after a long, slow chipping away at the humble satisfactions of everyday life. The moral of this story is that a society that pursues any all-consuming purpose will inevitably neglect those things that make people most fully human. There will be little time for such "useless" pursuits as philosophy, liberal learning, or conversation. All energies must be directed toward a prosperous future. Such a life, moreover, has need of "forever-recurring obstacles and of ends that are more and more inaccessible."[3] Their very inaccessibility makes them the more desirable, but it also means that there can never be repose. The good thus consists in a delayed eschaton, the appeal of which "lies in the implicit thought that a time will come when there will be no further consequences about which to be concerned."[4] But Oakeshott was quite clear that there could be no such time. The nature of daily practical life, he thought, was bound up with change and consequences.

Both Tower of Babel essays highlight the irreligious quality of pursuing an unattainable goal at the expense of a lived life. And although the language of ideals is now the preferred currency in religion, politics, and university education, Oakeshott thought it ought to be viewed at least with circumspection, if not outright skepticism. This view of life as service to an ideal consistently downplays individuality in favor of collective action, and what becomes important is to be part of a movement greater than oneself. And this appears not just in politics but in all kinds of careerism: crusades for better scientific knowledge or more advanced technology or a cure for cancer. None of these goals are in themselves objectionable, but they all incline one to recall a poetic quote from *Faust* that appears in one of Oakeshott's early essays: "*Und eh man nur den halben Weg erreicht, Muss wohl ein armer Teufel sterben*" (and long before the halfway point is reached they bury a poor devil in the ground).[5] If we conceive of life principally as one long investment, then what is it worth if the payoff is missed?

In his retelling of the Babel story Oakeshott also emphasized the tyranny of the concept of achievement, which he once called "the diabolical element in human life."[6] He was of course well aware that the achievement of many good things requires significant effort, and that in this sense the "investment theory of happiness" cannot be avoided. Such is the paradigm for learning anything of great value such as an instrument or a language; Oakeshott's own writings on education continually emphasized the apprenticeship necessary for initiation into a tradition of thought. Yet there is a strong human tendency to focus so much on some future outcome that the present is altogether abandoned. "The world's ideal is achievement," wrote Oakeshott. "It asks for accomplishment, and regards each life as a mere contribution to some far-off result. The past reaches up to the future, and the present, and all sense and feeling for the present is lost" (*RPML*, 36).

And this, moreover, is understood to be virtuous: it is self-denial and self-sacrifice for a cause about which one is passionate. Nevertheless, such an approach to life requires tremendous sacrifices, and for what? More often than not, the achievement of the stated goal yields little by way of contentment, but only more impatience to be about one's next project. As a contemporary of Oakeshott's observed, the essence of this kind of restless passion, whether in love or career, "is to feed on obstacles, and to aspire not to such or such a concrete realization, but to some objective infinitely distant—to an aspiration always more intense—even though the end, when all is said or done, is beyond all material or human possibility." Such passion "appears as a choice of intense and even mortal torment, in preference to the happiness and sorrows of daily life."[7] And so human beings find themselves continually hoping that some final and complete happiness will appear just around the next corner.

Perhaps what is most notable about the Tower of Babel myth, in both of Oakeshott's essays, is the perfectionism inherent in the story. Whether one wants to contribute to a great and noble cause or to change the world through human action, pride and overestimation lie at the center of this myth. The idea that humankind can eliminate poverty, that women and men can achieve absolute equality (whatever that might mean), that any such "perfect" outcomes could occur in the world is a misunderstanding of the character of human experience. Like Augustine, Oakeshott was inclined to see such perfectionism as the epitome of worldliness—dangerous enough in an individual but impossible to sustain in political life. At every moment an orientation of this kind "calls upon those who practise it to determine their behaviour by reference to a vision of perfection. . . . We are never suffered to escape from perfection. Constantly, indeed on all occasions, the society is called upon to seek virtue as the crow flies" (RP, 475). The desire for excellence and achievement had to be balanced, Oakeshott thought, with the imperfections of real human beings.

Nevertheless, as wrongheaded as this kind of Pelagian striving might be, there is a still worse alternative, which Oakeshott designated as the pursuit of "barbaric affluence" (VLL, 99). The residents of Oakeshott's Babel are consumed with acquisition rather than moral or intellectual perfection, "ready to drop the bone [they] have for its reflection magnified in the mirror of the future" (RP, 414). In this critique of acquisitiveness Oakeshott followed Augustine quite explicitly, since both thought that it was the most fruitless way to live a life. Such "barbarism" promises only various versions of midlife crises.

RELIGION

An alternative to these unacceptable and irreligious ways of life is the approach that Oakeshott proposed in a provocative 1929 essay titled "Religion and the World." The essence of the religious life, here, is the cultivation of individual sensibility and insight, recognition of the fleetingness of life, and a radical embrace of the here and now. Worldliness, on the other hand, is the pursuit of career, security, and various ideals. The here and now of the religious person, however, is understood not as mere pleasure but as a kind of intense and purposeful living. *Ars longa, vita brevis* (art is long, life is short) goes the Latin translation of Hippocrates's famous aphorism. But for Oakeshott life *is* itself the art. When we are young, Oakeshott wrote, the most important goal is "to preserve, at all costs, our integrity of character, for we believe that men, and not the things they create, are permanent and lasting. The length of art does not dismay us, for we are not conscious of the briefness of life" (*RPML*, 34). Achievements here take a clear second place; they become not primary goals but rather the "secondary manifestation(s) of a lived life."[8] To live religiously, then, meant not to postpone satisfaction to a next life, nor "to keep unspotted from the world" (27). The religious person was instead oriented toward the present.

This is indeed an unusual approach to religion. There is no theology, no church, and no mention of belief. And so we cannot say it is particularly Christian. But in one sense it is perhaps not incompatible with Christianity. Viewed in a certain way, Christian faith means precisely the putting aside of one's anxieties for the future and engaging, with mindfulness, in the living of one's life. Something like this would seem to be *the* primary challenge of practical experience. In this sense, Oakeshott's idea of sublimating concerns about the future seems compatible with Christianity. Yet it is not clear that his view is coherent in the absence of religious faith or, more particularly, of a certain kind of hope. Oakeshott once designated mortality as "the central fact of life," and as such it makes it extraordinarily difficult to live in the present. The prudent person must always prepare for the future by investing, planning, and protecting what is already owned. But Christian faith, by contrast, promises more than merely worldly rewards, and in this respect it might assist in the attempt to relieve our anxieties. It might, indeed, be essential to living in the present, although Oakeshott himself did not say this.

With respect to the moral life, however, Oakeshott's ideas about religion seem to be at odds with Christianity as it is often understood. He disdained the idea that the models for virtuous conduct are limited, and so he was inclined to be indulgent of eccentricities, and even of the moral radical. He thought one of the most essential features of human experience is the creative and aesthetic aspect of human conduct, which admitted of no limitations. To approach religion as an ideology or as a set of moral rules, as is often done today, is "rationalism in religion." But how does one strictly draw the line between moral rules as ideology and the creeds and beliefs that seem essential to any kind of orthodox faith? Would an answer lie in some kind of theological speculation that might distinguish the essential from the nonessential, or the merely ideological from the true?

The answer to this is definitely no. Oakeshott would not have denied that a religious person might well be thoughtful. Indeed, living religiously seems to require that one come to an understanding about what is most valuable. And yet he clearly did not think that theologizing could somehow substitute for the kind of life he called religious. Oakeshott's distinction between theology and religion parallels a similar one he made between philosophy and the practical life.

As Oakeshott famously observed in *Experience and Its Modes*, philosophy is a "parasitic activity" that arises to examine the various arrests or modes of experience such as history, science, and practical life. It is explanatory, not instructive. In the same way, theology is philosophy turned to theorizing religion, and thus Oakeshott thought that theology, understood in this way, could not instruct the religious person in religious conduct. It could only attempt to explain the religious experience. "The two forms of sought-after satisfaction, philosophical and religious, differ by reason of the two different conceptions of the experience of dissatisfaction to which they respectively respond."[9] If religion offered a type of "wholeness" or completion to remedy the deficiencies of abstract morality, as he put it in his early writings, Oakeshott was clear that such a "felt" wholeness is categorically different from a theoretical understanding. Theologizing is as different from religious conduct as philosophizing is from other kinds of moral activity. Oakeshott remarked on this distinction in several places: "the language . . . is that of religion and not of theology" (*CPJ*, 48); "it is a study of modern theology rather than of modern religion" (80); "merely a confusion between religion and theology" (*EM*, 293); and so on. He returned to this also in *On Human Conduct*, where he observed that "a religion may evoke a reflective consideration of its postulates and a theology may emerge from this engagement; but, although a faith is an understanding, a theoretical understanding of a faith is not itself a faith" (*OHC*, 81).

Oakeshott's most ingenuous expression of this point surely comes from a formerly unpublished early work titled "An Essay on the Relations of Philosophy, Poetry, and Reality." There he set out the distinction between theology and religion by asserting that the intellect could know only "about" things and that truly to know God was something intellect alone could never achieve: "The idea of logic in one form or another is the basis of intellectual perception: but when we possess truth by a logical process it is as if we held in our hands a well-corded and sealed box enclosing precious things of which we have neither the sight nor the touch." We may, Oakeshott continued, "affirm that we possess them since we possess the box which contains them, but it is no possession worth the name. The truth is that the knowledge of the intellect is strictly limited to knowledge *about* the things it studies; it is wholly from the outside. As Spinoza says; 'Intellect, finite or infinite, in actuality, must comprehend the attributes of God and the modifications of God and nothing else.' God Himself, Reality is beyond its grasp or knowledge" (*WIH*, 101–2).

Although this passage comes from an early unpublished essay and thus must be approached with care, it expresses an idea that recurred throughout Oakeshott's career. He consistently identified the temptation to take refuge in theology rather than to engage in religious conduct. Perhaps because of its difficulty, theology is a kind of activity that *seems* to be religious and thus may be mistaken for religion itself. But this, Oakeshott thought, was exactly the problem of modern life: it consistently prioritized intellectual mastery and "system" over the discernment, judgment, and the true affection that may sometimes come from actually having an experience of something. How much easier it was, he once commented, to know all about a picture than actually to have cultivated a sensibility for it! But to substitute a sterile, academic knowledge for lived experience was to deny the poetic character of human life and, particularly, the poetic character of religion.

Thus a clear critique of contemporary religion emerges throughout Oakeshott's work—namely, either that it is rationalist in losing its original impetus and devolving into a moral ideology or that it tends to become excessively intellectual and systematic. We are left with the impression that religion has gone wrong in the same way as modern politics. People are motivated by the twin impulses of insecurity and pride—a sense that one is not good enough, on the one hand, and that one is capable of anything, on the other. In attempting to overcome these shortcomings we engage in Pelagian endeavors to change the world or seek to lose our sense of insecurity by becoming part of a movement or pursuing an ideal. At all events this is a view of the world in which individual human beings are destined for unhappiness, because they can never live in the present but must always look forward to some future satisfaction. But is there any alternative to living in a religiously rationalist world? Oakeshott was too subtle a thinker to recommend an easy way out of this dilemma; indeed, he rejected outright the idea that the moral and intellectual problems he recognized could be "solved" by applying some sort of technique. If there were any solution at all, Oakeshott thought, it would have to emerge from the understandings of individual human beings. And so he elaborated his own view of the world, and of the religious life, that remains available to anyone who wishes to see it.

PRACTICE

Oakeshott's characterization of the most satisfying human life does not lie on the surface of his writing. He was preeminently concerned to theorize the "practical mode" precisely as it is, since it encompasses a very great part of what most people think of as human experience. But practice is not the whole of experience, Oakeshott insisted; it is only one mode among others. And by appreciating the character and limits of the practical we begin to see how Oakeshott thought that certain nonpractical activities were of extraordinary value.

In *Experience and Its Modes* Oakeshott described modes as various well-defined ways of looking at the whole of experience. They are "homogeneous but abstract world[s] of ideas" (*EM*, 75). In the scientific mode, for instance, everything is as it appears to the scientist *sub specie quantitatis*, not as it is in the world of ordinary daily experience. Water is not water but H_2O; a breeze is not refreshing but amenable to measurement in terms of its height, duration, and speed. In the historical mode history is not some collection of facts but an independent world of ideas. It is "what the historian is *compelled* to think by the pattern of the [historical] evidence."[10] Practice is the most expansive of the modes, including not just everyday human interaction but politics, morality, and religion. Oakeshott's view of practice lies at the heart of his thought and is that against which all else is measured.

Practice is simply the realm of moral conduct—not just moral conduct in times of crisis (what ought we to do in a difficult situation?)—but moral conduct per se. It encompasses nearly all our daily activities, and the essential character of practice consists in the achievement of some desired change. Even the attempt to resist change is a practical activity, for to conserve and protect is still to concern ourselves with what ought to be.

Oakeshott saw clearly the limitations of practice. It offers tremendous possibilities, but it also tempts us toward inordinate worldliness. By worldliness Oakeshott meant the tendency to find one's true good in reputation, money, or material possessions, as opposed to making something of oneself. He would have liked the way A. G. Sertillanges put it in *The Intellectual Life*: "the most valuable thing of all is will, a deeply-rooted will; to will to be somebody, to achieve something; to be even now in desire that somebody, recognizable by his ideal. Everything else always settles itself."[11] The ideal, in this account, comes not prepackaged by politics or ideology but is a certain kind of self-chosen aim. It is the attempt to make something of oneself that is good or beautiful, to live an "artful" life.[12] Thus the accomplishments that may be pursued in the mode of practice range from the most mundane and necessary to the very highest, encompassing everything in between. Indeed, Oakeshott even placed religion in the practical mode, for he thought it offered a certain kind of completion. Religion was, for Oakeshott, "practical experience at its fullest." It was "the consummation of all attempts to change or maintain our practical existence" (*EM*, 294).

The drive to achieve something great or beautiful for its own sake—to possess, as Oakeshott put it in "Religion and the World," insight and sensibility—is, he thought, to live religiously. It matters little what others think. Like the truly just man in Plato's *Republic*, the religious man would choose such a life even if it offered no apparent reward. "It is only in the world's view that a man is better off for being known to be what he is; for religion it is enough to be it" (*RPML*, 37). The trick is to make something of oneself without at the same time making too much of oneself. In an essay on Hobbes, Oakeshott thus described an ideal person who

> would find greater shame in the meanness of settling for mere survival than in suffering the dishonour of being recognized a failure; a man whose disposition is to overcome fear not by reason (that is, by seeking a secure condition of external human circumstances) but by his own courage; a man not at all without imperfections and not deceived about himself, but who is proud enough to be spared the sorrow of his imperfections and the illusion of his achievements; not exactly a hero, too negligent for that, but perhaps with a touch of careless heroism about him; a man, in short, who (in Montaigne's phrase) "knows how to belong to himself," and who, if fortune turned out so, would feel no shame in the epitaph: *Par délicatesse / J'ai perdu ma vie.* (*RP*, 339)[13]

Oakeshott was careful to distinguish the pride that characterizes this moral personality from that which he found so abhorrent in the modern rationalist. Hobbes, he thought, recognized the twofold meaning of the word, and thus the kind of pride that he found admirable was a kind of justified and moderate self-love. It was not an overweening desire to control circumstances and other people but instead self-knowledge, self-respect, and magnanimity. It consisted in contentment with one's own want of greater perfection and, at the same time, in striving to be good and noble.

We can summarize this description of religion and practice, then, by observing that for Oakeshott a religious orientation meant a clear-sighted and candid assessment of the character of practice. Practical life is an unending series of efforts to change circumstances or to prevent those circumstances from changing. Religious conduct therefore requires a person prepared to confront both the limited character of practice—that nothing may ever be finally fixed or finished—and the possibilities it offers for a person who is full of neither pride (in the negative Augustinian sense) nor fear. There is sometimes in moral goodness, Oakeshott wrote, "a release from the deadliness of doing and a possibility of perfection, which intimates poetry" (*RP*, 538). This approach to human conduct offers opportunities for creative "self-enactment," which Oakeshott described as profoundly different from ordinary practical conduct. What are the differences, he asked, between normal moral conduct ("self-disclosure," to use his technical term) and this kind of exceptional conduct? The most important difference is that in self-enactment an agent "think[s] as he chooses to think" and enacts or reenacts himself "as he wishes to *be*." (*OHC*, 72). In this kind of conduct, doing is "delivered, at least in part, from the deadliness of doing, a deliverance gracefully enjoyed in the quiet of a religious faith" (74). It is an "undivided and indivisible life" (*CPJ*, 81).

POETRY

There is, however, an entirely different aspect of Oakeshott's thought about religion that arose not out of the mode of practice but rather from his appreciation for the ultimately nonpractical or "useless" engagement in poetic experience. As he observed in an essay about liberal learning, quoting Paul Valery, "Tout ce qui fait le prix de la vie est curieusement inutile" (Everything that makes up the value of life is curiously useless) (*VLL*, 28). And so he found poetry to be a useless art—quite completely and utterly useless, but vital. By poetry Oakeshott meant not only written verse but all kinds of art, including music, literature, and painting. Throughout the whole of his corpus one finds snippets of poetry from Shelley, Wordsworth, and Coleridge, and continually he makes reference to poetic images, as in the evocative final lines from his essay "The Voice of Poetry in the Conversation of Mankind." Poetry, Oakeshott wrote there, echoing William Blake, "is a sort of truancy, a dream within the dream of life, a wildflower planted among our wheat" (*RP*, 541).

But poetry was more than just artistic experience, though Oakeshott did not often say so explicitly. He understood well that to overstate a point was to kill it, and the beauty of the poetic vision Oakeshott provided was that it was never overdone. He proceeded by way of suggestion and "intimation," to use one of his favorite words. Being capable of appreciating the poetic meant a particular orientation toward the world, particularly toward what might, if we are fortunate, lead away from the practical. This was not so much a will to overcome the world as a disposition to value "things in themselves" rather than constantly think about utility and profit—or, indeed, about oneself at all. And so poetic appreciation could be transferred from art to friendship. Poetry could be found in love and in conversation. It could really be found anywhere. The images in children's literature provide many such examples of this kind of "purposeless" and poetic activity. Animals use language, cars and trucks take on outrageous and funny shapes, and grasshoppers engage in Augustinian pilgrimages that demonstrate to adult readers the value of contemplation and delight.

What is it about poetry that gives it its value, in Oakeshott's view? It is precisely that it does not conform to practical strictures, that it offers a kind of "escape" from the tyranny of practice. In his earlier writings this escape appears, as I have already noted, as a kind of self-mastery, a proper orientation toward the world, an astute assessment of oneself. It is very much a product of the will. To live religiously is to ignore the world's values, to cultivate a taste for beauty and excellence, to abandon the timid and commonplace concerns of the world. But as Oakeshott grew older, and seemingly also more reticent to talk about religion, he turned more and more toward the poetic as a way of expressing that desire to escape or transcend the practical. Indeed, his final statement about religion in *On Human Conduct* is itself thoroughly poetic, evocative, and even elegiac. Once again he spoke only in terms of intimations; there was no certainty. In religion the "fugitive adventures of human conduct," he wrote, "are graced with an intimation of immortality: the sharpness of death and the deadliness of doing overcome, and the transitory sweetness of a mortal affection, the tumult of a grief and the passing beauty of a May morning recognized neither as merely evanescent adventures nor as emblems of better things to come, but as *aventures*, themselves encounters with eternity" (*OHC*, 85).[14] Ordinary events of human experience may thus be transformed by viewing them as a kind of poetry, even if they remain liable to lapsing back into the ordinary demands of practical life. At certain moments, in poetry, "a self which desires and suffers, which knows and contrives, is superseded by a self which *contemplates*, and every backward glance is an infidelity at once difficult to avoid and fatal in its consequences" (*RP*, 535; italics added).

RATIONALISM

Throughout this essay I have argued that Oakeshott diagnosed the central problems of modernity as originating in a fundamentally religious mistake.

Having lost the original experience of Christian faith, those who would be religious tend either toward moral ideologies and perfectionism or toward a kind of hyperintellectualism. They are less inclined to accept the limitations of the human condition, enjoying the ordinary and looking for the poetic, than to seek some kind of permanent release from contingency. This diagnosis may begin to sound quite familiar to readers of Oakeshott's more explicitly political essays, such as "Rationalism in Politics," where he made a similar criticism of modern politics.

Oakeshott thought that a particularly virulent strain of gnosticism or, to use his term, *rationalism*, had emerged over the past several hundred years in the West. In particular the elites, as we might call them today, had begun to think that they possessed a kind of knowledge that would enable near-total control over the workings of politics. Oakeshott saw evidence of this not only in the totalitarian states of the twentieth century, but also in Europe and the United States as the political realm grew ever larger. But if the elites acted like overbearing parents, proudly confident in their knowledge of what was best for everyone, many others appeared to be overgrown adolescents. These "anti-individuals," as Oakeshott designated them, actually resented or feared the burden of self-determination. They preferred to ally themselves with some great project or cause, fearful that life without devotion to an ideal would prove insignificant and futile. And therefore the only political system that could account for this rejection of agency was an overbearing government that made decisions for them. Elites, then, fell into hyperintellectualism and prideful overestimation. The anti-individuals searched for an ideology that would solve their problems for them and alleviate the anxiety of the human condition. Both these views of politics were, in Oakeshott's view, pathological.

Although it would be too simple to say that Oakeshott was primarily a critic of modernity—he also thought our modern situation offered much to celebrate—we can now see how he fits into the larger mid-twentieth-century literature of critique. Like his philosophical contemporaries Eric Voegelin, Leo Strauss, and Hannah Arendt, he saw that something had gone wrong in modern politics. And although their diagnoses of what it was were different, each sensed that a philosophical mistake had been made along the road to modernity. Voegelin was explicit about the spiritual nature of this mistake; Strauss and Arendt were not. Where was Oakeshott? He was quite well aware of a certain kind of spiritual crisis, although unwilling to speak too explicitly about it. He did not conceive of himself as possessing a prophetic voice, like Voegelin. Yet Oakeshott consistently conveyed a sense that human beings ought to reject "worldliness," even as he also knew that nobody could escape the conditions of practical life. The primary task is to come to terms with this human predicament, facing it squarely and even embracing it. One cannot help but recall the quote from Augustine that Oakeshott included in his final discussion of religion in *On Human Conduct*: "Whoever thinks that in this mortal life one may so disperse the mists of the imagination as to possess the unclouded light of unchangeable truth understands neither what he seeks nor who he is that seeks it."[15] Augustine had it right once again.

One final comment is in order here. Some will want to know just what ought to be made of Oakeshott and his relationship to Christianity. Was he or was he not a Christian? He probably was not, in any ordinary sense. He was certainly no religious traditionalist. Was he then an atheist, as some have suggested, or an agnostic?[16] All these questions are difficult to answer, because he did not often speak explicitly about these subjects, and never in print. It has always been my sense that Oakeshott bewilders many, though not all, orthodox believers, who tend to view him with suspicion, because he falls into no tidy categories. As we have seen, he was not much drawn to theology, nor did he enter into the great debates over reason and revelation that engaged Strauss and Voegelin.[17] And yet his work is suffused with religious insight. Without recognizing this we have failed to grasp the man as a whole. This religious insight is, I would argue, the "single passionate thought" that pervades all of his philosophy.

As I suggested earlier, evident in his work is a certain orientation toward both poetry and practice that seems to be essential for engaging in any kind of spiritual life at all. It is a disposition—always a disposition, not a "philosophy"—to favor beauty and poetry and the enchantment they are at times capable of bringing to human life. If Oakeshott was reticent to specify any transcendent origin for the contemplative experience, others are not. Compare Josef Pieper, who in his meditation on Plato's *Phaedrus* observed the propensity of beauty to remove us, temporarily, from our ordinary existence: "When we receive beauty in the proper way . . . we are referred to something that is not-already-present. Those who submit to the encounter with beauty in the requisite spirit do not see and partake of a fulfillment but a promise—which perhaps cannot be kept at all within the realm of this physical existence."

Oakeshott at times longed for this kind of escape from the prison of practice, even as he recognized that human beings must live out their lives within this mode. Pieper appreciated precisely the same conflict, recounting a vision of Socrates as follows: "On the one hand man is of such nature that he possesses himself in freedom and self-determination. . . . He can and must give shape to his own life on the basis of his insights." On the other hand, Pieper continued, this same man is "nonetheless so much involved in the Whole of reality that things can happen to him and he can be dislodged from his auton-omy. . . . It may take such a form that in the very loss of his self-possession another fulfillment is granted to him, one attainable in no other way."[18]

All of this is perhaps a bit mystical in the context of the supremely level-headed Oakeshott. He did, after all, spend most of his scholarly life writing about the earthly pursuit of politics and disabusing the worst kinds of politi-cal dreamers of their illusions. Oakeshott called politics a necessary evil, "a second rate form of human activity, neither an art nor a science, at once cor-rupting to the soul and fatiguing to the mind, the activity either of those who cannot live without the illusion of affairs or those so fearful of being ruled by others that they will pay away their lives to prevent it."[19] And yet sometimes those most carefully attuned to the practical are the ones who also recognize the virtue of an entirely different sort of experience, whether that experience manifests itself as philosophy or poetry. As Oakeshott himself put it, "Having an ear ready for the voice of poetry is to be disposed to choose delight rather than pleasure or virtue or knowledge, a disposition which will reflect itself in practical life in an affection for its intimations of poetry" (RP, 540). There was, for Oakeshott, no permanent escape from practice, nor would he have desired a permanent escape. Nevertheless, a temporary emancipation from the practical was something to be seized and enjoyed, and he thought a dis-position to appreciate the poetic was well worth cultivating. It is a disposition that, seen in a certain light, might properly be called religious.

Oh, to love what is lovely, and will not last!
What a task
to ask
of anything, or anyone,
yet it is ours,
and not by the century or the year, but by the hours.[20]

NOTES

1. Arnold Lobel, *Grasshopper on the Road* (New York: HarperCollins, 1978).

2. A prime example of this in the present day is the Millennium Development Goals of the United Nations: "To meet the challenge of addressing global poverty in all its dimensions, world leaders in 2000 created the 'Millennium Development Goals' (MDGs), a set of eight quantifiable targets *designed to cut poverty in half by the year 2015*" (italics added). Episcopal Church's Office of Government Relations, "On the Issue: The Millennium Development Goals (MDGs)," Episcopal News Service, January 2006, http://archive.episcopalchurch.org/3577_71627_ENG_HTM.htm.

3. Denis de Rougement, "Passion and the Origin of Hitlerism," in *The Crisis of Modern Times*, ed. A. James McAdams (Notre Dame: University of Notre Dame Press, 2007), 77.

4. Timothy Fuller, "On the Concept of Change in Practical Conduct" (unpublished conference paper, presented at the 2009 American Political Science Association meeting, Toronto, Canada, September 3–6).

5. Johann Wolfgang von Goethe, *Faust*, trans. Walter Kaufmann (New York: Anchor Books, 1990), 106.

6. Ian Tregenza, *Michael Oakeshott on Hobbes: A Study in the Renewal of Philosophical Ideas* (Exeter: Imprint Academic, 2003), 147

7. De Rougement, "Passion," 77.

8. Timothy Fuller, "Editor's Introduction," in *RPML*, 3.

9. Ibid., 19.

10. Terry Nardin, *The Philosophy of Michael Oakeshott* (University Park: Penn State University Press, 2001), 149.

11. A. G. Sertillanges, *The Intellectual Life: Its Spirit, Conditions, Methods* (Washington, D.C.: Catholic University Press, 1987), 10.

12. There are clear echoes of Walter Pater here. As a young man, Oakeshott read Pater's work extensively.

13. "Through *délicatesse* I lost my life." The precise meaning of *délicatesse* is quite difficult to render in English.

14. Clearly Oakeshott is also evoking Wordsworth here in his use of the phrase "intimation of immortality."

15. The quote is from Augustine's *The Harmony of the Gospels*. Philip Schaf, ed., *St. Augustin on Sermon on the Mount: Harmony of the Gospels and Homilies on the Gospels* (Whitefish, Mont.: Kessinger, 2004), 235.

16. Mark Le Fanu, "Cowling and the English Intelligentsia," review of *Religion and Public Doctrine in Modern England*, by Maurice Cowling, *Cambridge Quarterly* 17, no. 1 (1988): 86. Le Fanu claims that Oakeshott was "probably an atheist."

17. See *Faith and Political Philosophy: The Correspondence Between Leo Strauss and Eric Voegelin*, trans. and ed. Peter Emberley and Barry Cooper (Columbia: University of Missouri Press, 2003).

18. Josef Pieper, *Enthusiasm and Divine Madness* (South Bend, Ind.: St. Augustine's Press, 1965), 85, 51.

19. Tregenza, *Michael Oakeshott on Hobbes*, 129.

20. Mary Oliver, *Why I Wake Early* (Boston: Beacon Press, 2004), 34.

7

WHATEVER IT TURNS OUT TO BE:
OAKESHOTT ON AESTHETIC EXPERIENCE

Corey Abel

Orbaneja, a fictional painter from a real town, is criticized by Don Quixote for painting so badly that he produces only "whatever emerges," so that he must append a sign to his work. He paints a cockerel "so unlike a real cockerel that he had to write in capital letters by its side: 'This is a cockerel.'" Cervantes uses the tale twice in the second part of *Don Quixote*, in which our hero confronts a literary representation of himself published almost simultaneously with his own adventures. Its representational accuracy concerns him, as does the disturbing possibility that his own "history" could be like Orbaneja's painting, "needing a commentary to make it intelligible."[1]

In "The Voice of Poetry in the Conversation of Mankind" (1959), Oakeshott uses Orbaneja to introduce beauty, friendship, and the "delightful insanity" of childhood. In *Don Quixote*, the tale of Orbaneja introduces a discussion of the relation between poetry and history. When Oakeshott's discussion turns to poetry in "The Voice of Poetry," the first footnote in the section cites passages in Aristotle's *Poetics*, differentiating poetry from "medicine or natural science" and from "history."[2] Orbaneja, the painter Oakeshott says all poets are like, allusively introduces us to Oakeshott's themes—creativity and imitation, signs, beauty, love and friendship, childhood, Aristotle, the relation of poetry, science, and history.

Commentators agree that "The Voice of Poetry" is important but disagree on whether Oakeshott wrote a theory of aesthetics. Most think "The Voice of Poetry" establishes poetry's distinction from practice, as it does, forcefully.[3] But in his remarks on childhood, friendship, and love, Oakeshott seems to rejoin poetry and practice. He also seems, in *On Human Conduct*, to rejoin poetry and practice in claiming that a religion's dignity resides, in part, in the "poetic quality" of its images.[4]

There are some problems with this approach. First, the remarks in *Experience and Its Modes* about art and practice might not be the only foolish sentences. Second, most assume history is a voice, but in "The Voice of Poetry," Oakeshott does not discuss history as a "voice." This needs to be explained. Third, some deny that Oakeshott intended to contribute an aesthetic theory.[5] Others call his effort "unsatisfactory."[6] It would be strange for Oakeshott to publish a lengthy essay as a book, titled as it is, if it was not on poetry. A count of pages, references, footnotes, and points made shows it to be undoubtedly about art. Those who find Oakeshott's aesthetics unsatisfying criticize him for not doing what he never tried to do.

The first and third problems are obviously related. Any "retractions" would have to relate to his aims in the essay. But the place of history is crucial. History's quality as storytelling, its grounding on invention, and its abstract relationship to the past make it seem akin to poetry.

Throughout the twentieth century there has been sustained interest in narrative, myth, and poetry on the part of thinkers such as Heidegger, Gadamer, and Ricoeur, who were trying to understand meaning and truth in a way that might preserve humane values and challenge science's dominance.[7] The resultant critique of rationalism is quite different than Oakeshott's. They insist that the one authentic voice of human experience is a blend of history, practice, and poetry. With the narrativists Oakeshott has what has been called a "hermeneutic" stance against scientism.[8] Against the narrativists Oakeshott defends the integrity of science as a universal system of knowledge and of history as a disinterested inquiry.[9]

Aesthetic theories often seek criteria for good art. The tendency is to blend empirical description, psychological observation, and ethical counseling. But Oakeshott never tried to tell scientists or historians how to proceed. In aesthetics he is not trying to dictate norms, analyze the participants' psychology, or describe the appearances but—as elsewhere—indicate the postulates of the experience.[10] This is what he means by saying "neither the poet nor the critic of poetry will find very much to his purpose in what I have to say" (*RP*, 495). While avoiding legislating, he believed philosophy could expose false views, such as the view that science is constituted in a method of examining the real world. In aesthetics he disposes of "false beliefs" and expresses certainty that these beliefs must fail if his theory has merit (521). Why would a theory about something other than aesthetics go to such pains to tell people they are wrong about aesthetics?

"The Voice of Poetry" is primarily on aesthetics. The other aims—to reposition the modes, outline an idea of civilized human intercourse, and support a theory of liberal education—have a place in relation to this.[11] If Oakeshott's aesthetics is "ambiguous," or his attack on moralistic readings of art "implausible," then the rest of Oakeshott's hopes are undercut.[12] I focus here on "The Voice of Poetry," the deepest expression of Oakeshott's ideas on art.[13]

Oakeshott alludes to Orbaneja three times in "The Voice of Poetry." The first allusion relates to beauty, the traditional concern of aesthetics. Oakeshott says, "Sequences, patterns, correspondences may give delight when they answer expectations, but only when they are poetic expectations. . . . There is no 'true,' or 'proper,' or 'necessary' order or concretion of images to which approximation is being sought" (RP, 527). Instead, Oakeshott says, all poets are like Orbaneja, creating "whatever it turns out to be."[14] "Consequently, 'beauty' . . . is not a word like 'truth'; it behaves in a different manner." *Because* there is no necessary order, beauty cannot operate like truth. Judgments of truth determine logical relationships between signified identities. There is no signification in art: therefore no truth. Traditional aesthetic concerns about order, symmetry, and completeness are sublimated in a flourish of modern creativity. Beauty, if it means anything, must honor the rights of subjectivity. Order has become ironical.

Oakeshott's aesthetics is grounded in claims about the modality and abstraction of human experience. "The Voice of Poetry" is consistent with *Experience and Its Modes* but transforms its language. The essay is puzzling. Why does Oakeshott, while seeming to repudiate Plato's theory of contemplation, characterize all human activity as image making? Why does he tackle contemplation, if he is rescinding his "absolute idealism"? Why does Oakeshott, so attuned to tradition and history, make a seemingly timeless form of experience central to his defense of civilization? Why does he neglect history and demur comparing history to poetry (and to practice and science)?

In "The Voice of Poetry," Oakeshott denies that all experience is in one mode and insists that "activity is always a specific mode of activity," that "an image . . . belongs to a world or field of images," and that "imagining . . . is not a condition of thought; in one of its modes, it is thought" (RP, 496–97; cf. EM, 9). He also insists that the "real world" consists of "selves" and "not-selves," which "generate one another" (RP, 495). The self "appears as activity," and this activity "is primordial; there is nothing antecedent to it."[15] In all this he remains consistent with his early views. Making a change of terms, Oakeshott says he "shall call this activity imagining" (496).[16]

Oakeshott creates some confusion about the immediacy of contemplation. In "The Activity of Being an Historian," he says that contemplation occurs when whatever immediately appears is accepted for its own sake and not as evidence for something not present (RP, 157, 164). Oakeshott makes clear in

"The Voice of Poetry" that poetic images are not "immediate."[17] He says they are not facts, causes, effects, or implications (510). But this does not establish their immediacy. Oakeshott says, "every mode of imagining is activity in partnership with images of a specific character" (509, 514); in poetry, images "partner" the "contemplating self" (510, 513). Partnership implies mediation.

There may be a state akin to lethargy in which "what appears will be a mere sequence of images, . . . each entertained for its moment of delight but none held or explored" (*RP*, 513). This is as close to immediacy as Oakeshott gets, but he rejects immediacy by calling this "the nadir of contemplation, *from which the contemplative self rises* when one image . . . becomes the focus of attention and the *nucleus of an activity* in which it is allowed to proliferate, to call up other images and be joined with them and to take its place in a more extended and complex composition" (513; italics added). To have joining, complexity, extension, and proliferation of images in an ongoing activity, to "hold" and "explore" images, must involve mediation.

Another seeming departure from *Experience and Its Modes* is the claim that "properly speaking, 'truth' concerns propositions" (*RP*, 521). In 1933 he asserted, "[thinking or] judgment and explicit, conscious inference are not identical" (*EM*, 24). But "The Voice of Poetry" does not contradict the earlier claim: he is not saying thought is propositional, only that truth is propositional. He is expanding his exploration of the nonpropositional nature of thought.[18] He apparently narrows the scope of coherence within practice, science, and history. I say *apparently* because the modes are easily understood within a propositional context, insofar as they are inquiries and make objective claims about the world. To insist on thought's nonpropositional character seems unnecessary in *Experience and Its Modes*, since aesthetic experience has *not* been firmly set off from practice. In other words, to the extent that he is arguing that "experience, [as] Plato says, is dialectic; the true form of experience is argument" (37), the earlier book seems compatible with a claim that "thought" is, indeed, propositional. But that is not what he meant. So that line on dialectic may be another "foolish sentence."[19]

Art, however, is where the nonpropositional character of thought (or imagining) makes sense—but perhaps also practical experience. We note Oakeshott's hedge: "Practical statements *may* constitute propositions, and scientific and historical statements *always* do so, [but] poetic images are never of this character" (*RP*, 522). These claims about statement making and image making are at the heart of Oakeshott's view of experience and aesthetics.

Oakeshott argues that practical activity, like all others, is "a manner of imagining" and consists in "making and moving among images" (*RP*, 497). But in practice, mainly constituted in actions, "we also speak words" (503). He notes that the "language in which the business of practical life is conducted is a symbolic language." So, it is a mistake to think that practical speech is making images or that practical words are images. "Speaking here is expressing or conveying images, and is *not itself image-making*" (503; italics added).

Practical speech violates the general description of activity as image making (but still falls within "moving among" images). The practical self is semimute, able to exchange coins of fixed value but not to make any verbal images. Within a fixed semantic field, the practical self tries (as it did in 1933) to change the world through action, in terms of understood goods. If practical agents make any images, it must be in the domain of action; deeds, not words, are the practical agent's true language.

Science, like practice, is a manner of imagining. Here, Oakeshott writes of familiar images, such as "sound" being replaced by "the concept of undulations in the air" (*RP*, 505). Concepts replace images? Not exactly. "We are introduced to images which have no counterparts in our familiar world, the concepts (for example) of velocity, inertia and of latent heat." Concepts are images. Oakeshott later calls these "conceptional images" (505) and "conceptual images" (506, 507). He goes on to argue that the language of science is "a more severely symbolic language even than that of practice," because it transforms words by refining their meaning, and, "when they can be refined no further, they give place not to gestures but to technical expressions, to signs and mathematical symbols" (508). But it would appear that science is capable of making images—by making concepts, which it expresses in a severely symbolic language.

In "The Activity of Being an Historian," Oakeshott distinguishes two basic responses to our untutored awareness of the inchoate goings-on we find ourselves immersed in: to enjoy what immediately appears or to see what appears as evidence for what does not appear (*RP*, 157–58). Poetry and play belong to the former; practice, science, and history to the latter.[20] This ordering of experience refigures the critique of abstraction in *Experience and Its Modes* and paves the way for the introduction of the theory of symbolic language in "The Voice of Poetry." The taking of what appears as evidence for what does not appear is the introduction of reference—it introduces a "not-here," which we must go in search of. It posits disunity and sets out to resolve that disunity through language, either verbal or mathematical: generalization, specific narrative, or moral imperative.

Science, Oakeshott says, is a "conversable voice" (*RP*, 508, 505).[21] Yet it is ultimately nonverbal. Any literal idea of the "conversation of mankind" as a verbal engagement must give way, along with the idea that conversation brings modes, or theory and practice, together. When Oakeshott discusses how "one mode of imagining may give place to and supersede another," it is entirely a matter of lacunae. It is only "diminished or interrupted activity in one mode" that "may generate an opportunity for the appearance of another" (516). How can a moral argument about lying to shield innocents from harm ever respond in its own verbal terms to an expression like $W = Fx$?

Regarding symbolism and images, "*All* activity (except symbolic utterance) is imagining" (*RP*, 503, 516). It follows that symbolic utterance is not imagining. If all human experience is the activity of imagining and moving among images, then symbolic utterance would seem barely to qualify as experience, to have an external and limited relation to images; the ability to convey or move among but not make them.

"What we call a 'thing' is merely a certain sort of image recognized as such because it behaves in a certain manner and responds to our questioning appropriately" (*RP*, 497). For example, "the word 'water' stands for a practical image" (514). The relation of words to things is that of words to images modally specified: for practice, thing (undefined liquid) and word-symbol ("water"); for science, thing (undefined liquid) and symbol (H_2O). The truth claims of the modal voices lie in their symbols, but—and this radicalizes the critique of modal abstraction—the reality of symbolic modes is fractured. They can never say what they think the truth is. They only manipulate symbols. Images are only ever referred to and never find actual expression in words (or other symbols). The supposedly underlying "things" that a realist would wish to speak of are irredeemably out of reach.[22]

When are words images (not the signs of images)? Oakeshott's poet is not stating anything, not asserting a truth. But poetic images are often made of words. What sorts of words are statements and what sorts symbols? Practical statements and scientific statements are symbolic. Poetic images are non-symbolic; they do not point beyond themselves to anything else. In not pointing to anything else, they attain a reality of their own, which is "the fictitious as such" (*RP*, 532; cf. 528).

Oakeshott's definition of poetry includes several key points: there is no "distinction between the image generated and the experience contemplated" (*RP*, 524–25); the poetic image is not a sign or symbol (512) and has no referent outside itself, "no antecedents or consequents"; it has neither characteristics of usefulness or uselessness, nor "products or effects," nor a "history" (510). The poetic image is an "individual" that has "the appearance of being both permanent and unique" (508–10). On this crucial point Oakeshott adds, the poetic image "is permanent merely because change and destruction are not potential in it; and it is unique because no other image can fill its place" (510). "Poetry appears when imagining is contemplative imagining," when images are not recognized as "'fact' or 'not fact,' nor as provoking moral approval or disapproval, nor as causes, effects, or means to ulterior ends." Most important, a poetic image delights.

Furthermore, poetic images "are made, remade, . . . played with . . . composed into larger patterns which are themselves only more complex images and not conclusions" (*RP*, 516–17). Nearly anything can be a source of delight if "the manner in which it is imagined is what [Oakeshott] has called 'contemplation.'" Thus, "any scene, shape, pattern, pose or movement, in the visible or audible world, any action, happening or event or concatenation of events, any habit or disposition exhibited in movement, speech, any thought or memory" may all be images of delight (517). Commentators ask how contemplation relates to moral life. Habits, events, and thoughts (among much else) can all be images of delight. *Of course* poetry resembles the "real world."

Oakeshott's examples of artworks are traditional, representational, with characters, actions, events: *Figaro, Romeo and Juliet*, King David. His sole example of a Dada-style aesthetic perception comes from "a loaf of bread in paint," which he gives as an example of an image with an "ambiguously practical character" (*RP*, 515). Duchamp, Dali, Picasso, Pollock, and the maestros of abstraction are all absent. Despite his overwhelmingly realistic examples, Oakeshott's aesthetics is antirealistic. This gives insight into Oakeshott's theorizing. The epistemology is antirealist, but this does not mean that artworks must be nonrealistic.

Oakeshott's first salvo against those who would confine aesthetics to the real world is to suggest what criticism would look like if art were so confined: we should in that case ask what David actually looked like, what was Hamlet's bedtime, and so forth. Critics say he is being shallow, but he says these sorts of inquiries are "misconceived" (*RP*, 519).

Misconceived questions are commonplace. Reviewing a Rothko exhibition, Simon Schama relates Rothko's work to his struggles as a Russian Jew ("a scar on his nose . . . put there by a Cossack whip"); highlights his "melancholic temperament"; discovers his social context ("never really an *American* painter"); claims that Rothko would "bite your head off" if you took a formalist approach to his work; and observes his emotions ("he felt European calamity viscerally").[23] Apparently, to understand artists we must consult their feelings, their beliefs about aesthetics, their biography, and their political context. The paintings are mere vessels for psychosocial and historical messages.

We may still question Oakeshott's separating poetry and morality. Saying that art elevates our sympathies only throws ambiguous terms at the problem.[24] Some Nazi officers reputedly enjoyed classical music. There is the derangement of Don Quixote and Emma Bovary, who take lessons from literature. There is the philistinism that informs us perfunctorily about "the real point of the story." More ominously, we have T. S. Eliot "in the dock."

Critics of Oakeshott's amoralism have the burden of explaining why we should allow people to attain delight in public from witnessing the foul deeds of incestuous patricides, why we should *not* banish the poets, whose works foment civil war. Corey clear-sightedly raises Platonic censorship.[25] Are we prepared to go beyond private self-censorship of the company we keep? Should we require *The Chronicles of Narnia* be read as Christian allegories? Perhaps it is not that art elevates our sensibilities, but only those with adequately trained sensibilities can appreciate art. An adulteress, a thief, or a strange god can be a thing of beauty.

Oakeshott stresses that images are more apt to command our aesthetic attention when they are framed: "A work of art is merely an image which is protected in an unusual degree from being read (that is, imagined) in an unpoetic manner, a protection it derives from its quality and from the circumstantial frame within which it appears." Such frames may be "a theatre, or a picture gallery, or a concert hall, or the covers of a book" (*RP*, 518, 518n15). What goes on in the frame?

Oakeshott applies his theory of symbolic utterance to all the arts: the "enemies of poetic imaging in music and in dancing are *symbolic sounds and movements*; the plastic arts emerge only when the *symbolism of shapes* is forgotten" (*RP*, 528–29; italics added). Realistic sculptures are nothing of the kind: "Donatello's David is not an 'imitation' King David as a boy; it is not even an imitation of a model: a sculptor's model is not a person, but a pose" (519). "Drama, is not 'acting.' . . . It is 'playing at acting'" (519n16). He applies his theory to the languages of literary criticism and poetic metaphor: "The so-called 'language of flowers'" as well as "imitation period architecture, character acting, or a good deal of pre-Raphaelite poetry" are without aesthetic merit and consist only in symbols (528, 528nn28, 29).

Since poetry is not about anything, titles are "never of any significance." It is not that titles are per se invalid, only titles that purport to tell us poems are statement-making utterances. Similarly, "the table of contents of a book of musical compositions often (and not inappropriately) consists of the opening bars of the compositions themselves" (*RP*, 526). Different arts may vary in the degree of aesthetic security of their images: "A musical image is more secure than a pictorial image" (518). Oakeshott's theory makes this clear since music is neither making statements about nor depicting the world.

Regarding relative aesthetic security, Oakeshott notes the interesting case of photography: "A photograph (if it purports to record an event) may 'lie,' but a poetic image can never 'lie' because it does not affirm anything" (*RP*, 519). The use of photography's clarity may put it outside the domain of art and in that of journalism or history, the domain of symbolic utterance.

Oakeshott's examples of poetic images make up whole and partial works: "a pose or a phrase of movement of Nijinski" (*RP*, 517) may be a poetic image. Poetic delight may take root in what is usually understood as a part of a work. Oakeshott stresses artworks as loci of delight, since they stand apart, framed; yet the work's boundaries are not final. The idea of form/content unity replaces the part/whole relationship. To say a perfect work is that to which nothing may be added or subtracted can mean only that a form and content so thoroughly interpenetrate one another as to render the distinction between them impossible to establish definitively.

Oakeshott comments on artists' activity: "The changes poets are apt to make in their work are not, strictly speaking, 'corrections.' . . . They are attempts to imagine more clearly and to delight more deeply" (*RP*, 525n24). This is not how poets describe themselves, but it follows from Oakeshott's premises. (The practice of exhibiting studies turns out to be more than merely satisfying our biographical curiosity.) Instead of describing how artists work, he offers a postulate of artistic agency. If artworks are neither fact nor not-fact, are not contained within the modal universes of practice or science, are not about anything but themselves, then artists are not expressing anything or trying correctly to render a mental picture.

The artist and the spectator in Oakeshott's account are described as doing the same thing. This is a departure from speaking of the artist as making something, and the audience enjoying, judging, or being moved, corrupted, or shocked by it. There is often a third term, the performer. If an "entrance of Rachel," or "Tom Wall's leer" may be objects of delight, then these too must be works. As works, these movements or gestures are not simply the implementations of a work by indifferent thespiological mechanics. Rehearsals are analogous to drafting, performances to finished works. The distinction between draft and work is one of degree.

Examining art, artist, and audience, Oakeshott identifies "false beliefs" about poetry. The first is that poetic images are "in some sense true, or representations of 'truth'" (*RP*, 521). Oakeshott's denial of art's representation of truth has relevance to each of the other modes.

The distinction between art and practice, which seems implausible, is crucial. Emma Bovary is not an utterance of desire; Emma's statements (at least some of them), however, are. A reader who falls in love with Emma is mad—not because she is unfaithful or silly, but because she exists only in the text. Such a reader's prospects are even worse than Pygmalion's: Aphrodite has learned the difference between art and life and answers no irrelevant prayers.

In respect to history, every historical work triggers a campaign to correct the record. This would be nonsensical but for the public's belief it is learning about history. A work such as Michael Frayn's *Copenhagen* tempts us to conflate history and fiction. The play ingeniously plays with characters who are dead but who gather to remember certain events. Superficially, history provides the form and content of the drama. Leaving aside the differences between remembering and criticizing survivals, we can see that Frayn has in a radical way affirmed the character's fictional status. We cannot think of the characters as real because we know they are dead. Frayn only sows confusion by saying, "the central event in the play is a real one."[26] The central event in the play is a fiction.

A small number of works, such as *Hapgood* and *Copenhagen*, seem to rest on science. A brief consideration shows the science to be no more than a conceit, which opens a space for aesthetic delight, because it is not truly scientific. Stoppard, with superb irony, tells us so when he has Kerner, a physicist, complain about spy novels: "I don't understand this mania for surprises. If the author knows, it's rude not to tell. In science this is understood."[27]

The second false belief is that poetry involves "seeing things as they really are." This is "a denial of the interdependence between the self and its images" or "a confused representation of the mistaken view that all experience is inquiry" (*RP*, 522). The error is the assertion that all utterance is symbolic. But the poet is not saying anything at all about "things." To inhabit a world of truth is to miss the voice of poetry: "When you know what things are really like you can make no poems" (523). And yet, says Oakeshott, there still can be poetry, even "after Auschwitz."

The third false belief is that poets are "expressing emotion." Referring to Keats's "Ode on Melancholy," Oakeshott says, "this poem could have been written by a man of sanguine temperament who never himself felt the touch of melancholy. . . . It is not designed to elicit melancholy in the reader . . . and it cannot be said to tell us what melancholy 'really is'" (*RP*, 526). This expressive error remains pervasive. One recent example is Sarah Kane's "Psychosis 4:48." Reviewers always mention Kane's depression. One asserts, "It is impossible not to feel the weight of the author's suicide behind the work."[28] Must the audience be informed of Kane's suicide as a condition of appreciating the play? (Must an audience of *Antigone* be informed of Sophocles's sanguinity?) If the author's depression is really expressed in the work (making it a suicide note), without being transmuted into something nonpractical, then it cannot be an object of delight. Oakeshott can admit there is emotion "in" art—what are *Anna Karenina* or "Crazed Girl" without emotion?—but not the artist's personal emotion expressed truly.[29]

The fourth false belief is that poetic images "have a special quality named 'beauty'" (*RP*, 521). Oakeshott says little about beauty in this essay. But rejecting the claim that there is some necessary order of images makes it either beside the point to discuss beauty or requires him to do so in some unusual way. This he does, with the vocabulary of contemplation and delight. Oakeshott's refusal to define beauty is an effort to immunize art from the "infection of symbolism" (528). Is there a positive account of beauty? Perhaps beauty is the actuality of the self-recognition of the creative self in its creativity.

Oakeshott's theory seems to be well suited to capture the nonrepresentational, nonnarrative forms of art. This seems to be his major point. Artists do not tell true stories or make accurate representations of reality. Yet he ignores all the "-isms": cubism, Dadaism, surrealism, and so on. His exemplary artworks are traditional dramas, novels, operas, and poems. Among the most obvious features of real life such works represent (aside from persons and actions) are time, events, and change.

What if the differentia of poetry is not so much its nonpracticality, but its timelessness, its enjoyment of what is present, its refusal to engage reality from the point of view of work, use, or causation? Why did Oakeshott, historiographer par excellence, come to believe there was a major form of experience that consists in suspending, ignoring, or overcoming our immersion in time and contingency?[30]

Oakeshott makes striking claims about the absence of time and history from poetic images and contemplation: change and destruction are not potential in poetic images; they have no past; their pastness is ignored in contemplation; the contemplative past is "specious" (*RP*, 164–65); practical space, time, and memory are not involved.

At least four elements of aesthetic experience involve questions of time and history: the artist, the spectator, the image, and (colloquially) past images. The artist and the spectator have awareness of past images. Images apparently refer to time—the tense of narration, emplotment, musical tempo, sunsets in paintings. "Holding" and "exploring" images, delight endures—the time we spend before the bust of Apollo (while it "changes our life").

To ask what it means that change is "not potential in" poetic images, is not to ask about the history of poetry or the history of morals, of which poetry may form a part (*RP*, 533n33). Since a delightful image is not put into a symbolic-discursive story, it is nonreferential. One way to approach the problem is to ask how we read, since many artworks are written.[31] Oakeshott's references to reading in "The Voice of Poetry" are mostly in the context of symbolism, of taking reality as evidence for what does not appear and interpreting it (517–18). In "The Activity of Being an Historian," reading means taking the present as evidence for what does not appear: "'The past' . . . is a certain way of reading 'the present'" (162).

What would reading in a poetic manner involve (cf. RP, 523)? We know that the world of symbolism, the world of reference, is also the world that introduces time: "what appears" is evidence for what has happened or what is going to happen (161). Reading appearances as evidence is the interpretive move in human consciousness that introduces temporal awareness.

If delighting is "not-reading" (even when actually reading), it must be an encounter with a timeless world. The narrator's clues give evidence for what has not yet appeared in the story, but this symbolic interpretation is contained within the text. We do not expect characters to step from the pages (it is a function of the boundlessness of delight that authors play with these expectations). In the "world of the text" there may be emplottment, narrative tense, and characters' memories, yet no potential for change in the work itself. The time sense of the text, while analogous to the time sense of the real world, is not assimilated to it or "interwoven," as Ricoeur insists they must be.[32]

Is the world of the text in fact timeless? One of the pillars of Oakeshott's idealism is "the interdependence between the self and its images." We appear to change. How can images interdependent on a changing self not themselves change? Oakeshott says change is not potential in a poetic image. Must we say that we change and merely circle round a changeless thing? That would be a brand of Platonism Oakeshott did not wish to defend.

If a poetic image says only itself, must it give always the same delight in the same way? Or can it acquire new meanings as the spectator changes? If it said something about reality, the way a proof of the area of a triangle says something, its saying would be fixed. But if it says only itself, can it be enjoyed repeatedly and differently? Or is there a different kind of fixity in the realm of the nonsymbolic? Perhaps, like tradition, poetic images remain the same while undergoing change, except tradition is "neither fixed nor finished," while artworks give delight in appearing permanent and unique.

Another approach is by way of memory, which Oakeshott says is tied to practice. There must be a modal analogue—aesthetic memory. What is our relationship to images we have already contemplated, if it is not a historical (or practical) relationship? We could compose a history of our aesthetic encounters, but we are not creating a historical narrative when we delight in our third reading of *Hamlet*.

Oakeshott says, in contemplation, the "pastness" of the image "is ignored," and a "contemplative past" is "specious" (*RP*, 164–65). Since the past itself is a reading of the present, to ignore the past can only mean to give presentness free rein to ignore the time-scheme we ourselves have given to experience. This does not change the fact that we recall *Hamlet* when we see *Rosencrantz and Guildenstern Are Dead*.

For practical memory the sense of time is inseparable from desire: longing means the time is too long. For history, time is chronology, past is a world that changes only in virtue of historians' criticism. For science, time is a variable in equations describing timeless patterns (*RP*, 157, 164).

Aesthetically suspending practical time and space (*RP*, 520, 525n23) must involve complex cognition. Oakeshott's point in saying contemplation makes no distinction between present and past is that delighting is not an awareness of time. Yet he cannot mean our awareness of *David*'s beauty obliterates our awareness of King David. In the loosening of images from their practical and historical contexts, there may be a forgetting or a misidentification: statues no longer relevant as objects of worship become eligible to give delight to those who either do not know or do not care about their practical-historical provenance. But we do not simply forget what we know about the past. It seems that we deliberately suspend knowingness and grant the imagination license to play in the world of the fictitious.

Is the suspension of knowingness, the deliberate overturning of historicity, also what artists are doing when they delight? Is there an analogy to aesthetic memory across extended periods? If spectators see Titian's *Venus* alluded to in Manet's *Olympia*, it may contribute to their delight—assuming it does not lead them into a reflection on history. The historical time, place, and context of the earlier artist is not what matters. If the work's allusion succeeds, it succeeds by contributing to delight (cf. *RP*, 540).

Artists are aware of what we call past images. In alluding to them they are not narrating a passage of change, or explaining the history of painting, much less painting's historicity. They are taking it into their own activity of delighting. For them, as for viewers, the combination of images contributes to delight. One artist described his sense of the past as "a perception, not only of the pastness of the past, but of its presence . . . a simultaneous existence . . . compos[ing] a simultaneous order."[33]

The experience of delighting must involve complex forms of temporal awareness. A historical awareness destroys delight, pushes us into a symbolic-explanatory world. Delight may involve no consciousness of the historical provenance of the object; ignorance may help us in delighting. Can delight also be coupled with a sophisticated awareness of historical provenance? If so, the structure of delight is the suspension of knowingness, the negation of historicity, the formation of a timeless moment in the stream of time.

Oakeshott's aesthetics are part of a serious effort to find (or preserve) a place for timeless experience, to deny historicity, while also rejecting structuralist and functionalist theories of human nature and society. To be sure, there is historicity (contingency) enough in Oakeshott's accounts of conduct and historical explanation. Though he defends the integrity of history as a mode of understanding, he also places it (modally) behind a firewall, so historicity cannot seep into all forms of experience, as in the school of Gadamer and Ricoeur, who insist, after Heidegger, that all forms of experience are essentially historical and we must recognize their historicity. Oakeshott's denial of the claims of history is strong enough that he says, "there is nothing that can be regarded *only* in [a historical manner]" (*RP*, 161). Certainly, he feels under no pressure to assimilate fiction and narrative.

Ricoeur's dialectic subtlety leads him into some strange gaffes: "One and the same book can thus be a book of history and a fine novel." He develops this idea at great length, but the crucial point is that he finds, in the similarity of narrative form, that "fiction is quasi-historical" and "history is quasi-fictive." "Is not every [fictive] narrative told as though it had taken place?" he asks, entirely missing the modal differences present within similar grammatical and semantic structures. The "as though" is everything.[34]

Like Gadamer and Heidegger, Ricoeur finds the "lifeworld" to be the final horizon of experience. Denying, for example, the separation of ethics from fiction, he says, "no neutrality is possible" in reading fiction.[35] But this fails to explain how we judge Iago to be bad while delighting in him and in the way Shakespeare's art discloses him. Delight in villainy, like delight in depression, is ethically problematic if we cannot separate poetry from practice. These remarks add force to and extend the observations of Luke O'Sullivan that Oakeshott "did not make 'narrativity' a postulate of historical understanding" and of Franco that Oakeshott does not identify philosophy with historical knowledge, though he makes it sensitive to context.[36]

Although Oakeshott emphasizes our historical embeddedness, he does not make historical consciousness the condition of all thinking. He is sensitive to context but hardly enslaved to it, finding evidence of "civil association" in Aristotle, Hobbes, and Hegel (*OHC*, 109). He even asserts that "there have always been poets . . . in the sense in which I have used the expression" (*RP*, 530), even though they have not always been recognized. How can he define aesthetics apart from the history of aesthetics? For Oakeshott what something has become reveals a logical structure that may be always there though circumstantially not always recognized; time and history have the secondary role of bringing about propitious circumstances that reveal an inner logic. We are what we learn to become, but we are in some decisive respects not historical creatures. Oakeshott even says, "Practical experience is most often in danger of perversion by the irrelevant intrusion of history" (*EM*, 316).

Oakeshott's epistemology makes an unusual claim about human finitude. It is not our "throwness" in time that matters so much as our predicament of being creatures who cannot experience anything—except in art—without creatively postulating, taking what appears as evidence for something not-present. Yet as soon as we do this we fall into symbolic-discursive worlds of interpretation. This is the limit of human existence: the tendency to lapse into saying. Creation began in the Word; we create only words.

An epigraph to "An Essay on the Relations of Philosophy, Poetry, and Reality" is from Pascal: "It is good to be wearied in the vain search after the Ethical Reality (*le vrai bien*), that we may stretch out our arms to the Redeemer."[37] This Oakeshott seems foolishly to have forgotten when making this overconfident Hegelian sneer: "The doctrine, then, that the real is what is independent of experience should be distinguished from the doctrine that the weakness and imperfection of our human faculties place a permanent barrier between knowledge and reality; but it is difficult to say which is the more ridiculous" (*EM*, 54). The latter view may be less than ridiculous after all.

In "The Study of Politics in a University" Oakeshott distinguishes between language and texts or literatures. Languages, he says, are paradigms of manners of thinking, are spoken, and allow us to say new things. Literatures, on the other hand, are concretions of what has been said in a language from time to time (*RP*, 192, 197–98). There is an analogy to reading in symbolic modes and making poetic utterances that "set going a chain of linguistic reverberations" (503). We are creatures whose experience is mediated through living languages but whose very use of them produces deathly abstraction.

So another foolish line may be, "Interpretation requires something to interpret, but when we speak of *it* our language slips under our feet, for there is never in experience an *it*, an original, distinguishable from the interpretation, and consequently there can be no interpretation" (*EM*, 31–32). This is true of experience in general, in the sense that form and content are always implicated in one another, even in modes. For example, scientific method implies a world conceived in terms that make such a method possible and fruitful. It turns out that only for poetry (and philosophy?) is it true to say "there is no interpretation." For every other mode, every symbolic discourse, experience is essentially interpretive.

This suggests another foolish line: "Instead of a gospel, the most philosophy can offer us (in respect of practical life) is an escape, perhaps the only complete escape open to us" (*EM*, 3). The folly would be to specify that there is only one escape, philosophy. "The Voice of Poetry" shows that there is at least one other escape, poetry.[38]

To escape symbolism and interpretation one needs a form of experience that unifies form and content. Poetry fits the bill. It also transcends, ignores, or denies temporality. Yet, as O'Sullivan notes, there are similarities between narrative arts and the worlds of practice and history. Despite noticing these similarities, Oakeshott "came to think history could not literally be written by employing literary genres, as distinct from style."[39]

To add yet another candidate of sentential folly: "The historian, in short, is like a novelist whose characters (for example) are presented in such detail and with such coherence that additional explanation of their actions is superfluous" (*EM*, 141). Oakeshott later wonders if the historian can satisfy Don Quixote's desire to be put into a story that needs no commentary to make it intelligible. He decides (decades before Ricoeur's pronouncements) that poetry is *not* like history, which deals with truth or fact. The line errantly suggests that history is nonsymbolic. The historian's stories, no matter how much like fiction from the point of view of their artistry, cannot be poetic in the sense of nonsymbolic. There is a necessary lacuna between historical words and historical realities.

It is often thought that "The Voice of Poetry" modifies Oakeshott's early view of the relation of art to practice. I have suggested that several sentences could be retracted. Yet instead of radically changing the core doctrines of 1933, they bring into focus the profound skepticism implicit in Oakeshott's modal idealism.

In *Experience and Its Modes*, practice was the attempt by individual agents to modify existence in terms of understood better conditions. A rigid line within practice separated fact and value. Oakeshott later considers this an overly prosaic characterization of practice but sees that practice cannot be the effort to change the world *and* be poetic. "The Activity of Being an Historian" (1958), "The Voice of Poetry" (1959), and "Work and Play" (1960?) reflect a new focus on "play." In "The Voice of Poetry," the irredeemably worklike character of practice is exaggerated (part 3) to emphasize its differentia. Whatever else practice is—we get an idea of that in Oakeshott's comments about love, friendship, and religion—it must ultimately be the effort to change the world for the better.

Giving playfulness its due and emphasizing timelessness suggest that Oakeshott is exploring something analogous to the life world, or Lebenswelt (terms he never used). At one point he laments the loss of "the poetic character of human conduct" (*RP*, 485). But practice and the Lebenswelt must not be identified.

Oakeshott's theory of modes is unusual, but especially so is making practice a mode. In 1933 the "abstractions of practical experience" included "morality and religion, good and evil, faith and freedom, body and mind, the practical self and its ambitions and desires" (*EM*, 310). In 1959 he still thought "there is nothing sacrosanct about practical enterprise, moral endeavour, or scientific inquiry that 'escape' from them is to be deplored" (*RP*, 535). Only when we accept the modality of practice can we see why fiction cannot be derived from it. Fiction is as real as any of the other modal dreams that compose the collective dream we call civilization.

All modes, practice included, are constructions atop a mysterious realm—we could call it the Welt des Spiels, or "play-world." Oakeshott's accounts of experience as imagining, activity, energy, and goings-on all suggest that this mysterious realm is being acknowledged as the realm out of which modal constellations of experience flow, "like games children play." Oakeshott's (unstated) critique of Lebenswelt theorists is that their account of experience is, in the end, quasi-practical (*RP*, 165; *OHC*, 62; *OH*, 20–25, 20n5, 23n8). They take the modal for the finally real. They end up destroying *theoria* in the bonfires of care.

We should be wary of anyone who speaks about timeless experience, even if only within modal dreams. We should become agitated when he says his work resuscitates any portion of the Platonic doctrine of theoria. Oakeshott rejects the notion of art as expressive or imitative. He appears completely to reject Plato, but his critique turns out to be reconstructive. He denies that art (or any human activity) is the copying of eternal models. Nonetheless, Oakeshott calls poetry (and all human activities) "image making," which sounds both craftlike and imitative.

The image, for Oakeshott, is not a copy of anything, yet it resembles real life. Its status as image suggests something detached from any ontological base. If all activity is imagining, and all modes are constituted in images, this only makes matters more profoundly mysterious. Only against this mysterious background can we make sense of Oakeshott's use of "image" and his claim that he presents "all that can, in the end, survive of the Platonic conception of *theoria*" (*RP*, 512). To sustain this oblique connection to Plato, he invokes "a concept of creative activity," citing work by Michael Foster. It would seem that the *what* (of which a poetic image is an image) is our own achieved self-understandings. In this very narrow sense, we might say art reveals the truth about the human condition, except it does so nonpropositionally, nonsymbolically; therefore it can never be expressed as "truth."[40]

Aristotle is not ignored in Oakeshott's appropriating raid on the philosophical past. Oakeshott cites passages of the *Poetics* where Aristotle explains that poetry is a manner of activity (*RP*, 509). In section (i) Aristotle defines poetry (drama) as a kind of "representation" and points out that a work of natural science or medicine in verse is not poetry and that (section [ix]) Herodotus in verse is still history. Aristotle, distinguishing the historian and poet, also says, "The difference is that the former relates things that have happened, the latter things that may happen."[41] The contrast concerns the factual and the possible. In this sense, Aristotle conceives imitation as creative. Poetry may imitate action but it does so by exhibiting what has not actually happened. The poet is a maker of plots, hence, not a mere copier of models.[42] We may see in this a distant intimation of Oakeshott's suggestions about the worlds of fact and fiction and about the strange relationship of fiction to history.

Oakeshott writes, a good story "is the expression of some unchanging human predicament" (*OH*, 179). This is possible only if his approach to finitude is as I have suggested. Poetry can, then, show the universal, or the concrete universal. It can be a form of theoria, though one that accounts for a Pascalian skepticism about *le vrai bien*. Humankind can make images that are not copies, and when their images attain a nonsymbolic self-sufficiency of meaning, they may find in them leisure, freedom "from care," *schole* (*RP*, 514). Poetry is the timeless moment in time, or perhaps the disclosure of the ephemerality of the category "Time."

Leisure reminds us of Oakeshott's desire to emancipate the conversation of humankind from the boredom into which it has fallen from being assimilated to practice. Oakeshott separated aesthetics from practice because the effort to change the world can never be fully playful, and practice's time-sense is structurally future oriented even if not (histrionically) *being-toward-death*.

Nonetheless, Oakeshott also says that several areas of practical life are akin to poetry. Instead of asking how they fit with poetry, we should revisit the symbolism of practical speech. May practical agents make verbal images? Oakeshott indicates several areas where practical language may develop its nonsymbolic potentialities.

Oakeshott says, in an oft-quoted line, "Everybody's young days are a dream, a delightful insanity, a miraculous confusion of poetry and practical activity"

(*RP*, 539). For children "everything is 'what it turns out to be.'" Crucially, Oakeshott stresses language:

> To speak is to *make images*. For, although we spend much of our early years learning the symbolic language of practical intercourse, . . . this is not the language with which we begin as children. Words in every-day use are not signs with fixed and invariable usages; they are poetic images. We speak an heroic language of our own invention, not merely because we are incompetent in our handling of symbols, but because we are moved not by the desire to communicate but by the delight of utterance. (539)

Before we learn the symbolism of practice, we are poetic image makers. Is there some realm of experience for children and maybe also for adults that is nonpractical without being anything else? This is Oakeshott's opening-up of a play-world, but it is not the same life world in which German woodsmen make their homes.[43]

In adulthood playfulness is attenuated, symbolism encroaches. But friends and lovers may ease the regrasping of delight. "The image in love and friendship . . . is, more than any other engagement in practical imagining, 'whatever it turns out to be'" (*RP*, 538, 417). Where else but childhood has practical language such poetic range? This is where "secret worlds" are built, like fictive worlds—except here, lasciviously or elegantly, with courage or abandon, we actually live in them. Here, our speech may turn from mere symbolism and approach poetry; it may "set going a chain of linguistic reverberations" (503). Here is flirting, waxing eloquent, standing beneath balconies. But there is an inescapable component of desire and aversion, of approval, perhaps shame.

Though children invent heroic languages, lovers write sonnets, and friends invent nonsymbolic discourses, none is truly poetic. "Poetry has nothing to teach us about how to live or what we ought to approve. Practical activity is an endless battle for noble or for squalid but always illusory ends. . . . Poetic activity has no part in this struggle and it has no power to control, to modify, or to terminate it" (*RP*, 540).

Poetry's lack of power over the world is a warning against the expectation that politics could be poetic. But in a footnote Oakeshott says that politics has, in modern times, been assimilated to practice. Furthermore, "in ancient Greece (particularly Athens) politics was understood as a 'poetic' activity in which speaking (not merely to persuade but to compose memorable verbal images) was preeminent" (*RP*, 493–94n2). In his political writings, there are hints of a poetic dimension to politics in the noninstrumentality of law and morality, in ritual forms, the purposelessness of civil association. But civil association, the politics of skepticism, self-enactment, and individualism are always paired with their opposites. They are ineluctably tied up with serious endeavor, enterprise, and achievement. Beyond politics, we find religion, the culmination of practice, the intimation of salvation from the "deadliness of doing."[44] Here, again, is a place of poetic irruption in the worklike realm of practice.

There are intimations of poetry in religious faith and even "moral goodness" (RP, 538). Oakeshott's comments on religion in "The Voice of Poetry" point out that religious art is symbolic (530–32). Is religion itself poetic though religious art is not? Is religious language image making, nonsymbolic? Salvation is often understood as the conquest of the fatality of conduct by faith, works, or grace—an achievement to end all achievements. "Sinners Repent!" is a sign. Nonetheless, in the parables of Jesus, the cryptic utterances of Confucian masters, the writings of mystics, there are, perhaps, hints of a language that remains a "delightful insanity." A language that allows "what appears" to be contemplated and enjoyed, that does not posit evidential disunities of time, of grammar, of logic. Such a language may reveal to us our true and present salvation. Of course, a religion that offered only timeless enjoyment would seem to have forgotten its raison d'être.

Taking religion, politics (in one of its modes), love, friendship, childhood, in short, all the playful and noninstrumental aspects of practical life, and adding the disinterested inquiries that pursue knowledge in their own way and for its own sake, we see that much human experience springs up from the Welt des Spiels. But poetry above all retains its playfulness. Other modes never escape the tyranny of consequentiality. Science and history properly understood are nonpractical, but like practice, they divide the world into fact and not-fact; present, past, future. They are symbolic. Poetry alone among the modes is playful and disinterested and refrains from making signs. Don Quixote did not wish to be put into a history; what he wished was to be a story, to transform his conduct into a work of art, needing no commentary to make it intelligible. The project is mad, though the motive pure. An image of our unchanging predicament sent across the ages, from a real town where lives a fictional painter, Orbaneja.

NOTES

1. Miguel de Cervantes, *The Ingenious Hidalgo Don Quixote de la Mancha*, trans. John Rutherford (New York: Penguin Books, 2001), 2:iii, 507. The gap between symbol and meaning vexes, not the intrusion of writing into painting: Don Quixote later identifies Orbaneja as a "painter or

writer—it comes to the same thing" (2:lxxi, 965). Don Quixote is inseparable from *Don Quixote*—it is the character's first and highest aspiration to be in a "story" (1:ii, 30).

2. Oakeshott rejects "universality" as poetry's differentia, apparently rejecting Aristotle. He replaces it not with particulars, but with "individuals," which are, for him, "concrete universals" (*RP*, 512).

3. Oakeshott called "The Voice of Poetry" "a belated retraction of a foolish sentence in *Experience and Its Modes*." This is widely understood as concerning art's relation to practice (*EM*, 257, 296). W. H. Greenleaf, *Oakeshott's Philosophical Politics* (London: Longmans, 1966), 30; Paul Franco, *Michael Oakeshott: An Introduction* (New Haven: Yale University Press, 2004), 126; Robert Grant, *Thinkers of Our Time: Oakeshott* (London: Claridge Press, 1991), 104; Martyn Thompson, "Intimations of Poetry in Practical Life," in *The Intellectual Legacy of Michael Oakeshott*, ed. Corey Abel and Timothy Fuller (Exeter: Imprint Academic, 2005), 281–82.

4. The seven-line sentence is more complex than this isolated phrase.

5. See Thompson, in Abel and Fuller, *Intellectual Legacy*, 281–92.

6. Robert Grant, "Oakeshott on the Nature and Place of Aesthetic Experience: A Critique," in Abel and Fuller, *Intellectual Legacy*, 303. Elizabeth Campbell Corey argues that Oakeshott's aim was not to write a comprehensive aesthetics, and to the extent he did, his effort is "odd and unsatisfying." *Michael Oakeshott on Religion, Aesthetics, and Politics* (Columbia: University of Missouri Press, 2006), 112, 114. She faults him for not giving a "description of art or artists," denying moral questions, and neglecting the poet's role in society. He did all that on purpose. These denials allow him to offer an aesthetic theory that is not a piece of psychology, "thick description," or sermonizing in masquerade.

7. See Paul Ricoeur, *Time and Narrative*, 3 vols. (Chicago: University of Chicago Press, 1984–88).

8. See Terry Nardin, *The Philosophy of Michael Oakeshott* (University Park: Penn State University Press, 2001).

9. See Oakeshott's remarks against Heidegger (*OH*, 20–25, 20n5, 23n8).

10. Oakeshott agrees with Plato that poets do not really know what they are doing; it is pointless to ask them about aesthetics.

11. Thompson stresses the nonaesthetic agenda but concedes critics have been led astray by bogus understandings of art. Abel and Fuller, *Intellectual Legacy*, 288.

12. Franco, *Michael Oakeshott*, 130–32; Grant, *Thinkers of Our Time*, 104–9; Grant, "Aesthetic Experience," 303.

13. Others have traced the development of Oakeshott's ideas on art. See Glenn Worthington, *Religious and Poetic Experience in the Thought of Michael Oakeshott* (Exeter: Imprint Academic, 2005); Corey, *Oakeshott on Religion*, 100–111; and Efraim Podoksik, "The Voice of Poetry in the Thought of Michael Oakeshott," *Journal of the History of Ideas* 63 (2002): 717–33.

14. Cf. T. S. Eliot on the "order" of *The Waste Land*. In his footnote to line 309 of *The Waste Land*, Eliot asserts, "The collocation of these two representatives of eastern and western asceticism [Augustine and the Buddha], as the culmination of this part of the poem, is not an accident." To explain why it is not accidental, I would turn to Eliot's comments in "Tradition and the Individual Talent" (1917) and "The Function of Criticism" (1923), both in *Selected Essays: 1917–1932* (New York: Harcourt Brace, 1932); and "Ulysses, Order, and Myth," quoted in Jane Mallinson, *T. S. Eliot's Interpretation of F. H. Bradley* (Dordrecht: Kluwer Academic Publishers, 2002), 66.

15. In part 2 of "The Voice of Poetry," where Oakeshott discusses the real world, he does not speak about language at all. His complaint about Plato's recourse to "wordless experience" is ironic (*RP*, 516n13).

16. There are other redescriptions. In "Rational Conduct" (1950; *RP*), experience is "energy" and in *OHC*, "goings-on."

17. Greenleaf finds it strange that Oakeshott's earlier emphasis on thought has been dropped. Despite Oakeshott's saying "imagining . . . is thought" (*RP*, 497), he suggests "poetry" is akin to Coleridge's "*unthinkingness*" (*Philosophical Politics*, 32).

18. "The Voice of Poetry" develops, in the vocabulary of "image–making" and "contemplation," the claim: "In its full character, thought is . . . the self-revelation of existence" (*EM*, 24); cf. Greenleaf on *Geist* (*Philosophical Politics*, 33).

19. To assert that argument is the character of experience misstates modality. In his 1920s notebooks Oakeshott translates "dialectic" as "conversation." To translate it as "argument" is a foolish mistake. A view that Oakeshott especially wants "to avoid" (as opposed to others' errors that he with relish exposes) is Plato's *theoria* understood as copying models: "to make an experience of this sort supreme seems to entail *a belief in the pre-eminence of inquiry*, and of the categories of "truth" and "reality," a belief which I would wish to avoid" (*RP*, 512; italics added). Note the similarity of that demurral to the line about dialectic.

20. "The Voice of Poetry" suggests three basic responses: *to use* (practice); *to understand* (science); *to enjoy* (poetry). To use and to understand would alike involve symbolizations.

21. Oakeshott also states that science is the "voice of argumentative discourse" (*RP*, 489).

22. Grant finds Oakeshott's mystical idealism unrealistic; see "Aesthetic Experience," 299–300.

23. Simon Schama, "Rothko's Revenge," *Financial Times*, April 24–25, 2010, Life and Arts, 10, http://www.ft.com/cms/s/2/6e96e136-4e63-11df-b48d-00144feab49a.html.

24. Franco, *Michael Oakeshott*, 130–32. Oakeshott says poetry can do this, citing Schiller (*RP*, 533, 534n35), but this is not its differentia; cf. Grant, *Oakeshott*, 107–8.

25. Corey, *Oakeshott on Religion*, 113.

26. Michael Frayn, postscript to *Copenhagen* (Garden City, N.Y.: Anchor Books, 2000).

27. *Copenhagen* plays with history and science. *Hapgood* is a spy drama. On *Hapgood*, see Corey Abel, "Stoppard's *Hapgood* and the Drama of Politics and Science," *Perspectives on Political Science* 35, no. 3 (2006): 143–48; and Tom Stoppard, *Hapgood* (London: Faber and Faber, 1988).

28. Alison Croggon, "Review: 4:48 Psychosis," *Theatre Notes*, August 2, 2007, http: http:// theatrenotes.blogspot.com/2007/08/review-448-psychosis.html.

29. Cf. T. S. Eliot, *The Sacred Wood and Major Early Essays* (Mineola, N.Y.: Dover, 1998), 30, 32.

30. Since there is "no *vita contemplativa*" (RP, 540, 541), any overcoming of our temporality would be transient.

31. Oakeshott's oeuvre is marked by terms suggesting speech rather than writing: voices, invocation, hearing, provocation, conversation, idioms, having an ear, utterance.

32. Ricoeur, *Time and Narrative* 1:79–82; 3:180.

33. Eliot, *Sacred Wood*, 28.

34. Ricoeur, *Time and Narrative*, 3:186, 190; 1:82.

35. Ibid., 1:59.

36. Luke O'Sullivan, *Oakeshott on History* (Exeter: Imprint Academic, 2003), 105; Franco, *Michael Oakeshott*, 78–79. Oakeshott's work is rife with denials of genealogy: *EM*, 39, 73, 149, 182.

37. Pascal, *Pensées*, 422, quoted in *WIH*, 67.

38. Any of the voices may be an escape from the others (*RP*, 535).

39. O'Sullivan, *Oakeshott on History*, 80; cf. 103, 105, 164, 178–81.

40. On theoria, cf. Wendell John Coats Jr., "Michael Oakeshott and the Poetic Character of Human Activity," in *Intellectual Legacy*, ed. Abel and Fuller, 309–11. There are other Platonic surfacings: Plato's desiring soul (*RP*, 536) and *Laws*, 672b (*RP*, 151).

41. Aristotle, *Poetics*, trans. Richard Janko (Indianapolis: Hackett, 1987), 1, 2, 12.

42. Ricoeur, *Time and Narrative*, vol. 1, pt. 1, chap. 2, sees a creative imitation in Aristotle.

43. On childhood as a time of delight and the primacy of poetic experience against Heidegger's pragmatism, see *OH*, 20–25, 20n5, 23n8.

44. On myth and saga, see *RP*, 166, 182, 530; *OH*, 179–80; and "Leviathan: A Myth" (*HCA*, 159–63).

8

Un Début dans la Vie Humaine:
MICHAEL OAKESHOTT ON EDUCATION

Paul Franco

Michael Oakeshott's writings on education form one of the most attractive aspects of his philosophy and have duly garnered considerable attention.[1] They evoke an ideal of liberal learning for its own sake, freed from the narrowing necessities of practical life and social purpose. This ideal is summed up in Oakeshott's famous image of the university as a "conversation" between the various modes of understanding that make up our civilization, a conversation that has no predetermined course or destination, an "unrehearsed intellectual adventure" (*VLL*, 39). Of this ideal, Noel Annan wrote, "It was the finest evocation of 'the idea of the university' since Newman; and more subtle and persuasive."[2] As I hope to show, however, Oakeshott's philosophy of education is not without its difficulties, and these difficulties largely mirror the ones that run through his philosophy as a whole. In its formalism, conceptual compartmentalization, and rigid separation of theory and practice, Oakeshott's philosophy of education does not adequately address the problems of specialization, intellectual fragmentation, and cultural isolation that currently afflict education, especially higher education, today.

I break up my analysis of Oakeshott's philosophy of education into three parts, based largely on the chronological development of his writings. In the first section, I take up his earliest writings on education: "The Universities" (1949) and "The Idea of a University" (1950). In the second section, I discuss a number of essays from the 1960s: "The Study of 'Politics' in a University" (1961), "Learning and Teaching" (1965), and "The Definition of a University" (1967). Finally, in the third section, I consider Oakeshott's later essays on education, whose limpidly abstract language echoes that of his late masterpiece *On Human Conduct*: "Education: the Engagement and Its Frustration" (1972) and "A Place of Learning" (1974). By proceeding in this way, I do not mean to suggest that Oakeshott's ideas on education change radically from the late 1940s to the mid-1970s. Nevertheless, there are subtle differences, and in each period certain themes and emphases come to the fore.

I

Oakeshott's earliest essays on education, "The Universities" and "The Idea of a University," come from the period of his early rationalism writings between 1947 and 1950. Like his early rationalism writings, these essays are animated by a deep hostility to plans, purposes, missions, principles, and ideals. Indeed, "The Idea of a University" begins with an admirable encapsulation of Oakeshott's entire critique of rationalism: "It is a favourite theory of mine that what people call 'ideals' and 'purposes' are never themselves the source of human activity; they are shorthand expressions for the real spring of conduct, which is a disposition to do certain things and a knowledge of how to do them" (VLL, 95). Delivered as a talk for the BBC, "The Idea of a University" is largely a distillation of the ideas that appeared the year before in the much more substantial essay "The Universities." This latter essay deserves careful attention because it reflects both Oakeshott's profound originality and some of the characteristic weaknesses of his philosophy of education.

The essay is notable in the first instance for its polemical ferocity. The target of Oakeshott's attack was a book titled *The Crisis in the University* by Sir Walter Moberly. Now largely forgotten, Moberly was a prominent academic administrator in England in the second quarter of the twentieth century, serving as the vice-chancellor of Manchester University from 1926 to 1934 and as the chair of the University Grants Committee from 1935 to 1949. Even more relevant, he was a member of a group of Christian intellectuals known as the "Moot," who met for periodic weekend discussions between 1938 and 1947. The two most influential members of the Moot were T. S. Eliot and Karl Mannheim, and the group's discussions largely revolved around issues of cultural leadership and education.[3] With respect to the latter, considerable concern was expressed about increasing specialization in academic disciplines and the lack of coordination in the university curriculum. Not surprisingly, this is a major theme in Moberly's book on the contemporary crisis of the university.

Before considering Oakeshott's polemic, it is important to have a handle on Moberly's argument as he himself presents it. Oakeshott succeeds in making this argument look ridiculous only by a fair amount of distortion and exaggeration, as Moberly's later reply to Oakeshott makes clear.[4] As the title of his book suggests, Moberly believes the modern university is in deep crisis, which consists chiefly in the university's inability to provide intellectual, moral, and spiritual guidance in a world increasingly under the sway of uncontrolled scientific, technological, and economic forces. The universities, he claims, "are not now discharging their former cultural task." Instead of providing moral and spiritual guidance, they merely mirror the chaos of the world around them. The specialization of academic disciplines and the fragmentation of the curriculum leave students without deep convictions or clear standards of value; as a result, they become prey to the simplifying slogans and faddish ideas—what Newman called the "parti-colored ingenuities"—in which our world abounds.[5]

What can be done to resolve this crisis? Though Moberly calls for some sort of integration and unification of the modern university to counteract its fragmentation and collapse into a chaos of specialisms, he is careful not to seek a degree of unity or coherence impractical for or inappropriate to modern life. He rejects both classical and Christian humanism as models of integration, and he criticizes another Christian writer's call for the teaching of a "unified conception of life" in the universities: "if by a unified philosophy of life is meant a coherent system, even remotely reminiscent of St. Thomas's *Summa*, it may be a legitimate long-term objective; but . . . it is an impossible goal of practical policy in the near future." Moberly's proposals for overcoming the disintegration of the modern university are for the most part quite modest. He suggests that the university should serve as an open forum where fundamental issues about the ends and meaning of life are raised and debated; he argues for opening the lines of communication between the different disciplines; and he asserts that, although no agreed-on philosophy of life is possible in current circumstances, there are certain academic and communal values that we can all agree on.[6]

Moberly's diagnosis of the crisis of the modern university is by no means eccentric; it certainly was not so in the 1940s.[7] At several points Moberly refers to José Ortega y Gasset's *Mission of the University*, the English translation of which appeared in 1944. Like Moberly, Ortega highlights the problem of academic specialization and seeks to restore the university to its role as a spiritual power. The mission of the university is "culture," understood as the "vital system of ideas" that provides unity and direction in the midst of the chaos and confusion of life. Indeed, Ortega goes so far as to say that he "would make a Faculty of Culture the nucleus of the university and of the whole higher learning."[8] Closer to home, F. R. Leavis made the same point in his 1943 collection *Education and the University*. He too points to the problem of specialization and argues that the university must serve as a "centre of coordination and consciousness" to "bring the special sciences and studies into significant relation" and "train a kind of central intelligence by or through which they can, somehow, be brought into relation."[9] The master thinker who stands behind Leavis and the whole diagnosis of our situation in terms of spiritual anarchy and the need for some sort of cultural unity and authority is, of course, Matthew Arnold.[10]

With this background, we may now turn to Oakeshott's critique of Moberly. He begins with what he calls the major premise of Moberly's argument, "the alleged critical character of the times in which we live." Though Oakeshott distorts the degree to which Moberly thinks our current crisis is the result of physical insecurity, he accurately portrays Moberly's diagnosis of our spiritual predicament as one in which our intellectual, moral, and spiritual resources have failed to keep pace with the extraordinary development of scientific, technological, and economic power: "we possess immense power but lack discrimination in its use." In a characteristic move, Oakeshott dismisses this diagnosis as hysterical crisis mongering of the sort that always precedes rationalistic reconstruction. Not only does the diagnosis exaggerate the moral and intellectual chaos of our own age, it also exaggerates the coherence and stability of previous ages (VLL, 108–10). Moberly sensibly responds that Oakeshott may be missing the big picture here: "No doubt the mental security of the Middle Ages can be exaggerated . . . [but] to assert that the medieval universities were chaotic in anything like the same sense and degree is surely quite implausible."[11]

More generally, Oakeshott finds Moberly's diagnosis of our situation to be "at once too alarmist and too optimistic." As he sees it, our situation "is far more desperate than Sir Walter thinks," and therefore there is no reason to be alarmed about what we cannot change; "a more profound diagnosis of our situation . . . would offer no place for the optimism that supposes a 'revolution' can be conducted that would 'save' us." In a remarkable passage, Oakeshott discloses the darkly pessimistic outlook that lies at the bottom of his resistance to radical reform:

> When what a man can get from the use and control of the natural world and his fellow men is the sole criterion of what he thinks he needs, there is no hope that the major part of mankind will find anything but good in this exploitation until it has been carried far enough to reveal its bitterness to the full. This . . . is not an argument for doing nothing, but it is a ground for not allowing ourselves to be comforted by the prospect, or even the possibility, of a revolution. The voyager in these waters is ill advised to weigh himself down with such heavy baggage; what he

needs are things that will float with him when he is shipwrecked. (*VLL*, 109–10)

Oakeshott next takes up what he calls the minor premise of Moberly's book, which concerns the relationship between the university and the world. He ascribes to Moberly the view that the university should reflect the world and take it as a model to conform to. As Moberly's response makes clear, he nowhere advocates such a view in his book.[12] What he does advocate is that the university should become more aware of "the needs of the outside world" and that it should develop a "strong sense of responsibility in regard to them."[13] Even this more modest statement of Moberly's understanding of the relationship between the university and the world would not likely satisfy Oakeshott, who takes a more Manichean view of the matter. He maintains that the conflict between the university and today's world under the sway of the "plausible ethics of productivity" is "absolute" (*VLL*, 110–14). For the university to adjust to or in any way get involved with this world of "power and utility, of exploitation, of social and individual egoism" is to risk total corruption: "It is a very powerful world; it is wealthy, interfering and well-meaning. But it is not remarkably self-critical; it is apt to mistake itself for the whole world, and with amiable carelessness it assumes that whatever does not contribute to its own purposes is somehow errant. A university needs to beware of the patronage of this world, or it will find that it has sold its birthright for a mess of pottage" (103).

Oakeshott reserves his most acerbic comments for Moberly's diagnosis of the chaotic and fragmentary character of the modern university. He ridicules Sir Walter's lament that the modern university lacks a "unified conception of life," a Weltanschauung, a coherent system reminiscent of Saint Thomas's *Summa*, even though Moberly himself is rather circumspect about the possibility of such an integration of knowledge in today's circumstances. But Sir Walter is merely a pretext here for a more general critique of the rationalist mentality as it applies itself to the problem of higher education. According to Oakeshott, Moberly's diagnosis reflects the more general belief that a university must be guided by a self-conscious purpose or ideology. Instead of recognizing that universities are the product of long-standing and immanently rational traditions, Moberly supposes that they would be better off if they were self-consciously designed or planned. Oakeshott is especially withering about Moberly's proposals for general courses that seek to integrate the fragmentary specialisms by raising fundamental questions about the meaning and purpose of life: "As for these 'burning questions,' I suspect they are the sort which give a faint flicker about midnight and have burnt themselves out by the next morning. By all means let them be discussed, but let us also be aware of their triviality" (*VLL*, 117–24).

In opposition to Moberly's diagnosis that the modern university has degenerated into a miscellaneous assortment of specialisms and is in need of a more integrated conception of knowledge and life, Oakeshott offers (for the first time) his image of the university as a "conversation." The specialized studies that make up the curriculum of a university are united, not in some overarching purpose or mission, but in a "conversation in which each study [has] a distinctive voice" (*VLL*, 126). Oakeshott elaborates on this idea of conversation in "The Idea of a University," explicitly counterposing it to the idea of "culture" that had played such a prominent role in English reflection on education from Arnold to Leavis and Eliot and finally to Moberly. Though the "world of learning may have the appearance of a fragmentary enterprise," he comments, it need not call upon a "sticky mess called 'culture'" to fill in the interstices between the various branches of knowledge:

> The world of learning needs no extraneous cement to hold it together; its parts move in a single magnetic field, and the need for go-betweens arises only when the current is gratuitously cut off. The pursuit of learning is not a race in which the competitors jockey for the best place, it is not even an argument or a symposium; it is a conversation. And the peculiar virtue of a university (as a place of many studies) is to exhibit it in this character, each study appearing as a voice whose tone is neither tyrannous nor plangent, but humble and conversable. A conversation does not need a chairman, it has no predetermined course, we do not ask what it is "for," and we do not judge its excellence by its conclusion; it has no conclusion, but is always put by for another day. Its integration is not superimposed but springs from the quality of the voices which speak, and its value lies in the relics it leaves behind in the minds of those who participate. (98)

Oakeshott's image of the university as a conversation among many different specialized studies is an appealing one and contains many echoes of Newman's famous evocation of the university in the nineteenth century.[14] But Newman ultimately had Catholicism to fall back on to provide the university with a sense of shared purpose and ethical and spiritual unity. This is the security that had disappeared by the time Arnold came along, leading him to seek an alternative source of intellectual and spiritual authority in the protean (what Oakeshott calls "sticky") conception of culture.[15] The world and the university that Oakeshott confronts in 1949 more closely resemble Arnold's anarchy than Newman's religiously secured order. Therefore, we need to interrogate his notion of conversation to see if it adequately addresses the problem of academic specialization and cultural fragmentation that Moberly, among many others, highlights.

Toward the end of his essay on "The Universities," Oakeshott returns once more to the issue of specialization, this time in a less polemical, more thoughtful manner. Though he believes that Moberly has exaggerated the problem, he nevertheless acknowledges that the disintegration of the world of knowledge into a set of miscellaneous specialisms "is something we suffer from at the present time and that it is destructive of the university we are considering." Still, we must not look for quick or simple remedies. The problem of integrating the world of modern knowledge is "one of the most difficult of the current problems of philosophy: a century of pretty intense thought has already been given to it without much result."[16] For this reason, "to expect a university to provide an integration of its curriculum is asking for dishonesty" (VLL, 131–32).

Nevertheless, Oakeshott believes that the university can do something to relieve the problem of fragmentation and disintegration in undergraduate education. First, it should carefully select the specialisms to be studied "so that there is a chance that each may be seen, even by the undergraduate, as a reflection of the whole." Second, the university should teach these specialisms in such a way that the general objects of education—making one's thought clear, attending to what passes before one, being able to converse with oneself—are also conveyed. "Every 'true' techné, profoundly studied," Oakeshott comments, "knows something of its own limits . . . because it has some insight into its own presuppositions." Such insight is far more valuable than the bogus "integration generated ab extra" called for by Moberly. "The world of knowledge never has been integrated by a Summa, and those who urge us to look for it in that direction are unreliable guides whose immoderate thirst has conjured up a mirage" (VLL, 132–34).

Whether this completely answers the problem of specialization and cultural fragmentation raised by Moberly—and Arnold, Leavis, Eliot, and Ortega before him—is a question that will continue to occupy us as we go on to consider Oakeshott's later educational writings. Before leaving his earlier writings behind, however, there are two further aspects of his discussion of the university that need to be mentioned. First, there is the beautiful passage—one of the most beautiful ever written about liberal education—in which Oakeshott evokes what he calls the "great and characteristic gift of the university . . . the gift of an interval." Here, poetically, he makes what may be his most convincing case against the ethical and cultural urgency expressed by the writers listed previously:

> The great and characteristic gift of the university was the gift of the interval. Here was an opportunity to put aside the hot allegiances of youth without the necessity of acquiring new loyalties to take their place. Here was an interval in which a man might refuse to commit himself. Here was a break in the tyrannical course of irreparable human events; a period in which to look round upon the world without the sense of an enemy at one's back or the insistent pressure to make up one's mind; a moment in which one was relieved of the necessity of "coming to terms with oneself" or entering the fiercely trivial partisan struggles of the world outside; a moment in which to taste the mystery without the necessity of at once seeking a solution. . . . One might, if one were so inclined, reduce this to a doctrine about the character of a university; one might call it the doctrine of the interim. But the doctrine would be no more than a brief expression of what it felt like to be an undergraduate on that first October morning. Almost overnight, a world of ungracious fact had melted into infinite possibility; we, who belonged to no "leisured class," had been freed for a moment from the curse of Adam, the burdensome distinction between work and play. What opened before us was not a road but a boundless sea; and it was enough to stretch one's sails to the wind. (VLL, 127–28)

It is in connection with the university's "gift of an interval" that Oakeshott finally touches on the practical, indeed transformative, effect of liberal education on the student. "Nobody," he writes, "could go down from such a university unmarked." Not only will the student have acquired a discipline of mind that "puts him beyond the reach of the intellectual hooligan"; he will also "have learned something to help him lead a more significant life. . . . He will have had the opportunity to extend the range of his moral sensibility, and he will have had the leisure to replace the clamorous and conflicting absolutes of adolescence with something less corruptible" (VLL, 102–3). Here Oakeshott echoes another one of the great themes of Cardinal Newman, who claimed that the reason why it is more proper to speak of the university as a place of "education" rather than of "instruction" is because education "implies an action upon our mental nature, and the formation of our character."[17] Oakeshott does not dwell at length on this practical and transformative effect of liberal education in the two essays we have been considering—no doubt partly because it muddies his polemic against Moberly's emphasis on the university's role in providing students with existential meaning and purpose—but it plays an increasingly larger part in his later writings on education.

The second aspect of Oakeshott's earlier writings on education concerns the issue of expanding access to the universities. This is the real crisis in the universities, he claims: the influx of students unprepared to take advantage of the opportunity to "stretch one's sails to the wind" offered by a university. Here we encounter one of the least attractive features of Oakeshott's philosophy of education: its refusal to consider the claims of equity or what he scornfully refers to as "social justice." He dismisses Moberly's suggestion that, in the past, universities like Oxford and Cambridge have been bound up with "privilege" and a "leisured class"—hence the reference in the passage quoted earlier to "we, who belonged to no 'leisured class.'" And his characterization of the new class of students entering universities in the postwar years presents a grossly distorted picture: "The leaders of the rising class are consumed with contempt for everything which does not spring from their own desires, they are convinced that they have nothing to learn and everything to teach, and consequently their aim is loot—to appropriate to themselves the organization, the shell of the institution, and convert it to their own purposes" (*VLL*, 120, 130). Oakeshott softens this judgment in some of his later writings, but he never exhibits more than tepid enthusiasm for the expansion of educational opportunities for the less wealthy.

II

More than a decade passed before Oakeshott returned to the subject of university education in his 1961 essay "The Study of 'Politics' in the University." In this essay, along with two others from the same period, "Learning and Teaching" and "The Definition of a University," many of the ideas and concerns from the earlier essays reappear. Oakeshott still emphasizes the nonpractical, nonutilitarian character of university education. And he still envisages the world of learning in terms of the image of conversation; indeed, the definitive expression of this understanding of the world of learning and of civilization in general appeared in the 1959 essay "The Voice of Poetry in the Conversation of Mankind." Nevertheless, one can also discern some new ideas, or at least some slightly different emphases, in these essays as well. The most important of these is a new emphasis on education as an initiation into a historical inheritance and the role such an initiation plays in human self-realization.[18] Here Oakeshott taps into the notion of education as self-cultivation, or Bildung, that runs through a good deal of reflection on education in the nineteenth century, from Humboldt, Schiller, Goethe, Hegel, and Schleiermacher in Germany to Newman and Arnold in England.[19]

The new emphasis on self-cultivation and self-realization is evident from the outset of "The Study of 'Politics' in a University," where Oakeshott defines education as the "process of learning, in circumstances of direction and restraint, how to make something of ourselves." Learning how to make something of ourselves, however, is not something we can do simply on our own or independent of a particular context. Self-realization or self-cultivation necessarily involves initiation into a particular, historical civilization, in the process of which we "discover our own talents and aptitudes in relation to that civilization and begin to cultivate and to use them" (RP, 187).

How are we to understand this civilization in the mirror that we learn to recognize and cultivate ourselves? Oakeshott insists that it is not to be understood as a stock of things, like books or pictures or buildings or scientific inventions. It is better understood as a "stock of emotions, beliefs, images, manners of thinking, languages, skills, practices and manners of activity"; but even this description does not quite capture the meaning of a civilization. The word *stock* suggests something fixed and finished, when in fact these emotions, beliefs, and manners of thinking that compose a civilization are much more open-ended and fluid. For this reason Oakeshott suggests that a civilization is better thought of as a capital, "something known and enjoyed only in use." And with respect to the relationship that subsists between the components of such a civilization, he once again recurs to the image of a conversation: "A civilization (and particularly ours) may be regarded as a conversation being carried on between a variety of human activities, each speaking with a voice, or in a language of its own. . . . And I call the manifold which these different manners of thinking and speaking compose, a conversation, because the relations between them are not those of assertion and denial but the conversational relationships of acknowledgement and accommodation" (RP, 187).

Oakeshott goes on to characterize the different levels and types of education in terms of their relationship to the intellectual capital that makes up a civilization. In school education, for example, this capital is not yet recognized as capital but instead regarded as an inert stock of ideas and beliefs that has to be learned without the student even understanding why or what for. The education that comes after school education, on the other hand, is marked by a different attitude toward the capital of our civilization. This education takes one of two forms, either vocational education or university education. In the former, the capital of a civilization appears as a collection of skills to be used, but this capital is regarded as something already known, authoritative, and accepted; it does not look outside of itself or concern itself with anything beyond current practice. In university education, on the other hand, the intellectual capital of our civilization does not appear as something known and accepted but, rather, as something to be explored and investigated. Oakeshott employs the distinction between a "language" (or manner of thinking) and a "literature" (what has been said from time to time in a language) to bring out the contrast that he has in mind. In a vocational education, it is mainly a literature that is being studied; students are required to master a body of information, not to understand the manner of thinking that generated it. In university education, on the other hand, it is the manner of thinking of the historian or the scientist, not simply the results of their activity, that occupies the attention of the student (RP, 188–94).

The distinction Oakeshott draws here between vocational education and university education ultimately bears on the issue of specialization raised in his earlier essay on "The Universities." There he sought to address the problem of the degeneration of the university curriculum into a welter of narrow specialisms without having recourse to the integrating courses or unifying notion of culture advocated by Moberly. Specialized study at the university level need not be inimical to the general objects of a liberal education: "no true and profoundly studied *techne* raises the distinction between acquiring a knowledge of some branch of learning and pursuing the general objects of education" (VLL, 133). The distinction between vocational education and university education in "The Study of 'Politics' in a University" suggests how. Whereas a vocational education is necessarily a specialized education, an education in the current achievements and authoritative information of a particular skill or practice, a university education is not specialized, or at least not specialized in the same way. Insofar as the latter is an education in languages rather than literatures, it imparts not a body of authoritative information to be accepted but a manner of thinking to be explored. What differentiates university education, according to Oakeshott, is that it offers the student "practice in thinking: and not practice in thinking in no manner in particular but in specific manners each capable of reaching its own characteristic kind of conclusions. And what undergraduates may get at a university . . . is some understanding of what it is to think historically, mathematically, scientifically or philosophically, and some understanding of these not as 'subjects' but as 'living languages'" (RP, 197).

When Oakeshott finally turns his attention to the study of politics in a university, the reader is not unprepared for the conclusion that follows from his analysis. The study of politics in a university should concern itself with

languages rather than literatures, and these languages should be explanatory rather than prescriptive. The explanatory languages that Oakeshott finds
most relevant to the study of politics in the university are those of history
and philosophy; the quest for a science of politics has failed to yield anything
remotely resembling a scientific mode of thinking. Unfortunately, this is not
the direction that the study of politics has taken in the universities. From the
moment politics was introduced into the university curriculum, it was taught
in a manner appropriate to a vocational education. Information was imparted
that "could have no conceivable interest to anyone except those whose heads
were full of the enterprise of participating in political activity or to persons
with the insatiable curiosity of a concierge." To this were added works of
political philosophy read in a manner that Oakeshott describes as a "mixture between the manner in which one might read an out-of-date textbook
on naval architecture and the manner in which one might study a current
election manifesto." Though this has long been recognized as inadequate,
Oakeshott claims that the study of politics in universities has never shaken
its original vocational and practical orientation (RP, 207–18).

The other two essays that belong to this period of Oakeshott's reflection on
education, "Learning and Teaching" (delivered as a lecture in 1965) and "The
Definition of a University" (delivered as a lecture in 1967), overlap with each
other in many respects and in some places repeat verbatim the same ideas.
Both begin in the same way as "The Study of 'Politics' in a University," defining education as an initiation into an inheritance of human achievements, an
inheritance composed of emotions, beliefs, images, ideas, languages, skills,
and practices—"what Dilthey called a geistige Welt." And like "The Study of
'Politics' in a University," both essays insist that initiation into this inheritance or geistige Welt is necessary for self-realization and self-cultivation.
Indeed, Oakeshott goes so far as to say here that such initiation "is the only
way of becoming a human being." There is no opposition between entering an inheritance of human achievement and making the most of oneself:
"Selves are not rational abstractions, they are historic personalities . . . and
there is no other way for a human being to make the most of himself than
by learning to recognize himself in the mirror of this inheritance" (VLL,
45–48).[20]

In "Learning and Teaching," Oakeshott elaborates on the nature of the
inheritance into which students are to be initiated, emphasizing its historicity
and contingency. This inheritance, he writes,

> is an historic achievement; it is "positive," not "necessary"; it is contin-
> gent upon circumstances; it is miscellaneous and incoherent; it is what

human beings have achieved, not by the impulsion of a final cause, but by exploiting the opportunities of fortune and by means of their own efforts. . . . The notions of "finished" and "unfinished" are equally inapplicable to it. It does not deliver to us a clear and unambiguous message. . . . It has been put together not by designers but by men who knew only dimly what they did. It has no meaning as a whole; it cannot be learned or taught in principle, only in detail. (*VLL*, 49)[21]

Because this inheritance is so contingent, miscellaneous, and incoherent, the teacher may be tempted to substitute for it something more solid and super-human. But Oakeshott insists that he must "have the courage of his circum-stances. This man-made inheritance contains everything to which value may be attributed; it is the ground and context of every judgement of better and worse" (49).

Clearly Oakeshott is some sort of historicist, but we must be careful not to construe his historicism too crudely. The historical *geistige Welt* into which a student is to be initiated does not consist merely of what is present and immediately useful. Rather, "to initiate a pupil into the world of human achievement is to make available to him much that does not lie upon the surface of the present world. An inheritance will contain much that may not be in current use, much that has come to be neglected and even something that for the time being is forgotten." For this reason the teacher's task is not to expose the student to what is merely dominant or currently successful; it is not to hold up the "mirror of the present modish world." Rather, the "busi-ness of the teacher . . . is to release his pupils from servitude to the current dominant feelings, emotions, images, ideas, beliefs and even skills, not by inventing alternatives to them which seem to him more desirable, but by making available to him something which approximates more closely to the whole of his inheritance" (*VLL*, 48–49).

In "Learning and Teaching," Oakeshott does not speak explicitly of univer-sity education, but he draws a distinction between "information" and "judg-ment" that parallels the distinction between literature and language used in "The Study of 'Politics' in a University" to differentiate university education from vocational education. Information refers to the "explicit ingredient of knowledge," consisting of the authoritative and relatively inert facts and rules found in dictionaries, encyclopedias, manuals, and textbooks. Judgment, on the other hand, refers to the "tacit or implicit component of knowledge" that, like connoisseurship, cannot be specified in propositions; it is the "know-ing how" that necessarily accompanies the "knowing what" of information in any concrete skill or ability. Although there is an element of judgment or connoisseurship in every concrete activity, this element is "immeasurably greater" in the activities that form the basis of a university education: art, literature, science, history, and philosophy. It is in learning to speak and manage these great languages of our civilization that students learn to think for themselves—again, the most important of the general objects of a liberal education—and to appreciate the intellectual virtues of patience, accuracy, economy, elegance, and style (*VLL*, 50–62).

The implications for university education of Oakeshott's analysis in "Learning and Teaching" are drawn explicitly in "The Definition of a University." As in "The Study of 'Politics' in a University," he distinguishes between a vocational education that views our inheritance as a collection of skills to be used to sustain a current manner of living and a university education that views our inheritance as a collection of enterprises designed to understand and explain ourselves and the world. Whereas the former is concerned with authoritative information consisting of already established and usable facts, the latter is concerned with manners of thinking to be explored. In connection with the great enterprises of understanding and explaining—science, history, and philosophy—Oakeshott makes clear here that, even for people who are not destined to become scientists, historians, or philosophers, it is important to have some understanding of what it is to think like a scientist, historian, or philosopher. Not only does this afford these individuals a glimpse of the whole of their human inheritance, it also sustains the explanatory enterprises themselves, which "depend upon the appreciation of men who can recognize them, and even be excited by them, but who do not and cannot actually participate in them."[22]

This, of course, raises the question of who is to be given the opportunity to enjoy a university education of this kind. Oakeshott gives a slightly more generous answer to this question than he gave in "The Universities." After briefly evoking what he earlier referred to as the university's "gift of an interval," he concedes that it would be difficult to deny "so valuable an experience" to anyone. But he hedges. He continues to worry about the influx of unprepared students who have wants and expectations that do not correspond to the academic opportunities a university has to offer. "I could not have written off as merely illegitimate the wants and expectations of such invaders," he writes. But a university handed over to students who desire only "well-digested useful information to be handed to them on a plate" or who are actuated by the desire "not to learn how to think, but to shout mindless and barbaric slogans to one another" will have ceased to be a university in any meaningful sense.[23]

Oakeshott concludes "The Definition of a University" by wondering about the fate of the university as he understands it in a civilization that has "sold itself to the plausible ethics of productivity" and become dominated by the "vulgarity of a single-minded devotion to the exploitation of the world and the barbarism of instant affluence."[24] We are reminded of his contention in "The Universities"—against Moberly's plea that the university assume some sort of responsibility for the world—that the conflict between the university and the corrupt world of today is "absolute." This same stark opposition between the noninstrumental university and the thoroughly instrumental world appears in an undated speech Oakeshott gave to undergraduates upon their arrival at the London School of Economics. He advises the undergraduates to forget the propaganda that urges them "to learn how to be a more efficient cog in the social machine. . . . That is not what you have come here to learn; you have come here to get acquainted with truth and error, not with merely what is and what is not serviceable to a lunatic productivist society." And he encourages them to take advantage of the gift of the interval that the university has to offer and of the freedom it affords "from having to take that attitude towards the world in which it is regarded merely as material for satisfying human wants" (*WIH*, 333–36).

The speech is charmingly iconoclastic. But it also raises the question of whether the stark opposition between the university and the world that Oakeshott draws is ultimately viable. Does it deprive the university of the possibility of any sort of salutary influence on the world? And does it also erode the possibility of the world's providing any sort of support for the university?

III

Oakeshott's last essays on education, "Education: The Engagement and Its Frustration" (1972) and "A Place of Learning" (1974), come from the period of *On Human Conduct* and reflect the abstract language and some of the theoretical preoccupations of that late work. These essays also reiterate many of the themes from the earlier ones: for example, the idea of liberal education as an initiation into a historical inheritance of human achievements and the insistence that such an education has nothing to do with social utility or the practical transformation of the world. With respect to the latter theme, we see in these essays the same stark opposition between the noninstrumental university and the thoroughly instrumental and materialistic world that we observed in earlier essays. Indeed, if anything, the opposition is even starker in these writings, and the tone more bitter. A note of despair sometimes creeps into Oakeshott's analysis, as he watches the protective walls surrounding the university slowly being breached by the barbaric forces of an obsessively productivist society.

In these later essays, Oakeshott makes even clearer than he did before the inseparability of education and being human. This contention is grounded in a thoroughly historicist and Hegelian understanding of the human being. Human beings are distinguished by mind, *Geist,* or intelligence and inhabit a world composed entirely of meanings and understandings. Not only is the world what they understand it to be, they themselves are what they understand themselves to be. They are *in themselves* only what they are *for themselves.* This self-understanding of the human being does not, of course, come about naturally; it has to be learned. Therefore, a human being "is what he learns to become"; "he has a history but no 'nature'" (*VLL,* 17–23, 64; see also *OHC,* 36–41).

Because human beings are what they learn to become, education is not a merely redundant engagement but one absolutely crucial to self-realization, self-cultivation, or *Bildung.* Human beings are more or less developed or fulfilled according to the degree to which they have appropriated the "inheritance of human achievements of understanding and belief" that constitutes a civilization, an inheritance composed of "historic languages of feelings, sentiments, imaginings, fancies, desires, recognitions, moral and religious beliefs, intellectual and practical enterprises," and so forth. The aim of education, therefore, is to initiate human beings into this rich inheritance and teach them to recognize themselves in its multifaceted mirror (*VLL,* 65–67).

In "A Place of Learning" Oakeshott elaborates on this inheritance that is to be appropriated by human beings. It consists, first, of a vast variety of skills and practices concerned with "exploiting the resources of the earth for the satisfaction of human wants." It is not with these, however, that a liberal education is concerned; rather, it is concerned with that portion of the human inheritance that consists of "adventures of intellectual inquiry, of moral discrimination and emotional and imaginative insight." Oakeshott allows that we might denote this aspect of the human inheritance with the word *culture,* but only if we are not misled by this word into attributing a unity or coherence to our inheritance that it does not possess. "A culture," he writes, "is not a doctrine or a set of consistent teachings or conclusions about a human life. . . . [It] is a continuity of feelings, perceptions, ideas, engagements, attitudes and so forth, pulling in different directions, often critical of one another and contingently related to one another." It is a "historic contingency," but it ought not to be despised on that account. It is all we have, and it contains everything that we can ever hope to be (*VLL,* 24–29).

Oakeshott also characterizes a culture as a collection of different languages used to understand the world and ourselves: the languages, for example, of natural science, history, philosophy, and poetic imagination. Nor are we

surprised to hear that the relationship between these languages is not argumentative or hierarchical but conversational. The components of a culture
may be understood, Oakeshott writes,

> as voices, each the expression of a distinct and conditional understand-
> ing of the world and a distinct idiom of human self-understanding . . .
> joined, as such voices could only be joined, in a conversation—an end-
> less unrehearsed intellectual adventure in which, in imagination, we
> enter a variety of modes of understanding the world and ourselves and
> are not disconcerted by the differences or dismayed by the inconclusive-
> ness of it all. And perhaps we may recognize liberal learning as, above
> all else, an education in imagination, an initiation into the art of this
> conversation in which we learn to recognize the voices; to distinguish
> their different modes of utterance, to acquire the intellectual and moral
> habits appropriate to this conversational relationship and thus to make
> our *début dans la vie humaine*. (*VLL*, 37–39)

This is a beautiful passage, and these late essays on education, especially
"A Place of Learning," are full of them. But there is also a note of bitterness in
these essays that occasionally explodes into derisive scorn. This is especially
the case with "Education: The Engagement and Its Frustration," in which the
emphasis falls far more on the frustration than the engagement. Oakeshott
identifies two main culprits in the subversion of the educational engagement
in the twentieth century. The first involves the assault on the idea of "school"
as a "place apart," where students explore their moral and intellectual inheritance without regard to utility. Oakeshott picks out for special ridicule here
various Deweyite proposals that seek to replace "school" as a place where children learn under "conditions of direction and restraint designed to provoke
habits of attention, concentration, exactness, courage, patience, and discrimination" with an "arena of childish self-indulgence" where learning is reduced
to "experimental activity," personal "discovery," and "group discussions."
In an uncharacteristically apocalyptic tone, he claims that these proposals
amount to nothing less than a design for the "abolition of man" (*VLL*, 68–78).

The second major source of subversion of the modern educational engagement springs from the project of substituting "socialization" for education.
Here education is understood not as an initiation into a historical cultural
inheritance, but as integration into current society, an apprenticeship to
adulthood and commercial and industrial life. This project got started in the
eighteenth century, when many European states sought to equip the poor
with skills that would allow them to become productive members of society,

and ever since it has not ceased to attract the attention of governments. This is perhaps not surprising, but what particularly irks Oakeshott is the role that educators themselves have played in this project of substituting socialization for education. He sees the 1963 Robbins Report on higher education, which greatly expanded the universities in Britain and created the polytechnics, as a particularly egregious example of such "self-betrayal" of the educational engagement. Once again, he concludes on an apocalyptic note: "The design to substitute 'socialization' for education has gone far enough to be recognized as the most momentous occurrence of this century, the greatest of the adversities to have overtaken our culture, the beginning of a dark age devoted to barbaric affluence" (*VLL*, 78–93).

In his excoriation of the project of transforming education into an adjunct of modern technological society, Oakeshott resembles no one more than his famously vituperative contemporary, F. R. Leavis. For all of their differences on the role of the university in providing cultural and spiritual guidance, both these thinkers agreed on the dangers of scientism to the university. One can imagine that Oakeshott must have delighted in Leavis's savage skewering of C. P. Snow's 1959 Rede Lecture on "The Two Cultures," with its philistine and thoroughly unself-conscious endorsement of the ideal of technological progress and economic productivity.[25] Oakeshott actually refers in "A Place of Learning" to the "silly doctrine of the 'two cultures'"; like Leavis, he is quite suspicious of the role played by science in the university curriculum, not because it doesn't represent a legitimate mode of intellectual inquiry, but because it tends to be pursued in a purely utilitarian and vocational manner and often represents itself as the "model of all valid human understanding" (*VLL*, 32–33, 88–89). Interestingly, the Robbins Report, which Leavis, like Oakeshott, also had unmitigated contempt for, referred approvingly to Snow's diagnosis of the two cultures.[26]

Apart from the corruption and self-corruption of the modern university, Oakeshott points to one other condition that undermines the possibility of a genuinely liberal and liberating education in today's world. In a passage toward the end of "A Place of Learning," he captures with deadly and depressing accuracy the circumstances in the contemporary world that make it exceedingly difficult for the young to respond to the invitation of liberal learning. This passage is worth quoting at length both because of its sociological acuity and because it raises once again certain questions that have run through my analysis of Oakeshott's philosophy of education:

> The world in which many children now grow up is crowded, not necessarily with occupants and not at all with memorable experiences, but

with happenings; it is a ceaseless flow of seductive trivialities which invoke neither reflection nor choice but instant participation. A child quickly becomes aware that he cannot too soon plunge into this flow or immerse himself in it too quickly; to pause is to be swept with the chilling fear of never having lived at all. There is little chance that his perceptions, his emotions, his admirations and his ready indignations might become learned responses or be even innocent fancies of his own; they come to him prefabricated, generalized and uniform. He lurches from one modish conformity to the next . . . seeking to lose himself in a solidarity composed of exact replicas of himself. From an early age children believe themselves to be well-informed about the world, but they know it only at second-hand in the pictures and voices that surround them. It holds no puzzles or mysteries for them; it invites neither careful attention nor understanding. . . . It is a language composed of meaningless clichés. It allows only the expression of "points of view" and the ceaseless repetition of slogans which are embraced as prophetic utterances. Their ears are filled with the babel of invitations to instant unspecified reactions and their utterance reproduces only what they have heard said. Such discourse as there is resembles the barking of a dog at the echo of its own yelp. (*VLL*, 41)

It is remarkable to think that Oakeshott wrote this passage in 1974, before the advent of personal computers, the Internet, e-mail, cell phones, Facebook, and Twitter. But for all its insight into the world in which children now grow up, the passage unwittingly raises a question about the sharp division Oakeshott draws between the university and that world. Nothing would seem to be clearer than that the university Oakeshott prizes cannot survive in a world degraded in this way. The university must exert some sort of cultural influence on this world if only to secure the conditions of its own existence. Oakeshott himself asks how the university should respond to the current hostility to intellect and spirit that prevails in today's world; he answers, by "a quiet refusal to compromise" (*VLL*, 42). But such a response seems to fall short of what is really needed. To remain a lonely island (or interval) in an otherwise hostile sea is ultimately to accede to the inevitable and engulfing flood.

All of this suggests that the university must once again become a source of cultural authority, providing standards of moral and intellectual excellence to a world that currently lacks any. This brings us back to Moberly's diagnosis of the crisis of the modern university and to the even more profound analyses of Newman, Arnold, Eliot, Ortega, Leavis, and—I might add—Nietzsche. Interestingly, Oakeshott invokes the latter thinker's "wonderful lectures" *On*

the Future of Our Educational Institutions in a couple of places in his late essays
(*VLL*, 31, 79). He is particularly taken with Nietzsche's scathing critique of
the utilitarian reduction of education to the task of keeping people "up to
date" with "all the ways in which money can be made." He quotes Nietzsche
to the effect that the goal of such an education is "to rear the most 'current'
men possible, 'current' in the sense in which the word is used of coins of
the realm."[27] This, however, is only one of the two major problems Nietzsche
identifies with respect to modern education. The other has to do with exces-
sive specialization, which enables scholars to achieve unbelievable virtuosity
in a particular science (*Wissenschaft*), but at the expense of knowing anything
outside of that science or of having any sense of the whole into which their
activity fits. Worst of all, according to Nietzsche, such a specialized or scientific education renders human beings incapable of addressing the most fundamental philosophical questions about morality and the meaning of human
existence.[28]

Here one recalls Oakeshott's sarcastic remark about Moberly's "burning questions," which "give a faint flicker about midnight and have burnt
themselves out by the next morning" (*VLL*, 122). In many ways, Oakeshott's
treatment of the problem of specialization and of intellectual and cultural
fragmentation—the problem that exercised not only Moberly but also Newman, Arnold, Eliot, Leavis, and Nietzsche—remains the least satisfying
aspect of his educational philosophy. This aspect is partnered by an equally
problematic opposition between the purely intellectual university and the
excessively instrumental and materialistic world. To be sure, one of the great
contributions of Oakeshott's philosophy of education is its eloquent defense
of liberal learning for its own sake. But, as in so many other aspects of his
philosophy, Oakeshott's determined effort to avoid utilitarianism and instrumentalism leads him to hive education off from any sort of moral or practical
or societal effect. The result is a certain formalism or aestheticism: the idea
of the university as a kind of "interval" between the crudities and urgencies
of the world. But in the end, the university can be—indeed, must be—more
than that: not merely an interval but a transforming power.

NOTES

1. See R. S. Peters, "Michael Oakeshott's Philosophy of Education," in *Politics and Experience: Essays Presented to Professor Michael Oakeshott on the Occasion of His Retirement*, ed. Preston
King and B. C. Parekh (Cambridge: Cambridge University Press, 1968), 43–63; Timothy Fuller,
"Introduction: A Philosophical Understanding of Education," in *The Voice of Liberal Learning*,
ed. Timothy Fuller (New Haven: Yale University Press, 1989); David Bromwich, "The Art of

Conversation," *New Republic*, July 10, 1989, 33–36; John Searle, "The Storm over the University," *New York Review of Books*, December 6, 1990, 40–42; Noel Annan, *Our Age: English Intellectuals Between the World Wars: A Group Portrait* (New York: Random House, 1990), 394–400; David McCabe, "Michael Oakeshott and the Idea of Liberal Education," *Social Theory and Practice* 26 (2000): 443–64; Efraim Podoksik, *In Defence of Modernity: Vision and Philosophy in Michael Oakeshott* (Exeter: Imprint Academic, 2003), 211–29; Paul Franco, *Michael Oakeshott: An Introduction* (New Haven: Yale University Press, 2004), 116–25; and Kevin Williams, *Education and the Voice of Michael Oakeshott* (Exeter: Imprint Academic, 2007).

2. Annan, *Our Age*, 395.

3. On the Moot, see Stefan Collini, *Absent Minds: Intellectuals in Britain* (Oxford: Oxford University Press, 2006), 316–22; and Roger Kojecky, *T. S. Eliot's Social Criticism* (New York: Farrar, Straus and Giroux, 1971), 161–97.

4. Walter Moberly, "The Universities," *Cambridge Journal* 3 (1949–50): 195–213.

5. Walter Moberly, *The Crisis in the University* (London: SCM Press, 1949), 15–29, 50–70; John Henry Newman, *The Idea of a University*, ed. Frank M. Turner (New Haven: Yale University Press, 1996), 10.

6. Moberly, *Crisis in the University*, 107–40, quote on 115.

7. Nor is it now. In his unlikely bestseller, *The Closing of the American Mind: How Higher Education Has Failed Democracy and Impoverished the Souls of Today's Students* (New York: Simon and Schuster, 1987), Allan Bloom argued that the universities are in crisis as a result of a pervasive "relativism" and that they need to once again provide a "unified conception of life" to save democracy and the souls of students. More recently, Anthony Kronman, in *Education's End: Why Our Colleges and Universities Have Given Up on the Meaning of Life* (New Haven: Yale University Press, 2007), also criticizes universities for harnessing themselves exclusively to the modern research ideal and abandoning the central question of the meaning of life. It must be admitted that the rhetoric of these books, as evidenced in their titles, makes them even more vulnerable than Moberly's book to Oakeshott's withering critique of the crisis-mentality and vague talk of *Weltanschauungen*.

8. José Ortega y Gasset, *Mission of the University*, trans. Howard Lee Nostrand (Princeton: Princeton University Press, 1944), 56–61, 85–86. In his 1946 *Die Idee der Universität* (Berlin: Springer-Verlag), Karl Jaspers makes similar points about specialization and the need for an integration of knowledge in the university.

9. F. R. Leavis, *Education and the University: A Sketch for an "English School"* (London: Chatto and Windus, 1943), 15–32. An earlier version of "The Idea of a University" appeared under the title "Why Universities?" in *Scrutiny* 3 (1934): 117–32. Oakeshott wrote several essays for *Scrutiny* during the 1930s.

10. See Matthew Arnold, *Culture and Anarchy*, ed. Samuel Lipman (New Haven: Yale University Press, 1994). The epigraph to Leavis's "Mass Civilization and Minority Culture" comes from *Culture and Anarchy*; see Leavis, *Education and the University*, 143.

11. Moberly, "Universities," 196–97.

12. Ibid., 197–98.

13. Moberly, *Crisis in the University*, 225.

14. Newman writes in *The Idea of a University*: "It is a great point then to enlarge the range of studies which a University professes, even for the sake of the students; and though they cannot pursue every subject which is open to them, they will be gainers by living among those and under those who represent the whole circle. This I conceive to be the advantage of a seat of universal learning, considered as a place of education. An assemblage of learned men, zealous for their own sciences, and rivals of each other, are brought by familiar intercourse and for the sake of intellectual peace, to adjust together the claims and relations of their respective subjects of investigation. They learn to respect, to consult, to aid each other. Thus is created a pure and clear atmosphere of thought, which the student also breathes" (77). Newman is careful, though, not to enlarge the range of studies in a university too much or too indiscriminately: a university "professes much more than to take in and lodge as in caravanserai all arts and science, all history and philosophy. In truth, it professes to assign to each study, which it receives, its own place and its just boundaries; to define the rights, to establish the mutual relations, and to effect

the intercommunion of one and all . . . to keep the peace between them all, and to convert their mutual differences and contrarieties into the common good. . . . Thus to draw many things into one, is its special function" (219).

15. See Stephen Marcus's essay "*Culture and Anarchy* Today," in Arnold, *Culture and Anarchy*, 165–85.

16. Included in this "intense thought" is Oakeshott's own *Experience and Its Modes*.

17. Newman, *Idea of a University*, 85.

18. This emphasis is not entirely absent in Oakeshott's earlier educational writings (see *RP*, 38; *VLL*, 133).

19. Both Podoksik and Williams relate Oakeshott to this neohumanistic tradition of self-realization, or Bildung; see Podoksik, *In Defence of Modernity*, 213–19; and Williams, *Education*, 7–11.

20. See also Michael Oakeshott, "The Definition of a University," *Journal of Educational Thought* 1 (1967): 130–32. This essay reproduces the text of a lecture Oakeshott gave at the University of Calgary on April 4, 1967. This text can also be found under the title "The Character of a University Education," in Luke O'Sullivan's edited collection *What Is History* (*WIH*, 373–90).

21. See also Oakeshott's "Reply to Raphael" (also from 1965) on the multifarious and miscellaneous character of a tradition (*VMES*, 183–84).

22. Oakeshott, "Definition of a University," 135–39.

23. Ibid., 140–41.

24. Ibid., 141–42.

25. F. R. Leavis, "Two Cultures? The Significance of Lord Snow," reprinted in Leavis, *Nor Shall My Sword: Discourses on Pluralism, Compassion and Social Hope* (London: Chatto and Windus, 1972), 41–74.

26. See quote from the Robbins Report in Leavis's essay "Luddites? Or There Is Only One Culture," in Leavis, *Nor Shall My Sword*, 99. For Leavis's contemptuous attitude toward the Robbins Report, see Leavis, *Nor Shall My Sword*, 80, 96, 104–5, 107–10, 119–20, 149, 151.

27. Friedrich Nietzsche, *On the Future of Our Educational Institutions*, trans. Michael W. Grenke (South Bend, Ind.: St. Augustine's Press, 2004), 36–37.

28. Nietzsche, *Our Educational Institutions*, 38–40; see also Nietzsche's essay "Schopenhauer as Educator," in *Untimely Meditations*, trans. R. J. Hollingdale (Cambridge: Cambridge University Press, 1983), 131–32, 141, 169–75.

PART TWO

POLITICAL PHILOSOPHY

9

MICHAEL OAKESHOTT ON THE HISTORY OF POLITICAL THOUGHT

Martyn Thompson

My concern is twofold. First, I outline what I take Oakeshott to have meant by the phrase "the history of political thought," and then I consider some criticisms from Oakeshott's perspective of the theory and practice of Quentin Skinner, the leading figure in the so-called Cambridge School of historians of political thought.[1] Oakeshott was impressed by his work. But there are significant points of disagreement. I focus on two: first, Oakeshott's disagreement with Skinner about the historical interpretation of Hobbes's *Leviathan*; and second, more generally, Oakeshott's objections to Skinner's reduction of the history of political thought to "the history of ideologies."[2] The two points are closely connected.

I

I do not attempt to compare any of Oakeshott's historical narratives with any of Skinner's, because Oakeshott published nothing which, in his own account of the logic of historical inquiry, might properly be characterized as an exclusively historical narrative.[3] Even the posthumously published works that many have taken to be histories, such as *The Politics of Faith and the Politics of Scepticism* (1996), are not.[4] Included among these posthumously published writings are Oakeshott's undergraduate lectures that appeared in print with the misleading title of *Michael Oakeshott: Lectures in the History of Political Thought* (2006). I must begin, then, by correcting the false impression that these lectures are likely to give to anyone interested in Oakeshott's understanding of the history of political thought. There is much in the lectures that is relevant to my concerns, but it has to be extracted from a work of a quite different character.

The published title is an invention of the editors.[5] Anyone even partly familiar with Oakeshott's published writings on the logic of history is bound to be surprised by some aspects of the lectures. They contain much that is unhistorical, some of which will be obvious to everyone. His decision to reverse the historical sequence of intellectual influence by examining Aristotle's political philosophy before considering the ideas of Socrates and Plato is one example. Other unhistorical moves will be apparent only to those with some familiarity with Oakeshott's ideas. Examples here include his relatively frequent recourse to "ideal types" as organizing ideas in the lectures (especially the lectures on medieval monarchies and on modern ideas of "telocracy" and "nomocracy"). Ideal types, for Oakeshott, were the analytic tools of philosophers, not historians (*LHPT*, 111–12).[6]

The fact that nonhistorical elements were interwoven into the lecture course strongly suggests that Oakeshott was doing something other than offering his students an outline history of Western political thought. And this suggestion is in part confirmed by the fact that Oakeshott's own title for the lectures did not mention "history." They were simply lectures on "political thought."[7] Their purpose, Oakeshott noted, was to offer undergraduates "a study of political thought, or aids to the study of political thought." To be sure, he went on immediately to say that in "the main" what he proposed to offer was a "historical study" (*LHPT*, 31). But the appropriate context for understanding what he meant by this is his clearly articulated view, part of his philosophy of education, of what is involved in the study of politics at a university.[8] The "problems" of the lectures as history disappear, and an immensely important set of observations for understanding Oakeshott's conception of the history of political thinking becomes clear when they are seen, as Oakeshott intended them to be, as "aids" to the study of politics at a university.[9] So what are the main components of this more appropriate context?

The key distinction is between the ideal types of vocational and university education in politics. A university education in politics is exclusively focused on the explanation and understanding of domestic and foreign traditions of political activity and political philosophy. It is not at all concerned with developing the vocational skills believed necessary from time to time to formulate policy and engage successfully in political activity. The appropriate explanatory "languages" for understanding political activity are those of history and philosophy; there is next to nothing in political activity capable of genuinely scientific explanation. So the undergraduate lectures provide students with examples of historical and philosophical explanation. They are sophisticated lectures, but their purpose is introductory. They are, indeed, neither more nor less than a series of wide-ranging aids for the historical and philosophical analysis of Western political thinking from ancient Greece to the modern sovereign state. Their mixed and introductory status is underscored by the fact that Oakeshott offered an advanced course, a graduate course, titled the "History of Political Thought." This course is a much more reliable guide than the lectures to what Oakeshott meant by the "history of political thought." So I draw mainly on the graduate course and Oakeshott's published writings, especially the last formulation of his "logic of historical inquiry" in *On History* (1983), to outline his ideas.[10]

But although the lectures are not the best source for Oakeshott's conception of the history of political thought, they do contain some important observations central to that conception. Thus history is a "mode of thought in which events, human actions, beliefs, [and] manners of thinking are considered in relation to the . . . circumstantial context" in which they first appeared. There is no single, "continuous history" of political thought; instead, there are as many histories as there are historical answers to historical questions that historians of political thought pose for themselves. Each of these histories necessarily focuses on "different peoples, at different times, in different intellectual and physical circumstances, engaging in politics in different ways and finding different things to think about." Notions of progress, regress, and evolution have no place as organizing ideas in histories of thought. A "history of thought is a history of men thinking, *not* a 'history' of abstract, disembodied 'ideas,'" theories, or concepts (*LHPT*, 31, 32, 33, 42).[11] All of these propositions, at least at this level of generality, would seem more or less compatible with the methodological contextualism and methodological conventionalism of the Cambridge School.

But the same cannot be said for two further sets of observations crucial for Oakeshott's understanding of the history of political thought. First, in both his published writings and his graduate course, Oakeshott insisted that the crucial characteristic of historical questions and historical answers was that they were designed to elicit the "pastness" of their objects of inquiry. Furthermore, the pastness sought in historical inquiries is nothing if it is not categorically different from the present meanings and present significance of the surviving relics of the past.[12] Second, Oakeshott frequently notes in the lectures and elsewhere that there "are many different levels of political thinking" (*LHPT*, 39) and in distinguishing between them it is always helpful to refer to something like the classical distinction between practical thinking (thought in the service of acting—that is to say, recommendation, moral evaluation, justification, etc.) and theoretical or explanatory thinking (thought in the service of understanding, making comprehensible, clarifying, etc.).[13] The distinction allows a historian, he claims, to see that the "preeminent voice" in Machiavelli's *Prince* and in Locke's *Two Treatises* is the voice of practical political argument, whereas the preeminent voice in Hobbes's *Leviathan* and Hegel's *Philosophy of Right* is the voice of explanatory political thinking.[14] Historians, Oakeshott concludes, should never confuse the two. "They belong . . . to two different histories" (43).

Now, on the face of it, Oakeshott's last observation seems untenable. If he means that historians interested, say, in seventeenth-century contract theorists cannot write a history featuring both Hobbes and Locke without committing a logical error, that would be preposterous. But that is not what he is saying. What he is in fact saying and why it is important to say it become apparent only through a review of his understanding of the logic of historical inquiry, an understanding that arises from a rigorous inquiry into both the pastness and the various levels of thinking in past political thought.

Oakeshott's graduate seminar pursued an inquiry into the logical presuppositions of history conceived as a distinctive mode of thinking and writing about the world. The relevant essays in *On History* offer Oakeshott's answers.[15] The essays begin and end with the observation that "historical inquiry is the invention of historians" (*OH*, 3, 118). Thus the philosophical interrogation of historical writings was designed "not only to assemble a distinct, coherent, ideal mode of understanding in terms of its necessary conditions" but also to "sustain the contention" that it was the ideal mode of *historical* understanding "by relating these necessary conditions to the identifying marks" characteristic of current, disciplined historical writing (6).

These "identifying marks" were the organizing ideas and technical vocabulary of narratives and analyses generally acknowledged to be historical. The identifying marks of histories include the terms *past, event, cause, change,* and so on. The identifying marks of histories of ideas add further terms such as *mental dispositions, beliefs, concepts, ideas,* and so on. And the identifying marks of histories of political thought add the key but slippery concepts of the political. Since, however, each of these concepts has a place in a variety of different discourses (practical, aesthetic, philosophical, social scientific, and so on), the question arises, "What, if anything, is distinctive about them in *historical* discourse?" If history is, as Oakeshott argued, a distinctive mode of understanding the world, then its key concepts must bear distinctive meanings, meanings different in some ways from the meanings they carry in other, nonhistorical kinds of discourse. Identifying what these distinctive meanings were led Oakeshott, among much else, to his controversial conception of the historical past. I concentrate on this concept in elucidating what I take him to have meant by the history of political thinking.

For Oakeshott the emergence of critical, disciplined history in the nineteenth and twentieth centuries was marked by a self-conscious concern with the pastness of the past. The intention to study the past "for its own sake" expressed the intention *not* to study it for any present practical or other ulterior purposes. Ranke's often quoted ambition to show what really happened in the past ("was eigentlich geschehen ist") and how it really was and came to be ("wie es eigentlich gewesen ist") expressed the intention to free the study of the past from anachronism, myth, and legend and to construct a past that had not survived from the relics of that past that had survived (*OH*, 66n18). But to the extent that these intentions and ambitions were realized by historians, the reality of this "historical past," as Oakeshott calls it (to distinguish it, for example, from the "practical past" that satisfies a present utilitarian impulse or the "contemplative pasts" of poets and historical novelists that satisfy an equally present aesthetic interest), is necessarily a peculiar reality. It is a past that exists nowhere but in history books. And this is so, Oakeshott argues, because history books consist of inquiries "in which authenticated survivals from the past are dissolved into their component features in order to be used for what they are worth as circumstantial evidence from which to *infer* a past which has not survived; a past composed of passages of related historical events . . . and assembled as themselves *answers to questions about the past formulated by an historian*" (33; italics added).

This, I take it, is what we mean when we say that history is made by historians. And if we do say this, if we do say that historians construct their historical objects (and from them they construct historical narratives and historical analyses), we mean something entirely different by the word *history* from its meaning in similar-sounding statements such as, for example, "Yuri Gagarin made history when he orbited the earth" or "Shakespeare was the greatest dramatist in the history of English literature" or "Napoleon was a world-historical figure."

So what is the character of the historical past constructed by historians of political thought? I illustrate Oakeshott's answer by reference to Althusius's *Politica methodice digesta*. I then consider Oakeshott's disagreements with Skinner on Hobbes's *Leviathan*.[16] Oakeshott's main observations about the historical past were the following. Historical inquiry begins with the analysis of a "recorded past," that is, "with a past which has itself survived and is present. It is composed of actual utterances and artifacts which have survived, which are understood as survivals, and are now present exactly as they were uttered or made except for any damage they may have suffered on the way." They are the "utterances and fabrications of long-dead human beings . . . in which their authors were responding to their current situations." These once-current situations have not survived, because they could not have survived (*OH*, 30).

The circumstances current, for example, when Althusius as professor of law in Herborn read and responded to Bodin's *De republica libri sex* in his *Politica* have not survived. Nor have the very different circumstances in which Althusius (this time as syndic in Emden) read and responded to, say, Arnisaeus's *De jure majestatis libri tres* and recast the argument of the first edition of his *Politica* into the greatly different, much more revolutionary, second edition of 1610.[17] And nor have the circumstances survived in which Althusius (still as syndic in Emden) expanded and recast once again his arguments for the third edition of 1614. What have survived are the three editions of his work as well as other related circumstantial evidence of the current situations in which Althusius found himself and to which he was responding on each of these separate occasions. His responses produced a significantly different work each time. But such survivals as these, as Oakeshott notes, are the "only entry into the past" that historians have available. And thus

> the first concern of an historical inquiry is to assemble them [the surviving relics] from where they lie scattered in the present, to recover what may have been lost, to impose some kind of order upon this confusion, to repair the damage they may have suffered, to abate their fragmentariness, to discern their relationships, to recognize a survival in terms of its provenance, and thus to determine its authentic character as a bygone practical or philosophical or artistic etc. performance. (*OH*, 32)[18]

The historical questions that historians of ideas are disposed to ask of a surviving record of the intellectual past are "What did this object or utterance mean in the circumstances in which it was made or uttered?" and "What may it be made to report indirectly about a past which has not survived?" (36). Answers to the first of these questions always require "reading" the object or utterance that has survived within the historically constructed situations (what all the relevant, available historical evidence obliges the historian to believe those situations and circumstances were and to which the object or utterance was a response) that have not survived. The answers to the first question, then, are what all the available evidence obliges the historian to believe the objects or utterances meant to their makers or authors at the time they were made or uttered.

In the case of Althusius's *Politica*, the surviving text of the first edition and the circumstantial evidence of its composition at the Hohe Schule in Herborn strongly suggest it be read as a textbook for students of political science, designed, at least in part, to promote the novel enterprise of state building: in this instance, the building of a small, highly cohesive Calvinist principality in Nassau-Dillenburg in the middle of Reformation Europe. It was, then, in Oakeshott's terms, primarily a systematic textbook "devoted to administrative invention" (*VMES*, 288).[19] The surviving text of the second edition and the circumstantial evidence surrounding its composition in Emden from 1604 to 1610 suggest a very different reading of the considerably reworked text. The projected constitutional framework that constituted one of the main organizing ideas of the original text was modified to reflect the institutional arrangements in existence in Althusius's new location in Ostfriesland. And Althusius added a lengthy penultimate chapter justifying armed resistance to tyrants, exactly the kind of armed resistance currently being pursued by the Calvinist city of Emden under Althusius's leadership against the Lutheran prince of Ostfriesland.[20] The political science textbook had become a *monarchomach* tract.

The first and second editions of the *Politica* are very rare. Only the still further expanded third edition was and is (though now in truncated form) readily available.[21] It, too, is at least two different books in one: a political science textbook and a monarchomach tract for the times. Small wonder, then, that the reception histories of the *Politica* display a marked bifurcation between those who read the work as a rigorous, "scientific" inquiry into the logical composition of an early modern state and those who read it as a polemical intervention in the practical political and religious controversies of its time. But this is not my primary point in considering the Althusius example in the present context. Rather, my point is twofold: first, the example illuminates the difference between a historically constructed "historical past," as Oakeshott understood it, and a past once experienced as a present; second, it helps illuminate a key characteristic of all relics of the intellectual past, including the relics of the past of political thinking.

As to the first: a moment's reflection reveals that it would be a mistake to think that the historian's creation of the relevant circumstances in which Althusius composed his three editions and that allow the historian to identify their "authentic" voices and original meanings corresponds to the actual circumstances that constituted Althusius's ever-changing present as he wrote.[22] Rather, the construction of the relevant circumstances is inevitably a very selective enterprise by the historian. Althusius may or may not have been ill, poor, or hungry at the relevant times; the text may have flowed or faltered; he may have composed the editions undisturbed or been frequently interrupted by his duties as *rektor*, as syndic, or by any number of other things. All these considerations and many others will have contributed to what Althusius understood his present situations to have been. But next to none of them have any relevance in the historian's quest to identify what Althusius's texts meant at the times they were composed. So the historical construction of the relevant circumstances (in this instance, in central Europe in the late sixteenth and early seventeenth centuries) is not a reconstruction of a past once experienced as a present. Rather, it is the construction of a past based exclusively on authenticated historical evidence *selected* by a historian to help answer the question the historian has posed about the original meanings (always plural) of Althusius's texts.

Second, Althusius's *Politica* exemplifies in an especially dramatic way a common characteristic of all the objects and utterances that are the surviving components of the recorded past and that are therefore the potential starting points for a whole variety of distinct and different historical inquiries. That is to say, each of them from the simplest to the most complex (from, say, a user's guide to a seventeenth-century ink pot to Hobbes's *Leviathan*) expresses a variety of different, explicit and implicit, meanings. In other words, as Oakeshott puts it, "none of these objects which compose the present of historical concern has an exclusive character or speaks with a single voice." No doubt, each may be recognized as having a "pre-eminent voice" such as that of "a musical composition, a philosophical argument, a scientific theorem, a religious ritual or a contribution to a political debate." No doubt, too, the identification of this preeminent voice may invite certain kinds of historical questions rather than others to be addressed to the objects concerned: say, questions that relate them to a historical past of musical composition or philosophical arguments or practical political engagement and so on. But it need not do so. Since each of the objects is a "heterogeneous utterance each is eligible to be used in a variety of historical enquiries some far removed from that suggested by whatever may be recognized as its pre-eminent voice" (*OH*, 48).

This, then, is the first question that the logic of the history of political thought requires historians to address to the relics of the recorded past: "what did this object or utterance mean in the circumstances in which it was made or uttered?" The answer always reveals multiple meanings and which of these is most relevant to a historian depends on the specific questions that the historian has posed and is seeking to answer. Hence, the second question: "what may these historically identified meanings 'be made to report indirectly about a past which has not survived?'" (*OH*, 36). The historical past that exists nowhere else but in history books, that is to say, is constructed by historians exclusively on the basis of historically "authenticated" evidence composed to answer the historical questions that the historians themselves ask. These questions may or may not be similar to those addressed explicitly or implicitly by the authors of the relics of the recorded past. As an empirical generalization, more often than not they are not. But the crucial point here is that the logic of historical inquiry does not require them to be so. For each of the surviving relics, when their historical meanings have been authenticated (that is, when they have been transformed from relic into historical evidence), remains "an oblique source of information which may be used in seeking answers to a variety of historical questions about the past, but was certainly not designed to supply any such information" (48).

Althusius's *Politica* may again illustrate the point. All three editions of Althusius's work discuss political matters. But questions concerning the history of political thinking (as considerably varied as these may be) are by no means the only kinds of historical questions that might lead historians to turn to Althusius's writings for relevant evidence. Anyone familiar with the texts would readily accept that they provide evidence for historians concerned with a great variety of intellectual histories: histories of religious (especially Calvinist) ideas; histories of logic (especially Ramist logic); histories of educational ideas; histories of rhetoric; histories of racial ideas (especially anti-Semitism); histories of early modern Latin; histories of the early modern book trade; and so on and so forth. Each of these different historical inquiries results in constructions of different historical pasts. The cast of characters and what they were doing, saying, and meaning that a historian, say, of ideas of sovereignty in the early seventeenth century would study are very different from the cast of characters and what they were doing, saying, and meaning that a historian, say, of logic would consider. And yet Althusius's *Politica* could feature prominently in both.

II

I now return to Oakeshott's contention that Hobbes's *Leviathan* and Locke's *Two Treatises* belong to "two different histories" and to his disagreement with Skinner on the historical interpretation of *Leviathan*. On the first point, Oakeshott identifies the preeminent voice of *Leviathan* as philosophical and the preeminent voice of *Two Treatises* as that of practical political argument. *Leviathan*, that is to say, is primarily concerned to offer a systematic explanation of the logic of sovereignty in an early modern state, whereas *Two Treatises* is not primarily concerned to offer much of an explanation of anything (save, perhaps, for the right to private property).[23] Hobbes's system of civil science,

in other words, was designed to demonstrate the "logical necessity" for absolute, undivided sovereignty in an early modern state (*CPJ*, 120). Locke's *Two
Treatises*, by contrast, "was designed to be convincing in a pragmatic manner."
Locke's design was to persuade his readers of the attitude they should adopt
toward the prospect of revolutionary action being taken against the reigning
monarch. So *Two Treatises*, Oakeshott observes,

> is not a work of political philosophy, like *Leviathan*, but a work of "politi-
> cal theory"—the questionable enterprise of recommending a political
> position in the idiom of general ideas. . . . Locke, like many other writ-
> ers, recognizes no firm distinction between explanation and prescrip-
> tion; he moves, often inadvertently, between these two disparate worlds
> of discourse, giving a spurious air of principle to his recommendations
> and a false suggestion of practical applicability to his explanations.
> (*VMES*, 163)

This difference in the character of their arguments, Oakeshott notes, is
reflected in their authors' different choices of discursive idiom. Two of the
predominant idioms of practical political argument in the seventeenth century were theological and juristic. Locke chose that of "theology" (*LHPT*,
393–94). Hobbes, by contrast, chose the altogether different idiom of science.

In support of this characterization of Hobbes's argument, Oakeshott could
quote Hobbes himself (*HCA*, 132), for Hobbes was quite explicit about the
systematic character of his philosophical inquiries, as well as about their nov-
elty and about the place of his "civil science" or "Civil Philosophy" within
them. In the "Epistle Dedicatory" to the *Elements of Philosophy*, for example,
Hobbes asserts that "Natural Philosophy" had only recently, with Galileo and
Harvey, achieved a scientific foundation and that a genuine "Civil Philosophy" was *"no older . . . then my own Book* de Cive." Having made this dramatic
claim, Hobbes immediately anticipated an objection: *"But what? Were there
no Philosophers Natural nor Civil among the ancient Greeks?"* And his answer
was that of course there were those called philosophers and who engaged in
something akin to philosophy. But these were writers like Plato, Aristotle,
Zeno, and Epicurus who had been *"derided,"* quite properly in Hobbes's view,
by the ancient Greek satirist Lucian of Samosata.[24] They were men who taught
"in stead of Wisdome, nothing but to dispute" and who decided *"every Question
according to their own fancies."* The result of their teachings, then, was a "Pernicious Philosophy" that had perverted all of the philosophical inquiries of
the Christian Middle Ages and that had only now, with the scientific revolution and with Hobbes's own works, been exposed as the catalog of errors that
Hobbes adjudged them to be.[25]

Here, then, is Hobbes's account of what he was doing in *De corpore, De homine,* and *De cive,* and in the reworking of the latter in *Leviathan.*[26] He was correcting the errors of all previous philosophers and establishing philosophy for the first time in its proper, systematic form. And this is what Oakeshott, like many others before and since, took the "pre-eminent voice" of *Leviathan* to be, and so he concluded that the appropriate context for explaining the predominant meanings of the text historically could be "nothing narrower than" the whole of "the history of political philosophy" down to Hobbes's own times.[27]

The case is far different with Locke's *Two Treatises.*[28] Few, if any, would deny certain structural similarities between Hobbes's argument in *Leviathan* and Locke's in the *Second Treatise.* But, at least since Laslett's remarkable work in the 1950s on the genesis and character of Locke's argument in *Two Treatises,* no one would mistake what Locke was doing in the *Second Treatise* for an attempt to pursue a Hobbes-like project to restructure systematically or replace altogether inherited philosophical accounts of the nature of civil society. Locke's principal opponents were Tory Filmerians, and, ostensibly at least, his main intellectual supports were the Bible and "the judicious Hooker." The appropriate context, then, for a historical account of the pre-eminent voice in *Two Treatises* would consist, mainly, of the complex cross-currents of seventeenth-century practical political argument.

This contrast between Hobbes's main concerns in *Leviathan* and Locke's in *Two Treatises* is what Oakeshott had in mind when he claimed that their works "belong to two different histories." The cast of characters (and what they were doing, saying, and meaning), which a historian would need to invoke to explain the main questions Hobbes was addressing in *Leviathan* and the way he went about answering them, would include earlier political philosophers such as "Aristotle, Epicurus and Aquinas" (*CPJ,* 182). Historical explanations of *Two Treatises,* by contrast, would need to invoke a very different cast of characters, a set of political theorists and polemicists (and what they were doing, saying and meaning) which might include writers such as Hooker, Hunton, Lawson, Filmer, Milton, Pufendorf, and Algernon Sidney. Of course, the voice of practical political argument is not entirely absent from Hobbes's *Leviathan,* just as the voice of philosophical explanation is not entirely absent from the *Second Treatise.* But any historian who attempted to explain *Leviathan* as simply a polemical tract or the *Second Treatise* as simply a work of philosophy, in Oakeshott's view, would be guaranteed to miss most of their historical meanings and most of their historical significance.

I can now turn to consider Oakeshott's disagreement with Skinner on the historical interpretation of *Leviathan* in a little more detail. Oakeshott's *Leviathan* is certainly different from Skinner's, but the two, from Oakeshott's perspective, are not utterly irreconcilable.[29] From Skinner's perspective, how-ever, they are. Skinner's great service to Hobbes studies has been to uncover various ways in which Hobbes's works were related to the practical political arguments of his day. The results have been fascinating, but the ambition behind them, from Oakeshott's perspective, is inappropriately one-sided. In the preface to *Hobbes and Republican Liberty*, for example, Skinner states,

> I approach Hobbes's political theory not simply as a general system of ideas but also as a polemical intervention in the ideological conflicts of his time. To interpret and understand his texts, I suggest, we need to recognize the force of . . . Wittgenstein's maxim that words are also deeds. We need, that is, to put ourselves in a position to grasp what sort of an intervention Hobbes's texts may be said to have constituted. My aim . . . is accordingly to give an account not merely of what Hobbes is saying but of what he is doing in propounding his arguments. My governing assumption is that even the most abstract works of politi-cal theory are never above the battle. With this in mind, I try to bring Hobbes down from the philosophical heights, to spell out his allusions, to identify his allies and adversaries, to indicate where he stands on the spectrum of political debate.[30]

In Oakeshott's terms, apart from the misplaced ambition to "bring Hobbes down from the philosophical heights" to which he clearly aspired and which, on Oakeshott's reading, he fully succeeded in reaching, there need be little to object to here.[31] Skinner has simply elected to explore the "voice" of prac-tical political engagement in Hobbes's "heterogeneous" text. This becomes unacceptable to Oakeshott only if the voice of practical politics is taken to be Hobbes's only "authentic" voice and this, indeed, turns out to be the thrust of Skinner's argument. Skinner's concern as a historian who construes the his-tory of political thinking as a history of ideologies, he says, is "to illustrate the extent to which *Leviathan* is itself a partisan political tract, albeit a large and ambitious one."[32] In other words, Hobbes's "general system of ideas" and the "philosophical heights" to which he climbed are apparently just "deceptions." They are the "deceptively smooth surface" covering a "seething" polemical core.[33]

It might be tempting to explain these differences between Oakeshott's Hobbes and Skinner's Hobbes by reference to their different conceptions of the relationships between political philosophy and political practice. For Oakeshott, developing the tradition of philosophical idealism, the scope and limitations of philosophy are best summed up in Hegel's famous terms: "To comprehend what is, this is the task of philosophy"; it is not to change what is into something better, something that "ought to be."[34] So philosophy for Oakeshott is a "parasitic activity," one that sets out to explain the world but that makes "no specific contribution" to the various activities it reflects on (*RP*, 491).

In this view, to read a philosophical inquiry as a partisan political argument is simply to misread it. For Skinner, by contrast, philosophical accounts of politics are always, in part at least, polemical interventions in practical political controversies. They are "never above the battle." In arriving at this conclusion, Skinner often invokes Wittgenstein's observation that "words are also deeds" and that "concepts are not timeless entities with fixed meanings, but should rather be thought of as . . . tools (Wittgenstein's term), the understanding of which is always in part a matter of seeing who is wielding them and for what purposes."[35] But these are observations entirely compatible with Oakeshott's views.

Furthermore, Wittgenstein's ideas about the relationship between philosophy and practice are much closer to Oakeshott's than they are to Skinner's. In the *Tractatus Logico-Philosophicus* (1921), for example, Wittgenstein insists, "Philosophy aims at the logical clarification of thoughts. . . . A philosophical work consists essentially of elucidations. . . . Without philosophy thoughts are, as it were, cloudy and indistinct: its task is to make them clear and to give them sharp boundaries."[36] And in the posthumously published *Philosophical Investigations* (1951), Wittgenstein asserts, "A philosophical problem has the form: 'I don't know my way about.'" And he continues, "Philosophy may in no way interfere with the actual use of language; it can only describe it. . . . It cannot give it any foundation either. It leaves everything as it is."[37] So, despite suggestions to the contrary, Skinner's conception of the relationship between philosophy and practice is not the same as Wittgenstein's. Rather, his conception of political philosophy and its relationship to political practice seems much more compatible with the perspectives and doctrines of modern proponents of critical theory and Ideologiekritik.[38] It is here, at least, that one finds assertions that all thought is ideological. It is here that knowledge is indissolubly linked to practical (often material) interests. And it is here that intellectual controversies are always part of the battle, inescapably part of the fray.[39]

But although all this might be of interest to anyone concerned to understand the differences between Oakeshott and Skinner as philosophers and theorists of the history of political thought, it is (from Oakeshott's standpoint) irrelevant to questions about the historical interpretation of Hobbes or, indeed, any other past political thinker. The relics that compose the recorded past of philosophical thinking from ancient Greece to modern times are replete with all sorts of arguments about the relationships between philosophy and practice.[40] What matters for the historical interpretation of Hobbes is not what Oakeshott and Skinner think those relationships to be. Theirs, after all, are views developed within the context of twentieth- and early twenty-first-century intellectual controversy.

What matters for Oakeshott's understanding of the history of political thought is what Hobbes understood those relationships to be within the context of mid-seventeenth-century intellectual controversies. Given the fact of seventeenth-century controversies about whether or not philosophical reason could have any practical applicability, it seems an unnecessarily arbitrary move to reduce from the outset the history of early modern reflection on politics to a history solely of ideology, where ideology is understood, as it usually is, as a kind of practical political thinking.[41] As I consider in a moment, it is unclear to me whether Skinner really needs to do this, although he often enough says he does.[42] With respect to Hobbes, as Oakeshott would have argued, the point Skinner has been making is that Hobbes's "general system of ideas" is related to seventeenth-century practical political arguments in ways historians have hitherto tended to overlook. But he has not shown that Hobbes's general system can be reduced to nothing but polemics.[43]

To be sure, *Leviathan* certainly can be read as taking sides in mid-seventeenth-century practical, political controversies (many readers, especially among Hobbes's first, have done so) and certainly, too, Hobbes does offer some practical recommendations. The most obvious recommendation is that *Leviathan* itself should be the only text of civil science taught in the universities.[44] But all this means only, on Oakeshott's understanding, that (apart from possible misreadings) *Leviathan* is a "heterogeneous text" speaking with more than one voice and that some readers are inclined to privilege one of the voices over any of the others.

Yet it is certainly worth recalling, in support of Oakeshott's interpretation, that when Hobbes himself came to recommend the study of his philosophy to the general reader, the reasons he gave did not include the provision of any specific guidance for the conduct of practical affairs. The reader, Hobbes said, should not expect to find "Philosophers Stones" or guides like those "found in the Metaphysique Codes." Rather, readers should only find the "Natural Reason of Man" at work. And so "Philosophy . . . , the Childe of the World and your own Mind, is within your self; perhaps not fashioned yet, but like the World its Father, as it was in the beginning, a thing confused." Then he continued with an image that would not be out of place in any of the philosophers from the ancient Greeks to Wittgenstein and Oakeshott, who take the defining characteristic of philosophy to be to explain and elucidate the world, not to change it. "Do therefore as the Statuaries do, who by hewing off that which is superfluous, do not make, but find the Image. . . . If you will be a

Philosopher in good earnest, let your Reason move upon the Deep of your own Cogitations and Experience. Those things that lie in Confusion must be set asunder, distinguished, and every one stampt with its own name set in order; that is to say, your Method must resemble that of the Creation." Then having noted the subject matter of the three sections of his own philosophical system, the last of which was already published as *Leviathan*, he concluded in a typically seriocomic fashion:

> But whatsoever shall be the Method you will like, I would very fain commend Philosophy to you, that is to say, the study of Wisdome, for want of which we have all suffered much damage lately. For even they that study Wealth, do it out of love to Wisdome; for their Treasures serve them but for a Looking-glass, wherein to behold and contemplate their owne Wisdome. Nor do they that love to be employed in publike business, aim at anything but place wherein to shew their Wisdome. Neither do Voluptuous men neglect Philosophy, but onely because they know not how great a pleasure it is to the Mind of Man to be ravished in the vigorous and perpetual embraces of the most beauteous World. Lastly, though for nothing else, yet (because the Mind of Man is no less impatient of Empty Time, then Nature is of Empty Place) to the end you be not forced for want of what to do, to be troublesome to men that have business, or take hurt by falling into idle Company, but have somewhat of your own wherewith to fill up your time, I recommend unto you the Study of Philosophy, *Farewell*.[45]

So philosophical inquiry, including political philosophy, was designed to dispel confusion by identifying (finding) the rational truth about the world. It was an exercise in self-realization, since philosophy is a "child of the world" and of everyone's "mind." Its practical use to the general reader was to keep idle minds profitably occupied and increasingly cultivated by revealing the shallowness of those who think themselves wise simply because they are rich or famous and by displaying the world's exquisite beauty. In the process, the real wisdom that philosophy has to impart could not but serve the interests of peaceful, civil intercourse and thereby help to avoid the severe "damage" that accompanies the breakdown of civil order. The contrast with Locke's immediately practical design in writing *Two Treatises* as a manifesto for a prospective revolution and then publishing it to "*establish the Throne of our Great Restorer, Our present King* William" could hardly be greater.[46]

So if the evidence suggests, as it seems to, that Hobbes did not share Skinner's view about what he was doing in *Leviathan*, how does Skinner justify reducing Hobbes and the whole of the history of political thought to the history of ideology? Oakeshott raised this question in a critical remark on Skinner's *The Foundations of Modern Political Thought*. Skinner's recent response, however, misrepresents Oakeshott's position in a possibly revealing way. Let me, then, conclude with a few, tentative remarks on this.

In his review of Skinner's *Foundations*, Oakeshott noted that there was, of course, a "very extensive literature" of the kind Skinner had called "ideological" and which he had treated in an exemplary historical fashion in the book. He then added, "But it would be going too far to suggest that reflexion of this kind, on these topics, comprises the whole of 'political thought.' It leaves out of account both the instrumental reflexion devoted to administrative invention and philosophical reflexion concerned with reasons of a different kind from mere justifications or rebuttals of the circumstantial claims of rulers" (*VMES*, 288). Skinner's recent response was dismissive. Oakeshott had "berated" him, he claimed, "for failing to understand that 'genuine' political theory occupies an autonomous philosophical realm." And he added, "Nor was he the only critic to make things easier for himself by inserting his preferred conclusion into his premises."[47] But Oakeshott had said nothing of the kind, and it was certainly not his "conclusion" that "genuine" political theory (whatever that might be) occupied an "autonomous philosophical realm."

Oakeshott's point was one I have been making all along. Political thinking is not and never has been all of a piece. To paraphrase Oakeshott, the history of political thought consists of different people, at different times, in different intellectual and physical circumstances, engaging with politics in different ways and finding different things to think about. Of the different ways of engaging with politics, some are directly practical (as, for example, "reflection *in the service of politics*" of the kind that generates "*policy*") and some are explanatory. Among the explanatory, some are directed toward the construction of "*political doctrine*," and others pursue the path of "radical reflective subversiveness," which Oakeshott considered characterized philosophical reflection alone (*RPML*, 146–55).

"Political theory," as Oakeshott understood the phrase, might encompass policy and political doctrine, two varieties of practical political thinking, although the latter, Oakeshott believed, offered only spurious guidance for political conduct. And even though the term is highly contested, these kinds of political theory might be called "ideological." But they could in no way display the radical subversiveness of philosophical thought. They would collapse under the weight of their own incoherence. So "political theory" of a practical political kind does not occupy an autonomous philosophical realm, according to Oakeshott. It is anchored in the world of practical politics, and what coherence it does have is derived from that anchorage. And this, one might say, is what makes it amenable to the methods of historical interpretation that Skinner's *Foundations* exemplify so splendidly.

But nor does political philosophy inhabit an autonomous philosophical realm. It is, in Oakeshott's view, "radically subversive" of everyday ideas about political life, as well as of those kinds of political reflection that generate policies and political doctrines. Like political engagement, philosophy is a practice that has to be learned. But it is a practice of a very different kind. So its history, too, will be of a different kind from the history of "ideologists." To be sure, philosophers do things with words. But they do different things as philosophers from the things ideologists do as ideologists. So a historian of political philosophy certainly has to take seriously Wittgenstein's observations that "words are also deeds" and that "concepts are not timeless entities . . . but tools." If words were not deeds, philosophy would not be a practice. And if concepts were timeless entities, they could have no place in a history marked by the differences between past and present meaning.

Now most, if not all of this, will be perfectly familiar to Skinner. So the question remains why he ignored Oakeshott's criticism that his conception of the scope of political thought was arbitrarily limited to include only ideological reflection and instead recast that criticism as an assertion about an autonomous philosophical realm for "genuine political theory." I can offer only one speculative thought. It seems possible, I would suggest, that Skinner read into Oakeshott's criticism much of the unhistorical or antihistorical baggage that marred the theory and practice of the history of political thought at the time that he and John Pocock began revolutionizing the field in the late 1960s. In particular, he may have taken Oakeshott to have been advocating the study of "a canon of 'classic' texts," assuming that those texts contained "a 'dateless wisdom' in the form of 'universal ideas.'" And that they should be read "as if 'written by a contemporary' for our own edification and benefit."[48] If this is the case, I hope at the very least that my review of Oakeshott on the history of political thought has succeeded in showing that nothing could have been further from Oakeshott's mind.

NOTES

1. Quentin Skinner, *Liberty Before Liberalism* (Cambridge: Cambridge University Press, 1998), 101–20; and Mark Goldie, "The Context of *The Foundations*," in *Rethinking the Foundations of Modern Political Thought*, ed. Annabel Brett and James Tully (Cambridge: Cambridge University Press, 2006), 3–19, provide helpful sketches of the emergence of the Cambridge School.

2. Quentin Skinner, *The Foundations of Modern Political Thought* (Cambridge: Cambridge University Press, 1978), 1:xi. Several commentators have addressed questions of the relationship between history and ideology in Skinner's work. But, as in the recent review essay by Nadia

Urbinati, the concern has tended to be about the relationship between Skinner the historian and Skinner the supposed ideologist. Oakeshott's question, by contrast, concerned the range and scope of Skinner's conception of "political theory"; Urbinati, "The Historian and the Ideologist," *Political Theory* 33, no. 1 (2005): 89–95.

3. I agree with Kenneth B. McIntyre's analysis in *The Limits of Political Theory: Oakeshott's Philosophy of Civil Association* (Exeter: Imprint Academic, 2004), 117–19.

4. The editor, Timothy Fuller, quite rightly notes that this "book, although neither an historical monograph nor a strictly philosophical essay, includes elements of both, and more. It is as close to a book of advice for the practice of modern politics as Oakeshott ever produced" (*PFPS*, x).

5. Here I happily correct my own misleading characterization of Oakeshott's lectures as lectures in the history of Western political thought. Martyn P. Thompson, "Michael Oakeshott: Notes on 'Political Thought' and 'Political Theory' in the History of Political Thought, 1966–69," in *Politisches Denken Jahrbuch, 1991*, ed. Volker Gerhardt, Henning Ottmann, and Martyn P. Thompson (Stuttgart: Metzler, 1992), 103.

6. For a convincing argument that Oakeshott rejected recourse to ideal types in historical inquiry, see Gene Callahan, "Ideal Types and the Historical Method," *Collingwood and British Idealism Studies* 13 (2007): 53–68. On ideal types and philosophy, Oakeshott once remarked of Hegel's philosophy that "unlike [Benjamin] Constant, Hegel was a philosopher concerned not merely to identify a 'State' in terms of desirable characteristics (e.g., religious freedom, 'representative' government etc.) but to distinguish an ideal *mode* of association and to theorize it in terms of its postulates" (*VMES*, 230). In introducing his lecture on Aristotle's political philosophy, Oakeshott told his students that here "we will get our first glimpse of what it is to reflect philosophically about politics" (*LHPT*, 117).

7. See the relevant annual *Calendars* (London: London School of Economics and Political Science, 1966–67) and *Sessional Timetables* (London: London School of Economics and Political Science, 1966–67).

8. The most relevant essays are "Political Education" and "The Study of 'Politics' in a University: An Essay in Appropriateness," in *RP*, 43–69, 184–218.

9. The editors do note some of these unhistorical and historically questionable elements. But much that they say by way of explanation misses Oakeshott's point. Their suggestion that Oakeshott presents a "liberal" account of the history of toleration is an example (*LHPT*, 27). For Oakeshott such qualifiers as liberal, conservative, socialist, and so on belong to the language of practice, not explanation. Other putative "problems" identified by the editors arise from their own lack of care. Thus, for example, they note that Oakeshott identified "first three and then four Aristotelian approaches to politics" (11n19). But they fail to note that the reference to "three" came in Oakeshott's daytime lectures, the reference to "four" in the evening lectures, usually, perhaps always, given by someone else. In fact, all of the lectures in the edition are the morning lectures, except for this one (lecture 7, the second one on Aristotle). Furthermore, it is somewhat troubling that the edition contains thirty-two lectures, but the series only ever consisted of thirty (ten per term over three terms). Lecture 18 is clearly too short to have been delivered in the series. And in all the live "performances" that I witnessed (and in the copies of the lecture notes in my possession), lectures 21 and 22 were combined into a single lecture.

10. *On History*, of course, is dedicated to "all who, over the years, have been members of the seminar on the history of political thought in the LSE." I was fortunate enough to have attended the undergraduate lectures and to have participated in the graduate seminars over many years.

11. Skinner's qualified embrace of Begriffsgeschichte makes the last point admirably. The "fundamental point we need to grasp if we are to study the phenomenon of conceptual change," he says, is the "almost paradoxical contention . . . that the various transformations we can hope to chart will not strictly speaking be changes in concepts at all. They will be transformations in the application of the terms by which our concepts are expressed." *Visions of Politics, Regarding Method*, vol. 1 (Cambridge: Cambridge University Press, 2002), 179.

12. The categorical distinction between past and present meanings is the central theme of Oakeshott's discussion of "historical experience" in *EM*, 86–168.

13. For further references, see *LHPT*, 99, 160, 176, 322–23, 392–94. An early sketch of these distinctions has been published in *MPME*, 13–15.

14. The phrase "pre-eminent voice" is deployed in *On History*, not in the lectures.

15. The next few paragraphs summarize and extend part of my argument in "The Logic of the History of Ideas" (forthcoming).

16. Johannes Althusius, *Politica methodice digesta* (Herborn, 1603); Thomas Hobbes, *Leviathan* (London, 1651).

17. Jean Bodin, *De republica libri sex* (Paris, 1586); Henning Arnisaeus, *De jure majestatis libri tres* (Frankfurt, 1610).

18. This is an admirably succinct description of what, for example, Merio Scattola was doing with the original three surviving editions of Althusius's *Politica* in his essay "Von der *maiestas* zur *symbiosis*: Der Weg des Johannes Althusius zur eigenen politischen Lehre in den drei Aufla-gen seiner *Politica methodice digesta*," in *Politische Begriffe und historisches Umfeld in der "Politica methodice digesta" des Johannes Althusius*, ed. Emilio Bonfatti, Giuseppe Duso, and Merio Scattola (Wiesbaden: Harrassowitz Verlag, 2002), 211–49.

19. Much of the evidence about the Herborn edition is discussed in Howard Hotson, "The Conservative Face of Contractual Theory: The *Monarchomach* Servants of the Count of Nassau-Dillenburg," in *Politische Begriffe*, ed. Bonfatti, Duso, and Scattola, 251–89. Hotson's conclusion, however, that the first edition of Althusius's *Politica* was designed as a "conservative" work is somewhat misleading. It was certainly not designed to foment resistance or to justify armed resistance in the manner, say, of the *Vindiciae contra tyrannos* (1579). But the activity of Calvinist state building, for which it was designed, was an altogether novel enterprise. It was, then, not at all conservative in any meaningful sense of the word.

20. The standard account of these circumstances is Heinz Antholz, *Die politische Wirksamkeit des Johannes Althusius in Emden* (Leer, Ostfriesland: Verlag, 1954). But see also Corrado Mal-andrino, "Il *Syndikat* di Johannes Althusius a Emden: La Ricerca," *Il Pensiero Politico* 28, no. 3 (1995): 359–83.

21. None of the modern editions reproduce the whole of Althusius's text. But they are all based on the third edition.

22. The notion that historians are in the business of reconstructing bygone times that were once experienced as present times is untenable. It ignores the "fluidity," the lack of "fixity" and the "constructed" character of both the past and the present. A classic set of reflections on the fleeting nature of the present and the "fluidity" of time past, present, and future is to be found, of course, in Saint Augustine's *Confessions*, trans. Richard S. Pine-Coffin (London: Penguin, 1961), bk. 11, esp. chs. 14–31.

23. "Property," Locke wrote in 1703, "I have nowhere found more clearly explained, than in a book entitled, Two Treatises of Government." Quoted in Peter Laslett, ed., *John Locke: Two Trea-tises of Government* (Cambridge: Cambridge University Press, 1960), 3.

24. Hobbes's reference is in all likelihood to Lucian's *Hermotimus or the Rival Philosophers*, in Henry W. Fowler and Francis G. Fowler, eds., *The Works of Lucian* (Oxford: Clarendon Press, 1905), 2:41–90.

25. Hobbes calls "Pernicious Philosophy" "Vain Philosophy" in *Leviathan*, ed. Michael Oake-shott (Oxford: Blackwell, 1946), chap. 46. Hobbes, *Elements of Philosophy, the First Section, Con-cerning Body* (London, 1656). "The Authors Epistle Dedicatory, to the Right Honorable, My Most Honored Lord, William Earl of Devonshire," London, *April* 23, 1655, n.p. The original Latin ver-sion was published in 1655.

26. Thomas Hobbes, *De corpore* (London, 1656); Hobbes, *De homine* (London, 1658); Hobbes, *De cive* (Paris, 1642).

27. Hobbes, *Leviathan*, ch. 8.

28. John Locke, *Two Treatises* (London, 1690).

29. Eric S. Kos argues a similar point in *Michael Oakeshott, The Ancient Greeks and the Philo-sophical Study of Politics* (Exeter: Imprint Academic, 2007), 124–36.

30. Quentin Skinner, preface to *Hobbes and Republican Liberty* (Cambridge: Cambridge Uni-versity Press, 2008), xvi.

31. Famously, for Oakeshott, *Leviathan* was a rare "masterpiece of political philosophy" (*HCA*, 8).

32. Skinner, *Modern Political Thought*, 1:xi; Quentin Skinner, "Hobbes on Representation," *European Journal of Philosophy* 13, no. 2 (2005): 155.

33. Skinner, *Hobbes and Republican Liberty*, xvi.

34. G. W. F. Hegel, *Philosophy of Right*, trans. T. M. Knox (London: Oxford University Press, 1952), 11.

35. Skinner, *Hobbes and Republican Liberty*, xvi; and *The Return of Grand Theory in the Human Sciences*, ed. Quentin Skinner (Cambridge: Cambridge University Press, 1985), 13.

36. Ludwig Wittgenstein, *Tractatus Logico-Philosophicus*, trans. David F. Pears and Brian F. McGuiness (London: Routledge and Kegan Paul, 1961), prop. 4.112.

37. Ludwig Wittgenstein, *Philosophical Investigations*, trans. G. E. M. Anscombe (Oxford: Basil Blackwell, 1976), secs. 123, 24.

38. For a brilliant, very brief, and critical survey, see Ruediger Bubner, *Modern German Philosophy* (Cambridge: Cambridge University Press, 1981), 173–79. See also Jürgen Habermas, Dieter Henrich, and Jacob Taubes, eds., *Theorie-Diskussion: Hermeneutik und Ideologiekritik* (Frankfurt am Main: Suhrkamp Verlag, 1971).

39. A forceful presentation of all this can be found in Jürgen Habermas, *Toward a Rational Society*, trans. Jeremy J. Shapiro (London: Heinemann, 1971).

40. For the emergence in ancient Greece of philosophy as a purely "theoretical exercise" and not a practical one, see the splendidly succinct survey by Michael Frede, "The Philosopher," in *Greek Thought*, ed. Jacques Brunschwig and Geoffrey E. R. Lloyd (Cambridge: Harvard University Press, 2000), 3–19.

41. For references to seventeenth-century debates about "the practical applicability of philosophical reason," see Jonathan Israel, *Enlightenment Contested* (Oxford: Oxford University Press, 2006), 471–95.

42. See, for example, Skinner's concluding essay, "Surveying the *Foundations:* A Retrospect and Reassessment," in *Rethinking the Foundations*, ed. Brett and Tully, esp. 242.

43. A similar observation seems to be behind Peter J. Steinberger's recent critique of the limitations of Skinner's method. I cannot see, however, how his suggested remedy, which involves a fairly arbitrary distinction between "analysis" and "interpretation," can help. See "Analysis and History of Political Thought," *American Political Science Review* 103, no. 1 (2009): 135–46.

44. At least one of Hobbes's contemporaries, the rather eccentric Seth Ward, almost agreed. In attacking the use of Aristotle in the universities, he suggested that much better guides for students of "political learning' were offered by Bodin, Machiavelli, and "our own Countreyman master *Hobbs.*" *Vindiciae Academiarum* (Oxford, 1654), 88.

45. "The Authors Epistle *To the Reader*," in Hobbes, *Elements of Philosophy*, n.p.

46. Laslett, *John Locke*, 137. When Hegel, in his famous *Lectures on the History of Philosophy* from 1805 onward, came to discuss modern philosophy, Hobbes and Locke featured relatively large in the discussion. Locke, in fact, was treated much more extensively than Hobbes. Of all of Hobbes's works, the only two that merited philosophical attention were *De cive* and *Leviathan*. As for Locke, the only work that Hegel found of philosophical interest was the *Essay Concerning Human Understanding*. After a relatively thorough review of the essay, Hegel concluded, "This is Locke's philosophy. Locke's other achievements in terms of education, toleration, natural law and the general theory of the state are of no concern to us here. They are matters of general culture." Oakeshott would not have dissented. *De cive* and *Leviathan* were appropriate kinds of texts for historians of philosophical thinking, but *Two Treatises* was too uninteresting philosophically to warrant such attention. Hegel, *Werke in zwanzig Bänden* (Frankfurt am Main: Suhrkamp Verlag, 1971), 20, 221 (my translation).

47. Skinner, "Surveying the *Foundations*," in *Rethinking the Foundations*, ed. Brett and Tully, 244.

48. Ibid., 241.

10

OAKESHOTT AND HOBBES

Noel Malcolm

I

Even those who know only a little about Michael Oakeshott know that he had a strong and abiding interest in the philosophy of Thomas Hobbes. His edition of *Leviathan* (1946) became the standard edition for several generations of students, and his substantial introduction to that volume, which was reissued in a revised version in 1975, remains one of the classic texts of modern Hobbes interpretation. Oakeshott's special interest in Hobbes had developed more than a decade before the appearance of that edition; his first publication devoted to Hobbes was a long essay in the literary-critical magazine *Scrutiny* in 1935, in which he surveyed a range of recent publications on Hobbes's political thought and emphasized that the old caricature of Hobbes as a philosopher of "despotism" was now completely untenable.[1] In 1937 Oakeshott returned to this subject with a review of another book, a study of Hobbes's political philosophy by Leo Strauss; here he agreed with Strauss that Hobbes's political thought was not grounded on a crudely "naturalistic" kind of science, while disagreeing with Strauss's attempt to derive it from a set of purely moral assumptions. After the introduction to *Leviathan*, Oakeshott wrote another lengthy exploration of Hobbes's moral theory (with an "appendix" on his theory of the formation of the state), an essay entitled "The Moral Life in the Writings of Thomas Hobbes," published in *Rationalism in Politics and Other Essays* (1962). With the exception of the *Scrutiny* article, these items were gathered (together with a short essay, originally a radio talk, entitled "*Leviathan*: A Myth," which Oakeshott described as "a conversation piece, a flight of fancy") in a volume published under the title *Hobbes on Civil Association* in 1975. And from the same period (1974) dates also a substantial book review, of a monograph on Hobbes by Thomas Spragens, which was later reprinted under the title "Logos and Telos" in the expanded edition of *Rationalism in Politics*; here Oakeshott once again challenged the idea that Hobbes's philosophy was simply modeled on natural science, emphasizing that it explored, rather, a world of human intentions and human meanings. In every one of these texts it is evident that Oakeshott wrote about Hobbes not merely as a historian of ideas, but as a philosopher who found, in Hobbes's central arguments, something valid and philosophically important.[2]

But herein lies a problem. Those who know only a little about Michael Oakeshott also know that he was deeply opposed to "rationalism" in political theory and practice; yet most of the attitudes and beliefs which he identified as rationalist are also to be found in Hobbes. And this is not a matter of some minor or secondary features of Hobbes's thinking that happen to overlap, coincidentally, with rationalist positions; rather, the whole portrait of the rationalist in the opening pages of Oakeshott's essay "Rationalism in Politics" reads like a list of central features of Hobbes's approach to political theory.

The rationalist, Oakeshott writes, "stands . . . for thought free from obligation to any authority save the authority of 'reason'" (*RP*, 5–6). Compare Oakeshott's own characterization of Hobbes: "For Hobbes, to think philosophically is to reason; philosophy is reasoning. To this all else is subordinate"; "the inspiration of his philosophy is the intention to be guided by reason and to reject all other guides."[3] The rationalist, we are told, is "sceptical," "optimistic," and "something also of an individualist" (*RP*, 6). Again, both Hobbes's skepticism and his individualism are emphasized in Oakeshott's introduction to *Leviathan*; as for optimism, we have only to turn to the dedicatory epistle of Hobbes's *De cive*, where he wrote that if philosophy were applied to human actions with the same degree of certainty as that achieved by geometers in their study of geometrical figures, "ambition and greed, whose power is founded on the false opinions of the common people about right and injury, would be disarmed, and the human race would enjoy such secure peace that . . . it seems unlikely that there would ever be a reason for fighting."[4]

According to Oakeshott, the rationalist has "no sense of the cumulation of experience"; to the rationalist, "nothing is of value merely because it exists (and certainly not because it has existed for many generations)" (*RP*, 6, 8). This chimes with Hobbes's polemical attacks on the alleged authority of custom, such as his comment in *Leviathan* that "When long Use obtaineth the authority of a Law, it is not the Length of Time that maketh the Authority, but the Will of the Soveraign signified by his silence. . . . Many unjust Actions, and unjust Sentences, go uncontrolled a longer time, than any man can remember."[5] In his *Dialogue . . . of the Common Laws of England*, similarly, Hobbes dismissed the claims made by the leading Common Lawyer Sir Edward Coke about "an artificial perfection of Reason gotten by long Study, Observation and Experience," and insisted that, by applying his own reason and consulting the statute-book, he could become a perfectly competent judge "in a Month, or two."[6]

The rationalist, Oakeshott writes, campaigns against prejudice and "the fumes of tradition" (RP, 8–9). Hobbes devoted much of the fourth part of Leviathan to his campaign against the whole classical-scholastic heritage of metaphysics, physics, ethics, and political philosophy; he believed that only when this entire tradition of thought was cleared out of people's minds could human beings achieve lasting political stability, founded on true civil science. And when Oakeshott says that the rationalist believes in "the blank sheet of infinite possibility," and adds that "if by chance this tabula rasa has been defaced by the irrational scribblings of tradition-ridden ancestors, then the first task of the Rationalist must be to scrub it clean" (9), it is hard to believe that he is not mindful of Hobbes's famous remark that "the Common-peoples minds, unless they be tainted with dependance on the Potent, or scribbled over with the opinions of their Doctors, are like clean paper, fit to receive whatsoever by Publique Authority shall be imprinted in them."[7]

The "hidden spring" of rationalism, as Oakeshott explains, is a belief in technical knowledge—which, by its very nature, is "susceptible of precise formulation"—as the sufficient or even the sole form of knowledge. This goes with a "preoccupation with certainty" and an obsession with method, of the sort that can be expounded in a book; what it excludes is the kind of practical knowledge that is acquired only through prolonged contact with an experienced practitioner (RP, 11–17). Here one is reminded of Hobbes's frequent insistence that true "science," which yields certain knowledge, is different from "prudence," which merely extracts probabilities from experience.[8] Hobbes believed that geometry was the prototype of a true science, and that his own civil science was modeled on it; at the end of his English Optical Treatise he expressed the hope that he would be recognized as "having beene the first to lay the ground of two Sciences, this of Opticques, the most curious, and that other of naturall Justice, which I have done in my booke de Cive."[9] The contrast with "practical" knowledge was made by Hobbes himself: "The skill of making, and maintaining Common-wealths, consisteth in certain Rules, as doth Arithmetique and Geometry; not (as Tennis-play) on Practise onely: which Rules, neither poor men have the leisure, nor men that have had the leisure, have hitherto had the curiosity, or the method to find out."[10] In that passage the key phrase is "certain Rules": true civil science, according to Hobbes, could operate with a certainty as absolute as that supplied by the mathematical sciences. And as Oakeshott says, "The heart of the matter is the pre-occupation of the Rationalist with certainty. Technique and certainty are, for him, inseparably joined because certain knowledge . . . not only ends with certainty but begins with certainty and is certain throughout" (*RP*, 16).

Oakeshott's essay on "Rationalism in Politics" does make some attempt to locate the birth of rationalism historically. He observes that "the moment when it shows itself unmistakably" is in the early seventeenth century, and he identifies both Bacon and Descartes as foundational figures in the rationalist tradition (*RP*, 18, 19–22). In this account, Hobbes, whose philosophical formation took place in the early seventeenth century, and who enjoyed personal relations with both Bacon and Descartes (friendly with the former, rivalrous with the latter), is passed over without even a mention. In Oakeshott's introduction to *Leviathan*, on the other hand, Hobbes is briefly identified as an exemplar of "rationalism," but only in order to emphasize the gulf that separated his kind of rationalism from that of a thinker such as Descartes: "The lineage of Hobbes's rationalism lies, not (like that of Spinoza or even Descartes) in the great Platonic-Christian tradition, but in the sceptical, late scholastic tradition. He does not normally speak of Reason, the divine illumination of the mind that unites man with God; he speaks of reasoning. And he is not less persuaded of its fallibility and limitations than Montaigne himself."[11] There is some tension between this discussion and the account given subsequently in "Rationalism in Politics": in the later essay, Descartes is himself characterized as an exponent of "scepticism," whose role as a founding father of rationalism was to a large extent foisted on him by later generations of vulgarizing Cartesians (*RP*, 21–22). More puzzlingly, that account also portrays the "reason" of the rationalists as something very different from "Reason, the divine illumination of the mind that unites man with God": an important footnote in "Rationalism in Politics" declares that "The 'reason' to which the Rationalist appeals is not, for example, the Reason of Hooker, which belongs still to the tradition of Stoicism and of Aquinas. It is a faculty of calculation by which men conclude one thing from another and discover fit means of attaining given ends not themselves subject to the criticism of reason" (*RP*, 22–23)—a description which, while no doubt formulated with twentieth-century social engineers in mind, seems to match quite closely the Hobbesian notion of "reasoning."

While Oakeshott entertained different ideas at different times about the notion of "reason" held by the rationalists, the one unchanging criterion on which he seems to have distinguished their notion from Hobbes's was that of certainty. Hobbes's concept of philosophical knowledge, he argued, was doubly disqualified from providing certain truth about the world: first, because it depended on "names" (linguistic terms) that were arbitrary impositions and, secondly, because it consisted only of conditional or hypothetical statements.[12] This part of Oakeshott's interpretation of Hobbes does not stand up well to scrutiny. When he attributes to Hobbes the view that "Truth is of universals, but they are names, the names of images left over from sensations; and a true proposition is not an assertion about the real world," he misrepresents Hobbes's nominalism, which declared only that universals were names as opposed to real entities; truth was a property of statements, not things, but those statements could indeed be true statements (whether particular or general) about the world.[13] As for philosophical knowledge being only conditional or hypothetical, this was the case, in Hobbes's view, in two quite different ways. First, all universal truths about things were conditional or hypothetical as to the existence of those things: to say that "a crow is a bird" is a necessary truth does not mean that any crow necessarily "is," and the truth can always be reformulated as "if there is a crow, it is a bird." Secondly, the particular sort of philosophical knowledge that concerned the causes of physical phenomena was always hypothetical, always just the knowledge of a possible cause, because the same things could be produced by different causes.[14] But philosophical knowledge, for Hobbes, was not confined to postulating the causes of physical phenomena. According to Hobbes, there was another kind of knowledge of causes, a kind of science in which certain knowledge was possible because human beings were themselves the causes of the objects of that science. His first example of such a science was geometry, in which human beings make circles, triangles, etc., and determine the nature of those geometrical objects by the way they think of them; and his second example was civil science. "Geometry therefore is demonstrable; for the Lines and Figures from which we reason are drawn and described by our selves; and Civill Philosophy is demonstrable, because we make the Common-wealth our selves."[15]

II

Thus far, it may seem that Oakeshott's admiration for Hobbes can be rendered compatible with his hostility to rationalism in politics only on the basis of a misunderstanding: apparently, Oakeshott was prepared to overlook the many obvious similarities between Hobbes and the rationalists because he believed, wrongly, that on one fundamental issue—that of certainty—Hobbes represented a contrary point of view. But to leave the matter there would be to fail to acknowledge the most important way in which Oakeshott regarded

Hobbes as a representative of the non-rationalist or anti-rationalist position. The essential nature of his interest in Hobbes was summed up in the title he chose for the collection of his writings about him: *Hobbes on Civil Association*. More than anything else, what attracted him to the earlier philosopher was Hobbes's account of the nature of a political community as something constituted by a web of mutual understandings and mutual commitments of a peculiarly open-ended and unconditional kind. In Oakeshott's eyes, Hobbes was an archetypal non-rationalist in politics because he had a rich understanding of the non-instrumentality of the state.

The first signs of Oakeshott's interest in this aspect of Hobbes's thought can be found in an early work, the essay on "The Authority of the State" (1929). Readers of Oakeshott who know how strongly his early thinking was anchored in the tradition of British Hegelianism will of course be inclined to read this essay as a purely Hegelian text. Its argument is that what has genuine authority for us is never merely external to us; on the contrary, the only final authority must be "our world of ideas as a whole." The state, in its fullest sense, is much more than an apparatus of government; it is the "totality" in which all human activities (economic, religious, intellectual, etc.) find their meaning. "If it is to be a concrete fact, the state must be self-subsistent, something which carries with it the explanation of itself and requires to be linked on to no more comprehensive whole in order to be understood" (*RPML*, 79, 83). So far, so Hegelian. But readers with an interest in Hobbes may well be struck by a passage in which Oakeshott attacks the notion that it is possible to separate the "state" from society, since this would leave us with "on the one side, mere government, political organization for its own sake . . . and on the other side, a society without organization, which again is an abstraction and nowhere to be found in the concrete world" (84). This corresponds quite closely to Hobbes's constant argument that "sovereign" and "people" are correlative terms: unless it lives under the authority of a sovereign representative, a people is not a people at all, but merely a "multitude," an aggregate of individuals. And the suspicion that Oakeshott himself may also have had Hobbes in mind here is strengthened by the pronouncement about the authority of the state in the essay's final sentence, "Of this authority, and of no other, can it be said, *Non est potestas super terram quae comparetur ei*"—where the Latin is the phrase from Job 41:24, "There is no power on earth that may be compared to him," which appears at the head of the famous engraved title page of *Leviathan*.[16]

If Oakeshott was combining Hegel and Hobbes here, the key to the combination was the idea that the state not only embodied the "totality" of all the meanings and values of those who belonged to it, but was in some sense the ground or condition of their having those values at all. With this idea as a

starting point, the argument could go in either of two quite different directions. A teleological approach would portray the state as something embodying a higher value, so that individuals would enhance their own value as they
aligned themselves more fully with it; a non-teleological approach would
argue that the state's value is merely the inherent value of everything that
takes place within it, and that the state itself can have no telos. Oakeshott's
own phrasing in this essay ("the state must be self-subsistent, something
which carries with it the explanation of itself and requires to be linked on to
no more comprehensive whole in order to be understood") is perhaps ambiguous, not least because it is framed in terms of meanings rather than values,
but it does clearly exclude the idea that the state should be seen as serving
some overarching aim or value of a kind that can be separately conceived or
described. The citizens' allegiance to the state, therefore, cannot be ascribed
to, or made conditional on, the fact that the state fulfills some separately
describable purpose or value. That allegiance is unconditional because the
state is understood to be the condition of any and every purpose or value that
an individual citizen might hold. And here, at the moment when a Hegelian
concept of the state receives a Hobbesian nudge in a non-teleological direction, we see what may be the origins of Oakeshott's ideas about the peculiar
nature of "civil association."

Hobbes, certainly, was non-teleological and anti-teleological in his entire
pattern of thought. This in itself makes him an opponent of one type of "rationalist" thinker, the type that assumes that reason can intuit supreme values
or goals, and that the aim of politics is to construct a state and a society that
will fulfill them. In this category are to be found all political idealists and
utopians, both secular and theologically grounded, and all those who come
under Oakeshott's description of the "politics of faith"—believers in the possibility of "human perfection," who think that the role of government is either
to lead people towards perfection, or to force them to conform to a perfect
pattern (*PFPS*, 45). Such people might be described as grand rationalists, and
in their case Oakeshott's characterization of Hobbes as an anti-rationalist
was clearly correct. But it is surely also possible to be a rationalist without
subscribing to any such high-flying ideals, or indeed to any teleology at all.
Non-teleological rationalism—what might be called petty rationalism—prefers to describe political activity using more modest metaphors drawn from
engineering: the task of government is to make an endless succession of
small-scale adjustments and improvements to the mechanisms of economic
and social life (what Karl Popper famously described as "piecemeal social
engineering"). Most of Oakeshott's essay on "Rationalism in Politics" is concerned with petty rationalism of this sort. And while it may be true that a
belief in teleology stimulates a stronger kind of rationalism, it may also be the

case that a lack of belief in teleology, for many people, leads easily towards a rationalist approach to politics: in the absence of any overall goal, it is easy to think of politics merely in terms of "problem-solving."

For some of Oakeshott's contemporaries, Hobbes's anti-teleological stance was a guarantee of his essential liberalism. Thus R. G. Collingwood, who in the draft preface to his *The New Leviathan* described Hobbes's treatise as "the first book in which the idea of a civilised society was consciously and systematically expounded," wrote that a belief in liberalism and democracy "means renouncing all Utopias and all millenniums: all hope of omnipotence or omniscience, whether in relation to Nature or in relation to man. It means believing that human beings will never have solved all their problems, overcome all their difficulties, or settled all their quarrels; but that they need never lack the wits, the power, or the good will to solve the problems which at any given moment they most urgently need to solve."[17] But the contours of liberalism do not map exactly onto those of anti-rationalism, as conceived by Oakeshott. Although the liberal-democratic attitude described by Collingwood here would no doubt have seemed, in Oakeshott's eyes, hugely preferable to Utopian pseudo-omniscience (Collingwood was referring to fascism and Nazism in particular), it was nevertheless an essentially rationalist attitude, with its portrayal of true politics as "problem-solving." Oakeshott could not have agreed, therefore, with Collingwood's idea that Hobbes was one of the prime exponents of this liberal tradition.

For some writers, on the other hand, the absence of teleology in Hobbes's thought was part and parcel of his extreme illiberalism. Indeed, the traditional view of Hobbes as a defender of "despotism" took his eschewal of ultimate guiding values as the basis of what was so objectionable about his politics: the absolute power of the sovereign could not be limited or controlled in the name of any higher or transcendental value (such as religious truth, or the values enshrined in traditional natural law theory), because Hobbes had eliminated all such values from his account. The point here was not that Hobbes would have had any enthusiasm for the self-proclaimed teleology of, say, the Third Reich, but merely that he offered no set of objective values on which to base resistance to it, other than that of mere self-preservation. In the mid-1930s, when Oakeshott's ideas about Hobbes were forming, a strong version of this criticism of Hobbes was put forward by the French Catholic philosopher Joseph Vialatoux: his book *La Cité de Hobbes: Théorie de l'état totalitaire* accused Hobbes of expounding a "totalitarian naturalism" which, by eliminating higher values, paved the way towards the totalitarian ideologies of the twentieth century. He was answered by a young law professor, René Capitant, who insisted that Hobbes was a founder of the modern "individualist" tradition, and that individualism led not to totalitarianism but to its opposite, liberalism.[18] In this debate, Oakeshott would certainly have found himself siding with Capitant against Vialatoux; he regarded Hobbes neither as a herald of totalitarianism nor even as a defender of absolutism, declaring in his introduction to *Leviathan* that "Hobbes is not an absolutist precisely because he is an authoritarian. His scepticism about the power of reasoning . . . together with the rest of his individualism, separate him from the rationalist dictators of his or any age. Indeed, Hobbes, without being himself a liberal, had in him more of the philosophy of liberalism than most of its professed defenders."[19] But at the same time that last qualification, insisting that Hobbes was not himself a liberal, indicates that Oakeshott could not have been a wholehearted supporter of Capitant's approach.

Also in the 1930s, a more complex debate about Hobbes's political philosophy was taking place in Germany. The key figure here was the jurist Carl Schmitt, who found in Hobbes's writings a prefiguration of his own radical analysis of the nature of politics and the state. Hobbes, for him, was important because he had understood what was specially and irreducibly political about the realm of political action; he had shared Schmitt's view that the fundamental distinction on which all politics was based was that between friend and foe; he had understood the vital role of conflict as that which generates, and guarantees the validity of, the state; he had, similarly, understood the importance of fear as a motive force; and he had seen the need for a kind of authority that could not be constrained by fixed rules, as it would always be needed to make decisions in those special circumstances—moments of political crisis, and of threat to the state itself—for which no rules could be provided. Above all, Hobbes had grasped that there was an essential difference between the nature of the political and the nature of all particular interests within civil society.[20] Schmitt's fear was that modern liberalism had undermined that essential difference. It had, he thought, mechanized and neutralized the state, making it little more than an instrument, a servant of the needs of various competing interest groups. This, he felt, was what had happened in Weimar Germany, with (in the words of one modern writer), "trade unions versus company goons, communist mobs versus fascist gangs, political party versus political party. . . . Each had declared the right to evaluate self-protection in one's own way, and to act accordingly. Each had claimed the right to judge the political."[21]

Responding to Schmitt in 1932, the young Leo Strauss agreed that the liberal-pluralist approach to politics had neutralized the state, but disputed the claim that Hobbes's political philosophy belonged to the opposite tradition. On the contrary, he thought that Hobbes's argument, with its individualism, its emphasis on the subjective human will, and its portrayal of the state as a product of human choice, had contained the essential principles of the liberal-neutral view.[22] In his book on Hobbes, published in 1936, Strauss emphasized this point: Hobbes's political philosophy rested on a radically new moral vision, and thus formed the starting point of modernity in political theory.[23]

Oakeshott took a close interest in Strauss (as we have seen, he wrote a lengthy review of Strauss's book); he was also aware of Schmitt's views, commenting in his 1935 *Scrutiny* article on Schmitt's discussion of Hobbes in his *Politische Theologie* (1922; 2nd ed. 1934). At some level, it is possible to identify a degree of kinship between Oakeshott's thinking and Schmitt's. Oakeshott could not be entirely satisfied by the theory of the liberal-pluralist "framework" state (even though he was happy to live in something that was largely indistinguishable from it in practice); for it was a theory which, in his view, failed to capture the distinctive nature of what was involved in being subject to the authority that constitutes and binds a political community. And Oakeshott seems also to have felt a certain distaste (though nothing like Schmitt's visceral revulsion) when he contemplated the modern ideology of liberalism in its simple form: in 1939 he commented on "the crude and negative individualism which is apt to be associated with Liberalism," and remarked that "the Fascist criticism of Liberal Democracy is far too acute to be merely ignored" (even though he made it clear that he had no sympathy for what fascism sought to put in its place) (*SPD*, xvii, xxi).

But there were important differences between Oakeshott and Schmitt on these matters. Schmitt sought to take the essential features of political life and strip them down to the raw elements of existential fear and hostility. Oakeshott wanted to understand political life as it is lived in a functioning, civilized state, where rules are followed and traditions of behavior are understood. Schmitt read Hobbes's account of the origins of the state in reductive terms: the state of nature was the deeper reality, always present beneath the surface. Oakeshott read Hobbes's account in much more Humean terms, taking the story of the original covenant as merely a heuristic device or a "myth." What mattered was the sort of agreement that was implicit and inherent in a political community: the civil state, not the state of nature, was the reality from which our understanding of these matters must be drawn.

The point can best be illustrated by means of the analogy with language which Oakeshott developed in his 1935 *Scrutiny* article:

> The creation of language and the establishment of the state are, for Hobbes, inventions of the same character and serve the same end. . . .

> The necessity of an absolute sovereign in the community . . . is a neces-
> sity exactly paralleled by the necessity of fixing the meanings of names
> if language is to serve any useful purpose at all. . . . A language which
> is understood by only a single person and a way of behaviour which is
> pursued by one man independently of all other men are, for Hobbes,
> examples of the same kind of anarchy.[24]

From a Schmittian perspective, to establish that language is arbitrary is to
reduce it to a product of sheer will. From the Oakeshottian point of view, it is
to understand that language is a matter of convention, a system of behavior
that rests merely on its own internal rules, without being grounded on anything else. Language has developed over time, and each person who uses it
today is inheriting centuries of its use. Each user is constrained by its rules;
yet those rules do not reduce the user's freedom, as they do not tell the user
what to say. Language can be used instrumentally for any and every purpose
(promising, begging, buying a loaf . . .), but language as such, and its rules,
are not instrumental: it was not invented for a particular purpose, although
it is obviously true to say that, as language developed, it became supremely
useful. Oakeshott saw Hobbes's whole vision of "civil association" in similar
terms. Like language, civil association involved a system of rules, arbitrary
in some fundamental sense, but not constraining freedom, and enabling the
fulfillment of all kinds of purposes without having any purpose itself.

   If one keeps this analogy in mind, it may become a little easier to see
why Oakeshott regarded Hobbes as a political non-rationalist. In his essay
on "Rationalism in Politics" he put the argument largely in terms of epistemology: what was wrong with rationalism was that it made a mistake about
human knowledge, reducing everything to the technical and the instrumental. In his later works, the argument acquired more of a moral character: the
problem with rationalism was that it threatened human freedom, undermin-
ing the agent's ability to act as a fully human being. These two lines of argument were, it seems, not fully separable. For the idea that all knowledge is
technical, instrumental knowledge reduces all human activity to the supplying of means to statable ends. This is what is morally objectionable: treating
people's activities only as means to ends, even if the ends are their own ends,
demeans their nature as human beings. It implies that others can know the
means better than they do, and it also has the effect of making the ends they
have chosen merely arbitrary, without any real meaning or value.

   What appealed to Oakeshott about Hobbes's vision of the state was, above
all, its non-instrumentality. In Hobbes's story (or "myth") of the covenant that
founded the state, there was a transfer of rights that was entirely open-ended,

without specific conditions or purposes attached to it. The artifice that created the state consisted of non-substantive intentions; the only intention at work there was the intention that there be a sovereign authority. In Oakeshott's view, an enterprise association was also a product of artifice, but one based on substantive intentions. Using the distinction outlined earlier, we might say that a grand rationalist state—a totalitarian one—was one in which the substantive intentions were structured in such a way that all intentions were subsumed under one highest intention, whereas a petty rationalist state—a mechanistic-liberal one, in which politics was the art of piecemeal social engineering—was one in which the role of the state was to adjudicate between particular substantive intentions, bundle some of them together, and find ways of fulfilling them.

Hobbes's state, according to Oakeshott, differed from all of these. His reason for constituting sovereign authority was precisely that there was *no* particular substantive end in view (indeed, if there were, the authority would fail to be sovereign, as it would be limited to whatever was necessary for achieving that particular end, with the result that some other body would be needed to judge whether it had gone beyond those limits). The substantive ends of particular individuals or groups within the state were of no concern to the sovereign. The state did not exist to solve problems; it existed, rather, to be the condition of civilized life.

How did this differ from the neutral liberal "framework" state, which might be described as the one general means towards enabling individuals to pursue their own particular means to particular ends? Oakeshott's answer to this question seems to have been located in the concept of law. If the framework state has only an instrumental value, its laws must have, ultimately, an instrumental value: the framework state can thus shift towards being a facilitator state, which means that law loses its special nature as law and becomes mere policy. Only a state where authority remains fully non-instrumental can maintain a full and proper concept of law. Hence it is that Oakeshott's final, and strongest, claims on Hobbes's behalf are to be found in his essay on the rule of law. Perhaps his most extreme claim about Hobbes—and certainly his most Oakeshottian—is that Hobbes's "Natural Laws," his "maxims of rational conduct," are "no more than an analytic break-down of the intrinsic character of law, what I have called the *jus* inherent in genuine law which distinguishes it from a command . . . or a managerial instruction" (*OH*, 159).

Oakeshottian this may be, but it is not really Hobbesian. Hobbes derived his natural laws not from an analysis of the intrinsic character of law, but from studying and systematizing the means to self-preservation: his definition of a law of nature was "a Precept, or generall Rule, found out by Reason, by which a man is forbidden to do, that, which is destructive of his life, or taketh away the means of preserving the same; and to omit, that, by which he thinketh it may be best preserved." Since peace was the optimum general condition for self-preservation, the fundamental law of nature was "*to seek Peace, and follow it*"; the other laws of nature were statements of the optimum general ways of achieving and maintaining peace.[25] Hobbes thought of his political science as a body of certain and necessary truths not only because it analyzed and established certain meanings (as Euclidean geometry did), but also because it rested on a causal science: it demonstrated a relationship between cause and effect. Human beings who desired to achieve any particular goal in their lives must recognize, if they reasoned correctly, that being alive was a necessary condition of achieving it, and that peace was the best guarantor of that condition. Some actions would always have the long-term effect of endangering peace, and were therefore wrong. The transfer of rights that constituted the commonwealth was something dictated by the laws of nature, and those laws were "Immutable and Eternall" because they stated general truths about the consequences of actions: "For it can never be that Warre shall preserve life, and Peace destroy it."[26]

So there was, underlying Hobbes's concept of the state, a substantive aim: peace. And this aim was itself a means to a substantive end for each human being: self-preservation. Of course it could be argued that these aims are so open-ended that they hardly seem substantive at all; Hobbes makes no attempt to tell the individual what to do when he or she is at peace, or what goals to aim for, given that he or she is alive. But they do have *some* shadowy substantive content. And this in turn has some practical effect, for example, where the right of resistance is concerned. Oakeshott gave a glancing recognition of this in his introduction to *Leviathan* when he observed that "For example, no subject is obliged to kill or to injure himself. . . . The appeal here is from what the law ordains to the end for which the legal order was instituted."[27] And, having noted Hobbes's definition of "felicity" as continual success in the satisfaction of one's desires (whatever the contents of those desires might be), he did devote one lengthy passage to describing the creation of the state as "the means by which a number of men may procure felicity." But that entire passage, significantly, was omitted from the revised version of his text.[28]

Underlying Hobbes's concept of the state, then, was a substantive-intention view of the purpose it was meant to serve. It was a view that arose out of a psychology of means-ends calculations and a (would-be) scientific account, in causal terms, of human nature and human actions. That account was also combined with a different notion of "science," modeled on the definitions and deductions of Euclidean geometry, which was meant to yield certain and necessary truths. For these reasons, Hobbes's whole cast of mind was much closer to that of the rationalist—as portrayed in Oakeshott's essay on "Rationalism in Politics"—than Oakeshott seems to have been willing to admit. On the other hand, the substantive intentions that Hobbes saw as underpinning the state (being alive, and being at peace) were so open-ended that they did indeed seem tantamount, for most practical purposes, to non-substantiveness. Nevertheless, the completely non-substantive version of the theory belonged to Oakeshott, or to Oakeshott's Hobbes—not to Hobbes himself.

NOTES

1. Michael Oakeshott, "Thomas Hobbes," *Scrutiny* 4 (1935–36): 263–77 (reprinted in *CPJ*, 110–21).

2. For valuable accounts of Oakeshott's philosophical engagement with Hobbes, see Paul Franco, *The Political Philosophy of Michael Oakeshott* (New Haven: Yale University Press, 1990), 82–95; Steven Gerencser, *The Skeptic's Oakeshott* (Basingstoke: Macmillan, 2000), 77–123; and, most fully, Ian Tregenza, *Michael Oakeshott on Hobbes: A Study in the Renewal of Philosophical Ideas* (Exeter: Imprint Academic, 2003).

3. Thomas Hobbes, *Leviathan*, ed. Michael Oakeshott (Oxford: Blackwell, 1946) (hereafter cited as Oakeshott ed.), xx, xxvii.

4. Thomas Hobbes, *De cive: The Latin Version*, ed. Howard Warrender (Oxford: Clarendon Press, 1983), 74: "ambitio & auaritia quarum potentia falsis vulgi circa *ius* & *iniuriam* opinionibus innititur, inermes essent, fruereturque gens humana pace adeo constante, vt non videatur . . . vnquam pugnandum esse."

5. Thomas Hobbes, *Leviathan* (London: Crooke, 1651), 138 (Oakeshott ed., 174).

6. Thomas Hobbes, *Writings on Common Law and Hereditary Right*, ed. Alan Cromartie and Quentin Skinner (Oxford: Clarendon Press, 2005), 9, 11.

7. Hobbes, *Leviathan*, 176 (Oakeshott ed., 221).

8. For example, Hobbes, *Leviathan*, 21, 34–35 (Oakeshott ed., 29, 45–46).

9. Elaine C. Stroud, "Thomas Hobbes' *A Minute or First Draught of the Optiques*: A Critical Edition" (PhD diss., University of Wisconsin–Madison, 1983), 622.

10. Hobbes, *Leviathan*, 107 (Oakeshott ed., 136).

11. Hobbes, *Leviathan* (Oakeshott ed., xxvii).

12. Ibid., xxiv–xxvii.

13. See Noel Malcolm, *Aspects of Hobbes* (Oxford: Oxford University Press, 2002), 152–53.

14. See ibid., 183–84, 186–89.

15. Thomas Hobbes, *Six Lessons to the Professors of the Mathematiques* (London: Crook, 1656), sig. A2r-v (punctuation emended). Cf. the comments on this point in G. F. Seifert, "The Philosophy of Hobbes: Text and Context and the Problem of Sedimentation," *Personalist* 60 (1979): 177–85, esp. 178–79.

16. Hobbes's phrase is a slightly reordered version of the Vulgate wording of Job 41:24; in the Authorized Version this is Job 41:33, "Upon earth there is not his like."

17. R. G. Collingwood, *Essays in Political Philosophy*, ed. David Boucher (Oxford: Clarendon Press, 1989), 193, 228. On Collingwood's views on Hobbes, see Paulette Carrive, "De *Leviathan* à *The New Leviathan*," in *Materia actuosa: Antiquité, âge classique, lumières; Mélanges en l'honneur d'Olivier Bloch*, ed. Miguel Benítez, Antony McKenna, Gianni Paganini, and Jean Salem (Paris: Honoré Champion, 2000), 731–41. On the context of Collingwood's *New Leviathan*, see Fred Inglis, *History Man: The Life of R. G. Collingwood* (Princeton: Princeton University Press, 2009), 293–303.

18. Joseph Vialatoux, *La Cité de Hobbes: Théorie de l'état totalitaire* (Paris: Lecoffre, 1935); René Capitant, "Hobbes et l'Etat totalitaire: À propos d'un livre récent," *Archives de philosophie du droit et de sociologie juridique* 6 (1936): 46–75. On the controversy between Vialatoux and Capitant, see Luc Foisneau, "Authoritarian State vs. Totalitarian State: *Leviathan* in an Early Twentieth-Century French Debate," in *Leviathan Between the Wars: Hobbes's Impact on Early Twentieth-Century Political Philosophy*, ed. Luc Foisneau, Jean-Christophe Merle, and Tom Sorell (Frankfurt: Lang 2005), 77–94.

19. Hobbes, *Leviathan* (Oakeshott ed., lvii).

20. Carl Schmitt, *Der Begriff des politischen* (Munich: Duncker and Humblot, 1932).

21. John P. McCormick, "Fear, Technology and the State: Carl Schmitt, Leo Strauss, and the Revival of Hobbes in Weimar and National Socialist Germany," *Political Theory* 22 (1994): 619–52 (here 624).

22. Ibid., 627–29.

23. Leo Strauss, *The Political Philosophy of Hobbes: Its Basis and Its Genesis*, trans. Elsa M. Sinclair (Oxford: Clarendon Press, 1936), esp. chap. 7 ("The New Morality") and chap. 8 ("The New Political Science"). See also the discussion in Daniel Tanguay, *Leo Strauss: An Intellectual Biography*, trans. Christopher Nadon (New Haven: Yale University Press, 2007), 99–109. Schmitt shifted slightly in this direction in his subsequent article "Der Staat als Mechanismus bei Hobbes und Descartes," *Archiv für Rechts- und Sozialphilosophie* 30 (1936–37): 622–32, where, influenced to some extent by Capitant, he agreed that Hobbes's state was merely a humanly designed machine, not a "Totalismus."

24. Oakeshott, "Thomas Hobbes," 276.

25. Hobbes, *Leviathan*, 64 (Oakeshott ed., 84–85).

26. Hobbes, *Leviathan*, 79 (Oakeshott ed., 104).

27. Hobbes, *Leviathan* (Oakeshott ed., xliii).

28. Ibid., xxxvi–xxxix.

11

THE FATE OF RATIONALISM IN OAKESHOTT'S THOUGHT

Kenneth Minogue

I

Michael Oakeshott is perhaps best known as the foe of a political vice called "rationalism," and it is a vice because, in believing that all knowledge is technical, it fails to recognize the crucial role of what Oakeshott calls "practical knowledge." The famous distinction between technical and practical knowledge, however, obscures the sheer complexity of Oakeshott's understanding of political activity. We can, indeed, find a simple theme running through much of Oakeshott's criticism at this period: namely, that the contingencies of the human world cannot be reduced to a simple, abstract (and manageable) plot. Rationalism does this, and Oakeshott detects it also in Whig history as analyzed by Herbert Butterfield: "What is, in fact, a resultant, or even a byproduct, of conflicting purposes and interests is made to appear as the consummation of a single homogeneous stream of activity triumphing over opposition and obstruction" (*WIH*, 221). But this general theme becomes recessive as he developed his political philosophy in the years after the famous inaugural. He seeks a more complex understanding.

Recognition of complexity always recalls Oakeshott to his philosophical vocation after his holiday excursions into condemnation. Rationalism itself therefore demanded a broader treatment. Indeed, the more Oakeshott developed his thought, the more he became a kind of rhapsodist of complexity, and this can be observed no more strikingly than in *The Politics of Faith and the Politics of Scepticism*, the manuscript he wrote after his inaugural and had probably finished in 1952.[1] It remained unpublished until after his death. What happened to the idea of rationalism in this new context?

In approaching political rhetoric, we learn in a typical passage, "it is not only the habits and institutions of modern European government which are alloys composed of diverse elements; the language, the political vocabulary in which we speak of the activity of government and make it intelligible to ourselves, is also hybrid. It is a modern language, and like all modern languages it is an amalgam of words and expressions (derived from diverse sources), each of which is in turn a complex world of diverse meanings. There are no simple expressions in our political vocabulary" (*PFPS*, 9). Alloys, amalgams, diversities, hybrids—we are almost into self-parody here. Western political talk is understood throughout this manuscript as exhibiting ambivalence toward two "extremes" or "polarities," between which political practice oscillates without ever touching either. Such discourse is a "predicament" issuing from the complexities of our practice of government. The sheer delicacy with which Oakeshott conveys these complexities is likely to generate both admiration and irritation. Yet, like a writer of detective puzzles, having led us into confusion, he leads us (with appropriate cautions) toward his clarifying distinction: that between the politics of faith and that of skepticism.

Oakeshott was passionate about ideas, and in casual conversation he did not stint on expressing his disdain for folly, but his philosophical instincts were always to discover some element of rationality in what he most detested. Living in a generation of philosophers, some of whom were so enthusiastic about criticism that they adopted it as a self-identifying slogan, Oakeshott always regarded criticism as merely a preliminary to further understanding—not, of course, in the sense of *tout comprendre, c'est tout pardoner*, but as a vision of the world in which everything is a necessary evil. In the essay "Rationalism in Politics," "rationalism" has few if any redeeming features. The interesting question is how he rethinks its character as he goes along.

Rationalism featured in the original essay as a vice of practical life, parasitic on history, science, and poetry—indeed, particularly on philosophy itself. The busy rationalist is unmistakably the most crashing bore in the conversation of humankind. Rationalism confuses part and whole. It corrupts the mind because it is both false and debasing (*RP*, 37). It offers a false dream of competence to the ignorant and cuts them off from whatever tradition is relevant to their enterprises, making them fancy that a doctrine is more flexible and responsive to reality than the inventive tradition that it merely abridges. Rationalism is idolatrous. In its political appearance it becomes a device for mechanically imposing some limited dream on an entire population. Individuals are corralled into abstract categories that suppress variety and aspire to uniformity. Rationalist projects inevitably fail, but in a rationalist atmosphere, an ignorant population can conceive of no better response to failure than to embrace some new collective project, so long as it promises an abstract social perfection. The outcome is an unstable political world, in which what Tocqueville called *la république,* "the slow and tranquil action of society on itself," is lost.[2]

It might well seem that no rationality could be discovered in a dominant political fashion leading to such comprehensive mischief. And yet: our civilization is so remarkable that the significance of books is hardly to be exhausted by looking to the vulgarities of autodidacticism. Our modern world has not ceased to flourish, even during modern times, when rationalism was inescapable.

To understand such an entity as rationalism requires transcending the judgment of mere error to find some element of reality that explains its appearance and possibly reveals that its vices may even be understood in some context as virtues. In this way, Oakeshott regarded Marx with appropriate disdain as a mere vulgarizer of Hegel but dismissed the judgment that Marxism was bad history with the objection that Marxists were not historians at all. They were, rather, political actors, brilliant expositors of mobilizing rhetorical prose.

What, then, might one say that might redeem the rationalist? One solution is simply to let the inadequate formulation drop out of one's treatments of the relevant themes, and it is indeed true that rationalism as a term did indeed drop out of Oakeshott's writings as they developed. It does not appear in *The Politics of Faith and the Politics of Scepticism.* The subject of this work is no longer "the most remarkable intellectual fashion of post-Renaissance Europe" (*RP,* 5) but rather an analysis of the entire tradition of European politics in terms of oscillation between two extremes or "polarities," as rulers respond to circumstances. The politics of faith is identified with the passion to move toward perfection by political means, while the politics of skepticism is circumstantially responsive, partly because of a sense that extensive political changes dangerously undermine our political world.

This distinction is such that sympathetic readers of Oakeshott are likely to regard skepticism as the essence of political wisdom. Most would be inclined to dismiss the politics of faith as folly. The initial layout of the work, in other words, suggests that it will become an intramural argument to be explored in terms of familiar Oakeshottian categories: it is political wisdom identified as skepticism. In fact, quite the contrary. The argument is a revisionist exercise in demonstrating that the "politics of faith," which many readers disdain as being the "son of rationalism," must be accorded an essential place in Western political life.

In other words, mere condemnation of rationalism (like any other form of evaluation) was in danger of irrelevance by mistaking the category of what was being condemned. As Oakeshott remarks late in *The Politics of Faith and the Politics of Scepticism,* "mere denunciation is out of place," and he goes on to insist that we must recognize the politics of faith not on its own terms "as a final simplification of politics" but as the exclusive pursuit of one political potentiality (127). The argument is, as Tim Fuller points out in his introduction, ultimately Aristotelian, because it locates the activity of governing as a mean between the two "polarities" referred to in the title (x). Of course, *faith* and *skepticism* are both terms that license a certain distance from certainty and commitment. Faith here (as in the case of the Christian religion) is a term that refers to a strong conviction not necessarily backed by appropriate evidence available to us.

II

It might well seem that the natural order of discussion would be to consider faith first, because skepticism exercises itself on beliefs already in play, and our modern world is awash with abstract projects for moving society closer to perfection. Such a procedure would be to mistake Oakeshott's design. It is essential to his argument that both the politics of faith and the politics of skepticism must arise independently out of specific circumstances making each plausible in its own terms.

In Oakeshott's view, the "politics of faith" is a response to power, especially to the constantly increasing powers available to modern governments. It explores the "intimations" that emerge from this situation. To find some such independent basis for the generation of skepticism is not so easy. Where can it be found?

Oakeshott finds it in the balanced government of medieval times, when the power available to kings was limited. Such limitation of power was partly a practical result of the available technology and the social arrangements of feudal society, but it also corresponded to a widespread preference for living according to law rather than be subjected to the will of others. The politics of skepticism might arise from a variety of circumstances, but medieval attitudes allowed such a practice to entrench itself.[3] In medieval England we have Parliament itself understood as a court whose business was to deal with petitioners and thus redress grievances. And the body of thought by which these grievances were understood and settled assumed that an established law already existed. We have not at this time entered a modern era in which the easy response of legislation expressed a sovereign will. Violating customary standards of right was a clear mark of injustice.

The medieval world, however, was far from changeless. How then did the authorities of the time deal with new situations requiring new forms of response? The answer is that they enforced an already established law. Such a thing was obviously not always to hand, and the typical recourse was to inquests seeking to infer from existing norms what the possibly forgotten rule might be or must have been. This sustained the fabric of law, even as it facilitated modification of the detail of laws. In any case, power in England moved, for a time (especially after the Lancastrian succession), away from the masterful domination of a king to the more responsible custodianship of Parliament. Oakeshott, in treating the politics of skepticism, sought its genesis in a version of political reality rather than as (what is likely to seem more plausible to us) a reaction against the ambitions of the politics of faith.

This view of the sources of the two styles of politics might suggest that skepticism belongs essentially to the medieval period and that faith dominates our modern world. Faith is indeed currently dominant, but Oakeshott characteristically resists temporal patterning of this kind. Skeptical assumptions, often taking a legal form, survived into the seventeenth century. They survived, that is to say, even the emergence of sovereign power under the Tudors. We find, then, for a long period of government, a fully coherent understanding of society in legal terms, and within its limits it carries with it a conviction about the proper as well as the possible limits of the power of rulers.

Skepticism survived, particularly, to reappear in the eighteenth century. But even before that, it made periodic appearances, often in unlikely places. Oakeshott notes, for example, that excesses of policy during the English Civil War provoked elements of skepticism in figures such as Cromwell and Ireton, figures whom one would more generally associate with the politics of faith (*PFPS*, 71). Like the Levellers they hesitated in their support for a saintly realm, when it began to require the abandonment of formalities, such as honoring commitments.

Toward the end of the English Revolution, the political principle of what Oakeshott calls "the mean in action" made an explicit appearance as part of a general conversation concerned with the place of enthusiasm not only in politics but also more generally in civil life as a whole. This is a conversation whose participants, he tells us, included Locke, Berkeley, Shaftesbury, Halifax, Boyle, Saint Evremond, Fontenelle, and Hume. It even included wits such as Mandeville "to provide the comedy" (*PFPS*, 122). In this company, Halifax is accorded a special place in advancing "the principle of the mean in action" by virtue of his distance from mere partisanship. And what Oakeshott means is the virtue of exploiting the middle range of our political opportunities (123). But Halifax is taken to have circumstantially misunderstood the polarities of this principle by identifying one extreme not with skepticism but with moderation.

More specific articulation of the politics of skepticism is to be found in Hobbes, Hume, Montesquieu, and others, among whom philosophical skeptics such as Montaigne and Pascal are important. Locke features here, as often in Oakeshott, as a skeptic in a bit of a muddle. He was, we learn, "the most ambiguous of all political writers of modern times; a political sceptic who inadvertently imposed the idiom of faith upon the sceptical understanding of government." He thought to entrench skepticism in a theoretical framework by converting historical rights into natural rights (*PFPS*, 83), a mistake from which the tradition had to be rescued by Burke and Hegel. What he failed to understand, in Oakeshott's view, was that the attempt to found the politics of skepticism on some theoretical structure was "an infection caught from faith." For it is of the essence of the politics of skepticism to be "a recognition of the contingency of every political arrangement and the unavoidable arbitrariness of most" (80).

Here, then, is an account of the European political tradition as a ceaseless tension between two polarities or extremes, in which the triumph of either would be self-defeating and amount to the destruction of politics altogether. It is a subtle and complex account of our situation, and it is one in which the politics of faith, which has almost all the characteristics of rationalism in earlier writings, is domesticated and recognized as having an essential place in our political tradition. Skeptical politicians are taken as strongly averse even to changes that may be necessary. The politics of faith thus plays a salutary role in sustaining the balance required in the activity of government. To what extent, we may ask, is this a plausible parceling out (as it were) of the virtues necessary for political balance? The vice of the politics of faith is its passion for perfection, which must necessarily take the form of espousing abstract change. Skepticism, by contrast, responds to contingency. But this raises the question of whether a skepticism understood in legal terms can entirely free itself from abstraction in its understanding of the state.

III

The legal historian Maitland once remarked that the Greeks never managed to generate a satisfactory system of law because they sought the philosophically ideal solution to every case. Here we have a suggestive paradox in which error seems to be understood as a virtue. But it is not, of course, "mere error." A system of law cannot be anything else but a set of rules effective in sustaining a social order, and those rules must, of course, generalize the contingencies of social experience so that they constitute ideas manageable by lawyers and rulers and understandable by everybody else—ideas such as crime, contract, punishment, mitigation, rights and duties, negligence, and so on. These generalized ideas become technicalities to be used in classifying events within a legal framework.

For Oakeshott the politics of skepticism is, at least in England, historically generated by legal assumptions and constitutes an escape from the abstractions of the politics of faith. Skeptical politics recognizes human beings as creatures responding to wants and ideas and as living in a contingent world whose spring of action is responsiveness to situations rather than in a world in which social conditions actually determine how people behave. It might well seem, however, that in escaping from the politics of faith by moving toward a politics of skepticism generated by legal thought, Oakeshott had merely substituted one kind of abstraction for another.

For it will be clear that the categories of law are from one point of view no less abstract than those of political projectors. Such categories sit uneasily with the complexities of real human conduct and can produce odd results. Indeed, if our ideal is that the punishment should fit the crime in any absolute sense, then legal categories fail to generate ideal justice. They assume for a start that a stable human identity underpins the move from the commission of a crime to the imposition of a penalty. And the acts categorized as criminal must be understood as intentional, which cannot be established psychologically with any degree of confidence. An intention, even a confession, is never much more than an inference from words and actions. None of them are entirely univalent. The judgment of criminality requires a complex apparatus recognizing degrees of guilt and types of mitigation, and psychiatrists are forever nibbling away at these judgments, because criminality and mental disorder are often difficult to distinguish.

These problems are intensified if one considers the point of punishment in terms of social and moral policy, and such questions can never be entirely absent. Retribution rests on quite different principles of punishment from deterrence, and rehabilitation from both. Each also mandates a different treatment of an offender. Retributive theories of punishment may be regarded as, in one sense, ideally just, but the whole idea of justice has become almost meaningless in modern times, as the proliferation of adjectival qualifications of justice reveals. Distinguishing climatic justice from economic is quite a feat, and marking off social justice from any other kind a virtual impossibility. Again, if the point of punishment is taken as deterring others, then the criminal is being used, perhaps unjustly, as a means to a more or less extraneous end. Even if we assume, in the deterrence case, that the offender himself, as a member of society, has a stake in his own criminal proclivities being discouraged, we have to recognize that the offender's own stake in this principle of self-government is pretty miniscule. As for rehabilitation, it deprives punishment of moral character and degenerates into an inefficient kind of social and moral engineering.

Such a system of law can produce only determinate results, according to the technicalities of the system. Some systems of law recognize indeterminacy more explicitly than others, and perhaps the adversarial practices of Anglophone common law societies are most at home with such skepticism. And they recognize it in both theory and practice. No one doubts that legal processes often fail to express ideal justice. And this is in part recognized in the discretion allowed to judges as they interpret the law. For all its technical sophistication, a legal system cannot escape practicality and approximation.

IV

Nor, of course, can it escape abstraction. The vice of rationalism lay in subsuming human beings under abstract formulae and in failing to recognize human agents as intelligently responding to their world. It was a politics that discarded contingency. But legal categories are no less abstract, as any classificatory system must be. In what sense, therefore, does law sustain a kind of skepticism that might put some limit on the drive to social perfection?

The answer lies in the fact that legal categories, particularly where we are dealing with common law systems, are instruments by which we respond to specific situations, and the resulting judgments are to a large extent limited to the circumstances from which they arose. No doubt precedent and principle are involved, but verdicts and decisions do not entail universal rules. Common law in particular constitutes a framework for responding to immediate problems. It does not legislate for an unpredictable future. While rationalist projects seek to create a transformed future, legal judgments are self-limiting to the present. Precedent and principle, we may say, trump perfection.

As we move from the medieval to the modern world, however, this manner of responding to the problems of public life changes because new kinds of disorder emerge, and the power and confidence of rulers increases vastly. In this rising world, sovereign power is imprescriptible. As Oakeshott reflected on this situation, he absorbed the distinction between rationalist projects and other styles of politics into the difference between an understanding of the state based on the analogy of *universitas* and one based on *societas*. A universitas as a corporation had to be managed in terms of the enterprise constituting it, while a societas as an association of individuals under law required a different form of government (*OHC*, 231).

The problem posed in *The Politics of Faith and the Politics of Scepticism*, however, takes its rise not from a typology of human association but from the ambiguity of modern political language as reflecting the ambivalence of Western life. The polarities of faith and skepticism constitute an equilibrium system, because if policy moves too close to one polarity, the system generates a balancing reaction toward the other. This is a system that anticipates Oakeshott's later account of the modern state as modally mixed. The politics of skepticism is distinguished from that of faith by its acceptance of the fact that societies, being composed of human beings, cannot help but be imperfect structures. For the politics of faith, however, an unremitting drive toward perfection entails a constant dissatisfaction with such a modern world. And just such a dissatisfaction with the imperfections of our society is not only an implication of the Oakeshottian account of what he calls "the politics of faith" but also a familiar feature of the world in which we actually live in the twenty-first century. And that situation tempts us to the question: is there, even in principle, a system of public life that might purge our society of its imperfections?

And indeed, in a sense, there is such arrangement: one might institute rulers having absolute and unchecked power, because their wisdom corresponds not to any technical legal system (for such a system would circumscribe their wisdom) but to the essence of the social system over which they preside. This will seem a ridiculous idea, even to Western readers familiar with the reputation of King Solomon, and of course it is. Yet contemporary readers will also observe that just such rule (in the guise of one kind of vanguard party or another) is precisely the solution espoused by twentieth-century exponents of the politics of faith. Such readers had better realize, indeed, that recourse to such a figure, either in a literal or figurative form, has been almost universal in human affairs. It is certainly the basic idea actualized in most of the grand non-European civilizations of the past. Such a figure would be exemplified by an Ayatollah expressing the principles of the sharia, or a Mandarin enjoying the mandate of heaven. We Westerners would recognize such rulers as despotic, but we ought also to recollect that the same image of a possible perfection was just what bewitched the aspirations of many political idealists in recent times. For it is almost a theorem of social perfection that it can be actualized only by a ruler disposing of the entire quantum of power available. And subjection to a ruler disposing of such power, we could hardly help thinking, would be a notable imperfection of its own. But we are, of course, merely thinking in theoretical terms.

Or are we? Is the politics of faith currently held in balance by the politics of skepticism? In both modern thought and practice, power takes an ever-greater interest in the concrete details of personal lives. The movement for so-called social justice in normative political thought increasingly judges that general arrangements are inadequate to deal with the imperfections of our society, where imperfection covers even such subjective phenomena as the happiness of individuals. Some radicals have become interested in the psychology of happiness as an object of public policy. Unhappiness has turned up in the politics of faith as a prima facie reason for diagnosing injustice. And in the practical world, the supposedly increasing problem of child abuse and of the crimes of pedophiles have generated large departments of state. Nor are these organizations charged merely with enforcing legal principles. They include large numbers of people such as social workers and probation officers whose duties are to supervise quite closely the personal lives of those thought to be vulnerable to these evils. Some of these evils would certainly have been found back in the mists of time, but they seem to have multiplied mightily in recent times. The liberated twentieth century relaxed the rules of family life, with the result that responsible conduct among some parents and children became distinctly fitful. Thus does one social change, often presented as a reform, lead on to others. And the consequence in our time has become that the ideal model of enlightened despotism, as incarnated by a state intruding into ever more personal, indeed intimate, areas of modern life, has become the rule.

Oakeshott takes the view that the essence of the politics of faith is the failure to keep religion and politics apart. In all other cultures but our own, however, no such separation ever took place. In our current circumstances, "religion" has in any case become an ambiguous word. Humanism and secularism are beginning to take on many of the features of a faith. They increasingly parade their sensitivity to the presence of religious symbols (the cross, rosary beads, etc.) and demand an environment free of religious symbols. It is true that their concern is almost exclusively with Christian symbols, those of other religions being tolerated under the rubric of multiculturalism. For that reason, secularism has in part the character of a spiritual civil war within European states, and a secularism making such demands is clearly taking on faithlike attributes. We thus find ourselves in a rather paradoxical situation, in which for all our value of freedom, increasing numbers of Western people come to be subject to forms of supposedly enlightened despotism.

This paradox of antireligious groups taking on the character of faiths dissolves if we recognize that what Oakeshott has called "the politics of faith" (perhaps with deliberate irony) is just what its name suggests: namely, a policy in which society is based on universal agreement about the one right system of belief. Salvation is, he tells us, a condition in which nothing further may be desired, and should the politics of faith attain its extreme, then we would all, in principle at least, enjoy salvation. Such a perfectionist drive has long been at the heart of Western societies, and it necessarily takes the form of some kind of collectivism. After the horrors of twentieth-century totalitarianism, this drive tactically withdrew to a more piecemeal ambition. Vanguard parties and supreme leaders are today out of favor in free states. The perfectionist drive, however, may well be found attractive to the large numbers of immigrants to Western states from other civilizations, many of them accustomed to despotic rule. The freedom we associate with being able to pursue our own individual projects increasingly lacks the political conditions from which it originally developed.

We need, therefore, to broaden our concerns beyond Oakeshott's austere concentration on the character of political language. We need to consider the significance of the culture that mandates such a language. The ambiguity of our political language, Oakeshott notes, corresponds to the ambivalence of our attitudes, and in fact such ambivalence is found in nearly every aspect of our culture. The notional perfection of a single ruler—caliph, bodhisattva, mandarin, guru, chief, and so on—in other cultures rests on unanimity of general beliefs. We in the West do not usually claim even a notional perfection, but the imperfections we enjoy rest not on some right doctrine but on an equilibrium such as Oakeshott describes in politics, one that in all fields balances conflicting institutions, ideas, and interests. Such is the way we cultivate science, religion, productive enterprises, and the right thing to do about our national interests. We live in a society full of conflict, contestation, and competition, which is exactly why European societies have so widely been regarded in the rest of the world as highly dangerous models. Our civil associations are not held together by any kind of unanimity. But that seems to be changing.

The ambiguity of our political vocabulary merely reflects our world, and such reflection is revealed by Oakeshott as the reason why ambiguity has not—yet!—collapsed into the simplifying virtues of some notional right order. The reason for this, he argues, is that whenever we approach the extremes of one or other style of politics, self-defeat looms for the style that approaches too close to a polarity (*PFPS*, 92). Each style is thus the nemesis of the other. And the notion of a policy becoming self-defeating must here be understood historically. Both faith and skepticism, pushed toward their extremes, are self-defeating—but only because we are the kind of people we are, and so long as we remain so.

The problem is that in the twenty-first century, styles of politics can be pressed a very long way indeed without quite encountering self-defeat. I pluck from the current headlines a proposal made in Britain by the current minister for Schools and Children—a title that would have provoked notable Oakeshottian derision. New guidelines for schools should require that boys from the age of five onward must be taught respect for girls as one element in a curriculum aimed at something called "personal development." Oakeshott knew, as most of us do unless we are ministers of the crown promoting a faith, that men refraining from acting violently toward women is part of the absorption of manners they acquire in the interstices of early life, partly by imitation of adults and partly by absorbing elements of the chivalric convictions that have almost perennially been a presence in European life. The notion that such subtle and central modes of conduct can be disseminated propositionally, by a taught course of a didactic kind, is a piece of rationalism that no sophisticated person would take seriously. And if sophistication were lacking, as often it seems to be, a little empiricism would make the point that endless appeals instructing us in better conduct (for example, campaigns against bullying) have been correlated in recent times with an actual increase in the conduct criticized. What, one wonders, has led to such rationalist obtuseness? Could it be connected to a linguistic lacuna in English: namely, the absence of a distinction between *connaitre* and *savoir*?

In Oakeshott's hypothesis, faith and skepticism balance each other. But the evidence is accumulating that some version of the politics of faith has overridden the hesitation even of the political skeptics. This is the way politics ends. Our resources of skepticism seem to have been lost.

V

The great value of *The Politics of Faith and the Politics of Scepticism* is that it develops Oakeshott's conception of political activity as an endless movement between two limiting possibilities of action and policy. It is these extremes that both explain and set limits to political possibility. But are faith and skepticism the only plausible extremes between which politics oscillates? Other dichotomies feature in Oakeshott's exposition. Complexity and simplicity, for example, constitute another of these central dichotomies. Oakeshott uses them as characterizing political language, though simplicity, at least, manages to make its escape from semantics later in the work and is revealed as a possible consequence, and a destructive one, of the politics of faith. Such a consequence is exemplified in Marxism as theory and in the Soviet Union as a practice. And on the other wing of the simplicity/complexity polarity, we might well identify complexity as a conceivable real extreme in such a case as the enlightened despot attempting (no doubt impossibly) to actualize perfect justice by responding to each problem in all its contingency.

Moderation and extremism constitute another dichotomy that appears within Oakeshott's argument, and these are polarities long recognized in practical political discussion. "Extremist" in our talk covers a multitude of positions and is often useful in obscuring details (such as the Muslim inspiration of jihad) that various people would prefer not to notice. Oakeshott is, of course, wary of moderation as a polarity because it threatens to turn into an actual policy rather than a mere orienting extreme. That, I think, is one of the reasons why he prefers skepticism, in spite of its liability to be confused with a philosophical position.

Faith and skepticism, however, certainly constitute a highly suggestive version of the polarities between which policy swings in our endlessly contestatory practice of government. Yet there remains a problem about how much content such polarities themselves should have, and that problem becomes focused as we observe Oakeshott manipulating, as it seems, the meaning of skepticism in pursuit of an ulterior purpose. Characterizing the way in which modern European states should be governed, he writes,

> an appropriate manner of government will be one which not only recognizes multiplicity but one that is also alive to change. It is at this point that the characteristic failure of the politics of scepticism appears: it is a style of government pre-eminently suited for a complex but relatively static condition of society. The government of faith is alive to change. . . . The government of scepticism . . . having no authority to prevent it, is relatively indifferent to change of any kind, and consequently is apt to be insensitive even to those effects of change which come within its province. (*PFPS*, 107)

He goes on to observe that skepticism will be "insensitive" in particular to the need for change to sustain the current system of rights and duties. This is not a contingent failing of skepticism: it is, he tells us, an inherent defect of the virtue of this style of government. Yet actual exponents of the politics of skepticism, such as Burke, are famously alive to the need for change to sustain a desirable structure of rights and duties as it currently exists. Real thinkers are not, of course, to be identified with abstract polarities, but they do test the plausibility of the abstraction. Furthermore, in recognizing the politics of faith as supplying a defect of skepticism, Oakeshott is attributing to the politics of faith something less dangerous than its addiction to perfectionist change.

The unavoidable question is whether we ought to accept an argument that seeks to domesticate the politics of faith as the balancer of the politics of skepticism. Must we attribute an absolute aversion to change as part of the essence of the politics of skepticism? Skepticism here must be taken not so much as the abstract extreme in the balance of politics but as a style of government. The question becomes why must we equip skepticism in practice with an insensitivity to one of the major elements of political wisdom—namely, the need for change—if it is intimated in the circumstances of the time? If the politics of faith is, as it were, a mindless appetite for a change leading to perfection, must the politics of skepticism exhibit an equally mindless aversion to change?

Oakeshott is not at all unaware of this difficulty, and we find that the defects of the politics of skepticism in this area are attributed to the current dominance of the politics of faith: "In this activist climate (in which the government of faith seems so pre-eminently relevant), the sceptical style must appear as an unintelligible piece of sophistication. . . . In short, the intellectual distinctions which constitute this style of government are foreign to the activist climate of opinion" (*PFPS*, 109–10). If that is the case, then the defect of the politics of skepticism becomes an outcome of particular contingent circumstances in contemporary politics. But if this is true, then it weakens Oakeshott's ideal characterization of modern politics as moving between these polarities. That characterization then loses its ideal status and becomes a hostage to the fortunes of contemporary politics. It would reveal a changed situation in which the ideal balance has dissolved, and we find ourselves face-to-face with the nemesis of a triumphant faith. And that does indeed seem to be our situation in the twenty-first century.

It seems to me, then, that in this particular enterprise Oakeshott has made a move that can be understood only in terms of an overriding desire to find in the structures of politics some legitimate place even for rationalism, at whatever cost. It is only by this move that he is saved from asserting (what his instincts and those of many of his readers desire) that the politics of skepticism, with its responsiveness to the concrete, is itself one complete account of political wisdom. Real political skeptics would think that the politics of skepticism must include a sensitivity to what is intimated. If so, they would not need, as a condition of political skill, the balancing readiness for change found in the politics of faith.

VI

My argument has been that Oakeshott characteristically moves from condemnation of something to a more philosophical understanding of it as exhibiting at least some limited rationality. Has the idea of rationalism exhibited this pattern? It has to some extent in that rationalism turns, largely without modification, into the politics of faith and is domesticated as part of a broader theory of modern politics. It thus finds a useful role to play. On the other hand, this theory is part of an account of modern politics that has a practical character: it is, as Tim Fuller remarks in the introduction, as close to a book of advice for the practice of modern politics as Oakeshott ever produced (*PFPS*, x). As books of advice go, it is highly philosophical and very modest in its claim to usefulness, but practical is certainly what it is. And the practical justification of an undesirability is usually a matter of making the best of a bad job rather than discovering new aspects of the thing in question.

The problem with Oakeshott's solution to the problem of domesticating rationalism is that the limited rationality discovered in the politics of faith, alias rationalism, results not from any philosophical development in the way in which it is understood, nor in any new virtue discovered in some aspect of it, but merely by locating it in a context in which it has a rather odd function. And the creation of this context relies on a high degree of abstraction such that faith's partner, the politics of skepticism, must be equipped with an inertia such as may (when the equilibrium works) be corrected by the passion for perfecting society. Hence the central interest of *The Politics of Faith and the Politics of Scepticism* must be in what it tells us about Oakeshott's view of the activity of governing.

My conclusion must be that while Oakeshott has indeed attempted to move beyond condemnation to a broader understanding of the phenomenon of rationalism, he has not modified his essential view of its nature. He has merely found a slightly implausible framework, in which it achieves the saving grace of a respectable place in political life.

As ever with Oakeshott, the detail of the argument is marvelously suggestive, and its development so subtle that it can be criticized only by the most brutish grasp of what he might actually be up to. But if I am at all on the right track, I think I understand why he chose not to publish so remarkable a work.

NOTES

1. That this work was completed by 1952 is Professor Fuller's judgment in his introduction (*PFPS*, ix).

2. Alexis de Tocqueville, *Tocqueville on America After 1840*, ed. and trans. Aurelian Craiutu and Jeremy Jennings (Cambridge: Cambridge University Press, 2009), 14.

3. Skepticism may, of course, occur in a variety of political circumstances; the Middle Ages are not the time of some once and for all "invention" of the politics of skepticism. Thus, in discussing *salus populi suprema lex esto*, Oakeshott observes that in its military context, "the word *salus* . . . begins its political life in the service of the politics of scepticism" (*PFPS*, 39–40). He also observes here that "salvation" as an account of social perfection means a condition in which nothing else can be desired.

12

OAKESHOTT AND HAYEK: SITUATING THE MIND

Leslie Marsh

It's a hazardous enterprise contrasting two figures such as Friedrich August von Hayek (1899–1992) and Michael Joseph Oakeshott (1901–1990)––similarities are often superficially drawn; divisions tend to be overstated.[1] But if one understands both men to be centrally concerned with the social nature of mind and with the distributed nature of knowledge, then this confluence of interest dissolves the somewhat rigid ideological lines that both followers and uninformed critics attribute to these two thinkers. Admittedly, these divisions are engendered by the misunderstandings and terminological confusion that the two thinkers themselves generate.[2]

Oakeshott and Hayek were both in the business of "situating the mind," that is, both understood rationality to be culturally saturated and modulated.[3] For both Oakeshott and Hayek, customs, practices, and traditions are the *fundamentum* and the *residua* of practical reasoning. Oakeshott was inspired by the Diltheyan hermeneutic tradition; Hayek was schooled within the Austrian hermeneutic tradition emphasizing the lived subjectivity of experience.[4] Both traditions take individuals to draw their self-understanding from what is conceptually to hand, a preexisting and dynamic web of linguistic, technological, social, political, and institutional constraints.

The embedded mind does not merely respond to a given world; it is enacted through a particularized history of socioenvironmental coupling. This dynamic conception of cognition is manifest as the exercise of skillful know-how. This externalist view of mind is in sharp contrast to the Cartesian tradition that both Oakeshott and Hayek took to task—a chauvinistic and imperialist apriorism they diagnosed as corrosive of sociopolitical and ultimately moral freedom.

It may appear eccentric to approach Oakeshott and Hayek from the perspective of cognitive science and the philosophy of mind, given that their reputations were established as social theorists.[5] This said, if one is to do justice to their explicitly anti-Cartesian stance, then mind and sociality—Janus-like—cannot be pried apart. The situated stance subscribes to the proposition that mind can coherently exist only at the nexus of the embodied, the social, and the artifactual. With this firmly in place, my motivation is to show that Oakeshott and Hayek

1. Offer a more sophisticated account of sociality than traditional sociology. They do not dispense with the vital methodological principle that retains the individual as a locus of cognition within a wider system—unlike a tradition of sociological theorizing that posits an inflated social ontology that makes no concessions to the mechanics of the mind and individualized learning patterns.[6]

2. Have a great deal of relevance beyond their usual sociopolitical constituencies—indeed, they are right at home in the non-Cartesian wing of cognitive science.[7] As heretical as it might first sound, Oakeshott's and Hayek's hermeneutical stance is compatible with a nonreductive naturalism as espoused by non-Cartesian cognitive science.

3. And that (1) and (2) jointly inform their notion of epistemic modesty: that is, the recognition that the individual is necessarily subject to cognitive—and therefore epistemic—constraint, which manifests itself as their critique of rationalism in matters of sociality. Therein lies their distinctive brand of liberalism, a liberalism that tends to get lost in the intellectual crosscurrents that can be found in Oakeshott and Hayek.

The order of business is as follows. The next section locates Oakeshott and Hayek within the non-Cartesian wing of recent cognitive science. This clears the space to make an attempt to unpack the intertwined notions of constructivism and rationalism that exercised both Oakeshott and Hayek in the following section. The penultimate section offers an assessment of the famous or, perhaps more accurately, infamous swipe by Oakeshott at Hayek in *Rationalism in Politics*. The final section offers a concluding perspective by drawing Oakeshott and Hayek together under what I take to be the distinctive feature of their liberalism—an embedded individualism.

SITUATING THE MIND

Oakeshott and Hayek are known, to use the current argot, as "situated" theorists. Situated theorists take seriously the idea that cognition has an embodied, social, and artifactual dimension.[8] Indeed, the perpetual cybernetic impact of the artifactual world on the brain has outstripped any adaptive alteration of the genetic code.[9] This distinctly non-Cartesian sensibility is captured by Oakeshott's slogans: "[a] history of thought is a history of men thinking, not a 'history' of abstract, disembodied 'ideas'" (*LHPT*, 42) and "a man's mind cannot be separated from its contents and its activities" (*RP*, 14, 106). Hayek's more famous slogan pretty much sums up his lifelong project: "It is probably no more justified to claim that thinking man has created his culture than that culture created his reason."[10] Hayek inherits from the Austrian tradition the emphasis on the subjective, socially embedded quality of action, along with the decentralization of knowledge (tacit and propositional).[11] Oakeshott tends to focus more strictly on the Cartesian inheritance manifest as the "unencumbered intellect" (11, 111, 120); the mind conceived as an engine or an independent instrument (106, 109–13); and the notion of reason hypostatized, an attenuated rationality (105, 113).

It might strike the reader as odd to say that neither Hayek nor Oakeshott was an individualist: in a word, Oakeshott and Hayek would be termed "externalists" in the philosophy of mind. Broadly speaking, externalism is the thesis that an individual's environment has some causal determinant on the content of the individual mind. By contrast, Cartesian individualism (or internalism) is internal in the sense that knowledge relies solely on, or is fashioned by, the operations of the cognizer's mental states without any appeal to external considerations. The methodological supposition that cognition can be studied independently of any consideration of the body and the physical and ambient social environment is characteristic of orthodox philosophy of mind.

Individualism has many, often overlapping, connotations across moral philosophy, political philosophy, philosophy of social science, epistemology, and the philosophy of mind. In moral and political philosophy, individual persons are the ultimate units of moral worth: society has as its proper end the good of the individual; there is no social good over and above that of individuals; and individual flourishing requires people to make their own choices as far as possible. Hayek and Oakeshott are both individualists in this sense. Individualism in the philosophy of social science centers on the question as to how one apportions the extent to which individuals' cognitive states are causally dependent on their social milieu. Furthermore, could all statements about political and other institutions be reduced to statements referring purely to individuals and their interactions? Individualism in analytic epistemology (i.e., the Plato-Descartes tradition) is normative: it is internal in the sense that knowledge relies solely on the operation of mental states without any appeal to external considerations. This is in sharp contrast to the sociological tradition of social epistemology, which gives priority to the manifold and ubiquity of social considerations. Hayek and Oakeshott are "compatibilists"—that is, they offer a hybrid version, whereby the individual is retained as a locus of cognition within a wider system, retaining the link between the epistemic and cognitive.

For Oakeshott and Hayek, cognition is always perspectival and sociality is always adjectival on intrinsic cognitive architecture, and thus agents are necessarily subject to epistemic constraint. For both Oakeshott and Hayek, selves (or minds if you will) are possible only when embedded in a matrix of practices and traditions in historically specific societies or civilizations (*RP*, 63; *VLL*, 19 41). Non-Cartesian agents augment their epistemic capacity by allowing information to remain outside the brain and exploiting environmental and social resources rather than having to encode everything relevant internally. For Oakeshott and Hayek, this is *the* mark of advanced cognition— humankind's ability to diffuse propositional and practical knowledge or wisdom through external epistemic structures. The irony will not be lost even on the most casual of readers: tradition here is understood as advanced cognition! For Oakeshott this knowledge is suspended in traditions and practices; for Hayek, knowledge exists within a network as spontaneous or complex adaptive orders.

Whatever a tradition, practice, or spontaneous order is, by definition it cannot reside solely within an individual—there is no direct brain-to-brain/ mind-to-mind memetic transmission—continuity can be mediated, albeit imperfectly, only through a web of social artifacts.[12] For Oakeshott the epistemic interrogation of, say, a political tradition is within and through the quasi-mystical ability to "pursue intimations" or the ability to enter into a "flow of sympathy" (*RP*, 57, 59–61, 129, 131), divining a pattern of behavior.[13]

The notion of situatedness intersects with the so-called knowing-how/ knowing-that distinction, a distinction that both Hayek and Oakeshott fully exploited.[14] It has been said that knowing-how is the "very essence of creative cognition" and the fault line dividing orthodox Cartesian representationalism and anti-Cartesianism.[15] Embodied know-how emerges as our primary way of gaining epistemic access to the word and takes epistemic primacy over knowing-that (propositional knowledge). Whereas the Cartesian cognizer is a fully decontextualized entity, for Oakeshott and Hayek it would seem to be an essential fact about human cognition that it always operates within a context of activity. Tradition (or culture) is of such complexity, a complexity generated by infinitely fine-grained constantly shifting local and ephemeral variables, that as a guide to action, social knowledge (or know-how) cannot be reduced, abridged, or restated propositionally (knowledge-that) without remainder. For

Hayek that means the twofold constraint: (a) no one mind can apprehend all the knowledge required because of the necessary dispersion of knowledge; and (b) no one mind can deal with the complexity or amount of detail that would be required to guide even the most banal of actions.

This dispersion of social knowledge is what Andy Clark calls the "spreading of epistemic credit."[16] "Being-in-the-world," to invoke a Heideggerian term, is one in which situated agents are perpetually responding to and redefining their environment without having recourse to an explicit range of alternatives. For Hayek abstract rules of which we are not aware determine the sensory world presented as conscious experience.[17] For both Oakeshott and Hayek, Gilbert Ryle's celebrated critique of the Cartesian project provided a useful conceptual underpinning to the rationalist propensity to view all intelligent performance as coextensive with conscious thought.[18]

For Oakeshott one is always dealing with a reflective tradition, not an inert pattern of habitual behavior, where there is no "changeless centre . . . everything is temporary but nothing is arbitrary" (RP, 61; OHC, 100). The emphasis on the importance of know-how therefore implies a strong dynamism or engagement: "Mind as we know is the offspring of knowledge and activity" (RP, 109; reiterated in 110–13). For Hayek mind "emerges" through a cybernetic relation between our conceptual creativity and the environment, to intimate, regulate, and inform concepts and action.[19] Hayek's nuanced conception of sociality has a strong evolutionary flavor to it. The dynamism characteristic of both Oakeshott and Hayek is fully consonant with a major theory of mind in current non-Cartesian philosophy of mind known as "enactivism" and bears no resemblance whatsoever to the ossified character attributed to conservatism by "conservatives" of a fundamentalist stripe and in turn by their "liberal" critics.

Enactivism is a term coined by neurobiologist Francisco Varela and his philosopher colleagues.[20] It refers to a theory of cognition very much more ecumenical in its concerns than (Cartesian) orthodox philosophy of mind; it's a theory that does not shrink from—or sideline—notions of autonomy, sense making, embodiment, emergence, and experience. The enactivist stance is a naturalistic nonreductive view of mind as embodied and embedded, giving due emphasis to biological autonomy and lived subjectivity—virtues surely consonant with Oakeshott's and Hayek's requirements. Cognition on an enactive account is the exercise of skillful know-how, a know-how that emerges from recurrent sensory-motor coupling and looping between the organism and the artifactual environment.

The epistemic modulation of knowledge through practices, traditions, and institutions that arise through cooperative endeavors is central to theorizing sociality. Most of our thinking is guided (or even operated) by rules of which we are not aware—"rational," or more precisely "conscious," thought is but one element. Consider this extract from the doyen of situated theorists—it expresses the very insights that Hayek and Oakeshott demand of theorizing sociality:

> This power of culture and language to shape human subjectivity and experience belongs not simply to the genetic constitution of the individual, but to the generative constitution of the intersubjective community. Individual subjectivity is from the outset intersubjectivity, as a result of the communally handed down norms, conventions, artifacts, and cultural traditions in which the individual is always already embedded. Thus the internalization of joint attention into symbolic representations is not simply an ontogenetic phenomenon, but a historical and cultural one.[21]

A situated cognitive science is not trying to sideline what has been disparagingly termed as folk psychology by reducing all experience to the level of physics. On the contrary, it accepts that a theory of mind has to accommodate our perceptual, conceptual, and emotional experiences—and as a nonreductive science it acknowledges that there are different levels of description appropriate for differing subject matter.

Earlier I contended that the hermeneutical stance is compatible with a nonreductive naturalistic stance. It is usually conceded that the greater complexity of social phenomena and the practical difficulties of controlled experimentation lessen the precision of the social sciences. This does not, however, drive a logical wedge between the social and the natural sciences. Antinaturalism of the sort that Oakeshott would endorse argues that the social world is filled with meaning and significance that render the methods of the natural sciences irrelevant. But a nonreductive stance such as enactivism takes meaning and significance very seriously indeed. Oakeshott can't surely be suggesting that mind is not a part of the natural world. It is here that a link between social complexity and mind is forged through hermeneutics: a hermeneutic approach to social explanation, the idea of the brain as a hermeneutic device, is highly consistent with enactivism's nonreductive theory of mind.

CONSTRUCTIVISM AND RATIONALISM

A prime example of the terminological confusion that bedevils comparisons between Oakeshott and Hayek revolves around the terms *rationalism* and *constructivism*. That both Oakeshott and Hayek took rationalism to task, at least in matters of sociality, is incontrovertible. Hayek's use of the term *constructivism*, or elsewhere as *intentionalism* or *artificialism* or even *intellectualism*, and Oakeshott's use of the term *rationalism* (*RP*) are, for all intents and purposes, coextensive—this despite Hayek's earlier use of the compound term *rationalist constructivism* and an even earlier reliance on plain and simple *rationalism*.[22] If there is a difference between Oakeshott and Hayek, it's perhaps more a matter of emphasis rather than a matter of substantive discontinuity. Things, however, are not that straightforward. Oakeshott and Hayek are both dyed-in-the-wool constructivists obfuscated by the very fact that it is so-called constructivism that Hayek takes to task. Furthermore, both reject the constructivist tendency to be found in the sociology of the (scientific) knowledge movement, the heirs to Marx and Mannheim.

Constructivism

Elsewhere I argued that there is a tension in Oakeshott: he accepts all of the philosophical preconditions of constructivism, yet he cannot accept its natural conclusion.[23] The problem is that writers in the social constructivist tradition by their own admission tend to be reformist and would thus qualify as rationalistic in Oakeshott's (and Hayek's) terms.[24]

The seeds of modern constructivism can be traced to Kant.[25] John Gray has stressed Hayek's "skeptical Kantianism," the idea being that though the mind is inherently a pattern seeker in an undifferentiated metaphysical world, this structure is itself subject to evolutionary malleability through the idiosyncratic factors of personality, culture, situation, and infinitely fine-grained permutations of other circumstances and considerations.[26] For Oakeshott experience requires not just the capacity for sensory awareness stressed by Locke and Hume but also the capacity to make judgments about what one is aware of. At a minimum this last condition means that observation is theory-laden. Hayek attributes to constructivists the belief that, since all aspects of sociality are in some sense artifactual (in being created by humans), sociality in all its forms must be amenable to alteration.[27] Implied in the constructivist viewpoint, according to Hayek, is the idea that because social phenomena are the residua of conscious minds at work, this consciousness connotes some notion of preconceived design. This of course is complete nonsense to both Hayek and Oakeshott.

Rationalism

I won't rehearse Oakeshott's all-too-familiar notion of rationalism. Both he and Hayek lay the blame for constructive rationalism at Descartes's doorstep (though not impugning Descartes himself).[28] Cartesian constructivism, or individualism, has contempt for tradition, custom, and history in general.[29] The familiar refrain (for both Oakeshott and Hayek) is that the Cartesian rationalist insists on the profoundly incoherent notion of abandoning all cultural inheritance.[30] Not only would this render one incapable of action, but to disregard an inherited body of knowledge is to be thoroughly irrational.[31]

THE MAN WITHOUT A PLAN

The Hayek-Oakeshott waters are muddied by four overlapping factors.[32] First, Hayek is taken by many supporters and critics to be a paradigmatic libertarian theorist. Second, Oakeshott is taken by some commentators to be sympathetic to or as endorsing libertarianism. Third, Oakeshott and some Oakeshott scholars ascribe a (pejoratively motivated) "economism" to Hayek. Last, and most problematic, there is Oakeshott's famous (and oft-uncritically repeated) swipe at Hayek: "A plan to resist all planning may be better than its opposite, but it belongs to the same style of politics" (RP, 26). This comment has overshadowed the Oakeshott-Hayek relationship within the secondary literature for nigh on fifty years.

Hayek the Libertarian

Hayek is perhaps the most prominent poster child for libertarianism, but a libertarianism that is profoundly at odds with his actual position. For Hayek knowledge and freedom exist within a manifold network of spontaneous or complex adaptive orders, in which situated agents are perpetually responding to and redefining their environment. Free (open and competitive) orders are, in effect, coordination and communications systems. Communication systems are mechanisms for cooperation among strangers with differing wants, preferences, and interests, mechanisms that offer epistemic (and computational) efficiencies in that knowledge is distributed and dynamic.

For Hayek the market has no special socio-ontological status—it is one spontaneous order among many; nowhere did he claim that the market should subsume or impinge on other orders, for a single or dominant communication system would impoverish the liberal condition.[33] Indeed, for Hayek the healthy functioning of a market presupposes institutions that cannot be provided by private enterprise. Hayek explicitly and repeatedly distanced himself from radical libertarianism, the view that the market is both coextensive with freedom and the universal panacea for all social ills. Even in the most charitable of interpretations, The Road to Serfdom (the very book that would feature on most contemporary libertarian lists) just doesn't support the libertarian stance.[34] Hayek was alert to this misappropriation: "Probably nothing has done so much harm to the liberal cause as the wooden insistence of some liberals on certain rough rules of thumb, above all the principle of laissez faire." This is hardly an isolated instance. Yet again Hayek writes, "It is important not to confuse opposition against this kind of planning with a dogmatic laissez faire attitude. The liberal argument is in favor of making the best possible use of the forces of competition as a means of coordinating human efforts, not an argument for leaving things just as they are."[35]

Let us get a few things straight regarding Hayek's alleged doctrinal laissez-faire stance. For Hayek whether the state should or should not "interfere" poses a false dichotomy: every state must act.[36] Issues that legitimately fall under the purview of government include the provision of signposts, roads, health and safety in the workplace, and environmental issues. Hayek was concerned to specify the proper functions of the state as well as the limits of state action. It might be surprising but Hayek, the supposedly paradigmatic individualist and capitalist apologist, has an environmentalist sensibility. The inference to be drawn is unambiguous: the market alone is not equipped to attend to these needs. To suggest otherwise would be perverse: "In no system that could be rationally defended would the state do nothing."[37]

Oakeshott the Libertarian

Oakeshott's supposed libertarianism takes wing from his endorsement of the economist Henry Simons in "The Political Economy of Freedom" (*RP*, 384–406).[38] Though one can't deny that this essay is replete with the term *libertarian*, a closer examination reveals that Oakeshott is using the term to connote something other than the mere conjoining of laissez-faire with the minimal state.[39] Oakeshott's invocation of the term *libertarian* is quite simply a term of art that connotes an individual who has "a passion for liberty" (386). Consider his reading of Simons: "Nevertheless, his proposals have, of course, nothing whatever to do with that imaginary condition of wholly unfettered competition which is confused with *laissez faire* and ridiculed by collectivists. . . . To know that to regulate competition is not the same thing as to interfere with the operation of competitive controls, and to know the difference between these two activities, is the beginning of the political economy of freedom" (*RP*, 403). It should, therefore, come as no surprise that some current libertarians view Simons as having the poorest of libertarian credentials.[40] Since in Oakeshott's account libertarianism is roughly coextensive with liberalism, his concern is much broader. By contrast, liberalism's "self-appointed friends"—collectivists and syndicalists, very often in uneasy complicity with each other—pose the greatest threat to freedom (386). Much like in Hayek's view, "libertarian" freedom is not any one characteristic but is part of a whole fabric of mutually supporting liberties (388). The Oakeshottian libertarian is someone who rejects any overwhelming concentrations of power, be it church, state, business/industrial corporation, or union (388–89, 393, 398, 401).

Hayek's Economism

Paul Franco takes Hayek (in Oakeshott's account) to be identifying economic freedom with "economism."[41] This interpretation is read off the following extract:

> Finally, the saddest of all the misunderstandings of a state as a civil association: that in which it is properly presented as an association in terms of non-instrumental conditions imposed upon conduct and specified in general rules from whose obligations no associate and no conduct is exempt, but defended as a mode of association more likely than any other to promote and go on promoting the satisfaction of our diverse and proliferant wants. Prosperity may be the likely contingent outcome of civil association, but to recommend it in these terms is to recommend something other than civil association. (*RP*, 457)

There's no misunderstanding on Hayek's part, at least on the data we've looked at so far, let alone a sad one. Hayek is not confused, no one less so. His defense of liberty is multilayered: the constitution of liberty is intrinsically valuable and also instrumentally valuable. Hayek's effectively single-value politics may be thin and unconvincing (he doesn't have an adequate idea even of that single value), but if, as seems likely, he is Oakeshott's target here, Oakeshott has misfired. For Hayek freedom is the supreme political value and the "constitution of liberty" embodies it. To the objection—"what about justice?"—he replies that transactions made under abstract general laws, necessary for freedom, will be just and that justice holds only between individuals. There can be no such thing as social justice between groups and classes. Now whatever one thinks of that position, it isn't a purely instrumental defense of civil association. It's reasonable to roughly equate Hayek's "constitution of liberty" with Oakeshott's "civil association." Certainly the constitution of liberty isn't an enterprise association. Neither Hayek nor Oakeshott is using politics as a vehicle to promote some social ideal.

But Hayek also believes that the constitution of liberty is more likely than any other to promote and go on promoting the satisfaction of our diverse and proliferant wants. Here his economic views, far more elaborate and sophisticated than Oakeshott's, come into play. It is true that Hayek defends civil association on this instrumental ground but it's a complete caricature to say that this is his sole or principal ground of defense. The central rationale of civil association/the constitution of liberty is the protection of freedom as an intrinsic value, and the constitution of liberty is itself intrinsic to that value. I don't therefore share Raz's confidence in characterizing Hayek's concern with freedom as exclusively instrumental in nature.[42] If, in Oakeshott's account, enterprise association assigns an overarching purpose to politics, then civil association would entail the view that politics has no purpose. He frequently stresses that the laws of a civil association are purely procedural: they have no purpose; they are simply instrumental to the purposes of the citizens. Then, of course, laws are purposive after all!

A society in which no conduct was exempt from the control of general rules would be one without freedom. Hayek is concerned with "actions towards other persons"—not just conduct—and he refers to a "person's protected sphere."[43] There wouldn't be such a sphere if no conduct was exempt from general rules. There's an ambiguity here: "no conduct is exempt" may mean that (a) all conduct is (actually) included or (b) more reasonably, no particular conduct is automatically excluded. Any conduct might in principle fall within the ambit of general rules—for example, there's no area marked out as protected by our natural rights. "All" or "any"—that's the ambiguity.

So if Oakeshott misattributes a doctrinal "economism" to Hayek, what possibly could have motivated that? Richard Ashley's analysis is that laissez-faire is a species of, or consistent with, or even synonymous with economism. Therein lies the conceptual confusion.[44] And Oakeshott does certainly equivocate between the two.[45] If we agree that, broadly speaking, economism "connotes an exaggeration of the importance and autonomy of the economic sphere" and that, furthermore, it's "a term that has no purpose other than to secure the boundaries of disciplinary discourse," then taking Hayek to task for his so-called economism loses its force.[46] Hayek wouldn't disagree with Oakeshott's words: "To know that unregulated competition is a chimera, to know that to regulate competition is not the same thing as to interfere with the operation of competitive controls, and to know the difference between these two activities, is the beginning of the political economy of freedom" (RP, 403).

Hayek's own diagnosis (with no particular target in mind) is that there is an ambiguity inherent in his invocation of the term *planning*. He acknowledges that there is a weak and rather trivial sense in which we are all planners. Hayek, however, is reacting to a coercive approach inherent in a command economy, the very same rationalistic ("consciously directed") tendency that Oakeshott identifies. It is this epistemological overreach that Hayek felt would lead us inexorably on the "road to serfdom." For Hayek the failing of collectivist thought is that it misconceives the very process on which the growth of reason depends—in other words, that which we call reason is very much a social phenomenon.[47] Hayek and Oakeshott are shoulder-to-shoulder on this.

Ascriptions of economism/libertarianism mistakenly turn on the notion of individuality and associated expressions of choice. Libertarians, in current understanding, regard the market economy as offering the best expression of the notion of individuality manifest as choice. While Hayek and Oakeshott are not out of sympathy with the importance of the market, for them it's a gross error to reduce all expressions of human freedom to this one area of human experience.[48] Individual freedom (or individuality) at its richest is about choice, but choice that only meaningfully exists at the matrix of art, literature, philosophy, commerce-industry, and politics (*RP*, 370)—and this is as true for Hayek as it is for Oakeshott.[49] True individuality (as opposed to the "individual manqué" or "anti-individual") embraces the inextricable link between choice and the contingency afforded by this choice. The libertarian, properly speaking, should not be merely *homo sapiens* nor *homo laborans* but *homo ludens*, as exemplified in Oakeshott's essay "Work and Play" (*WIH*, 303–14).[50] Hayek is certainly not complicitous in the "danse macabre of wants and satisfactions" (*VLL*, 93).

Oakeshott's Hayek: The Man Without a Plan

Quite how Oakeshott came to view Hayek as such a caricature is puzzling: even the most charitable of interpretations of *The Road to Serfdom* doesn't support his famous swipe at Hayek. Let us look at the context from whence the offending Oakeshott quote comes:

> How deeply the rationalist disposition of mind has invaded our political thought and practice is illustrated by the extent to which traditions of behaviour have given place to ideologies, the extent to which the politics of destruction and creation have been substituted for the politics of repair, the consciously planned and deliberately executed being considered (for that reason) better than what has grown up and established itself unselfconsciously over a period of time. This conversion of habits

and behaviour, adaptable and never quite fixed or finished, into comparatively rigid systems of abstract ideas, is not, of course, new; so far as England is concerned it was begun in the seventeenth century, in the dawn of rationalist politics. But, while formerly it was tacitly resisted and retarded by, for example, the informality of English politics (which enabled us to escape, for a long time, putting too high a value on political action and placing too high a hope in political achievement—to escape, in politics at least, the illusion of the evanescence of imperfection), that resistance has now itself been converted into an ideology. This is, perhaps, the main significance of Hayek's *Road to Serfdom*—not the cogency of the doctrine, but the fact that it is a doctrine. *A plan to resist all planning may be better than its opposite, but it belongs to the same style of politics.* (*RP*, 26; italics added)

Though the preamble to the punch line reveals much that Oakeshott has in common with Hayek, it must be admitted that Oakeshott was just plain wrong about Hayek. "The man without a plan" Hayek is the Hayek that has been misappropriated by libertarian ideologues.

But I think there is a different worry that Oakeshott was trying to express, and I think it turns on Hayek's notion of spontaneous order. The argument is usually expressed as follows: spontaneous orders (Hayek) are sometimes incompatible with, indeed corrosive of, traditional patterns of living (Oakeshott). But if, as Roger Scruton puts it—"Those who believe that social order demands constraints on the market are right. But in a true spontaneous order the constraints are already there, in the form of customs, laws, and morals"—then what's the problem? Scruton goes onto say: "Hume, Smith, Burke and Oakeshott—have tended to see *no* tension between a defence of the free market and a traditionalist vision of social order. For they have put their faith in the spontaneous limits placed on the market by the moral consensus of the community."[51] In this view, Oakeshott has set up a straw man. The question that has to be asked is, what is a traditional order if it is not a spontaneous order? It must surely be conceded that Oakeshott's account of tradition and practice is itself a species of spontaneous order. Patterns of traditional behavior, in Oakeshott's own terms, cannot be other than spontaneous—spontaneous order here taken to connote a cultural dynamism rather being the product of a rationalistic or constructivist mind set.

Whatever the misunderstanding of Hayek in 1947–48, when the essay was originally published, Oakeshott seems to have had a change of heart come 1960. In his "Reader's Report" for Hayek's *The Constitution of Liberty*, Oakeshott writes, "This work is a rehandling of one of the most notable idioms of European political experience and reflection—'liberalism,' 'libertarianism' or as Hayek himself is inclined to call it (in order to avoid the ambiguities which have overtaken these words) 'Whiggism'" (*WIH*, 301). Assuming it was in the version of *The Constitution of Liberty* that Oakeshott first came by, it is most odd that Oakeshott did not pick up on Hayek's explicit acknowledgment of the "rationalistic laissez faire doctrine" if taken literally and pushed to its logical conclusion.[52] Clearly, there is no attribution of the fetishism that Oakeshott earlier ascribed to Hayek.

Hayek, as I hope has been made clear, did not seek to give any priority to the economic realm. Though he was an economist, he was much more besides.[53] All Hayek sought to do was to sharply illustrate the mechanism of spontaneous orders, best articulated by the market. The free flow of knowledge best promotes the conditions for moral and political freedoms or autonomy, issues that Oakeshott was of course critically concerned with.[54] Jointly and severally, the discussion in these subsections takes the wind out of the misattribution of "economism" and "libertarianism" to Hayek.

LIBERALISM AS EMBEDDED INDIVIDUALISM

A more interesting issue concerns the vexed question of whether Oakeshott was a liberal conservative and whether Hayek was a conservative liberal. Despite Oakeshott explicitly touting his conservative credentials (*RP*) and Hayek explicitly touting his nonconservative credentials, I take both thinkers to be liberal thinkers.[55] Boyd and Morrison nicely capture the fluidity of Oakeshott's and Hayek's respective ideological positions: "Hayek is not as unambiguously 'liberal' as he suggests, nor is Oakeshott purely a 'conservative' of the variety that Hayek indicts."[56] This fluidity shouldn't be viewed as problematic.[57] Both Hayek and Oakeshott are well aware that much of the terminology deployed in political discourse has been emptied of any meaning—for Oakeshott, notably in the essay "Talking Politics" (438–61), these terms include *liberal*, *laissez-faire*, and *conservative*.

So the question that should be asked is, "What then separates a conservative (antirationalist) who favors incremental change in preference to large-scale change from a liberal who equally prefers incremental change?" Is there any way of prying Oakeshott and Hayek apart? Conservatism, broadly speaking, rejects the rationalist/ideological project of a radical reconstitution of society in the light of some political ideal such as the promotion of justice or equality. Liberals such as Popper equally reject such "large-scale social engineering."[58] The point is, however, that liberalism *does* want to promote socially transformative ideals—the ideal, say, of equal opportunity. So in having big ideas about how society can and should ultimately be changed, the liberal has common ground with the rationalist. Perhaps another way of looking at the problem is courtesy of the chaos and catastrophe theory, whereby small changes can have disproportionate (sometimes drastically so) effects. In this view, the conservative should also acknowledge that even incremental change isn't safe, since no one really knows what it will lead to any more than one knows with large-scale social engineering. It seems here that Oakeshott has an advantage over Hayek. Oakeshott has (whatever its sociological validity) an idea of tradition, and within a tradition probabilities can be assigned. Someone who understands, say, the British Constitution and British political culture has a pretty shrewd idea of political dangers and risks.[59] "Probability," as Bishop Butler said, "is the very guide to life."[60] With this in mind, a conservative should, can, or might have a good idea of what's feasible, desirable, or dangerous relative to a tradition of behavior.

But maybe there's a defense for Hayek, a possibility for him to appeal to limited predictability of the sort that Oakeshott would find in a tradition. Hayek stresses the spontaneous social order generated by a market economy but he also relies on a range of economic generalizations. His arguments with Keynes centered on how a monetary and fiscal system could be expected to behave. The "road to serfdom" also rests on certain inductive probabilities. I don't think Hayek believes that his spontaneous social order carries any implication of acausality, let alone total randomness. Economic systems have a logic, a set of inbuilt dispositions, of their own, and these yield limited predictability in the interests of political and social policy.

Let us reorient the discussion back to the socially embedded mind, for it is here that the inextricable connection between mind and knowledge is made, which I claim is the binding agent between Oakeshott and Hayek. Complexity for Hayek offers both the fabric of possibility and of inherent constraint. On the one hand, agents within a rich (complex) social tapestry have their conceptual and behavioral possibilities tempered by the partial cognitive and epistemic access to the (complex) manifold that informs the ambient culture (OHC, 58; RPML, 91). On the other hand, mind is itself constitutionally (and terminally) constrained in fully understanding its own (complex) mechanics—a mind significantly constituted by its (complex) social environment. Oakeshott specifically conceives of mind as "the intelligent activity in which a man may understand and explain processes which cannot understand and explain themselves" (VLL, 19). For Hayek the paradox is this: knowledge can become less incomplete only if it becomes more dispersed.[61] Epistemic and cognitive efficiencies, well beyond the capacity of any one mind, are facilitated through the ubiquity of sociocultural scaffolding and dynamic looping.[62] For both Oakeshott and Hayek, tradition, custom, and practice are the vehicles or scaffolding for "computational" efficacy. For Hayek, "cognitive closure," a mark of the human condition, can be ameliorated if the social and artifactual world functions as a kind of distributed extraneural memory store manifest as dynamic traditions, part of the resources for acting, thinking, or communicating. Put another way, the notion of cognitive closure entails the postulation of an open society—here Hayek makes the highly distinctive and direct link between mind and social liberty.[63]

So-called individualism for Hayek is an attitude of humility—he is talking about the methodological principle that whatever else cognition is, it is still undertaken by individuals, even though most, if not all, of what is cognized is the result of the activities of multitudes of others.[64] This is equally applicable to Oakeshott.[65] Antirationalists understand that to make reason as effective as possible requires an insight into the limitations of the power of conscious reason—and this modesty is conspicuously missing from a rationalist's conception: "Both freedom and justice are values that can prevail only among men with limited knowledge and would have no meaning in a society of omniscient men."[66] Oakeshott's invocation of Tacitus (*Histories* 1:83) as channeled though Ruhnken, "*tam nescire quaedam milites quam scire oportet*," is roughly translated as "There are things which we have to reconcile ourselves to not knowing" (*RP*, 6–7). For both Oakeshott and Hayek, the demand for a demonstrative and deliberate use of reason in matters of sociality exceeds the cognitive capacity available to any one or group of individuals.[67]

NOTES

1. The Hayek corpus on which I draw includes *The Road to Serfdom* (1944; repr., Chicago: University of Chicago Press, 1976); *Individualism and the Economic Order* (1948; repr., Chicago: University of Chicago Press, 1980); *The Counter-Revolution of Science: Studies on the Abuse of Reason* (1952; repr., Indianapolis: Liberty Fund Press, 1979); *The Sensory Order* (1952; repr., Chicago: University of Chicago Press, 1976); *The Constitution of Liberty* (1960; repr., Chicago: University of Chicago Press, 1978); *Studies on Philosophy, Politics, and Economics* (Chicago: University of Chicago Press, 1967); *Rules and Order*, vol. 1 of *Law, Legislation, and Liberty* (Chicago: University of Chicago Press, 1973); *The Mirage of Social Justice*, vol. 2 of *Law, Legislation, and Liberty* (Chicago: University of Chicago Press, 1976); *New Studies in Philosophy, Politics, Economics, and the History of Ideas* (Chicago: University of Chicago Press, 1978); *The Political Order of a Free People*, vol. 3 of *Law, Legislation, and Liberty* (Chicago: University of Chicago Press, 1979); *The Fatal Conceit: The Errors of Socialism* (Chicago: University of Chicago Press, 1988).

2. The most sustained and exemplary effort to contrast Oakeshott and Hayek has been Richard Boyd and James Morrison, "F. A. Hayek, Michael Oakeshott, and the Concept of Spontaneous Order," in *Liberalism, Conservatism, and Hayek's Idea of Spontaneous Order*, ed. Peter McNamara and Louis Hunt (New York: Palgrave Macmillan, 2007). Edmund Neill marks the surprising

paucity of literature comparing Hayek and Oakeshott. *Major Conservative and Libertarian Thinkers: Michael Oakeshott* (New York: Continuum International), 124n5.

3. To say that rationality is culturally saturated and modulated should *not* be understood as "socialization," a discussion of which is to be found in *VLL*.

4. Oakeshott's influences were much more besides, as this volume illustrates.

5. Oakeshott had a long-standing interest in consciousness, first manifest in his critique of the realist myth of the self-differentiating object (*EM*); his best-known statement being his mid-career anti-Cartesianism (*RP*), culminating with his identification of reflective consciousness as a postulate of conduct (*OHC*). Hayek's more empirical interest in consciousness was sketched out as early as 1920, as "Beiträge zur Theorie der Entwicklung des Bewusstseins" ("Contributions to a Theory of How Consciousness Develops") and "Within Systems and About Systems: A Statement of Some Problems of a Theory of Communication," 1952, folder 51, box 94, Hoover Institute Archives, Hoover Institution Library, Stanford, California), works that became more fleshed out in *Sensory Order*.

6. Stephen Turner, "Social Theory as a Cognitive Neuroscience," *European Journal of Social Theory* 10, no. 3 (2007): 358.

7. Identifying Oakeshott in these terms was first made by Keith Sutherland, "Rationalism in Politics and Cognitive Science," in *The Intellectual Legacy of Michael Oakeshott*, ed. Corey Abel and Timothy Fuller (Exeter: Imprint Academic, 2005); and Stephen Turner, "Tradition and Cognitive Science: Oakeshott's Undoing of the Kantian Mind," *Philosophy of the Social Sciences* 33, no. 1 (2003): 53–76.

8. Philip Robbins and Murat Aydede, "A Short Primer on Situated Cognition," in *Cambridge Handbook to Situated Cognition*, ed. Philip Robbins and Murat Aydede (Cambridge: Cambridge University Press, 2008).

9. I employ the term *artifactual* as a blanket term for all aspects of sociality, including the commonly understood conception of artifacts, such as pens. Bruce Wexler, *Brain and Culture: Neurobiology, Ideology, and Social Change* (Cambridge: MIT Press, 2006).

10. Friedrich Hayek, *Counter-Revolution of Science*, 155; cf. "A man is his culture" (*VLL*, 29).

11. Mario Rizzo, "Austrian Economics: Recent Work," in *The New Palgrave Dictionary of Economics*, ed. Steven Durlauf and Lawrence Blume (Basingstoke: Palgrave Macmillan, 2009).

12. Stephen Turner, *Brains/Practices/Relativism: Social Theory After Cognitive Science* (Chicago: University of Chicago Press, 2003), 3, 11.

13. See *VLL*, 155–58, for Oakeshott's unusually rare rejoinder to critics regarding this terminology.

14. Friedrich Hayek, *Studies on Philosophy*, 7, 43, 56, 60–62. See Leslie Marsh, "Hayek: Cognitive Scientist *Avant la Lettre*," in *The Social Science of Hayek's "The Sensory Order,"* ed. William N. Butos, Advances in Austrian Economics (Bingley: Emerald, 2010); Leslie Marsh, "Ryle and Oakeshott on the Know-How/Know-That Distinction," in *The Meanings of Michael Oakeshott's Conservatism*, ed. Corey Abel (Exeter: Imprint Academic, 2010).

15. Daniel Hutto, "Knowing What? Radical Versus Conservative Enactivism," *Phenomenology and the Cognitive Sciences* 4 (2005): 389–405.

16. Andy Clark, *Being There: Putting Brain, Body, and World Together Again* (Cambridge: MIT Press, 1997), 69.

17. Hayek, *Sensory Order*, secs. 6.15, 6.22–6.28.

18. Gilbert Ryle, *The Concept of Mind* (Harmondsworth: Penguin, 1949); Marsh, "Ryle and Oakeshott."

19. Hayek, *Rules and Order*, 37; *Sensory Order*, sec. 5.65.

20. Francisco Varela, *Ethical Know-How: Action, Wisdom, and Cognition* (Stanford: Stanford University Press, 1999); Varela, Evan Thompson, and Eleanor Rosch, *The Embodied Mind: Cognitive Science and Human Experience* (1991; repr., Cambridge: MIT Press, 2000).

21. Evan Thompson, *Mind in Life: Biology, Phenomenology, and the Sciences of the Mind* (Cambridge: Harvard University Press, 2007), 409. These sentiments are echoed in Alva Noë, *Out of Our Heads: Why You Are Not Your Brain, and Other Lessons from the Biology of Consciousness* (New York: Hill and Wang, 2008).

22. For the use of the term *constructivism*, see Hayek, *New Studies in Philosophy*; for *intentionalism* and *artificialism*, see Hayek, *Rules and Order*, 26–27; for *intellectualism*, see Hayek,

Counter-Revolution of Science, 378; for *rationalist constructivism*, see Hayek, *Studies on Philosophy*, 29; and for *rationalism*, see Hayek, *Counter-Revolution of Science*, especially the chapter "Conscious Direction and the Growth of Reason." There seems to be a consensus that Hayek's notion of scientism and his notion of rationalism were much the same; see Bruce Caldwell, "Hayek and the Austrian Tradition," in *The Cambridge Companion to Hayek*, ed. Edward Feser (Cambridge: Cambridge University Press, 2007); Caldwell, *Hayek's Challenge: An Intellectual Biography of F. A. Hayek* (Chicago: University of Chicago Press, 2004); and Andrew Gamble, "Hayek on Knowledge, Economics, and Society" in *Cambridge Companion to Hayek*. ed. Feser. Boyd and Morrison take Hayek's scientism to be almost identical with Oakeshott's rationalism. "F. A. Hayek," 92.

23. Leslie Marsh, "Constructivism and Relativism in Oakeshott," in *Intellectual Legacy*, ed. Abel and Fuller.

24. That Oakeshott is a constructivist is not open to doubt. For Oakeshott *everything* is a construction: "The starry heavens above us and the moral law within are alike human achievements" (*VLL*, 38). This constructivism is to be found across the Oakeshott corpus (*OHC*, 18; *VLL*, 9, 37, 65–66; *RP*, 506; *EM*, 42).

25. Hayek, *Philosophy, Politics, and Economics*, 95.

26. John Gray, *Hayek on Liberty* (Oxford: Basil Blackwell, 1984).

27. Hayek, *Rules and Order*, 5.

28. Ibid., 9, 11, 12, 17; *Counter-Revolution of Science*, 161; Hayek, *Philosophy, Politics, and Economics*, 85–86.

29. Hayek, *Rules and Order*, 10; *New Studies in Philosophy*, 8.

30. Hayek, *Fatal Conceit*, 61.

31. Hayek, *Individualism*, 24; *Counter-Revolution of Science*, 163; *Constitution of Liberty*, 61–62; *New Studies in Philosophy*, 18.

32. Unlike the tarnished Oakeshott-Berlin relationship (see Paul Franco, "Oakeshott, Berlin, and Liberalism," *Political Theory* 31, no. 4 [2003]: 484–507), the Oakeshott-Hayek relationship was very cordial; there was some substantive discussion of nomocracy and telocracy and civil and enterprise association but to my knowledge never any (at least documented) mention of the famous swipe against Hayek, the subject of this section. Two years after the publication of *Rationalism in Politics*, Hayek duly accepted an invitation from Oakeshott to deliver a lecture at the London School of Economics (folder 24, box 40, Hayek Archives, British Library of Political and Economic Science). By then Hayek had already left Chicago for Freiberg. I am told by Hayek's personal assistant in the 1970s (Kurt Luebe) that the two got on very well indeed and did engage in substantive and animated discussion in London and at the Mont Pelerin Society meetings. Hayek cites Oakeshott's lectures (supposedly the History of Political Thought Lectures, published as *LHPT*) approvingly in *Political Order*, 15. Oakeshott wrote a glowing "Reader's Report" on Hayek's *Constitution of Liberty*, to be found in *WIH*, 301–2. Was the postscript to *Constitution of Liberty* not available to Oakeshott? See note 55.

33. Hayek, *Counter-Revolution of Science*; cf. Oakeshott's *EM*.

34. Hayek, *Road to Serfdom*, 38, 17, 35, 36, 39, 42, 81; *Studies on Philosophy*, 61–62; *Mirage of Social Justice*, 151. See Gamble, "Hayek on Knowledge," 128.

35. Hayek, *Road to Serfdom*, 17, 36.

36. Ibid., 80–81; *Studies on Philosophy*, 162–63.

37. Hayek, *Road to Serfdom*, 54, 39. Adam Smith in *The Wealth of Nations* specifies three roles for the state: (a) protecting society from external threats, (b) protecting each individual of society from the injustices perpetrated by others of the society, and (c) the duty of "erecting and maintaining" certain public works and certain institutions, which can never be in the interest of any one individual or small group of individuals. Though current libertarianism looks to Smith's idea of negative freedom (or "natural liberty") for conceptual validation, it is far from obvious that Smith's three roles would reduce the level of state activity in current conditions. *An Inquiry into the Nature and Causes of the Wealth of Nations*, ed. Edwin Cannan, 5th ed. (London: Methuen, 1904), 4:9.51 and 5:1.69.

38. Henry C. Simons (1899–1946) is considered the progenitor of the Chicago School.

39. Two prominent commentators who have labeled Oakeshott as a libertarian are W. H. Greenleaf and Charles Covell: Greenleaf, *Oakeshott's Philosophical Politics* (London: Longmans, 1966), 82–83, 84–86; Covell, *The Redefinition of Conservatism* (Basingstoke: Macmillan, 1986),

212–13; and Covell, *The Defence of Natural Law: A Study of the Ideas of Law and Justice in the Writings of Lon L. Fuller, Michael Oakeshott, F. A. Hayek, Ronald Dworkin, and John Finnis* (London: St. Martin's Press, 1992), 114–21.

40. Walter Block, "Henry Simons Is Not a Supporter of Free Enterprise," *Journal of Libertarian Studies* 16, no. 4 (2002): 3–36.

41. Paul Franco, *Michael Oakeshott: An Introduction* (New Haven: Yale University Press, 2004), 172.

42. Joseph Raz, *The Morality of Freedom* (Oxford: Clarendon Press, 1988), 7. Though not specifically referring to Raz, a prominent Oakeshott scholar shares my view; see Elizabeth Campbell Corey, *Michael Oakeshott on Religion, Aesthetics, and Politics* (Columbia: University of Missouri Press, 2006), 223n10.

43. Hayek, *Constitution of Liberty*, 155.

44. Richard Ashley, "Three Modes of Economism," *International Studies Quarterly* 27, no. 4 (1983): 463–96.

45. Compare the aforementioned quotes from *RP*, 26 and 457.

46. Ashley, "Three Modes of Economism," 463.

47. Hayek, *Road to Serfdom*, 165–66.

48. Robert Grant, *The Politics of Sex* (Basingstoke: Palgrave Macmillan, 2000), 7.

49. Gray, *Hayek on Liberty*, 130. Hayek shared Oakeshott's view of the value of liberal education. Hayek, referring to himself, wrote, "exclusive concentration on a specialty has a peculiarly baneful effect: it will not merely prevent us from being attractive company or good citizens but may impair our competence in our proper field" (Hayek, *Philosophy, Politics, and Economics*, 123, 127).

50. Herbert Simon, as did Hayek and Oakeshott, rejected the fiction of *homo economicus* so favored by orthodox economics. See Leslie Marsh, "Mindscapes and Landscapes: Hayek and Simon on Cognitive Extension," in *Hayek and Behavioural Economics*, ed. Roger Frantz and Robert Leeson (Basingstoke: Palgrave Macmillan, 2012).

51. Roger Scruton, "Hayek and Conservatism," in *Cambridge Companion to Hayek*, ed. Feser, 219–20 (italics added).

52. Hayek, *Constitution of Liberty*, 60.

53. Hayek was one of the twentieth century's genuine polymaths; see Marsh, "Hayek."

54. Hayek, *Rules and Order*, 55.

55. It may well be that Hayek's postscript to *Constitution of Liberty*, "Why I'm Not a Conservative," had Oakeshott's "On Being Conservative" (*RP*) in mind. This said, the characterization of conservatism in *Constitution of Liberty* bore little resemblance to the brand of (dispositional) conservatism espoused by Oakeshott. Having just moved to Chicago, Hayek's target, I think, was the muddying of the conceptual waters of the terms *liberal* and *conservative* in transatlantic discourse (cf. *Political Order*, 136; Chandran Kukathas, "Hayek and Liberalism," in *Cambridge Companion to Hayek*, ed. Feser). This state of affairs still obtains fifty years on. Bruce Caldwell, the general editor of *The Collected Works of F. A. Hayek* (Chicago: University of Chicago Press), tells me that "We do know that Hayek was not happy about the fact that *Serfdom* was often taken to be a party document in the U.S., that is, one that Republicans would endorse and Democrats not." Wendell John Coats Jr., "Michael Oakeshott as Liberal Theorist," *Canadian Journal of Political Science* 18 (December 1985): 773–87; Paul Franco, "Michael Oakeshott as Liberal Theorist," *Political Theory* 18, no. 3 (1990): 411–36. Scruton offers a dissenting voice, taking Hayek's core arguments to be essentially conservative. See his "Hayek and Conservatism," in *Cambridge Companion to Hayek*, ed. Feser,.

56. Boyd and Morrison, "F. A. Hayek," 99–100. See Hayek in *New Studies in Philosophy*, 18–19. This view is pretty much shared by Kukathas, "Hayek and Liberalism," in *Cambridge Companion to Hayek*, ed. Feser, and by John Gray, *Post-liberalism: Studies in Political Thought* (New York: Routledge, 1993).

57. Michael Freeden, "Political Concepts and Ideological Morphology," *Journal of Political Philosophy* 2 (1994): 140–64; Steven Wulf, "Oakeshott's Politics for Gentlemen," *Review of Politics* 69 (2007): 244–72.

58. Karl Popper, *The Poverty of Historicism*, 3rd ed. (London: Routledge and Kegan Paul, 1961), 43.

59. Lord Salisbury and Stanley Baldwin would fall into this category.

60. Joseph Butler, *The Analogy of Religion, Natural and Revealed, to the Constitution and Course of Nature* (Charlottesville: Ibis, n.d.), intro.

61. Hayek, *Rules and Order*, 15.

62. Hayek, *Studies on Philosophy*, 34, 42.

63. Hayek, *Mirage of Social Justice*, 127. The philosopher of mind Colin McGinn, who coined the term *cognitive closure*, understands it as a mark of the richness of the human condition. See *The Problem of Consciousness* (Oxford: Blackwell, 1989), 22. In a similar vein Timothy Fuller sums up Oakeshott's critique of education as mere problem solving: "The human condition is a predicament, not an itinerary" ("Editor's Introduction" to *VLL*, 11).

64. Hayek, *Rules and Order*, 166.

65. Grant, *Politics of Sex*, 36.

66. Hayek, *Rules and Order*, 29, 32; Hayek, *Mirage of Social Justice*, 127. Variations on this occur in *Mirage of Social Justice*, 8; and *Political Order*, 71, 72, 130.

67. I am indebted to Bruce Caldwell (general editor of *The Collected Works of F. A. Von Hayek*) for granting me permission to use items from Hayek's intellectual estate; Peter McNamara for a preprint of Boyd and Morrison's chapter; Noel Reynolds for the Kurt Luebe lead; and Keith Sutherland for his generosity in making available Imprint's complete holding of Oakeshottiana. I'm also grateful for the most excellent service accorded me by Ronald Bulatoff (archival specialist, Hoover Institution Archives—Hayek) and Anna Towlson (assistant archivist, Library, London School of Economics—Oakeshott). Thanks to Paul Franco, Geoff Thomas, Steven Wulf, and Andrew Irvine for their insightful comments and to David Hardwick and Gus diZerega for such fertile ongoing discussion. Thanks are also due to Shannon Selin for transcribing Oakeshott's often illegible handwritten correspondence with Hayek.

13

OAKESHOTT AS CONSERVATIVE

Robert Devigne

The identification of Michael Oakeshott with conservatism is fraught with debate. To be sure, some analysts consider Oakeshott to be the modern incarnation of Burke. Moreover, during the closing decades of the twentieth century, conservative thinkers in the United Kingdom made the greatest claims to Oakeshott. Yet different features of Oakeshott's thought have made it possible for him to be read as a liberal, a pragmatist, a historicist, an existentialist, a postmodernist, and a conservative.[1] What, then, is conservative in Oakeshott's political philosophy?

Conservative political thought, as most fully expressed by Burke's response to the French Revolution, developed throughout the West in opposition to Enlightenment beliefs that societies could be guided along a secular, egalitarian, and self-governing path. Burke's thought was characterized by a respect for history as the source of progress, a rejection of the view that individuals and their rights existed prior to institutions, an extolling of the virtue of prudence when introducing political reform, an appreciation for habits and traditional modes of conduct, an opposition to institutions based on rational models of behavior, and distrust for Enlightenment political philosophy in particular and philosophy more generally.[2] Because Burke and others argued that history, not philosophy, is the source of a nation's most important institutions and values, the conservative outlook, unlike its liberal counterpart, did not constitute a set of substantive ideas or an "ought" concerning the best form of government or best form of society. It defined only a framework for a variety of the defenses being raised throughout Europe against an ascendant liberal outlook.

How does Oakeshott line up in relation to Burke? Does Oakeshott's thought, like Burke and traditional conservatism more generally, assume that individuals belong to some continuing and preexisting social order, and does this understanding influence his positions when determining better or worse political associations? We examine Oakeshott's middle and late works, written from the late 1940s to the early 1980s, to identify significant points of continuity and difference with Burke in the middle period.[3] On the one hand, Oakeshott and Burke develop similar assessments of the value of traditions, the dissolving effect of rationalism on those practices, and the importance of a prescriptive approach to political reform. On the other hand, unlike Burke, Oakeshott places high value on philosophy itself and the role it plays in identifying better or worse political practices. And contra Burke, Oakeshott identifies a problematic English history not necessarily leading to the political good.

Turning to the late works, we discover that the differences between each thinker become more pronounced, as Oakeshott moves in a more liberal direction, focusing on the role that law plays in preventing conflict among individuals and groups pursuing variegated ends. We also see Oakeshott explicitly distancing himself from Burke's thought. Despite these differences, however, a new line can be drawn between a current of Oakeshott's and Burke's thinking during this time as well, as Oakeshott develops a more traditional European conservative position: respect for modern European history, whereby the "is" is not quite the "ought" but is certainly close to it.

Finally, in conclusion, I contrast Oakeshott's thinking with the other seminal conservative thinker of the second half of the twentieth century, Leo Strauss. Here I explain how Strauss's different assessments of modernity, Burke, and history clarify the distinct character of their respective conservatisms and illuminate why Strauss has become associated with a more proactive neoconservatism, while Oakeshott is often linked to a more traditional, historicist conservatism.

MODES OF CONDUCT AND RATIONALISM

Burke's appreciation for long-standing practices anterior to the individual, as expressed by his view that the individual is born into the "ties and ligaments" of society, has a counterpart in Oakeshott's discussions on idioms of conduct in his postwar essays on politics.[4] Human activities, Oakeshott argues, are based on patterns. These patterns come not from an extrinsic source but rather from a pattern intrinsic to the activity itself, often identified as customs, traditions, maxims, or idioms. They integrate the individual into society by establishing the basis for appropriate and inappropriate behavior, not due to their correspondence with some objective reality but owing to their being the source of coherence in human activity. "They are not, properly speaking, *expressions* of approval and disapproval, or of knowledge of how to behave—they *are* the substance of our knowledge of how to behave. We do not first decide that certain behavior is right or desirable and then express our approval of it as an institution; our knowledge of how to behave is, at this point, the institution." An individual's will, whether it is expressed while engaging in a scientific experiment or a historical study, gardening, or shopping, acts in the context of the beliefs and activities that make up the individual's mind and are in part an inheritance from history. "A particular action, in short, never begins in particularity, but always in an idiom or a tradition of activity," states Oakeshott (*RP*, 120, 126).

Evoking themes found in Burke's prediction that metaphysics rooted in rationalism would destroy the "whole chain and continuity of the commonwealth," making individuals "little better than the flies of a summer," Oakeshott charges that the failure to respect the different types of traditions and idioms of conduct is *the* great problem in postwar British politics.[5] Political philosophers and practitioners—most notably those attracted to pseudoscientific outlooks—fail to recognize that the distinct practices of education, history, production, cooking, practical activities, science, and others are rooted in historically derived assumptions of which most practitioners are unaware.

Oakeshott predicts a tug-of-war between the rationalist pursuit of moral ideals and the unself-conscious assumptions that inform our actions. When the state or other powers attempt to direct different types of human conduct toward self-imposed political and moral goals, the assumptions that set procedures for the pursuit of private aims are torn asunder. "Activity springing from and governed by an independently premeditated purpose is impossible," states Oakeshott. "To suggest that activity ought to be of this character and to try to force it into this pattern, is to corrupt it without being able to endow it with the desired character" (*RP*, 120). Rationalists, according to Oakeshott, would learn the error of their ways only by an acceptance of what they stand opposed to: unreflective behavior! Short of this self-renunciation, "all the Rationalist can do . . . is replace one rationalist project in which he has failed with another in which he hopes to succeed." But the errors of rationalism in politics are more difficult to recognize than errors spawned by rationalism in other idioms. If you approach a machine or an electrical apparatus in a purely technical matter, "you are likely to be pulled up short by an explosion: but in politics all that happens is war and chaos, which you do not immediately connect with your error." Traditions initially cause trouble for the rationalists, but, increasingly, it is the problems of the rationalists that will cause trouble for the traditions. In time, Oakeshott warns, the program of rationalists will lead to the life of society losing "its rhythm and continuity" as it is thrown "into a succession of problems and crises . . . and all sense of what Burke called the partnership between the past and present is lost" (28, 37–38, 113–14).

Oakeshott's advocacy of preserving while reforming weakened modes of conduct in the postwar essays also is consistent with the political spirit of Burke, who argued that a troubled tradition could be restored if "we do not suffer ourselves to be entangled in the mazes of metaphysical sophistry," and the reform is restricted to the part of the tradition no longer acting as it did in the past. "Even then it is to be effected without a decomposition of the whole civil and political mass, for the purpose of originating a new civil order out of the first elements of society." This prescriptive approach to politics flows from a prudent response to broken practices in society, in such a way that that the reforms are seen by the public as the restoration of the necessary.[6]

Similarly, Oakeshott states that whenever innovation cannot be proved to be more beneficial than stability; whenever imposed change is deemed more important than change through growth; whenever general social conditions are more important for public policies to target than specific problems; whenever rapid political change is placed above incremental reform (and with adjustments along the way); and whenever unintended consequences are more likely than limited, intended, reforms, he prefers the activity of the present to the activity of the speculated future. Furthermore, even when the principles of prescription and prudence are implemented, Oakeshott maintains, success is dependent on the strength remaining in the idiom itself. "There is, in fact, no way in which a knowledge of how to behave can be made to spring solely from a knowledge of propositions about good behavior. In the end, the cure depends upon the native strength of the patient; it depends upon the unimpaired relics of his knowledge of how to behave" (RP, 128–29).

These manifest affinities between Burke and the postwar Oakeshott regarding tradition, rationalism in politics, and reform may tend to obscure important differences in their political and philosophical thinking, however. For example, Oakeshott did not reject philosophical thinking, while Burke did, declaring that, when it came to understanding politics and society, "I shall always advise to call in the aid of the farmer and the physician, rather than the professor of metaphysics."[7] In contrast, Oakeshott's critique of modern British politics is rooted in philosophy. Deeply influenced by Hegel, Bradley, and other thinkers of the idealist tradition, Oakeshott asserts that human judgments require the subordination of reality to ideas. Philosophy analyzes the different types of understandings developed by the mind to create a coherent reality and organize behavior.

But, like Burke, Oakeshott rejects the view that philosophy is a privileged form of knowledge that endorses, and dictates to, other kinds of knowledge. Indeed, Oakeshott insists that a philosophy of politics is irrelevant to political practice, as it stands beyond the assumptions and temperament necessary to that engagement and places the limited reality of political conduct in the context of all experience. Yet, unlike Burke, Oakeshott values philosophy as a distinct type of inquiry among the other idioms of knowledge in society: it seeks to understand the modes of thinking that different practices require, while also turning on itself and critically assessing the assumptions it adopts in identifying the idioms of other practices. Accordingly, a philosophy of politics can identify—but not create—the assumptions on which political activities are based.

Oakeshott also is far less positive than Burke about an unfolding moral wisdom growing organically out of the specific genius of English traditions, properly understood. "This idea of a liberal descent," Burke wrote, "inspires us with a habitual native dignity. . . . It carries an imposing and majestic aspect. . . . All your sophisters cannot produce any thing better to preserve a rational and manly freedom than the course we have pursued."[8] In contrast, Oakeshott devotes an enormous amount of mental energy to the task of identifying a polarized inheritance in regard to the assumptions and beliefs about political and social arrangements in the United Kingdom. On the one hand, Oakeshott identifies a habituated moral outlook, with very little self-awareness, which encourages, respects, and preserves the traditions and idioms that inform manifold ways of life. Individuals with this outlook have the "power to act appropriately and without hesitation, doubt, or difficulty," but they do not have the ability to explain themselves "in abstract terms or defend" their conduct as "as emanations of moral principles." On the other hand, Oakeshott also identifies a deeply rooted conviction that focuses on the techniques and methods deemed appropriate for this or that practice and, more ominously, for the realization of self-imposed moral ideals in the society as a whole. As Oakeshott believes that this latter outlook—the rational pursuit of moral ideals—is the dominant feature in the cultural landscape of postwar Britain, and as it is an antagonist to the "morality of habits," he sees the moral and intellectual inheritance of the United Kingdom as a predicament, not progress.[9] To be sure, Oakeshott, like Burke, does not believe that politics can transcend the entrenched assumptions rooted in historical practices. But to Burke, the "is" is the "ought," or the good. To Oakeshott, the "is" is contradictory and both good *and* bad (*RP*, 470, 473–74, 487).

OAKESHOTT'S SHIFT

Beginning with essays in the early 1950s and culminating in the magisterial *On Human Conduct*, there is a subtle, but very important, shift in Oakeshott's assessment and critique of modern politics: moral conflict, not epistemological confusion, is the great problem. Oakeshott explains that the primary impetus to modern Western political practice and thought was the breakdown of late medieval communal organizations, giving rise to a political division between a morality centered on individuals who find the occasion of making choices a readily agreeable opportunity and a morality based on individuals who find the freedom to make decisions a toilsome and onerous responsibility. The former is a disposition or sentiment to protect and cultivate human agency, while the latter outlook found the circumstances of the newfound freedom to be too challenging. Each outlook provides the foundation to an underlying division on the proper aims of the modern European state, which Oakeshott identifies through the categories of *societas* and *universitas*. "In short," states Oakeshott, "my contention is that the modern European consciousness is a polarized consciousness, that *these* are its poles and that all other tensions (such as those indicated in the words '*right*' or '*left*' or in the alignments of political parties) are insignificant compared with this" (*OHC*, 320). From this new starting point of contending moral outlooks and competing ideas of the state, Oakeshott's political philosophy moves in a decidedly more liberal direction, and his distance from Burke's thought becomes more pronounced in some dimensions, while becoming more proximate in another.

In Oakeshott's view, the morality of individual choice is expressed by the politics of societas, the view that seeks to specify and limit the functions of government so as to allow a great diversity of self-chosen enterprises. The government's primary task is to establish general rules of conduct that delineate the conditions that individuals and groups must subscribe to when pursuing their respective substantive or particularistic aims. Oakeshott identifies Montesquieu, Hobbes, Bodin, Spinoza, and Hegel as the most accomplished architects of this school of thought. He also identifies many other circumstances that have contributed to the politics of societas: lack of substantive unity among subjects, monarchs' establishment of courts and "distant law," the use of mercenaries for military purposes in the late medieval and early modern eras, and the decline of the papacy and landed aristocracy, among others. Still, Oakeshott insists that the fundamental impetus to this type of politics is the development of a human character with a "disposition to be 'self-employed' in which a man recognizes himself and all others in terms

of self-determination; that is, in terms of wants rather than slippery satisfactions and of adventures rather than uncertain outcomes" (*OHC*, 206–13,
233–66, 324).

Oakeshott explains that the counter morality to that of *societas* is expressed
by the politics of *universitas*, the drive to use state power and concomitant
availability of technology to alleviate humanity's weaknesses and fears, as
well as to organize society as a common enterprise. The most comprehensive engineer of this outlook, according to Oakeshott, is Francis Bacon, who
envisioned the state as a corporate enterprise for the exploitation of the earth,
and it was further developed by the Cameralists, Saint-Simon, Fourier, Owen,
Marx, and the Webbs. Oakeshott identifies many circumstances that contribute to the politics of *universitas*: "the unpurged relic of lordship" among rulers, the exigencies of modern war and the necessity of a mobilizing state,
modern science and the vision of "enlightened government," and the state's
replacement of the church as the source of moral education, among others.
Oakeshott maintains that the primary source of this type of politics is the formation of a human character with a "disposition to identify oneself a partner
with others in a common enterprise and as a sharer in a common stock of
talents with which to exploit it" (*OHC*, 213–24, 267–317, 324).

To be sure, Oakeshott's loyalty in regard to this division is clear, as he
focuses on developing an ideal picture of civil association, where the laws
create a framework within which individuals and groups interact but do not
specify substantive performances and actions. This *societas* is an association
in which members are joined, not in the pursuit of common goals, but only
in the common recognition of noninstrumental laws of conduct. Oakeshott
insists that the rule of law must be absolutely differentiated from commands.
Laws are determined by their form, and this form is imposed by setting
"known, non-instrumental rules (that is, laws) which impose obligations
to subscribe to adverbial conditions in the performance of the self-chosen
actions of all who fall within their jurisdiction." If the law does not have the
form of a rule, it is inconceivable to distinguish the rule of law from the pro-
grammatic aims of those wielding the most power. While commands specify
individuals and direct particular tasks, laws speak to the general public and
establish the same conditions for everyone in the association. And for laws to
be generally known by the public, they must be a product of a public order of
intelligible rules.

Finally, the rule of law, in Oakeshott's account, is *not* concerned with cultivating moral development or specific types of human qualities; these issues
are to be left to the discretion of groups and individuals outside of the public
sphere. In short, Oakeshott's ideal type of a civil association is designed not
to impose a pattern of life or to direct public activities or to make people good

but to set procedural conditions that make it possible for the public to inter-act and associate while pursuing their private projects (*OHC*, 127–30; *OH*, 148–61).

Oakeshott clarifies the meaning of civil association, as well as the politics of *societas* and *universitas*, in discussing two types of rules that govern distinct types of associations. First, there are associations of practice (for example, people speaking a common language or members of a science association or sports league), in which general rules allow members to pursue particular or substantive goals. Invoking the same themes he used in discussing idioms or traditions in the middle period, Oakeshott explains that "it is a relationship in respect of a common recognition of considerations such as uses or rules intel-ligently subscribed to in self-chosen performances." Furthermore, Oakeshott explains that the laws of a civil association mimic the two most important associations of practice—a common language and morality. As each of these is a practice without engaging any extrinsic purposes, they are not concerned with performances in terms of their results (*OHC*, 112–13, 119–24).

Second, there are enterprise associations (for example, trade unions and business companies), in which members are united by the pursuit of pro-grammatic goals. Their rules are prudential instruments for realizing such substantive goals. "These rules are contingently related to the purpose con-cerned," states Oakeshott. "It means . . . that if any of them were considered in terms of their desirability, it would be judged by its propensity to promote or hinder the pursuit of this purpose." Political problems arise when the enterprise mode of association is adopted by the state, as it develops instru-mental, rather than civil, laws. Furthermore, a state by definition is a nonvol-untary, coercive institution: it cannot allow its citizens to obey laws according to their preferences. Henceforth, the enterprise state forces its citizens to pursue substantive aims. "To be a member is to have surrendered choice in these matters," summarizes Oakeshott (*OHC*, 114–17, 263–66, 316). All of this discussion about contending moralities and different associations moves Oakeshott's thought well away from a Burkean-type thesis centered on the conflict between traditions and rationalism.

AUTHORITY

Indeed, Oakeshott's ideal type of civil association and his preference for soci-etas clearly sends him in the direction of the liberal tradition that emphasizes establishing civil interaction among individuals pursing different ways of life. Nevertheless, he adds some nuances of his own that prevent him from plac-ing both feet squarely in this camp. One difference centers in Oakeshott's views on authority and the state, in which he clearly rejects the traditional liberal view, most notably expressed in the theory of John Locke, where individuals are understood to have rights prior to society, and the state is erected as an instrument to protect those rights.[10]

When Oakeshott describes the ideal type of civil association, he explains that the authority of law does not derive from utility, desirability, consent, or public compliance. These consequences, opinions, and actions may result from the authority of law, but they do not provide the grounds of obligation to obey, as they render the laws instrumental and subject to arbitrary policy decisions. "Nor can the authority of *respublica* [the public order of intelligible rules] lie in the identification of its prescriptions with a current 'social purpose,' with approved moral ideals, with a common good or general interest," states Oakeshott, for "civil association has no such common purpose and the attribution of authority does not postulate approval of the conditions it prescribes." Finally, Oakeshott avoids invoking as authoritative either a Lockean natural law or deontological rights doctrine that upholds a norm of justice or liberty outside or above the sovereign, as both ultimately undermine authority. A civil association, Oakeshott concludes, recognizes that authority resides in the rules themselves—"the recognition of rules as rules"—and nothing else (*OHC*, 148–61).

While debunking extrinsic sources of authority for the law, Oakeshott seeks to avoid the value neutrality of the legal positivists, who believe that although laws are products of the will, they are just if they follow the proper legal procedures established by the sovereign; hence they require the obligation of citizens. Oakeshott recognizes that the justice "inherent" in the civil association contributes to the authority of the law. "The *jus* of *lex* cannot be identified simply with its faithfulness to the formal character of the law," Oakeshott explains. "To deliberate the *jus* of *lex* is to invoke a particular kind of moral consideration": the character of both the civility and the procedure that the law is establishing. But, he acknowledges that even in the ideal type of civil association, many of the laws will be at best "imperfect reflections" of justice. How should the subject respond? In Oakeshott's words, "The answer is that authority is the only conceivable attribute it [the laws] could be indisputably acknowledged to have. In short, the only understanding of *respublica* capable of evoking the acceptance of *cives* without exception, and thus eligible to be recognized as the terms of civil association, is respublica understood in respect of its authority (*OHC*, 152–54; *OH*, 152–54).

In Oakeshott's account, citizens in a civil association may feel that a law does not meet the requirements of justice, yet they are obligated to obey it for no other reason than that the sovereign state is the ultimate authority for all the rules and practices in society. In short, there is a subtle acceptance in Oakeshott that the state in civil association creates the framework within which all political and civil activities are conducted: the institution that is the end and fulfillment of politics. And where the state and the authority of the law are treated respectfully as an end and not a means, the civil association will be strengthened. Just as an idiom provides a procedure anterior to the individual for the pursuit of private, substantive goals, a rule created by the state "does not initiate a performance: it exists in advance of the situation of the agents. . . . It prescribe[s] norms of conduct; that is, abstract considerations proper to be subscribed to in choosing performances but which cannot themselves be "obeyed or performed" (*OHC*, 126).

CONSERVATISM

So how conservative is Oakeshott's late work? Do laws as general rules of conduct and a morality of individualism fit into a conservative framework? Does Oakeshott continue to discover wisdom in Burke's thought? Did Oakeshott completely abandon the traditional conservative reliance on history for establishing standards of right and wrong, good and bad? Answers to these questions can help us begin to identify the political character of Oakeshott's thought.

Oakeshott addresses some of these questions himself in "On Being Conservative," the 1956 essay where he unambiguously reveals his new emphasis on law and individuality. Here Oakeshott asserts that the rule of law is consistent with the conservative disposition: preserving while reforming, maintaining political stability in the face of change. That said, Oakeshott goes on to explain that the rule of law and the prescriptive approach to reform now revolves around preserving a decidedly more liberal agenda: inducing political restraint among a public energized around variegated pursuits in society and protecting the distinct English heritage of individualism.

First, Oakeshott makes the case that a government that focuses on making and enforcing laws as general rules of conduct sets up a prescriptive approach to change that combines reform with restoration. Laws, no doubt, require improvement, Oakeshott affirms, but the better known and more predictable they become, the more efficacious they are in providing a framework for the pursuit of private aims. To be sure, emergency conditions develop that may require a radical departure, but a desire to be incremental rather than extreme is unquestionably appropriate when there is an ensemble of laws. Again, a law is the product of thought and decision—there is nothing invulnerable about them; they are amenable to renovation—but if our orientation toward them were not incremental, or if we were inclined to fight over them one time after another, they would no longer perform their duties. Finally, Oakeshott states that it is highly inappropriate to think about rearranging all of the laws at once whenever there is a new experience or an unexpected crisis (*RP*, 430–31).

Next, Oakeshott states that a government focused on developing and enforcing laws as general rules of conduct exemplifies an indifference to the specific beliefs and particularistic actions of the public. This detachment can be expected to cultivate a habit of political restraint among a public consistently energized and active in the pursuit of this or that cause, idea, or interest. "Indeed," Oakeshott states, "it might be said that we keep a government of this sort to do for us the skepticism we have neither the time nor the inclination to do for ourselves. It is like the cool touch of the mountain that one feels in the plain on the hottest day" (*RP*, 433–34).

Finally, Oakeshott argues that the rule of law as general rules of conduct defends a distinct English inheritance: a morality of individualism. Many of the English engage in a variety of activities, hold an innumerable amount of opinions, buy and sell all types of products, and pray to God or ignore him. In short, significant sections of the English are people who make choices, and the rule of law preserves this way of life. Oakeshott concludes that "whether to be conservative in respect of government would have the same relevance in the circumstances of an unadventurous, a slothful or a spiritless people, is a question we need not try to answer: we are concerned with ourselves as we are." Here, a morality of individualism is the "is" and the "ought" (*RP*, 424–25, 428–30, 435).

With the new emphasis on the rule of law and individualism, Oakeshott's evaluation of Burke changes as well. When Oakeshott's analysis of modern politics centers on the tension between self-generating traditions and rationalism, he consistently praises Burke's foresight in recognizing the modern political predicament. Burke, according to Oakeshott, objects to the imposition of comprehensive plans on society, discusses principles of politics within an idiom of skepticism, adapts an unspoken English inheritance of political restraint and restates "its principle in a manner appropriate to its times," puts forth the politics of the mean, and—along with Hegel—roots the rights and duties of individuals within historically derived practices (*PFPS*, 80–83).

Yet in Oakeshott's reformulated view of the main tension animating modern politics, Burke's prescience is not acknowledged. Indeed, Oakeshott states that in terms of understanding a conservative government that defends the inheritance of individualism, "there is more to be learned . . . from Montaigne, Pascal, Hobbes and Hume than Burke or Bentham" (*RP*, 435). And when, in his late work, Oakeshott compliments Burke's thinking, it is for

Burke's "less known views about the office of government." It also is for a more liberal Burke. Here, Oakeshott appreciates Burke for recognizing that government's primary task is the common need of providing restraints on individuals engaged in a great variety of activities, while holding many different moral and religious views. "What a government provides is rules of conduct for all to follow equally, and an independent judge or umpire with the authority to settle disputes between individuals." To Oakeshott, Burke's thought expresses a "version of the political theory of individualism" (*MPME*, 69–72).

SOCIETAS AND UNIVERSITAS

If that were the end of matter, we would be left with a very unsatisfactory assessment as to whether Oakeshott can be identified as a conservative. The prevailing questions would be, is late or postmodern conservatism the protection of a liberal tradition that defends the rights of individuals and groups to pursue this or that interest, aim, or way of life? Does Oakeshott put forth a "conservative individualism" that differs substantially from other liberal ideas of free human conduct? To address these issues, we would be rightfully turning our attention to the question of whether the categories of liberalism and conservatism obscure more than they clarify.

But that is not the end of the matter, because as much as Oakeshott admires the politics of societas, and as much as he believes civil association represents the rule of law, he also argues that the politics of universitas cannot be written out of history; it is here to stay for—at the very least—a very, very long time. Just as Leo Strauss points out that Plato's just city in the *Republic* denies human nature, Oakeshott himself recognizes that his articulation of civil association denies history.[11] The ideal character of civil association, he states, is "not an association of ascertainable persons identifiable in terms of a place and time." It is "abstracted from the contingencies and ambiguities of actual goings-on in the world" (*OHC*, 108–9).

To wit, the underlying context of modern European political thought and practice is defined by two contending ideas and assumptions that have fostered an ambiguous and ambivalent political tradition, creating confusion and conflict over the meaning of democracy, law, freedom, and the common language of politics. "The recognition of these destinations [of societas and universitas] has never been so exact as to avoid all confusion, and there have been strayed travelers on each of these paths expecting to arrive where it does not lead" (*OHC*, 318). Consistent with his long-standing position that philosophical thinking and theorizing operate on a different plane from that of political practice, Oakeshott does not urge the political theorist to attempt a fruitless task, such as the formation of a political outlook that will clarify and distinguish the equivocal character of Western political thinking and practice. The most that a theorist can do, states Oakeshott, is to present these concepts as a vehicle for understanding the complex character of the modern European state, to provide historical evidence to buttress the view that this is an effective apparatus for appraising such states, "not to put upon them [the concepts] more weight than they can support, and to leave it at that" (323).

This is not Oakeshott's final say on *societas* and *universitas*, however. Oakeshott explains that when left alone, the two contending moral and political outlooks are incomplete. Indeed, the different type of human dispositions that provide the context for these entrenched moralities are "not friends, but nor are they exactly foes; . . . their relationship is that of 'sweet enemies'" (*OHC*, 326). Oakeshott is very careful here to avoid making a statement about the intrinsic character of politics, development, human nature, and history. He does not suggest, for example, like Plato in book 8 of the *Republic*, that the leading outlook of a regime ceases to be effective if it becomes the regime's sole guide. To Plato, oligarchic attachment to wealth produces citizens with a set of vices that hastens the slide to democracy, while democratic love for freedom and equality encourages character traits that open the door to tyranny. Nor does Oakeshott posit a Hegelian dialectic and claim that the modern European state is pulling together, harmonizing, and making whole a consciousness divided between its aspirations and actuality, setting the stage for a freer and more coherent way of life. Oakeshott also does not evoke a Nietzschean-type argument that both outlooks are endemic to human nature and that if one or the two were removed, it would only be a matter of time before it or they reappeared. And finally, Oakeshott does not present a Burkean-type argument where history is purported to mold an unchangeable constancy that prevents isolated problems from festering and inducing decay, because "the species is wise, and when time is given to it, as a species, it almost always acts right."[12]

But Oakeshott does state that each outlook reflects entrenched assumptions rooted in contingent responses to a distinct European historical situation that goes back to the late medieval era. He also intimates that there is a pendulum effect in modern politics, because the weakness of each view tends to create a movement back to the other. As he puts it in a posthumously published essay (believed to have been written in 1952), where he begins to articulate his new position that competing moral outlooks on the purpose of government provide the animating tension in modern European politics,

"Each, in the abstract, may have the virtue of simplicity; but neither, as we know them, is capable of being by itself a concrete style of political activity" (*PFPS*, 120).[13] For example, the politics of societas centers on establishing formal rules and protecting practices to ensure civil peace and free human conduct, yet this outlook contributes to periodic political problems, as it often responds too slowly to changing circumstances and emergencies. Here the politics of universitas provides a needed corrective, as it tends to bring enthusiasm and energy to government (*OHC*, 146). "And although," states Oakeshott, "even in these circumstances, the rule of law may (as Hobbes thought) be formally rescued by invoking such legal doctrines as that of 'eminent domain' of a government to be exercised *ex justa causa*, this is only another way of saying that necessity knows no law" (*OH*, 178). European history, as it turns out, is a source of the good after all, and Oakeshott's break from Burke on this issue is not so severe.

To be sure, Oakeshott continues to reject Burke's position that the good is intrinsic to the long-standing practices, institutions, and laws emanating from the nation. But he is claiming that an underlying social order animates the European political tradition—dating back well over six hundred years—creating a positive stalemate and a salutary political outcome. Oakeshott, unlike Burke, recognizes the contingent roots of a European history not bound by social laws or a teleological process. But Oakeshott also theorizes about those contingencies and identifies a relatively stable relationship between two modes of association and notes that—all in all—they have served modern Europe well. Our goal is to discover some way of being comfortable in the ambiguity that we have acquired and cannot now wish away. Oakeshott advises that as the character of our politics is "unavoidably complex—we must learn to exploit its virtues. And there can be no doubt that its virtues may be most fully enjoyed and its vices most certainly avoided while we hold back the extremes of which it is capable and explore the central area that lies between" (*PFPS*, 121). In sum, Burke recognizes that the grand design of English history promotes balance and equilibrium, while Oakeshott "elicits a coherence" on modern European history with the analogues of societas and universitas and also identifies balance and equilibrium (*RP*, 182).

Oakeshott submits that the twentieth century was dominated by the politics of universitas. He refutes the view—prevalent during much of the twentieth century—that there is an inevitable march toward a political association exclusively centered on universitas, and he looks forward to the politics of societas regaining ground in the future. No doubt thinking of himself, he states that this period of ascendance of the politics of universitas provides an opportunity for those concerned with the decline of societas to clarify their thinking on this subject. And Oakeshott states that one of the weaknesses of the politics of civil association is defining the standards for evaluating whether laws are contributing to such an association, a lacuna in political theory that Oakeshott says he is attempting to overcome (*OH*, 159–61; *OHC*, 161, 320–23).

Still, Oakeshott never establishes a clear line of demarcation on the proper relation between the modes of association of societas and universitas within the modern European state. To be sure, the Soviet politics of universitas in twentieth-century Russia indicate that there is a propensity for the modern European state to limit the practices of civil association. But it is also unlikely, according to Oakeshott, that a modern European state will be able to extinguish these enduring practices (*OHC*, 247, 313). "We should expect the manner of governing in modern Europe to range between these two extremes, settling upon one or other of them only when and where one of these dispositions got the better of the other," summarizes Oakeshott (*PFPS*, 43).

Oakeshott also does not clarify the proper relation between each mode of association, because he does not believe this knowledge could make a significant political difference. History, not politics or philosophy, is the principal source of modern Europe's most important institutions and values, according to Oakeshott. Politics is "the activity of attending to the general arrangements of a set of people whom chance or choice have brought together." Politics does not consist in founders or movements "making arrangements," because no individuals or groups can transcend the practices, or traditions, that condition all performances (*RP*, 44). A philosophy or an idea can only contribute to a society becoming "more conscious and critical of itself. . . . If a society is to be saved from a corrupt consciousness it will be saved . . . by knowing itself and having its values recreated" (*RPML*, 95). Oakeshott leaves us with the teaching that the past, present, and (probable) future of European morality and politics is not *the* good, but that this preexisting social and political order contains quite a bit of good and is certainly not bad. Ultimately, Oakeshott's conservatism centers on the realization that in modern Europe, history or the "is" approximates the "ought," and this "is" and "ought" are well worth understanding and preserving.

STRAUSS AND OAKESHOTT

Situating Oakeshott's thinking in relation to that of Leo Strauss clarifies the distinct character of Oakeshott's conservatism and helps illuminate why some commentators associate Strauss with a more proactive neoconservatism and

Oakeshott with a more traditional conservatism.[14] To be sure, Oakeshott and Strauss have many points of agreement. Oakeshott and Strauss both insisted on the separation of philosophy and politics; both helped introduce a new round of German philosophical thought into the more circumscribed Anglo-American philosophical environment; both challenged prevailing post–World War II political conventions in their respective countries, which each associated with the Left; both sustained polemical attacks from standard-bearers in the academy; both placed the history of political thought at the forefront of their concerns; and both recognized the seminal role of Hobbes in shaping modern political philosophy.

Where Strauss and Oakeshott differ at the most fundamental level is in their assessments of modernity. Oakeshott maintains that modernity is animated by a bifurcated political tradition, societas and universitas, producing a salutary stalemate between the mode of association that promotes human agency and the mode of association that promotes common enterprise. In contrast, Strauss argues that modernity tends to progressively deteriorate. In his account of Machiavelli, and then Hobbes and later thinkers, Strauss explains that modern thought goes through three waves or stages, eventually producing a radical historicism—the position that all modes of thought are local, contingent, and temporary—that kills reason and creates the preconditions for periodic political crises. All of this is a product of the core of the modern project: to have political philosophy rule practice and actualize the idea of freedom.[15]

This mission of the moderns broke with the twofold task of classical political philosophy, which in Strauss's observation was best expressed by Plato: protecting philosophical reason, while also contributing to the separate task of political reform. This twofold task leads to distinct orientations toward politics. On one plane, philosophers contribute to an environment that allows them to contemplate the meaning and best forms of human existence. While the philosopher is a member of the city, standing on the shoulders of its culture and using its opportunities for leisure, he is also driven by eros, the longing for a complete and self-defined existence, and he knows that the local laws, prejudices, and gods are far from the truth that he pursues. Here it is difficult to pin down a coherent and substantive political outlook in the ancients. In effect, the philosopher is parasitic, taking advantage of civil security to pursue his own ends even though he recognizes that such civil structures are not the highest ends. "The selfish or class interests of the philosophers consist in being left alone, in being allowed to live the life of the blessed on earth by devoting themselves to investigation of the most important subjects."[16]

On another plane, however, the ancients, in Strauss's view, recognize that since philosophy is dependent on the regime and since the philosophers themselves tend to love their own political society—especially if that society leaves room for philosophy—they cannot ignore politics, making "it necessary for the philosopher to descend again into the cave, i.e., to take care of the affairs of the city, whether in a direct or more remote manner." Here, the philosopher must "qualify" or "dilute" the quest for wisdom so as to help frame the mores, laws, and structures that will promote political stability, or better, political prosperity, addressing the city's need for standards of excellence and justice, as well as the public's desire for security. From this perspective, the classics posit a positive political outlook for philosophers around a consistent political framework. "To summarize, . . . the practically best regime is the rule, under law, of gentlemen, or the mixed regime" that pursues a variety of ends.[17]

The stimulus to the change in modern political philosophy, in Strauss's account, was frustration with premodern philosophy's limited political ambitions and willingness to abdicate political responsibilities to religious authorities. Rather than preserving the autonomy of philosophy from society, Strauss charges that Machiavelli redirects philosophy to conquer *fortuna*, or chance, to proceed from the starting point of how people live and to become actualized in society. Machiavelli makes the "decisive turn toward the notion of philosophy according to which its purpose is to relieve man's estate or to increase man's power. . . . The cave becomes the substance."[18]

Strauss's position that modern political philosophy's focus on actualization leads to subsequent problems has important continuities and differences with Oakeshott's position in his middle period of work. Here Oakeshott identifies Machiavelli, Bacon, and others as generators of a "modern rationalism" that sought certainty and actualization through the adoption of techniques that would control this or that practice and society as a whole. And like Strauss, Oakeshott explains that the rationalists would become increasingly frustrated by their inability to master these practices and society. Unlike Strauss, however, Oakeshott also identifies an alternative current in modern thought—most notably expressed by Hegel and Burke—that countered this rationalism and respected the historically derived idioms and traditions that provided liberty and order (*RP*, 19–21, 30–31; *PFPS*, 80–83).

In his account of modern thought, Strauss argues that Burke, Hegel, and other historicists intensify, rather than check, the modern predicament, because they themselves are as concerned with the actualization of wisdom as those they criticize. All of these historicists are responding to the Enlightenment philosophy of Hobbes, Locke, and others, who use reason to remold the political and moral world with a new "ought," or conception of natural right, centered on self-interest. In Strauss's account, Burke helps engender the "Historical School," which insisted that continuing the traditional order preserved wisdom, and Rousseau identifies the weaknesses of the Enlightenment with a view to reformulating it and thus *better* realizing its primary aims.

Despite their different political vantage points, both recognize that the Enlightenment's attempt to bring a universal, albeit narrow, conception of the good into different societies was failing because this universal does not respect temporality, locality, and individuality. But, Strauss contends, Rousseau's and Burke's responses to the Enlightenment further diminished the character of reason. Their mutual assertion that humanity is the product of history and their respective attempts to reconstitute a more robust political association—whether expressed by Rousseau's formal ethics of the general will or Burke's unfolding of history—raise a political or historical process over any substantive political ends. Rousseau and Burke identify the possible coincidence of the rational and the real, an outlook that would reach its apex in the thought of Hegel and Marx, both of whom proclaimed that the historical process was working itself out to produce a rational end state.[19]

All of this sets the stage, in Strauss's view, for Nietzsche's, Heidegger's, and Schmitt's comprehensive attacks on reason. Having learned from the century of historicism that followed Rousseau, these thinkers recognize that temporality and locality do not establish genuine freedom, an "ought," or progress. They turn on philosophy itself and embrace radical historicism: the charge that society and history create thought and not vice versa. Neither philosophy nor society is rational, nor does an "ought" characterize human associations. Instead, these thinkers turn to a vague but decidedly nonmoral focus and "action"—will as power for Nietzsche, Dasein for Heidegger, the political for Schmitt.[20]

Strauss insists, however, that the decline of reason in the West does not necessarily lead to political crises. Here the second leg of the classics' political philosophy, the legal and moral framework through which the statesman operates, is decisive in creating propitious conditions for stemming political decline. As Locke and Montesquieu, in Strauss's account, adapt conceptions of statesmanship from the ancients (and Machiavelli) and embed them in their respective modernist theories, they provide resources for political activities that augment modern liberalism's impersonal rule of law and institutions to fight off political deterioration. Equally important, the legal and moral frameworks of external enemies influence whether the philosophical crisis will lead to political crises. As different regimes are organized around sets of constitutionally irreducible organizing principles, "the regimes, themselves . . . force us to wonder which of the given conflicting regimes is better."

Religion, which remains a source of moral vibrancy and dissent in America, also limits political crises.

Finally, Strauss's references to America indicate a view that as the American founding reflects the first wave of modern thinking and is associated at least in part with texts—most notably, the Declaration of Independence, the Constitution, and the Federalist Papers—establishing inviolable principles and a designed constitution, the American political order has more powerful resources to withstand modernity's decline than other modern regimes.[21]

Where Strauss most clearly differs from Oakeshott in his political prescriptions for preventing the deterioration of modernity is in his understanding of the statesman. In *Natural Right and History* and in his commentaries on Plato and Xenophon, Strauss identifies the statesman as the ancients' highest form of nonphilosophical life. The statesman, for instance, respects the laws and mores that bind individuals in the political society; otherwise, a regime would be based exclusively on conflict and coercion. But the statesman also recognizes that even the best laws and political outlooks derive from past experiences and are not sufficient for addressing new challenges. The statesman also understands that relations among different regimes are based almost exclusively on power. Both of these factors require the statesman to recognize that creative political actions must periodically substitute for the rule of law and prevailing mores in crisis management and foreign policy, while maintaining a general commitment to the rules and principles of the political community. Accordingly, in February 1941—ten months before the United States enters World War II, and before his own thought has fully matured—Strauss points to the politics of Winston Churchill, and not the defense of a politically heterogeneous "Western tradition," as the alternative political pole to the dominant Nazi regime.[22]

In contrast, Oakeshott believes that only limited change can be induced through direct political means. Like Burke, he argues that history creates a set of arrangements superior to any that could have been founded. Such dramatic events, in Oakeshott's view—whether discussing the American, French, or Russian Revolutions, the enfranchisement of women, or the Magna Carta—are nothing but the realization of intimations already existent in society. This is why, in Oakeshott's account, the most capable leaders—the artist, poet, and philosopher—should eschew politics and remain true to their genius, thus creating conditions whereby they may contribute to the public good. "Societies," in short, "are led from behind, and for those capable of leadership to give themselves up to political activity is to break away from their genius," which is to contribute a little to a society's understanding of itself (*RP*, 52–53; *RPML*, 96).

And to be sure, Strauss himself primarily "led from behind," as he never offered specific remedies for either American politics or the corruption of modernity more generally. His writings primarily occupy the plane of high thought, preferring to elaborate on why ancient political philosophy is able to defend itself against the historicist critique of reason, to contemplate the tension between reason and revelation, and to identify how Machiavelli, Hobbes, and Spinoza establish the presuppositions of a modern political philosophy that relentlessly spirals downward into an attack on reason itself. That said, Strauss did step "out front" in pouring an enormous amount of energy to founding a school of thought that would eventually influence both the American academy and politics. This school would unfold around the twofold task of political philosophy that Strauss attributed to the ancients. Part of Strauss's school is contemplative and devoted to studying the history of political philosophy, and part of it is devoted to examining and defending the foundations of the American regime.[23]

STRAUSS'S AND OAKESHOTT'S BURKE

Strauss's differences with Oakeshott are crystallized by Strauss's assessment of the strengths and weaknesses of Burke. Strauss hails Burke as the individual who most vociferously denounced the destructive features of modern political philosophy. The English parliamentarian, while a proponent for a commercial economy along the lines envisioned by the Scottish Enlightenment thinkers, rejected the Enlightenment's singular focus on freedom, an instrumental view of reason, and the destruction of the traditional practices that induced moral restraint. Most important, Burke identified how philosophy actualized into practice produced political and moral evil. He opposes the "intrusion of the spirit of speculation or of theory into the field of politics." Burke vehemently rejects the proselytism of the new philosophy.[24]

Here Burke faced two choices, continues Strauss. One option was to wall off the dangerous tendency of political philosophers to remold society in the image of philosophy, while continuing to uphold political philosophy properly understood. A second option was to raise suspicion of political philosophy itself—both as a quest for wisdom and as a contributor to the legislator's art. According to Strauss, Burke chose the second route. Failing to distinguish good from bad philosophy, he conflated the calamity of the French Revolution with political philosophy and did not recognize the dignity of the political: "Burke is not content with defending practical wisdom against the encroachments of theoretical science. He parts company with the Aristotelian tradition by disparaging theory. He uses 'metaphysics' and 'metaphysician' frequently in a derogatory sense. . . . He rejects the view that constitutions can be 'made' in favor of the view that they must 'grow': he therefore rejects in particular the view that the best social order can be or ought to be the work of an individual, of a wise 'legislator' or founder."[25]

Strauss explains that, for Burke, if people would let go of their fascination with abstractions and look instead to the accumulated wisdom of their traditions, the modern goal of establishing safe and realistic standards of right and wrong would be secured. A turn to history is the cure for the malady of philosophy. Strauss charges that Burke adheres to a modern reference point, actualization in society, in distinguishing between real and sham wisdom. Burke's "intransigent opposition to the French Revolution must not blind us to the fact that, in opposing the French Revolution, he has recourse to the same fundamental principle which is at the bottom of the revolutionary theorems and which is alien to all earlier thought." This turn to history shifts the standard for evaluating political societies away from conceptions of high and low, better and worse. "It is only a short step from this thought of Burke to the suppression of the distinction between good and bad by the distinction between the progressive and retrograde, or what is and what is not in harmony with the historical process." Burke unwittingly paves the road to the Historical School and its nihilist offspring.[26]

It is likely that Oakeshott would not disagree with Strauss's assessment that Burke was a trenchant critic of modern rationalism, while neglecting philosophy himself. As to Strauss's challenge that Burke eschewed the role of founders and turned to history as the source of the good, it is likely that Oakeshott would state that Burke is guilty as charged, although not necessarily wrong. After all, Oakeshott himself holds similar positions on these questions. Modern European history, in Oakeshott's account, is largely a source of the political good, and this underlying political and social order establishes a set of arrangements superior in force to any that could be rearranged by founding-type individuals.

NOTES

1. Kenneth B. McIntyre, *The Limits of Political Theory: Oakeshott's Philosophy of Civil Association* (Exeter: Imprint Academic, 2004), 1–2.

2. Edmund Burke, *Reflections on the Revolution in France*, ed. Conor Cruise O'Brien (Harmondsworth: Penguin, 1968), 89–91, 100–110, 122–25, 148–53, 170–73, 181–86, 193–204.

3. Oakeshott's early work centers on philosophy itself, and there are few extended discussions on politics or political philosophy.

4. Edmund Burke, "An Appeal from the New to the Old Whigs," in *Further Reflections on the French Revolution*, ed. Don Ritchie (Indianapolis: Hackett, 1992), 141.

5. Burke, *Reflections*, 193.

6. Ibid., 105–6.

7. Ibid., 152.

8. Ibid., 121.

9. Indeed, Oakeshott refuses to develop a doctrine of defense for this "morality of habits" out of fear that he will contribute to the self-reflective outlooks uprooting it. See *RP*, 21–22

10. John Locke, *Second Treatise of Government*, ed. C. B. Macpherson (Indianapolis: Hackett, 1980), chap. 9, pp. 65–68. See also T. H. Green, "Liberal Legislation and the Freedom of Contract," in *Lectures on the Principles of Political Obligation and Other Writings*, ed. Paul Harris and John Morrow (Cambridge: Cambridge University Press, 1986), 194–212.

11. Leo Strauss, *The City and Man* (Chicago: University of Chicago Press, 1964), 11, 115, 127.

12. *The Republic of Plato*, trans. Allan Bloom (New York: Basic, 1968), secs. 547c–569d: 225–49; G. W. F. Hegel, *Science of Logic*, trans. A. V. Miller (London: Allen and Unwin, 1969), 106–8; Friedrich Nietzsche, *On the Genealogy of Morals*, trans. Walter Kaufmann (New York: Vintage, 1966), first essay, sec. 13, 44–46; Edmund Burke, "Representation of the Commons in Parliament," in *Edmund Burke: Selected Writings and Speeches*, ed. Peter Stanlis (Garden City, N.Y.: Anchor Books, 1986), 331.

13. See Timothy Fuller's discussion (*PFPS*, xii–xv) on how this essay captures the themes of Oakeshott's middle-period essays and late writings.

14. Alan Wolfe, "The Revolution That Never Was," *New Republic*, June 7, 1999, 34–42.

15. Leo Strauss, *What Is Political Philosophy?* (Chicago: University of Chicago Press, 1959), 47–48; Strauss, *City and Man*, 11.

16. Leo Strauss, *Natural Right and History* (Chicago: University of Chicago Press, 1953), 143; Strauss, *On Tyranny* (Chicago: University of Chicago Press, 1963), 84.

17. Strauss, *Natural Right and History*, 142–43, 152–63; Strauss, *City and Man*, 28–30.

18. Strauss, *What Is Political Philosophy?*, 45; Strauss, *Thoughts on Machiavelli* (Chicago: University of Chicago Press, 1984), 285.

19. Strauss, *Natural Right and History*, 272–77, 303–4, 316–19; Strauss, *What Is Political Philosophy?*, 50–54; Strauss, *An Introduction to Political Philosophy* (Detroit: Wayne State University Press, 1989), 89–94.

20. Strauss, *Natural Right and History*, 17–19, 26–28, 320–23; Strauss, *What Is Political Philosophy?*, 54–55; Strauss, *Spinoza's Critique of Religion* (New York: Schocken Books, 1965), 349–51; Strauss, *Introduction to Political Philosophy*, 94–98.

21. Strauss, *Natural Right and History*, 4, 164, 233; Strauss, *What Is Political Philosophy?*, 34; Strauss, *Liberalism Ancient and Modern* (Chicago: University of Chicago Press, 1968), 264–66; Strauss, *Introduction to Political Philosophy*, 98.

22. Strauss, *Natural Right and History*, 157–64; Strauss, *The Argument and the Action of Plato's Laws* (Chicago: University of Chicago Press, 1971), 86–87; Strauss, *City and Man*, 28; Strauss, *Thoughts on Machiavelli*, 5, 255–59, 264–65; Strauss, *On Tyranny*, 68–75, Strauss, "German Nihilism," *Interpretation*, trans. David Janssens and Daniel Tanguay, 26, no. 3 (1999): 363, 367. On Strauss's views on the proper relationship between the philosopher and the statesman, see Susan Shell, "To Spare the Vanquished and Crush the Arrogant," in *Cambridge Companion to Leo Strauss*, ed. Steven Smith (Cambridge: Cambridge University Press, 2009), 171–92.

23. On the relationship between Strauss and his school, see Robert Devigne, "Strauss and 'Straussianism': From the Ancient to the Moderns?" *Political Studies* (October 2009): 592–616; Heinrich Meier, "Why Leo Strauss? Four Answers and One Consideration Concerning the Uses and Disadvantages of the School for the Philosophic Life," in *Modernity and What Has Been Lost*, ed. Pawel Armada and Arkadiusz Gornisiewicz (South Bend, Ind.: St. Augustine Press, 2010), 19–32. For a survey by a self-described Straussian on the American civic philosophy established by Strauss's school and the debate within it, see Thomas Pangle, *Leo Strauss* (Baltimore: Johns Hopkins University Press, 2006), 104–23.

24. Strauss, *Natural Right and History*, 300–303.

25. Ibid., 311, 313.

26. Ibid., 316, 318

14

OAKESHOTT ON CIVIL ASSOCIATION

Noël O'Sullivan

The distinctive achievement of Western political thought since the seventeenth century is the ideal of the limited state. Despite extensive theorizing about this ideal, however, there has always been profound disagreement about its precise nature and implications. The full extent of this disagreement has been especially evident during the decades since World War II, in the course of which sustained efforts have been made by a variety of thinkers to construct a coherent alternative to totalitarianism. In Friedrich Hayek's view, for example, the limited state is principally characterized by a free market economy that facilitates human progress. For Karl Popper it is characterized by commitment to creating an open society that rejects absolute truth and asserts the conditionality of all knowledge. In the early writings of John Rawls, the limited state is characterized by commitment to rational principles of distributive justice. For Robert Nozick it means the minimal state. For Ernest Gellner it is the political structure appropriate to what he termed "modular man." For Jürgen Habermas, echoing Rousseau, it refers to a political order based on rational will formation. For Václav Havel what characterizes the limited state is the promotion of spiritual integration instead of the spiritual fragmentation associated with totalitarian regimes. Still other interpretations of the ideal of the limited state are found among theorists of globalization and the European Union.[1]

In light of this disagreement, Michael Oakeshott's interpretation of the limited state as civil association is of special interest, seeking as it does to give a degree of conceptual coherence to the ideal that is otherwise lacking. The principal obstacle to achieving this coherence, Oakeshott believes, is a deep division of opinion among modern political theorists about the nature of political science. To understand Oakeshott's identification of the limited state with civil association, it is therefore necessary to begin by considering his understanding of political science.

POLITICAL SCIENCE AND THE THEORY OF CIVIL ASSOCIATION

The core of Oakeshott's conception of civil association is his characterization of it as the only appropriate *moral* response to the problem of reconciling authority with freedom in a modern Western political order. Accordingly, civil association can be adequately theorized only by a political science capable of acknowledging and analyzing its moral presuppositions. Ever since the seventeenth century, however, many Western thinkers have aspired to transform the study of society into a science by applying the methods of the natural sciences to the study of human beings. For Oakeshott this project has been disastrous because it impoverishes the study of civil association by reducing political science to the study of facts, thereby rendering it impossible to theorize the moral dimension of the civil order.

This criticism was developed by Oakeshott at a relatively early stage when, shortly after graduating at Cambridge, he wrote a deeply disillusioned indictment of the teaching of politics, which provided the foundation for his subsequent philosophical work. What he had expected at Cambridge, Oakeshott wrote, was to study the part played by politics in the human condition, whereas what he had encountered was a narrowly institutional approach in which the political philosophers who might have given him the assistance he sought were not studied in any depth. Explaining precisely why the Cambridge syllabus was so impoverished, Oakeshott observed, "Where the Cambridge syllabus fails is in its attempt to make political science into a natural science which gives its definitions in terms of fact and not of meanings" (*WIH*, 57). Confining attention to the study of fact, he wrote, is unsatisfactory because it "leads simply to other facts, which may equally well be made the objects of further analysis. Indeed, by analysing a single fact into a number of separate elements, we are in general only multiplying our problems" (56–57). When political science is conceived in this way, Oakeshott caustically observed, the emphasis on facts means that the study of institutions is prone "to fly off into an irrelevant treatment of the habits of animals, of the marriage ceremonies of the inhabitants of Morocco or the islands of Fiji (subjects in which our 'sociologists' seem more deeply versed than in the institutions and thoughts of Englishmen to-day)" (59).

Turning from the critical to the constructive side of Oakeshott's rejection of the Cambridge syllabus, what must now be considered is his view of what a sound political science syllabus involves. Those responsible for the Cambridge syllabus, he wrote, had failed to realize that "if the term Political Science is to have any valid meaning at all, it must refer to a *moral* and not a natural science, that is, our subject is more properly named Political Philosophy than anything else" (*WIH*, 56). Neglect of political philosophy meant that when the Cambridge syllabus did happen to "spare a moment to treat of the State," it defined it "in terms of anthropology, psychology, or the anatomy of the body-politic," whereas "political science, properly so-called, must treat it from the view point of meaning and value" (59). Put slightly differently, the Cambridge syllabus could only ever explain politics at large, and the state in particular, in terms of a single language of power. It was quite unable, that is, to provide the ethical language required to explain such concepts as authority, law, and political obligation, which cannot be reduced to a language of power.

For Oakeshott, then, civil association can be properly theorized only within a conception of political science based on a philosophical standpoint that replaces the study of fact by "an analysis of meaning or explanation" (*WIH*, 56–57)—a standpoint, that is, which "seeks to discover the logical necessity for, and logical coherence of . . . a conception [such] as . . . the State" (57). Among those who had pioneered the study of civil society from the kind of philosophical standpoint of which he approved, Oakeshott credited the British idealist school of philosophy with providing "the only theory which has paid thoroughgoing attention to all the problems which must be considered by a theory of the State" (*CPJ*, 143). He noted approvingly, for example, that Green had indicated on the title page of his *Lectures on Political Obligation* that his book was about the logical grounds of political obligation, thereby clearly distinguishing his search for a philosophical understanding of the state from a more or less confused quest for origins and causes (*WIH*, 58). In particular, when Green wrote, "Will, not force, is the basis of the state," he had recognized that an ethical vocabulary, rather than a purely factual vocabulary of power, is required to analyze politics.[2]

For a similar reason, Oakeshott wrote approvingly of the ethical standpoint adopted by Bernard Bosanquet in *The Philosophical Theory of the State*, refusing to follow critics such as L. T. Hobhouse in dismissing that work as an unfortunate piece of Hegelian state worship (*CPJ*, 143).[3] Like Green, then, Bosanquet had recognized the need to avoid the Cambridge School's reduction of political science to the study of facts, since both realized that this would make it impossible to avoid presenting civil association as ultimately nothing more than a more or less benign system of power. Oakeshott also commended the idealist theory of the self, praising Bosanquet in particular for his distinguishing the self from the "so-called 'individualistic' theories'"—liberal theories, that is, that conceive of individual identity as existing apart from the relationships that constitute it (144).

Despite his early approval for British idealist philosophers, however, Oakeshott eventually disagreed with their theory of civil association in several crucial respects. In the first instance, he rejected their tendency to regard the state as more real than the individual. In addition, he rejected their tendency to emphasize the moral side of civil association to such an extent that they tended to ignore the inescapable nature of power. More precise, they ran the risk of submerging state sovereignty in a general will, in which power was concealed from sight. Finally, he considered that the idealist school tended to favor a substantive conception of the common good as the end of the state, whereas his own noninstrumental interpretation of civil association denied that it can have a purpose of any kind.

Although Oakeshott expressed qualified sympathy for the political philosophy of British idealism, this did not prevent him from becoming so disillusioned with the condition of modern political science as generally practiced at the time of World War II that he dismissed it as an almost entire disaster. Lamenting the general failure of European political thinkers to develop a philosophical account of "the meaning and possibility of a philosophy of law and civil society," he summarized the state of inquiry in this subject as "characterised by confusion and ambiguity" (*CPJ*, 154). It is against this background of almost complete disillusion with European political science near the middle of the twentieth century, then, that Oakeshott set out to clarify the structure of civil association during the remainder of his philosophical career. Beginning with two essays on "The Concept of a Philosophical Jurisprudence," he gradually developed a philosophical analysis of civil association of unprecedented rigor, which culminated in his magnum opus, *On Human Conduct*, and in the essay on the rule of law in the last book published during his lifetime, *On History and Other Essays* (1983). It is his mature view of this structure presented in the last two works in particular that must now be considered.

THE CONCEPT OF THE PUBLIC CONCERN (*respublica*)

For Oakeshott the principal problem of European political thought since Hobbes has not merely been the technical one of securing order as effectively as possible in the newly emergent nation states of the European world. It has been, rather, the normative one of how to constitute a state in conditions of cultural and social diversity without imposing coercive restraints on individual freedom. If a state is to be more than an organization possessing a monopoly of the means of coercion, the only possible solution to this problem, Oakeshott maintains, is for it to be based on a mutually shared sense of participation in a public order on the part of both governors and governed. But what, it must immediately be asked, is required for this shared sense of a public order to exist?

Oakeshott rejects the view that an answer can be given simply by referring to specific "persons, places, or occasions" as was the case, for example,
in ancient Greek political thought, where the concept of the public was tied
to the agora (*OHC*, 165). Instead, he identifies what is public in the political
sense with "a focus of attention and a subject of discourse" (165). What is
public refers, more precisely, to the "public concern" of *cives* (citizens), for
which Oakeshott adopts the Roman term *respublica*. Putting the same thing
slightly differently, a respublica exists only when a state is "constituted in
such a way that it can be considered as belonging to the governed, and not an
alien power" (*VMES*, 104).[4]

Without the existence of a public concern or respublica, then, a state lacks
a moral basis and is consequently indistinguishable from power or domination. It can accordingly be dismissed, as it was in the ancient world by the
Greek Sophist Thrasymachus, as embodying the interest of the stronger, or it
can be described, as it has been by modern Marxists, as merely a committee
of the bourgeois capitalist class. Exactly how the respublica necessary to rebut
these charges is to be structured, however, has been a matter for intense disagreement among modern political thinkers. At one stage of his intellectual
development, Oakeshott attributed this disagreement to a tension between
individualist and collectivist ways of thought in modern politics.[5] At another,
he attributed it instead to a tension between rationalist and pragmatic politics.[6] At yet another stage he theorized it in terms of a tension between the
"politics of faith" and the "politics of skepticism." In his mature presentation
of the tension in *On Human Conduct* (1975), however, he finally identified it as
lying between an essentially formal, nonpurposive concept of the respublica
embodied in civil association, on the one hand, and what he described as an
enterprise conception, on the other, which seeks to create a public concern by
imposing a substantive vision of the social good on all members of society. It
is this final statement of Oakeshott's position that is the main focus of attention here. Before considering the civil form of respublica, it is illuminating to
begin by considering Oakeshott's analysis of the enterprise version, according to which what is public is identified with a shared purpose in which all
citizens are compelled to participate.

RESPUBLICA AS ENTERPRISE ASSOCIATION

Many different shared purposes have been proposed as the basis of the modern state, beginning with the religious one favored, for example, by Calvin,
who wished to impose on Geneva the goal of promoting the faith and virtue

required for salvation. An alternative version of the enterprise state was the project outlined by Sir Francis Bacon in *The New Atlantis*, in which Bacon advocated the exploitation of nature by scientific means to create general prosperity. Although Bacon's vision had a religious foundation, secular versions of it have increasingly dominated subsequent Western history, allied more recently to, for example, the enterprise of implementing distributive justice portrayed by John Rawls in *A Theory of Justice*.[7]

In addition to enterprises for uniting modern societies of the kind just mentioned, there have been overtly totalitarian ones such as communism and Nazism. Oakeshott's response to these is of particular interest, since he rejects as wholly mistaken the conventional left/right spectrum classification, which takes at face value the claim by these ideologies that they are completely opposed to each other. For him the distinction between left and right is superficial because it ignores the fact that the seemingly opposed poles of the spectrum share an enterprise conception of respublica that makes it impossible to reconcile either of them with individual freedom (*LHPT*, 26).

But why, it must be asked, does Oakeshott maintain that freedom is always incompatible with an enterprise conception of the state: surely freedom is possible provided that the enterprise is a worthwhile one like social justice? In reply Oakeshott gives several reasons for rejecting the enterprise conception of respublica as incompatible with a free society. The most fundamental is that enterprise association lacks the moral basis of a free society, which is recognition of others as ends in themselves. As Oakeshott puts it, subjects in an enterprise state are reduced to the status of objects, because they are understood by the enterprise state as merely "the property of the association, an item of its capital resources," to be disposed of in whatever way the state believes best serves its purpose (*OHC*, 317). This remains true even if the enterprise state enjoys extensive popular support for such goals as economic growth or distributive justice, since the subjects who support them remain objects in the eyes of the state.

The implication is that those who reject the purpose pursued by the enterprise state are placed, in principle at least, in an extremely vulnerable position, since "it is not easy to rebut the view that the logic of a[n enterprise] state . . . assigns to the office of its government the authority to exterminate associates whose continued existence is judged to be irredeemably prejudicial to the pursuit of its purpose" (317n1). Although Oakeshott's concern about possible extermination may appear extravagant in relation to contemporary social democracies, it is justified to the extent that their instrumental perspective provides no intrinsic moral limits to the nature and scope of the actions of their governments.[8] If such limits are acknowledged, it is only because the enterprise state is qualified by the presence of elements of civil association.

There are, however, several other reasons for rejecting enterprise association as a possible way of creating respublica in addition to the lack of a moral perspective. One is that a purposive state that claims not to constrain freedom must secure universal consent to whatever enterprise it adopts, which is impossible to obtain in conditions of modern pluralism. Another is that this consent must extend not only to the enterprise the state pursues but also to the interpretation by rulers of its specific policy requirements. In practice, this is an equally impossible condition to realize. Finally, if an enterprise state is to be compatible with freedom, then citizens must be free to secede from it, should they cease to support its purpose. A state that granted that right, however, would prepare the way for its own dissolution.

If an enterprise state fails to meet these conditions, it follows that, strictly speaking, it has no genuine concept of respublica at all, since everything that purports to be of public concern is "privatized" by its subordination to the plans of the governors who impose and direct the state enterprise. The enterprise state, in other words, is simply a system of more or less benign power. To avoid possible misunderstanding, however, it must be emphasized that Oakeshott does not therefore reject all forms of enterprise association as undesirable: what he rejects is only the interpretation of *the state itself* as an enterprise association. In some circumstances, such as war, he fully recognizes that it is inevitable that a state will become an enterprise association and that even in peacetime any state must perform at least one function of an enterprise kind, namely, the levying of taxation. Even though the transformation of a civil into an enterprise state may be acceptable on occasion, insofar as it is necessary to defend or maintain civil association itself, the price to be paid must be clearly recognized: it is that the rule of law ceases to be the bond of citizens, and thus the state, for the time being, is no longer a free one.

RESPUBLICA AS CIVIL ASSOCIATION

The enterprise conception of respublica, then, cannot reconcile freedom with authority in modern societies characterized by a high degree of pluralism. How then is this reconciliation to be brought about? In its simplest form, Oakeshott's answer is that we can find glimpses of a possible solution in various aspects of the model of civil association found in the thought of Aristotle, Cicero, Hobbes, and Montesquieu, whom he explicitly acknowledges as precursors (*OHC*, 181).

What links these thinkers is the recognition that civil association consists of a complex of "rules and rule-like prescriptions to be subscribed to in all the enterprises and adventures in which the self-chosen satisfactions of agents may be sought" (*OHC*, 148). Hobbes, above all, is praised by Oakeshott for exploring the ideal character of civil association most profoundly. Nevertheless, Oakeshott criticized Hobbes on several counts. Hobbes failed, in the first place, to explain how self-seeking individuals could regard it as rational to make a covenant according to which each surrenders to all the other participants (as Hobbes requires) his natural right to interpret and enforce the law of nature as he sees fit. As Hobbes admits, to be a first performer in the kind of covenant he envisaged is feasible only for a few "magnanimous natures" such as Sydney Godolphin, to whom Hobbes dedicated *Leviathan*—wholly exceptional individuals willing to honor their promises even when a sovereign has not as yet been created to enforce laws that provide redress if others fail to keep theirs.

In addition, Oakeshott criticized Hobbes's use of contract theory for grounding obligation to law on an act of choice made by citizens. In fact, obligation to the laws of civil association does not involve an act of any kind: what it rests on is the acknowledgment by citizens of the authority of a legislator within whose jurisdiction they recognize themselves to fall (*OHC*, 183). This acknowledgment is not an act: it is, rather, simply an acceptance of the validity of rules made by an office holder whom citizens identify as their sovereign representative, whose status entitles him to make rules they acknowledge as obligating them.

Finally, Oakeshott criticized Hobbes for confusing the language of power with the very different language of authority, when he identified law with substantive commands by the sovereign, instead of with rules that specify formal conditions with which subjects must comply when they act. The outcome of this confusion is that civil association appears to be little more than a prudential arrangement for rescuing timid mortals from their fear of violent death.

Hobbes failed, in short, to provide a coherent moral conception of civil association—one, that is, which makes it more than a system of power expressing the will of the sovereign. Subsequent thinkers, Oakeshott maintains, have not succeeded in remedying the deficiencies of Hobbes's theory of civil association for a variety of reasons. In the first place, they have frequently adopted consequentialist perspectives that make the authority of law dependent on approval of its purposes and outcomes. In Locke, for example, the authority of law is made conditional on the implementation of natural rights. In Mill, it is made conditional on the willingness of governments to implement what Mill considered to be the requirements of human progress, especially the progress of truth. More generally, utilitarian versions of consequentialism treat civil association as primarily a means for achieving the greatest happiness of the greatest number, understood as personal security, prosperity, social welfare, or some combination of these ends. In every case, the consequentialist perspective fails to deal with the validity or legitimacy of legislation—with what is required, that is, for law simply to *be* law at all. This problem cannot be dealt with by indicating what makes laws desirable, since being desirable does not enable them to qualify as law. What then is required for legislation to be valid?

Answers often given to this question are that it must conform to a set of universally binding rational principles, implement principles of justice, or enforce universal human rights, for example. For Oakeshott, however, the relevant requirement is simply that law should have been made in accordance with procedures that the authority to legislate carries with it. This emphasis on procedural requirements might seem to imply that a Nazi regime that implements a genocide program, for example, would be immune to criticism provided that it complied with whatever formalities the will of the Führer might decide to acknowledge. This misgiving, however, ignores Oakeshott's insistence that enterprise states of the Nazi (or any other) kind lack any moral foundation, because they destroy the public realm (respublica) on which that depends. Such states, as has been seen, are merely power systems.

It is implicit in what has been said that civil association requires that subjects should not only observe the rule of law in their outward conduct but also regard their observance of it as obligatory, rather than merely compulsory. Liberal theorists have frequently met this requirement by trying to derive the authority of laws from an act of consent to them, but for Oakeshott the authority of law arises, rather, from mutual acknowledgment of it by both subjects and legislators as the source of a shared identity—a juridical identity, that is, created only through the law.

Civil association, then, is not merely an external structure of social integration: it is, rather, a rule-based language of self-interpretation that enables citizens to construct an identity for themselves as fellow members of it. This is why Oakeshott dismisses, in particular, all consequentialist attempts to theorize it on the ground that they assume that civil association "does" something or other, whereas all it does, insofar as that word can be used at all, is provide subjects with an identity through their mutual acknowledgment of the authority of the rule of law. Oakeshott acknowledged, however, that this is the most difficult aspect of civil association for the citizen of a modern democracy to understand—the fact that a liberal public order can exist only by virtue of impersonal constitutional forms and procedures that do not satisfy substantive wants and interests. Claiming to provide greater prosperity, security, and welfare benefits by satisfying those wants and interests, governments in search of votes indignantly claim that "modernization" is being obstructed when they find themselves impeded by these constitutional forms. Their indignation, however, sounds rather like that of the smiling fox in Aesop's story who is bent on persuading the chickens to abandon the protective structures that, the fox tells them, are preventing much needed improvements to the chicken pen. When the chickens foolishly allow themselves to be persuaded, the story ends with blood and feathers scattered everywhere. It is not only a sad story but, above all, one of folly. It is now necessary to examine more closely Oakeshott's view of the structure of civil association.

THE STRUCTURE OF CIVIL ASSOCIATION

Whereas the enterprise model of the state attempts to deal with diversity by identifying a common purpose that will restore substantive unity, the civil model explicitly seeks to accept and build on diversity in two related ways.[9] In the first place, it redefines the concept of the public in formal or procedural terms, in the manner originally foreshadowed in Aristotle's identification of the polis in terms of a shared constitution. Second, it drives a wedge between the authority of government, on the one hand, and approval of the policies the government pursues, on the other—the result of this wedge being that the acknowledgment of obligation to the law no longer depends directly on consent to the law or approval by those subject to it of those who make it. Precisely how these two features of the civil model permit it to reconcile order with freedom will become clearer, however, if the principal features of the civil model are outlined. Together, these constitute what may be called a nonfoundational theory of limited politics appropriate to conditions of social diversity. There are seven features that may be helpful to present in the form of the following list.

1. Civil association consists entirely of rules, in the form of laws, together with the institutional conditions necessary for making those rules, adjudicating them, and securing compliance with them.
2. These rules are noninstrumental: that is, they are not intended to serve any extraneous purpose, interest, or ideology. What they do is constitute or define civil association. In this respect, they are a bit like the rules of grammar, which do not require one to speak about any particular topic but define what is involved in speaking at all.

3. These noninstrumental rules are acknowledged as obligatory, simply because they are accepted as authoritative. What makes them authoritative is that they are acknowledged as the outcome of a procedure that is itself regarded as authoritative. The importance of this may be brought out by making the same point in the form of two negations:

   - The rules are not acknowledged as authoritative, because they have independently valid rational grounds, as in the philosophy, for example, of John Rawls or in the philosophy of more unqualifiedly utilitarian thinkers.
   - Nor are the rules accepted because they can be derived from some ultimate ethical norm, as in Hans Kelsen's theory of law, for example.[10]

4. Recognition of the authority of the rules of civil association does not entail personal approval of those laws by citizens or approval by citizens of the legislators who made them. Since there will, however, inevitably be a desire to change both the rules and the legislators who make them when these are not approved of, it is part of the nature of the civil model to provide procedures for permitting discussion of these subjects, as well as procedures for giving effect to the outcome of such debate.

5. The rules that constitute civil association entail, by their very nature, a distinction between public and private life, not in the sense of there being intrinsically different kinds of acts (as J. S. Mill thought) or intrinsically different spheres in which acts occur (as Hannah Arendt believed), but in the sense that there are two dimensions to every act, namely, a public dimension (insofar as every act can be seen from the standpoint of compliance or noncompliance with the rules) and a private dimension (insofar as every act is the successful or unsuccessful pursuit of some substantive purpose on the part of a particular agent).

6. The rules of civil association do not, in principle, exclude the simultaneous enjoyment of relationships other than the civil one itself. The only relationships they exclude are those incompatible with them; they do not, that is, exclude relationships that are only different from the civil one.

7. Finally, it is impossible to give a full account of civil association in terms of making and implementing a system of formal rules. For this reason, Oakeshott explicitly makes two vital qualifications to the model of civil association as a system of rule making and rule following.

- The first qualification is his recognition that civil association must include provision for an activity that goes beyond the activities of legislating and adjudicating. This is the activity of *ruling,* which is the executive activity of providing specific directives to particular groups or individuals to do particular acts in the interest of maintaining the civil order as a whole (*OHC,* 144).
- The second qualification is Oakeshott's recognition that there will inevitably be situations in which government acquires a purposive or "managerial' character. When a civil association is threatened with dissolution or destruction, as in time of war, he writes, "or when (in a lesser emergency) cives are deprived of the shelter or amenity of a civil order, in such circumstances that judicial remedy is unable to restore the situation, the common concern may become a common purpose and rulers may become managers of its pursuit." Oakeshott immediately adds, however, "For rulers to become managers even of an undertaking such as this, and for subjects to become partners or role-performers in a compulsory enterprise association such as this, is itself a suspension of the civil condition" (*OHC,* 146–47).

In addition to these two qualifications, Oakeshott adds an important clarification that seeks to remove a common source of confusion about the nature of government in civil association. Every government, he acknowledges, must acquire and maintain the material resources necessary to exercise the functions assigned to it in civil association. In the course of doing so, however, it will inevitably display some of the characteristics of purposive enterprise activity. It will, for example, become an employer of clerks and prison officers. This does not, however, mean that government has become an economic enterprise. What it means is that, insofar as managerial functions are assumed by the government, the relationship of subjects to rulers is no longer a civil one. This does not necessarily imply that the civil relationship is destroyed; indeed, it may ultimately be strengthened. The vital point, however, is that there is inevitably a tension between the civil and managerial relationship, and those who (as free citizens) regard the civil relationship as the key to human dignity are well advised to be aware of the dangers inherent in the situation, rather than gloss over them with the wishful idea that they have found a "middle way" that offers the best of all worlds. The belief that postwar Europe had in fact discovered just such a middle way was perhaps the most dangerous illusion cherished by Western social democracies in the quarter century after 1945.

SOME CONFUSIONS ABOUT OAKESHOTT'S THEORY
OF CIVIL ASSOCIATION

The model of civil association, then, is intended by Oakeshott to provide the only conception of the public realm, or respublica, that can reconcile order and freedom in a modern Western society whose citizens want to live self-chosen lives and reject any state that wishes to impose an overall purpose on them. A variety of theoretical objections to the civil model have been raised, however, by critics who claim that Oakeshott's theorization of civil association fails to make good his claims on its behalf. Some of the objections arise from confusion, but others are well-founded. An attempt must therefore now be made to distinguish the confused from the well-founded criticisms.

The first step in this process of clarification is to note the confusion about the nature of civil association that has arisen during the past three decades as a result of attempts made by Eastern European intellectuals to underpin their opposition to Soviet despotism by adopting the concept of civil association to describe the alternative for which they were fighting. The meaning they gave to it, however, usually had little connection with Oakeshott's version and was indeed incompatible with it in some crucial respects. Precisely how the Eastern European ideal differed from Oakeshott's may be illustrated by considering the political writings of Václav Havel, who is generally regarded as one of the leading Eastern European defenders of civil association. The grandeur of Havel's vision is unquestionable. The important point, however, is that he is committed to what Oakeshott terms an enterprise model of the state. Havel's enterprise, to be precise, is to promote spiritual renewal in what he regards as an age of dehumanization. From this, Havel says, it is "beside the point" to discuss topics such as socialism and capitalism, since the real concern is nothing less than salvation—"the salvation of us all, of myself and my interlocutor equally"—above all in the alienated relation to nature that has been created by modern industrial societies.[11] Elevated though Havel's words may be, a vision of this kind is incompatible with the formal, nonpurpose concept of civil association favored by Oakeshott.

The confusion caused by the Eastern European model of civil association, however, is only one of several that have resulted in the misinterpretation of Oakeshott's position. Another consists of the identification of civil association with the minimal state. This is the identification made, for example, by libertarian theorists such as Robert Nozick.[12] Civil association, however, is not committed to upholding the minimal state; its concern is to eliminate the arbitrary state. It is concerned, in other words, not with the quantity of government intervention but with the mode of intervention. Provided the mode of intervention does not conflict with the civil model, extensive government intervention is in principle not excluded by it. Precisely how much, however, and precisely which areas it occurs in, are matters for debate among citizens of civil association. They are not, that is, matters that can be determined by reflection on the civil ideal in the abstract.

Yet another confusion consists of identifying the civil model with capitalism. This confusion became widespread during the 1980s, when it was fostered in particular by such eminent neoliberal thinkers as Milton Friedman and Friedrich Hayek.[13] The confusion is easy to understand, since the free market seems in practice to thrive best in civil association. The difference, however, is clear: whereas the market is about economic growth, civil association is about restraints on arbitrary power. Failure to preserve that distinction has been a great misfortune for the newly liberated states of Eastern Europe. The assumption entertained by those countries was that a rapid adoption of liberal democratic institutions, accompanied by a program of deregulation, would automatically promote economic growth. When this growth failed to materialize as quickly as had been hoped, the civil model with which it had been identified was also discredited. The lesson is that the choice of freedom does not guarantee prosperity and may indeed conflict with it in many situations.

A further confusion consists of identifying the civil model with democracy. A tradition of civil association, however, existed in Britain in the eighteenth century, before the advent of democracy. And, as Tocqueville demonstrated long ago, when democracy emerged in the United States and Western Europe during the following century, it conflicted with civil association insofar as the dominant democratic concern is with equality rather than liberty. Equality, he noted, paves the way for a new kind of paternalistic despotism, since it permits democratic governments to use arbitrary power provided that they claim to be pursuing benign welfare policies.

Still other confusions require to be mentioned, among which is the confusion of civil association with liberalism. For Oakeshott, however, the civil ideal has no specific connection with liberal doctrine, mainly because liberal ideology has never escaped from a narrow concern with constitutional devices for protecting rights; from a tendency to interpret natural rights as substantive goods (such as employment, welfare, and education); and from a tendency to subordinate politics to a rationalist ideal of progress and human perfectibility (*OHC*, 245n2). In recent years, however, a number of scholars have claimed that Oakeshott himself is one of the finest theorists of liberalism. Insofar as the core of liberalism is a commitment to constitutionalism, hostility to concentrated power of any kind, and an ideal of limited politics, that claim is entirely justifiable.[14]

One more confusion consists in identifying the core of civil association with the arbitrary separation of a public from a private space or realm. Understood in this way, the distinction is plausibly attacked by feminist theory on the ground that it is merely a device for excluding women from the public realm. Behind it, feminists maintain, rests the indefensible assumption that their nature fits women only for private life. Chantal Mouffe, however, has rightly drawn attention to the fact that the private/public distinction made in the classical model of civil association does not, in Oakeshott's reformulation, attempt to make a distinction between two discrete, separate spheres, after the fashion of liberal thinkers like Mill. Oakeshott maintains, rather, that "*every* situation is an encounter between 'private' and 'public' because every enterprise is private, though never immune from the public conditions prescribed by the principles of citizenship."[15] In other words, every action inevitably has two aspects or dimensions, although no action can properly be classified according to a quasi-spatial separation between two spheres.

To this confusion may be added another that consists of assuming that the civil model entails an impossible ideal of political neutrality. This problem, however, arises only when the civil ideal is developed by liberal theorists who invoke a Kantian concept of reason as a foundation for legitimacy. As Hobbes made clear long ago, however, in the first great formulation of the civil model, the basis of civil association is not neutrality but authority, which needs no further ground beyond the fact that it is actually acknowledged. It is this nonfoundational position that Oakeshott has reiterated in his theory of civil association (*OHC*, 152–54).

Finally, two confusions remain to be noticed that have been left until last, because they are especially difficult to overcome. One of them arises when it is maintained that the formal or procedural character of the civil ideal means that it is indifferent to, and even destructive of, community. Civil association, however, is itself a form of community—the community, that is, of free men and women, insofar as they share a commitment to maintaining the civil conditions necessary for their own freedom and that of others. But it is not, of course, a community in the sense of that term that requires fellow members to share a common purpose within a voluntary organization. It may be added that the members of a civil association may also think of themselves as members of a community such as, for example, a nation. The only restriction that the civil ideal imposes on them in this respect, Oakeshott maintains, is that the communal identity must not conflict with the civil one. Members of

the Weimar Republic who thought of their primary identity in terms of commitment to Nazism, for example, could not reconcile this communal identity
with their civil identity, because the essence of the Nazi concept of community was that it entailed the destruction of the rule of law. This was regarded
as artificial and divisive and was to be replaced by the principle of personal
subordination to the Führer, regarded as the only natural and cohesive basis
for a racially pure society.

The remaining influential confusion to be considered, inspired by feminist political theory, consists of dismissing the civil model as fundamentally
gendered and hence exclusionist. Chantal Mouffe, however, has acknowledged that the civil ideal ceases to appear intrinsically exclusionist if feminist
politics are "understood not as a separate form of politics designed to pursue
the interests of women *as* women, but rather as the pursuit of feminist goals
and aims within the context of [the] wider articulation of demands."[16] Even
feminist philosophy, then, does not automatically mean the rejection of civil
association as intrinsically patriarchal and exclusionist.

Having examined some of the confusions about civil association that have
led to misunderstandings of Oakeshott's work, it is now possible to identify
four criticisms less easily dealt with.

WELL-FOUNDED CRITICISMS OF OAKESHOTT'S THEORY OF CIVIL ASSOCIATION

Perhaps the most plausible criticism of Oakeshott's model of civil association is that it is too "thin," in the sense that it is too narrowly procedural
and legalistic for it to have any motivating power for many citizens. In fact,
Oakeshott's own thought does not preclude broadening the attraction of civil
association by concessions to social democracy, provided it does not involve
a system of central planning that imposes a substantive vision of the good
society. Oakeshott's willingness to countenance at least some development in
that direction is indicated by the fact that he gave a very sympathetic review to
John Rawls's essay "Justice as Fairness," despite his later rejection of Rawls's
ideal of distributive justice in a footnote in *On Human Conduct* on the ground
that civil association is not about benefits but about the rule of law.[17]

There is, however, an element of truth in the claim that Oakeshott's model
of civil association is narrowly conceived. The narrowness lies, more precisely, in the fact that the model is above all a response to the problem of legitimation, which was the primary concern of classical political thinkers from
Hobbes to Rousseau. It is, accordingly, with the formal moral conditions for

legitimation, rather than the substantive conditions for political order, that Oakeshott is concerned. This is reflected in his insistence that his concept of a civil society is not intended to imply any particular kind of shape (such as social democracy) for a state but only to identify the formal conditions that must be satisfied for freedom to be reconciled with authority.

Chantal Mouffe, a sympathetic critic, has suggested that Oakeshott's narrowly conceived concern with civil association might be overcome by relocating the civil model within a radical democratic framework that would encourage active participation in politics, thereby removing Oakeshott's reliance on what may prove to be a minority consensus about forms and procedures. Mouffe fails to explain, however, why the agonistic conflict she wishes to encourage would ultimately contribute to political unity rather than to irresoluble conflict.[18] An alternative suggestion by David Boucher is that the apparent narrowness of Oakeshott's theory of civil association can be overcome by exploring the Roman model of republican sentiment on which Oakeshott implicitly relies. Even if Boucher's interpretation of Oakeshott is accepted, however, the trouble is that republicanism tends to presuppose a degree of civic virtue lacking in modern democratic states.[19]

The second persuasive criticism is that Oakeshott's thought is not only too thin to do justice to civil association but also ultimately too unpolitical, or even antipolitical. The chief source of this charge is Carl Schmitt, who did not level it directly against Oakeshott but argued that a model of civil association like Oakeshott's ignores the principal feature of politics, which is the element of decision in all political action—an element that cannot be subsumed under the rule following that Oakeshott regards as the defining characteristic of civil association.[20] To this charge of "depoliticizing" civil association, however, a telling response may be made on Oakeshott's behalf, which is that he did not eliminate decision from the theory of civil association; what he did was to insist, rather, that the aim of decision must be the creation and maintenance of civil association and that civil association ends once rule following ceases to be its constitutive feature.

The third criticism of Oakeshott's model of civil association that is difficult to rebut concerns his concept of the self. Although this concept of the self avoids many of the philosophical problems associated with modern individualist theory, it is open to the charge of identifying selfhood with a narrowly existentialist emphasis on choosing as the primary expression of human identity. This narrowness is particularly evident, for example, in a simplistic portrait Oakeshott once gave of modern European history as a struggle between two different kinds of self, namely, that of the individual, on the one hand, and that of the "individual manqué" or anti-individual, on the other.

Anti-individuals find individual responsibility a burden and turn to government to relieve themselves of the need to choose their own life.

Although there are no doubt many modern figures who fit Oakeshott's portrait of anti-individuals, the danger with such a picture is, of course, that it can easily lapse into a sweeping reactionary caricature of historical movements inspired by oppression. It also represented an evasion of a major problem posed by Oakeshott's defense of civil association. This problem, which had already been evident in Hobbes's thought, was to find a way of making civil association attractive to the mass of modern democratic populations, rather than writing them off as "anti-individuals." Hegel had attempted to do this by an optimistic presentation of the process of civic education that he thought civil society itself would engender, and Tocqueville had subsequently attempted to do so by outlining a program of decentralized government combined with local political participation. Oakeshott, however, remained silent on the issue of how an education for civil citizenship was to be conducted—with the exception, that is, of university students, for whom he outlined an appropriate academic syllabus. This, however, was too narrow an electorate for the purpose.

The final criticism of Oakeshott's model of civil association that carries weight is that it is rooted in the nation-state and has therefore become irrelevant to an age in which supranational entities such as the European Union are increasingly becoming the units of contemporary political life. To conclude that globalizing tendencies make civil association irrelevant, however, is incorrect. Although Oakeshott himself did not apply the civil model at a supranational level, a number of thinkers have defended the possibility of doing so from a philosophical standpoint.[21] Oakeshott's response, however, might be to accept the theoretical possibility of a supranational form of civil association, while noting that the concept of citizenship, as constituted by a shared commitment to the rule of law that he associates the civil model with, has thus far not been achieved beyond the nation-state, within which that ideal has in any case always been at best a fragile one.

THE FUTURE OF CIVIL ASSOCIATION

How relevant is Oakeshott's theory of civil association for the future of the ideal of the limited state in modern Western mass democracies? Throughout his life Oakeshott himself expressed varying degrees of pessimism on this score. At a relatively early stage, he identified mass democracy with the spread of anti-individualistic yearnings that would make citizens reluctant to accept the personal responsibility liberty requires. Subsequently, he expressed mis-givings about the future of constitutional government in an age in which the forms and procedures on which it depends are no longer regarded as having any intrinsic value. Toward the end of his life, his despondency deepened still further, finally finding expression in the last book published during his life-time, *On History and Other Essays*, in an essay on "The Tower of Babel," which displayed unalleviated gloom about the likely prospects of the civil model in the Western world. What created this gloom?

In brief, Oakeshott no longer identified the primary threat to civil associa-tion with the kind of ideological politics that had dominated his thought in the interwar and early postwar decades. Nor was he now primarily worried about the tentacles of the enterprise state. What troubled him was, rather, a malaise he believed extended far beyond the sphere of politics into the very heart of Western culture. This was the emergence of an all-pervasive instrumental mentality that he believed had come to pervade the whole of modern life. In this respect, it may be noticed, the vision of late Western modernity that dominated Oakeshott's final years converged with that of Nietzsche, Weber, Heidegger, and members of the Frankfurt School of neo-Marxist thought such as Adorno and Horkheimer, all of whom identified a predominantly instrumental conception of rationality as the source of profoundly dehuman-izing tendencies in contemporary Western culture. For Oakeshott what made the dangers inherent in this instrumental attitude almost incapable of being resisted by defenders of civil association is that they now present themselves in two forms that both claim to be allies of true freedom, and in that way conceal all the more effectively their incompatibility with the limited style of politics enshrined in the civil model.

The first danger is what is commonly termed *identity politics*, defenders of which profess an ideal of liberation that goes far beyond what can be secured by the purely formal achievement of legal rights or even by the redistribution of material benefits. True liberation, they maintain, is about recognition and respect. Although Oakeshott was deeply sympathetic to the concept of recog-nition as the moral foundation of civil association, what he rejected was the form of identity politics based on the claim that the personal is the political. He rejected it because, for those for whom the personal is the political, the principal aim of identity politics must be to destroy the public/private distinc-tion in any form at all.

In its place, identity politics seeks to place two things. One is a totally polit-icized view of every aspect of life. The other is a demand for total personal transparency as the only possible foundation for morality and politics in the contemporary world. When these two positions are combined, they yield a contemporary version of the enterprise state that was anticipated long ago by Rousseau's early presentation of the logic of identity politics. What Rousseau demonstrated was that the final result of equating the personal with the political, as he had in *The Social Contract*, for example, was most unlikely to be the sense of empowerment for which he had initially hoped. In practice, the outcome was much more likely to be not a morality of recognition based on mutual trust and sociality but a morality of mutual reproach and suspicion, in which everyone eyed everyone else with a view to identifying forms of selfishness and insensitivity that prevented genuine recognition from being achieved. To help oppressed groups, then, is one matter and is in principle quite compatible with civil association, even if civil societies fail dismally in this respect at times. As Oakeshott maintained, however, to seek a remedy in a form of identity politics that creates an intensely moralistic version of the enterprise state is at best to jump from the frying pan into the fire, and at worst to move into the world of universal mutual suspicion and unfreedom that Rousseau portrayed so graphically.[22]

The second form of instrumentalism that made Oakeshott especially gloomy takes the form of an intensely moralistic idealism that has established a profound influence over Western liberal doctrine during the past three decades. The essence of this idealism is the conviction that nothing that actually exists is entitled to command moral respect until it has been judged in the light of independently devised criteria that owe absolutely nothing to experience and pay no regard to felt wants or felt satisfactions. It is, in other words, an intensified form of the "rationalism" that Oakeshott had criticized earlier, but now in a more purely moralistic guise.

When applied to politics, moralistic idealism is characterized by a systematic refusal to provide a central place for prudence, the supreme political virtue, displaced by justice; for the unintended outcomes of actions that make up the greater part of human existence; for the inescapable contingencies of human existence, whether they relate to the individual or to society; and for the fact that habit and familiarity, rather than reason, are frequently the only things that give social and political relationships such acceptability as they possess. The precise danger Oakeshott believed to be created by this idealism is that in the name of justice, it is in practice more likely to foster a ressentiment that ends in a form of nihilism. This was the message contained in Oakeshott's retelling of the story of "The Tower of Babel" in the last book he published, *On History*.

Did Oakeshott, one may ask, see any remedy for this incipient nihilism? At the heart of his pessimism was a belief he shared with the Spanish philosopher José Ortega y Gasset and the Dutch historian Johan Huizinga, both of whom maintained civil association cannot survive in a culture devoid of any sense of play.[23] Only this can check the instrumental mentality and thereby make possible a regard for the constitutive role of rules on which civil association depends. Whether Oakeshott was right in lamenting the disappearance of play from Western culture and in fearing the end of civil association on that account is a matter for debate. In practice, the foreseeable future of Western political life is perhaps most likely to be marked, as Oakeshott himself believed it has been in the past, by a tension between the rule of law to which civil association is committed and the subordination of it to the administrative powers of governments bent on imposing substantive conceptions of the good society. If Oakeshott's misgivings about the survival of civil association prove to be well-founded, however, then his fate as a political thinker may ultimately be the fate Hegel suggested befalls all great political theorists when he remarked that the owl of Minerva flies only at dusk. Oakeshott may have clarified the requirements of civil association at the very time when the course of history has begun to turn decisively away from them.[24]

NOTES

1. Friedrich Hayek, *The Constitution of Liberty* (London: Routledge and Kegan Paul, 1960); Karl Popper, *The Open Society and Its Enemies* (London: Routledge and Kegan Paul, 1962); John Rawls, *A Theory of Justice* (Cambridge: Harvard University Press, 1971); Robert Nozick, *Anarchy, State, and Utopia* (Oxford: Blackwell, 1974); Ernest Gellner, *Conditions for Liberty: Civil Society and Its Rivals* (London: Hamish Hamilton, 1994); Jürgen Habermas, *Legitimation Crisis* (London: Heinemann, 1976); Václav Havel, "The Power of the Powerless," in *Living in Truth*, ed. Jan Vladislav (London: Faber and Faber, 1987).

2. T. H. Green, *Lectures on the Principles of Political Obligation* (London: Longmans, 1895).

3. Bernard Bosanquet, *Philosophical Theory of the State* (London: Macmillan, 1923).

4. This quote comes from Oakeshott's essay "The Concept of Government in Modern Europe," first published in Spanish as "La Idea de Gobierno en la Europa Moderna" (Madrid: Ateneo, 1955) as part of a series titled Tendencias actuales del pensamiento europeo.

5. See, for example, the essay "The Masses in Representative Democracy," in *RP*, 363–83.

6. See the essay "Rationalism in Politics," in *RP*, 6–42.

7. On Calvin and Geneva, see Paul Helm, *John Calvin's Ideas* (Oxford: Oxford University Press, 2004). See also Francis Bacon, *New Atlantis and the Great Instauration*, ed. Jerry Weinberger (Wheeling, Ill.: Crofts Classics, 1989); and Rawls, *Theory of Justice*.

8. See Alan Ryan, review of *On Human Conduct*, by Michael Oakeshott, *Listener* 93 (1975): 517–18; and David R. Mapel, "Civil Association and the Idea of Contingency," *Political Theory* 18 (1990): 409n14.

9. I am grateful to Professor Jyotirmaya Sharma for permission to rework some material in this section, originally published in an article on "The Political and the Concept of the Public," *Studies in Humanities and Social Sciences* (Journal of the Inter-University Centre for Humanities and Social Sciences, Indian Institute of Advanced Sudy, Shimla) 1, no. 2 (1997): 1–22.

10. Rawls, *Theory of Justice*; Hans Kelsen, *General Theory of Law and State* (Cambridge: Harvard University Press, 1949). A useful short overview of Kelsen's legal and political philosophy is provided by Kelsen in *Political Thought Since World War II*, ed. Wladyslaw Jozef Stankiewicz (New York: Free Press of Glencoe, 1964), 64–115.

11. Vaclav Havel, "Politics and Conscience," in *Conservative Thoughts*, ed. Roger Scruton (London: Claridge Press, 1988), 194.

12. Nozick, *Anarchy, State, and Utopia.*

13. Milton Friedman, *Capitalism and Freedom: Problems and Prospects* (Charlottesville: University Press of Virginia, 1975); Hayek, *Constitution of Liberty.*

14. On Oakeshott as a liberal thinker, see, for example, Wendell John Coats Jr., "Michael Oakeshott as Liberal Theorist," *Canadian Journal of Political Science* 18 (December 1985): 773–87; John Gray, "Oakeshott as a Liberal," *Salisbury Review* 10, no. 1 (1991): 22–25; Paul Franco, *Michael Oakeshott: An Introduction* (New Haven: Yale University Press, 2004), 172–82; Terry Nardin and Luke O'Sullivan, eds., "Editors' Introduction," in *Lectures in the History of Political Thought*, by Michael Oakeshott (Exeter: Imprint Academic, 2006), 24–25.

15. Chantal Mouffe, *The Return of the Political* (Verso: London, 1993), 84 (italics added).

16. Ibid., 87.

17. See Oakeshott's review of *Philosophy Politics and Society*, ed. Peter Laslett and W. G. Runciman, 2nd ser., in *VMES*, 191.

18. Mouffe, *Return of the Political*, 66–69.

19. David Boucher, "Oakeshott and the Republican Tradition," *British Journal of Politics and International Relations* 7 (2005): 81–96.

20. Carl Schmitt, *The Concept of the Political* (New Brunswick: Rutgers University Press, 1976).

21. Most notably, Terry Nardin in *Law, Morality, and the Relations of States* (Princeton: Princeton University Press, 1983).

22. Jean-Jacques Rousseau, *The Social Contract*, ed. E. Barker (London: Oxford University Press, 1956).

23. See José Ortega y Gasset, *The Revolt of the Masses* (London: Unwin, 1961); and Johan Huizinga, *Homo Ludens* (London: Paladin, 1970).

24. I am grateful to Professor Paul Franco for comments on a draft of this paper that greatly improved it.

15

OAKESHOTT ON LAW

Steven Gerencser

To write about law in relationship to Michael Oakeshott's ideas generally, or his thoughts on politics in particular, presents a complicated task, not because law is an obscure concept in Oakeshott and not because it is a topic about which he has written little. In fact, Oakeshott wrote about law and jurisprudence at the beginning of his life as a publishing scholar and was still writing essays on law more than half a century later. Rather, it is a challenge to write about Oakeshott and law because his ideas about law are so closely nested with related and interlocking concepts that it is very easy to start by thinking about law and find oneself considering authority or politics or his distinction between civil association and enterprise association. These concepts are woven together so tightly for Oakeshott that to pull one out and consider it on its own without attention to the others would badly misconstrue the idea. To express this idea in the terms that Oakeshott employs regarding Hegel and Hobbes, these ideas are related as in a system, and to attempt to understand any element of the system in isolation can generate only a limited and incomplete view, that is, a misunderstanding.

Yet this view of Oakeshott can itself lead to a misunderstanding, a mistaken belief that all he wrote about law over his life of analysis and commentary perfectly coheres. Instead, his thinking about law, as his thinking about politics, philosophy, and much else, changes over time, as we would expect from any complex and interesting thinker. His earliest published writing on law and jurisprudence comes before World War II, a period marked by the publication of Oakeshott's first book, *Experience and Its Modes*, and like much of his writing of that time, "The Concept of a Philosophical Jurisprudence" bears the stamp of British idealism. In that work Oakeshott is less concerned with law itself than with what it would take to develop a philosophical explanation of law; he states there that he is not interested in the usage of "'jurisprudence' that refers to 'case-law' or 'judge-made law,' or the practice of a court" (*CPJ*, 154). Instead, he reviews various schools of the philosophical explanation of law and, much as he did regarding history or science in *Experience and Its Modes*, finds them wanting. These all fail to achieve a true philosophical jurisprudence, because they cannot attain what a philosophical explanation must. Oakeshott states, "a philosophical explanation is one which, in principle, is the relation of its subject to what I have called the totality of experience" (175).

What Oakeshott himself has to offer as a philosophical jurisprudence at this time is less clear, as he is more involved with the critical review of the claims of others and theorizing what a true philosophical explanation must be like than with offering a theoretical explanation of law. He even suggests, "it is unnecessary for me to apply in detail my view of the nature of philosophy to the study of the nature of law; I have given the principle and the reader, if he cares, can easily apply it himself" (*CPJ*, 175). Oakeshott's early attention to law then is less about law than the nature of philosophical explanation and, like his writing on history or politics, in the period after the war, he would leave behind much of the attention to philosophical explanation according to the strictures of idealism and focus more on the actual consideration of law, history, and politics, among other matters.

Of course, differing judgments about how much and how significantly Oakeshott does change his views on various topics are a source of ongoing debates among various scholars who have interpreted his work. Yet it is not my intention here to rehearse those debates; rather, it is to suggest that discussing Oakeshott on law means encountering a dilemma that reflects one feature of those debates. Put simply and directly, two emphases can be found in Oakeshott's writing about government and politics, and seeing how these are reflected in his ideas about law reveals some conflicts between those emphases.

On the one hand, there is an Oakeshott, famous to many, who highlights the significance of practical knowledge over technical knowledge, who focuses attention on the traditional elements of a community, and who is suspicious of attempts to create de novo clear, simple ways of organizing community by means of universal principles, shorn of any local encumbrances; that is, this is the Oakeshott who cautions against what he calls rationalism, this we might call the traditionalist Oakeshott. On the other hand, there is an Oakeshott who reflects on human conduct, agency, and freedom in universal terms and who develops ideal understandings of human interaction and considers the terms of that engagement, most specifically law. The elements of that later view, which we might call the formalist Oakeshott, are exemplified in works such as *On Human Conduct* and "The Rule of Law"; I will suggest later that this formalist Oakeshott advocates a conception of law at odds with the views of the traditionalist Oakeshott, exhibited in works such as "Rationalism in Politics" and "Political Education." These two conceptions of law, a traditionalist and a formalist view, set up a potential conflict in Oakeshott's writings on law, a contradiction that he never acknowledges directly. Still, his manner of espousing these two approaches may offer a way to see them as complementary instead of contradictory and in doing so point to a way of thinking about law that escapes the confines of this common dilemma.

"RATIONAL JURISPRUDENCE," AN EXCURSION

In the essays collected in *Rationalism in Politics*, and notably in the eponymous essay of that collection, Michael Oakeshott provides a view of politics, government, community, and law that has secured his standing as a wide-ranging writer and insightful thinker and, perhaps in many persons' eyes, his reputation as a conservative as well. This last comes not only on the basis of his essay "On Being Conservative" but for his return again and again to themes regarding the importance of tradition and his emphasis on the local, customary, and practical knowledge that accompanies his critique of rationalism. In the essays collected therein, with the exception of his writing on Hobbes, Oakeshott actually addresses the law, as such, very little. What might we learn from those well-known essays about politics that would help to understand a view of the law? What conception of law might we draw from the signature themes in the essays of that volume?

A good starting place would be Oakeshott's well-known definition of politics from the essay "Political Education": "Politics I take to be the activity of attending to the arrangements of a set of people whom chance or choice have brought together . . . [and] the communities in which this activity is preeminent are the hereditary co-operative groups, many of them of ancient lineage, all of them aware of a past, a present, and future, which we call states" (*RP*, 44). There is much about the character of politics and the knowledge appropriate to it that Oakeshott develops from this passage, but one thing we can begin by noting is that those "arrangements" may be of many sorts (e.g., customs, habits, accommodations, agreements), but it would certainly appear that law is at least one of them, especially when "states" are the places where this activity, which he deems to be "pre-eminent," takes place.

Attending to these arrangements, then, for Oakeshott comes to be understood as a distinctly traditional activity. It is an engagement in which learning how to judge the character and appropriateness of these arrangements, how to perceive the need to address changes in circumstance that may require adjustments, and how to deliberate various possibilities requires acquiring knowledge of a certain character and employing it in a certain way. Oakeshott characterizes the knowledge needed for attending to the common arrangements of society as that based on "a genuine, concrete knowledge of the permanent interests and direction of a society" (RP, 27). What are those permanent interests, and what is the direction of society? Those questions cannot be answered in the abstract, because they involve the particular knowledge of and familiarity with a given society's traditions. This requires of a member of such a community "an initiation into the moral and intellectual habits and achievements of his society, an entry to the partnership of the past and present, a sharing of concrete knowledge" (38).

But the appropriate knowledge for attending to the arrangements of society is not simply the substance of a particular tradition, an intimate knowledge of the concrete character of a society and its past; it is also practical. That is, this type of knowledge comes from engaging in an activity, not learning about it in a book. This latter type of formal, written knowledge does indeed represent true knowledge about an activity, but that knowledge is also limited; it is an abridgment or abstraction from that activity. Oakeshott presents these as two components of knowledge of all sorts, practical and technical, yet the latter always comes second and is reliant on the first, not vice versa. Oakeshott explores this with the whimsical example of cooking: "The cookery book is not an independently generated beginning from which cooking can spring, it is nothing more than an abstract of somebody's knowledge of how to cook; it is the stepchild, not the parent of activity" (RP, 52). So too when it comes to the knowledge necessary for attending to the arrangements of society: there is the technical knowledge one can learn about the formal procedures for enacting business or the formal strictures of a law, and there is knowledge of how in a given time, with the possibilities, limitations, languages, and customs of a particular society, a law might come to be enacted or interpreted to apply in a particular situation.

I have tried to provide nothing original in this précis; it is a review that I hope would be unobjectionable to anyone familiar with some of Oakeshott's most famous writings and the reputation that redounds from them. Furthermore, from this account it is possible to piece together a recognizable and coherent understanding of law. Imagine an essay that Oakeshott did not write but might have written in accordance with the ideas in Rationalism in Politics. I call this fictional essay "Rational Jurisprudence." In this imaginary essay it would be reasonable to expect that Oakeshott would be a critic of approaches that understand law as nothing other than the explicit pronouncements of a rationally constructed, formally empowered state. He might have seen such a view as the development of an overly confident set of Enlightenment ideas about the power of the rational state and the capacities of rational legislators to rid society of messy, eccentric, local, legal customs and traditions. Here, a misguided "rational jurisprudence" would dismiss magistrates' courts and justices of the peace and instead the rationalist legislator would seek to replace the patchwork of precedent and common law with an organized, coherent system of legal statutes. In this "rational jurisprudence," the task of the judge is to be a mere administrator of the law, barely interpreting, rather mechanically applying the law in the most systematic fashion as possible to systematize not only the law but the behavior of the subjects of law.

In this imaginary essay, however, Oakeshott would suggest that such rationalist ideas misunderstand the character of law and the experience of those who live under it and employ it. Instead of being sloppy or inconsistent, those employing the reason of judges, whether in petty and police courts or in high appellate or even supreme courts, have daily experience of the interaction of the law and its subjects. They see the effects of statutory laws: when they achieve their purpose, when they do not, and where previous decisions or law still do or no longer reflect the beliefs and customs of the community from which they sprang. Furthermore, judges understood as such are responsible for deliberating on how their decisions will affect not only those before them but their own court in the future and other courts in the vicinage, and this responsibility keeps them modestly attuned to the sentiments about the law in their neighborhood and in other courts. Here the activity of judging reflects an element of politics, in which Oakeshott famously describes, "The enterprise is to keep afloat on an even keel; the sea is both friend and enemy; and the seamanship consists in using the resources of a traditional manner of behavior in order to make a friend of very hostile occasion" (*RP*, 60). Just as Oakeshott recommends that the best political education is one steeped in knowledge of a particular tradition, it would also seem that a legal education would be one based on a deepening acquaintance with a tradition as well, especially focused on the legal customs and precedents. I will not here repeat all the elements of that education that Oakeshott recommends in "Political Education," but I do suggest that in the imaginary essay "Rational Jurisprudence," Oakeshott would place historical knowledge as central to reasoned judging as well as politics.

> Every society, by the underlinings it makes in the book of its history, constructs a legend of its own fortunes which it keeps up to date and which is the hidden understanding of its politics [and law]; and

historical investigation of this legend—not to expose its errors but understand its prejudices—must be a pre-eminent part of a political [and legal] education. It is then in the study of genuine history, and of this quasi-history which reveals in its backward glances the tendencies which are afoot, that one may hope to escape one of the most insidious current misunderstandings of political [and legal] activity—the misunderstanding in which institutions and procedures appear as pieces of machinery designed to achieve a purpose in advance, instead of as manners of behaviors which are meaningless when separated from their context. (63)

It is in their daily engagement in the law, their investigation of its effects, and their building knowledge of how it develops incrementally over time that judges develop a sense of the law in which the immediate situation is comprehended through a practical understanding of what the law can—and cannot—achieve and how it fits into a broader historical context. Furthermore, those subject to the law, the suitors in a court, the plaintiffs and defendants, prosecutors and accused, witnesses and jurors, these all experience the law and respond to its agents as those judgments reflect, or do not reflect, the customs, habits, and traditions of the communities in which they are rendered. This would be a concrete understanding of law and the practice of judging, distinct from a more abstract view of what law must be by rational determination. Each case before a court offers an opportunity to review claims and activities under legal scrutiny not merely by applying a statute, but with an eye toward the legal traditions and moral expectations of a community.

This understanding of law would reflect the sort of conservative disposition that neither attempts to transform wholesale the arrangement of laws, rights, and duties that make up the legal life of a community, nor rejects changes to them; rather, it responds to fresh situations "by throwing our weight upon the foot which for the time being is most firmly placed, by cleaving to whatever familiarities are not immediately threatened and thus assimilating what is new without becoming unrecognizable to ourselves" (RP, 410). About this understanding of the law, Oakeshott might suggest, there is more to learn from Edward Coke and William Blackstone than from Jeremy Bentham or the great codifiers of the nineteenth century; it would be better seen in the English Common Law than in the Bürgerliches Gesetzbuch.

The ideas in the preceding paragraphs are mere suggestions based on familiar thoughts from some of Oakeshott's most famous essays. Nonetheless, in writings composed though not published during that time, Oakeshott does comment on how judicial activity in courts of law reflects an appropriate

approach to politics and governing, one that reflects the style of politics cau-
tiously espoused in essays such as "On Being Conservative," "Political Education," and "Rationalism in Politics."

In the posthumously published monograph *The Politics of Faith and the
Politics of Scepticism*, originally composed during the period when many of
the essays collected in *Rationalism in Politics* were being written, Oakeshott
identifies law courts as an example of medieval governance practices received
by modern Europe, an inheritance that reflects an appropriately skeptical and
modest attitude toward governing and politics, which he characterizes as the
"The Politics of Scepticism."[1] He writes, "And on any reading of its office and
competence, a court of law is not the kind of institution which is appropriate
to take the initiative in organizing the perfection of mankind: where governing is understood as the judicial provision of remedies for wrongs suffered, a
sceptical style of politics obtrudes" (*PFPS*, 77).

Elsewhere he gently mocks the American Revolution as "an instructive
chapter in the history of the politics of Rationalism," because its defenders
saw its principles "discovered in nature by human reason" (*RP*, 31, 33). Yet
here Oakeshott sees that in England, because of the skeptical, judicial style of
its politics, "the 'rights' and 'duties,' themselves, of course, were not recognized as natural or primordial; they were known to have been established by
a juridical process out of the tangle of personal relationships which preceded
their formulations'" (*PFPS*, 78n). An understanding of law seen through
the lens of courts and based on the organic development of the common
law is not only in keeping with the ideas expressed in *Rationalism in Politics*,
but explicitly reflects Oakeshott's advocacy of the politics of skepticism and
the proper understanding of important political issues like the foundations
of rights.

This matches directly with Oakeshott's view of a conservative disposition
regarding the proper attitude to governing articulated in "On Being Conservative," where he suggests, "To govern, then, as the conservative understands
it, is to provide a *vinculum juris* for those manners of conduct which, in the
circumstances, are least likely to result in the frustrating collision of interests; to provide redress and means of compensation from those who suffer
from others behaving in a contrary manner; sometimes to provide punishment for those who pursue their own interests regardless of the rules, and
of course to provide a sufficient force to maintain the authority of an arbiter of
this kind" (*RP*, 429). Oakeshott acknowledges that in England the growth of
Parliament had come to obscure this judicial and skeptical understanding
of governing, but only after it lost an understanding of itself as a judicial
body. "And the slowness of this change is one of the measures of the relative

weakness of the politics of faith (to which 'legislation' is indispensable) and the relative strength of the politics of scepticism" (*PFPS*, 78–79). Legislation is what Oakeshott here associates with the politics of faith and the rationalistic "imposition of a comprehensive pattern of activity upon all the subjects of a realm," while the character of judicial activity reflects not only an understanding of law but of the politics of skepticism (79).

I have proposed many of Oakeshott's views on law in a conditional mood, because, of course, he did not write an essay "Rational Jurisprudence"; furthermore, the discussions of courts and judicial activity I have provided come primarily from writings he did not publish while he was alive. Thus, I have titled this whole section an excursion, because the ideas about law expressed here, while in keeping with some of his most famous essays, are mere projections. While Oakeshott does dismiss the rationalist presumptions of natural law and the state-empowering temptations of modern legislation, he does not offer extended discussions of the advantages of common law; while he praises judicial activity as an example of the politics of skepticism, he also acknowledges that this vestige of the medieval period prevailed "in the early centuries of the modern period" but now is waning if not entirely disappearing (*PFPS*, 79).

RULES AND *LEX*

I suggested initially that understanding what Oakeshott says about law is difficult, not because he says so little, but because of how closely associated the idea of law is with his many other ideas. When we leave, then, the speculations of what ideas about law are implied in Oakeshott's early work and take up his formal explorations, we must note how explicit expositions of law are rooted in his discussions of special types of human associations, in particular that which he characterizes as the "civil condition," "civil association," or "rule of law."

Many other authors have explicated Oakeshott's thoughts on these topics, and it is not my endeavor here to replicate that important interpretive work. But because Oakeshott's most extensive discussions of law are found in his elaboration of his particular view of the civil condition, it raises the following question, to what extent are his ideas about law bound to that view? Is he saying that law is only truly law when it reflects the characteristics of the civil condition as he understands it? In other words, should we consider his thoughts on law as expressed in the second essay of *On Human Conduct*, titled "On the Civil Condition," and in his finely detailed essay "The Rule of

Law" as theoretical explorations of law in general, or rather only as law when found in the precise conditions he elaborates? If the former, then what do we make of common understandings of law dismissed by Oakeshott, yet held by various human agents and experienced as such? If the latter, then we must accept that most of his reflections pertain only to one uniquely understood type of law; then we must ask of what value is that view if the existence or even desirability of those conditions in which it is found come into doubt?

Oakeshott does address this issue after a fashion, but he does so to advance his discussion of the civil condition, not in a way that helps us answer these questions. He writes, "association begins and ends in recognition of rules. Such rules I shall call 'law'; and so that they may not be confused with the heterogeneous collection of rules and rule-like instructions, instruments, provisions, etc. which constitute those ambiguous associations we call states, I shall call them *lex*" (*OHC*, 128).[2] I will return shortly to discuss the substance of this conception of law as rules, but here I draw attention to his insistence that not everything that subjects in a state experience as law, that they may call a law or that might be called a law by the state, is for Oakeshott actually a law. Introducing the concept of lex helps him focus only on those aspects of law that reflect his understanding of the civil condition but dismiss (or neglect) any other conception. I register this not as a complaint against Oakeshott's views but as an acknowledgment of his insistence that his most developed discussions of law are not about law in general. Rather, his writings are about lex, law as a feature in one form of human association, variously labeled in Oakeshott's writings as the civil condition, civil association, societas, respublica, or rule of law.

So then, what is a law? As noted in the passage previously cited, Oakeshott simply claims laws are rules. What then is a rule? "A rule is an authoritative assertion, not a theorem. . . . It does not invoke approval or disapproval or offer itself as a reason or a plea of justification or as a subject of theoretical inquiry. It calls only for assent in any performance to which it may relate" (*OHC*, 125). Understanding more fully Oakeshott's distinctive use of rules requires exploring how a rule is a way to characterize the conditions that constitute a "practice," and a "practice is a set of conditions which qualify performances" (119–20). The "civil condition" in which one finds lex is a premier example of such a practice, as it shares central characteristics with all practices. Oakeshott explains, "And to be related in terms of a practice is precisely not to be associated in the reciprocal satisfaction of wants or in acknowledging 'managerial' decisions in the pursuit of common purposes; it is relationship in terms of a common recognition of considerations such as uses or rules intelligently subscribed to in self-chosen performances. It is formal, not substantial relationship" (121).

To be subject to a rule within a practice then does not require submitting to have one's actions chosen by the practice; rather, it requires those subject to the practice to qualify their individually self-chosen actions according to it. Oakeshott famously characterized these conditions as "adverbial considerations," claiming that a practice "is agents related to one another in actions and responses to actions qualified by the adverbial conditions of a procedure" (*OHC*, 57). A rule then is a component of a practice, the conditions that one must follow to participate in that practice; these rules do not require particular actions, they are not instructions, and they are not focused on achieving an outcome. Rules so understood are formal conditions agents must consider in their substantive choices or actions.

These are some of the unique features of the rules through which Oakeshott understands laws, and they share characteristics with other familiar rule sets, such as rules of a game or the rules of order of a business meeting. In each of these cases human agents are associated together under conditions that they share and whose authority over them they acknowledge; furthermore, the manner in which such associates engage with one another reveals different aspects or modes of behavior. Of course, the players of a game may seek healthy exercise or mental stimulation or the desire to win a prize; yet, for Oakeshott, the pursuit of these ends, whether individual or shared, indicates an enterprising engagement to accomplish something.

The pursuit of such goals is a significant part of human experience, yet focusing on the pursuits and goals teaches us little about law in a civil association. We may glimpse strategies, regularities of behavior, "instrumental precepts or maxims such as those enunciated by a trainer or coach," but each of these espouses a "prudential consideration" and has nothing to do with the following of the rules as rules (*OH*, 125–26). Still, a game is not just any arbitrary activity to win; it is participation in some distinct game with others who recognize they are playing that game as well. "And what is this game? It is nothing other than a set of rules" (126).

This understanding of the rules of a game—not its strategies, not observations regarding the skills it takes to play it, not the plans for a coming match or season of play—provides an analogy to laws and human agents' relationship to them. "To be related in terms of these non-instrumental rules is to be related in a mutual obligation to observe the conditions which themselves constitute the game, an obligation which cannot be evaded on the grounds of disapproval or conscientious objection" (126). This last is fundamentally important as well. Central to the playing of a game is accepting the obligation to follow the rules of a game. Players in a game do not properly think to themselves, "Is that a rule I like? If so I will follow it," but rather, "Is that actually a rule of the game? If so, I must follow it." The central questions regarding an obligation to follow the rule are "Is it an actually valid rule?" or "Can I be sure that is a rule I must follow?"

For Oakeshott this is true of all rules as rules, not just those understood as games: "All agents who fall within [its] jurisdiction are equal in respect of the rule and each has an obligation to subscribe to it. . . . If an agent refuses to be obligated there is but one valid reason he may give for his refusal, namely, that it is not a rule for him because he does not fall within its jurisdiction" (*OHC*, 126). There are then two manners of understanding a game and the players in it, what Oakeshott calls "two categorially distinct modes of association" (*OH*, 127). One draws our attention to the choices, strategies, plans, preparations, pieces of advice, and so forth regarding how to achieve success in the game. The other draws our attention to the authoritative rules that constitute the game and the official requirements of how players must conduct themselves. The former can be followed or ignored according to the instrumental or prudential judgments of the players; the latter must be observed or the game is not being played.[3]

Oakeshott suggests some other correspondences between the rules of a game and the character of law; for instance, rules of a game often require "some authoritative procedure" for settling disputes about whether a breach of the rules has occurred, and often some penalty is ascribed to recognized breaches of the rules (*OH*, 131). But while Oakeshott offers this discussion of the rules of a game as an analogy to understanding law, he recognizes it is merely "a glimpse . . . [into] the full character of association in terms of the rule of law" (128). While this glimpse of the rule of law through games offers insights, Oakeshott acknowledges that it has limitations as well. Most important, "The engagement [of playing a game] is intermittent and undertaken at will" (132). Once actually playing a game, participants may not randomly choose to follow the rules based on whether or not they likes the rules, but of course they can choose not to play the game at all, and thus be removed from their jurisdiction.

Furthermore, even when they choose to play a game, they are not always and forever playing that game; it begins, it ends, there are intervening periods when they are not playing, and participants might lose interest and no longer play the game. In these latter moments they are no longer bound to follow even the most surely authorized and clearly pronounced rules, simply because they have stopped playing, removing the obligation. Thus, in discussing the obligations of moral associations, finally, Oakeshott suggests that "they are not rules of a game the jurisdiction of which is settled in terms of an engagement (like a cricket match) which itself constitutes a relationship. . . . Here no game is being played and there is no common enterprise" (*OHC*, 128).

Because they are familiar and governed by rules, games offer some insights into the distinctive practice in which Oakeshott discusses rules as laws: civil association. A civil association is a type of moral association; that is, it is a practice in which those agents are related in what Oakeshott considers a moral relationship, an "association in terms of moral considerations" (*OHC*, 122). Among the many things that characterize a moral practice is that, unlike a game, it is not intermittent or related only to a single event or tournament; it is neither satisfied by the achievement of a substantive goal (winning or losing a game) nor is it avoided by stopping the game. Rather it is "a set of conditions to be subscribed to in all or any of an agents' [*sic*] actions or utterances . . . a continuous, not a once and for all enactment" (122).

A moral association binds the associates under its jurisdiction to follow its rules, and a moral practice may be characterized in terms of what constitutes "right" and "wrong" actions. But "moral association," Oakeshott claims, "is a relationship of human beings in terms of the mutual recognition of certain conditions which not only specify right and wrong conduct, but are prescriptions of obligations" (*OH*, 132). Having this understanding of a moral practice, and civil association as a moral practice, we can now return to Oakeshott's conception of law. Recall he wrote, "association begins and ends in recognition of rules. Such rules I shall call 'law'; and so that they may not be confused with the heterogeneous collection of rules and rule-like instructions, instruments, provisions, etc. which constitute those ambiguous associations we call states, I shall call them *lex*." He continues that passage by elaborating that law understood as lex identifies "rules which prescribe common responsibilities (and the counterpart of 'rights' to have responsibilities fulfilled) of agents and in terms of which they put by their characters as enterprisers and put by all that differentiates them from one another and recognize themselves as formal equals—*cives*" (*OHC*, 128). Law, then, understood in the frame of civil association and referred to as lex by Oakeshott, is that set or "system of rules," commonly acknowledged to have the authority to prescribe obligations to those who fall under its jurisdiction (129).

In bare outline we can now see the fundamental aspects of Oakeshott's conception of law or lex: law is a system of authoritative, noninstrumental rules. Yet this conception of law raises many further questions about the character of that authority, the creation of law, and its enforcement and adjudication.

AUTHORITY/AUTHENTICITY

Oakeshott has made it clear that the question of whether an agent is subject to a rule or law does not regard whether one approves of the law or not, but rather whether it is an authentic law and whether one is under its jurisdiction; that is, does it have authority over the agent? There is actually a self-reinforcing character to the authority of law and the binding of an association by means of common assent to the authority of laws, which all together he calls *respublica*. In the first instance, the shared acknowledgment of authority of law creates a civil community; yet the question regarding which rules have an authentic claim to obligate as law creates a central problem for all such associates. Thus Oakeshott claims, "Civil association is relationship in terms of the acknowledgement of authority of the manifold of laws and law-like conditions which constitutes *respublica*" (*OHC*, 158).

Yet he also suggests that "the first condition of this mode of association is for the associates to know what the laws are and to have a procedure, as little speculative as may be, for ascertaining their authenticity and that of the obligations they prescribe" (*OH*, 137–38). In *On Human Conduct*, Oakeshott emphasizes the self-justifying, almost self-defining character of authority of law. Authority is not a quality that attaches to civil association; rather "the authority of *respublica* is, then, a postulate of the civil condition" (*OHC*, 150). Authority here is a defining trait, and assent to the authority of the laws seems to be based on nothing other than the unexplained willingness of associates to assent to those laws. "And should it be asked how a manifold of rules . . . may be acknowledged to be authoritative, the answer is that authority is the only conceivable attribute it could indisputably be acknowledged to have" (154).

In *On Human Conduct*, Oakeshott refers to this explicitly as the "self-authenticating property of *respublica*," and he spends much more time dismissing various mistaken candidates for what might give lex authority than discussing what actually does so (150). The respublica as a system of acknowledged and authentic law does *not* rely on, among many things, "'will' of any sort," "common 'social purpose,'" "approved moral ideals, with a common good or general interest," "'scientific' information about the tendencies of human actions to promote the general happiness or about so-called 'laws of historical development'; finally, even "if a 'higher' law is postulated such that the authority of *respublica* is conditional upon correspondence with it, this 'law' must itself be shown to have *authority*: mere wisdom or rationality will not do" (152–53). In this list of denials, the actual source of the authority of the laws is evanescent. There is no substance to the authority of the laws, and nothing to check it against; this authority does not reflect anything. Authority is a product, and "the tie of civil association is continuous assent to this authority" (150).[4]

In the essay "The Rule of Law," however, Oakeshott does appear to provide a more explicit claim regarding the source of authority so that those subject to law are able "to know what the laws are and to have a procedure . . . for ascertaining their authenticity." The authority of laws Oakeshott directly locates in the recognition that "laws have been deliberately enacted or appropriated and may be deliberately altered or repealed by persons in regard to their occupation of an exclusively legislative office and following a recognized procedure" (*OH*, 138). Here Oakeshott potentially places the source of authority in the procedure for making law. What is an authentic law? Nothing other than the product of that person or body authorized to make it. "In short, the first condition of the rule of law is a 'sovereign' legislative office" (138).

Of course, this also may lend a "self-authenticating" character to the authority of laws as well. "Why is that rule an authoritative law for me?" an associate might ask. The answer here would seem to be "because a sovereign legislative office created it." But an associate might ask next, "Why is that office able to make rules obligatory and enforceable as law?" The answer again seems to be simply that is what the rule of law requires. "The rule of law, as a mode of human relationship, postulates an office with authority to make law," Oakeshott states, reflecting closely the language he earlier claimed about how authority is a "postulate of the civil condition" (*OH*, 139). It may be straightforward for an uncertain agent to address the question, "How am I to be certain whether or not that is a law I am obligated to obey?" by answering, "It is the product of a sovereign legislative office." But that answer merely displaces the inquiry to the question, "How am I to be certain that is the sovereign legislative office?"

This is not the place to focus the discussion on Oakeshott's ideas about authority for their own sake, yet authority is important here because Oakeshott's conception of law relies so heavily on it. Laws created by a state have the moral weight they do and the justifiable claim to be enforced because they are authentic; they are recognized to bear authority. We need not explore all of Oakeshott's philosophical ideas concerning authority to examine what Oakeshott says about it in relation to law.

Consider the claim that for a law to be seen as authoritative, it must be seen as "deliberately enacted or appropriated." This immediately precludes as law any form of rule claiming authority solely as a reflection of a customary or traditional way of acting, even if seen as obligatory and authoritative by agents submitted to it; instead, a law must have an explicit formal creation.

"Its authority cannot lie in its antiquity, in its current availability, or in the recognition of the desirability of what it prescribes" (*OH*, 138). The last in that list coheres with claims discussed earlier, since we have seen that rules' authority is never based, for Oakeshott, in their desirability; yet rejecting their "antiquity" and "current availability" as a source of authority is a bit harder to understand. Here the earlier discussion of games again shows its limitations. Oakeshott said there that "these rules [of games] have been made in a procedure of deliberation and may be changed or modified" (126). It may well be that some games' rules, like those of Olympic events, reflect just such features, and of course those rules are subject to constant deliberation and modification. Still, if the rules of other games such as poker or chess came into existence by any procedure, that procedure is long lost—except perhaps in the rarified world of tournament play—and it is surely not what gives them their authority. Furthermore, while one might find the rules for poker or chess in a book of rules for card games or board games, the publishers of such a book have neither created those rules nor could they amend them with any authority. Yet they are recognized as authoritative rules by card and game players because of their "antiquity" and "current availability."

What then of laws? Oakeshott again denies that the characteristics of "antiquity" or even "traditional acceptance" grant authority, and he asserts instead that not only must laws be deliberately enacted, but they must be the product of an "exclusively legislative office" (*OH*, 138). Only such a legislative office must be "recognized as the maker and custodian of the law"; however, "nor is it necessary for this office to be the sole *source* of law" (138). That is, whoever occupies a legislative office may look to habit, custom, and tradition and then reflect those in the deliberations of law and in that office's promulgations of law; yet the authority of those laws, Oakeshott claims, is not in their "traditional acceptance." Oakeshott does not deny that law may incorporate commonly held ideas or reflect traditions, but again, these are not what endow that law with authority: "where a law is to be recognized as *mos majorum* (or distinguished as a 'common law,' perhaps of unknown origin), it must be lodged within the custody of the legislative office" (138).

The authority of lex, then, has nothing to do with the character of the law, but with the procedures of its creation. That a law has been promulgated by a sovereign legislative office is all that is necessary for assuring any agent that it is an authentic and thus binding law. But are there no characteristics of the substance of a law that reflect on its authority or on the office that creates it? If a law does not reflect the sentiments and beliefs about proper conduct of the agents that it binds, can it still be authoritative? Oakeshott's answer to these question is that while these beliefs reflect significant qualities of a law, they speak not to its authority but to its justice or injustice or what Oakeshott refers to as its *jus* or *injus*.

Oakeshott rejects any discussion of the authority of lex in terms of the desirability of the conditions it imposes, yet he does see that qualities other than authority are also exhibited by law, and important among those is the character of jus. The challenge for a subject (or theorist) is not to confuse a judgment about whether a law is just or unjust with whether it is authentic. The authority of law is based in the properness of its enactment, whereas jus is a judgment about the character of law that is enacted, particularly what he calls its propriety. Oakeshott distinguishes the authority of lex from its jus thusly: "the *jus* and *injus* of law is composed of considerations in terms of which a law may be recognized, not merely as properly enacted, but as proper or improper to have been enacted; beliefs and opinions invoked in considering the propriety of the conditions prescribed in a particular law" (*OH*, 140–41). The quality of jus turns out to be the central characteristic in Oakeshott's understanding of the relationship of moral discourse and law, and importantly politics as well, as politics reflects deliberation about the desirability and propriety of the law.

Deliberation about what ought to be the law takes place on the terrain of jus as agents engage in debate over the appropriateness of various and particular conditions lex imposes and make suggestions for amendments. Here Oakeshott reviews and finds mostly unsatisfactory or confusing various endeavors to find "demonstrable, unambiguous, and universal criteria in terms of which to determine the *jus* of *lex*," preferring "an argumentative form of discourse in which to deliberate the matter" (*OH*, 143). Yet importantly, none of these debates relate directly to the authority of law. Certainly laws may be enacted that some agents might judge to be improper; such agents may indeed deem them to be injus because they do not reflect a "Law of Nature or of God" or "a set of inviolable human rights" or "unconditional human liberties" (142).

Yet centrally important for Oakeshott, such a judgment does not diminish the authority of that law if properly enacted. The jus of a law is then an important judgment about the character of a law, its desirability and its propriety; indeed it is in debate and differing judgments about just such qualities that Oakeshott identifies as the primary substance of politics. "In considering the engagement to deliberate the conditions prescribed in *respublica* in terms, not of their authority but of their desirability," Oakeshott maintains, "to imagine them different from what they are and to undertake or to resist their alteration, we are concerned with politics properly speaking. And that is how I shall use the word" (*OHC*, 163). However important to a respublica these deliberations, appraisals, debates, and disagreements about the jus of lex may be—and they appear to be the substance of creating and altering legislation—for Oakeshott, they are not to be confused with a judgment about whether a law is authentically binding or real.

LAW, COMMANDS, AND COURTS

Oakeshott cautions against confusing political deliberation with the consideration of a law's authority, and he also warns about other types of encounters with law or pronouncements about law that can create common misapprehensions about its fundamental character. We should, for instance, not confuse commands or authoritative judgments about particular actions with law itself. Both an authentic command and an authoritative interpretation (i.e., adjudication) of a particular action are given authority by law, but they are not themselves law. Oakeshott plainly states, "a rule is not, itself, a command" (*OH*, 129). Commands are directed to the specific actions of agents in particular situations, whereas a rule "relates indifferently and continuously to all who fall, or may in the future fall, within [its] jurisdiction"; furthermore, a command can be obeyed, and its requirements satisfied, but a rule or a law "is not used up in being invoked or subscribed to" (129).

Yet commands do have rulelike, and thus lawlike, features, in that if authoritative, their authenticity creates an obligation to be obeyed, and this obligation is not, of course, related to the approval or disapproval of the command. For Oakeshott commands are not exemplary of rules but dependent on them. "Commands are not themselves rules, but they postulate association in terms of rules" (*OH*, 130). Issuing a command may be described as ruling, but such ruling is different from a rule or its creation. Ruling understood as issuing commands is necessary in a civil association, and it shares in the same authority as lex, but the pronouncements of a command authorized by a rule are not lex. "To rule is to make utterances which require imagined and wished-for substantive responses from assignable persons in particular situations. It is not prescribing conditions to be acknowledged by unspecified (including yet unborn) persons in choosing what they shall do or say in unforeseen future contingent situations" (*OHC*, 141–42).

Commands are a necessary part of respublica, which requires the administering and enforcing of law that lex cannot do for itself. Lex can create only general obligations and address general conditions, whereas a ruling or a command takes these up "at the point where they are considerations not only to be subscribed to in acting but have become a requirement addressed to an ascertainable agent to act or desist. Generally speaking, this point is reached only when there has been a delinquency, putative or determined by an adjudicator" (144). A central element to a command is the need to attend to the particular, whereas lex must remain circumspectly and exclusively attentive to the general. What we see here then is the clear distinguishing of the offices of government, the executive from the legislative. This distinguishing element also attaches to the office of adjudication, for while it accomplishes a different task from ruling, likewise in contrast to legislating, it suffers from the same limitation as a command: it focuses on a particular agent or action.

Just as he rejects commands as law, Oakeshott thus also rejects the idea that adjudication produces law. Like with a command, a court in making a ruling does not produce rules that bind beyond the particular case before it, either on other agents or other courts. Again the office of adjudication is strictly separated from that of legislation. In doing so, Oakeshott clearly rejects the idea of the common law, and a court's role in calling on and maintaining it as a real law. In a passage cited earlier Oakeshott has already explicitly denied the common law as independent, authoritative, or true: "where a law is to be recognized as *mos majorum* (or distinguished as a 'common law,' perhaps of unknown origin), it must be lodged within the custody of the legislative office."

This judgment about common law, which essentially claims it is not law unless and until enacted by a legislative office, reflects a core holding of Oakeshott's view of law and jurisprudence. Already we have seen that law must be deliberately enacted, and its authority rests in that enactment by a legislative office, not in any other characteristics it might have. Then finally, the office that creates (or appropriates) such law must be "exclusively legislative." Oakeshott's rejection of common law and his emphasis on the "exclusive" character of the office that is "the maker and custodian of the law" announces a claim against courts as "makers" of law. This is not merely implicit in his emphasis on the exclusive legislative office; he also explicitly takes up the case against courts playing such a role in both *On Human Conduct* and "The Rule of Law." In each, while acknowledging the role for courts, Oakeshott circumscribes that role very narrowly, arguing not only that the legislative role must be understood differently from an adjudicative role, but that courts ought to have no participation in the making or authorizing of law.

In *On Human Conduct*, Oakeshott actually takes up the question of adjudication before discussing the proper role of the legislative office and the creation of law. There is no question that adjudication and the courts are of importance to Oakeshott's conception of respublica, with all the linked parts that create the rule of law. In regard to lex itself, adjudication is a very narrowly circumscribed authority. Lex for Oakeshott concerns only general conditions;

lex reflects rules that create general obligations, and particular agents need to account for these laws when making their choices and undertaking their actions. But whether or not a particular action by a given agent has or has not properly subscribed to such authoritative rules cannot be accounted for by the rules themselves or by a legislative office whose purview, again, must be general in scope. Law then needs "a means of settling uncertainties and disputes about the adequacy of contingent subscriptions" (131–32).

Oakeshott outlines a number of procedural elements to settling such disputes through a court (i.e., the identification of the parties of plaintiff, defendant, and judge), but primarily he calls for a type of judgment. This judgment is necessary because "relating a legal norm to a contingent situation" requires reflection in the context of uncertainty, and "*this* uncertainty is intrinsic to *lex* as the terms of human association" (*OHC*, 133). The task of dealing with the particular and the contingent cannot be done in advance but rather requires the complicated relaying between the general prescription and each new and unique instance. The legislator, of course, also exercises judgment and deliberation but does so while engaged in a different task than does the adjudicator. "Whereas a legislator deliberates the desirability of a change in some part of the existing system of general obligations . . . a court of law is concerned with a particular action or utterance in respect to conformity with the conditions of existing obligations" (*OH*, 144–45). Only a proper legislative office can create obligations and only a proper adjudicative office can evaluate unique occurrences.

Oakeshott emphasizes that not only are these different tasks with different conclusions, that is, the making or amending of a general rule or law and the rendering of a judgment in a particular case, but the reasoning and deliberation is, and should be kept, separate. "In seeking the meaning of a law in relation to a contingent occurrence this court cannot entertain speculations about the intentions of legislators or conjecture about how they would decide the case: to make law and to adjudicate a case are categorically different engagements" (*OH*, 146).

Oakeshott provides numerous other details regarding how a court should or should not make its decisions. For instance, he maintains that a court "may not regard itself as a custodian of a public policy or interest. . . . Nor may it consider a case in terms of so-called substantive 'rights.' . . . Nor again may the decisions of a court be attributed to what may be called the 'subjective opinion' of the adjudicator about what is 'just'" (*OH*, 146). And each of these restrictions reinforces the position that adjudicating says nothing about the law itself but rather is concerned only about the particular case. Judgments themselves, finally, bear the authority of law only as they apply

previously identified an understanding of the rule of law such as he
unded, Oakeshott suggests not only Hobbes and Hegel but also that
s in a slimmed-down version in the jurist Georg Jellinek. It hovers
eflections of many so-called 'positivist' modern jurists" (*OH*, 162).
at obscure German legal scholar might seem an odd choice to list
naries like Bodin, Hobbes, and Hegel, yet Jellinek, like Oakeshott,
conception of law that integrates a formal "positivist" view with an
o the traditional character of a particular society.

can Kelly suggests, Jellinek "developed a two-sided theory of the
he accepted . . . that positive law is a closed system and that private,
rights are essentially negative, self-limiting offerings or conces-
the state. Second, however, Jellinek attempted to offer an account
cepted the importance of real-world individuals and groups. In his
he state is a ruling legal entity, as well as political and associational,
e individuals under its reach are also its 'members.'"6 This "two-
ount at least attempts to reconcile these approaches, accepting a
racter and set of constraints to law but acknowledging that particu-
nities with unique individuals, with their given histories, provide
ce of those associations.

ott's writings on law, while not mimicking Jellinek, reflect some
this two-sided account. In the essays from the era of *Rationalism*
Oakeshott emphasizes the customary, traditional sides of politi-
nities; in *On Human Conduct* and "The Rule of Law" Oakeshott
e implications of ideal characters such as lex and he produces a
al account that reflects "'positivist' modern jurists." Early in *On*
nduct, Oakeshott suggests that theoretical understanding is based
ation, and "to identify . . . is to specify a *this* in terms of an ideal
omposed of characteristics; it is to understand a 'going-on' as a
rticularity and genericity. . . . And in every 'going-on' identified
ins an imperfectly resolved tension between particularity and
(*OHC*, 5). The themes regarding the "going-on" of law from the
s evince this "imperfectly resolved tension," reflecting two sides
d, as in Jellinek, if not unified.

ion in Oakeshott's discussion of law could have been an irresolv-
t, yet Oakeshott rescues it from this fate with his discussion of
local traditions of particular communities, the variations in legal
different courts, the arguments about what substantive elements
policies need legislative and executive pronouncements all have a
ics and the deliberations of what ought to be the law; meanwhile,
t create or undermine the authority of law, even while they suture

to each individual case on its own and not to any other case in the past or
future. Earlier decisions may provide insight to a given case because of "the
analogical force of the distinctions they invoked," but a court must not see
earlier decisions as binding: "it will not recognize them as precedents to be
followed" (146–47).

If a court were to recognize the judgment of an earlier court as an authoritative and binding restriction, then something other than lex would be creating obligations, and this, again, is a category error. "In respect of the rule of
law," Oakeshott holds, "the expression 'case law' is a solecism" (*OH*, 147).
Only a "'sovereign' legislative office" can create an authentic obligation;
the decisions of a court can create no such general obligation.5 Oakeshott's
strictly defined conception of such a legislative office then limits adjudication
as well and does so in a way that clarifies how different the idea of law in *On
Human Conduct* and "The Rule of Law" are from the speculative view of his
ideas about law that stem from the essays in *Rationalism in Politics*.

OAKESHOTT, COMMON LAW, AND LEGAL POSITIVISM

In the preceding pages I have highlighted a contrast. First, I reviewed an
Oakeshott whose works advocate the importance of traditional practices and
customs in politics; his approach there is wary of abstract approaches to
politics, those disconnected from or dismissive of a community's traditions
and customs, approaches that see law as something that can be rationally
developed on the engineer's chalkboard or applied as if from an architect's
blueprint. From this view, recognizable to anyone familiar with some of
Oakeshott's most famous works, I suggested a related understanding of law
that would reflect this traditional approach. This traditionalist view of law
would be less concerned with rationally distinguishing the various functions
or departments that inhere in the very idea of law and would rather be open to
the sometimes ramshackle ways in which particular peoples and communities develop institutions and laws to provide some stability and regularity to
their community's life. These laws would possess authority only to the extent
that they reflect customary beliefs and sentiments and only when those subject to the law experience it as reflecting those beliefs and sentiments. The
constable, the judge, the magistrate, or the member of a county council or
even Parliament or Congress, among many others, may each potentially play
a role as custodian of law.

While some may have the formal duty of creating law, the action of each
authoritative agent contributes to its ongoing re-creation. In a healthy polity,

law could then be adjusted to new conditions and changing customs and beliefs based on knowledge of what has been achieved; in an unhealthy or unlucky polity, much law may fall into desuetude when it is not amended to reflect new conditions or when legislators reject custom and tradition and try to create law anew. While nothing here mandates a role for judges, it would be easy to see them as uniquely positioned on an almost daily basis to assess how well the law and its subjects relate, to gain knowledge of how a particular case reflects previous cases and how previous decisions did or did not reflect settled understandings of justice, and to be aware of how their ruling contributes to ongoing expectations of what the law is. This is a roundabout way to suggest that the Oakeshott of his famous essays of the 1950s seems especially amenable to an understanding of the law deeply sympathetic to the common law. And it should be clear how far away this vision is from his formal writings on law.

When Oakeshott takes up the discussion of law in an essay such as "The Rule of Law" or in *On Human Conduct*, he explicitly rejects most of what I suggested was implicit in the earlier works. What gives law its authority? Neither its age nor its reflection of custom or common belief grants it authority, only that it is created in a formal legislative procedure. What makes such a formal procedure authentic? It takes place exclusively in an office of legislation explicitly authorized to make law—and nothing else. A law might be seen as just if it coheres with sentiments and beliefs about what the law should be, but this does not increase its authority; nor would a negative assessment of a law's justice undermine its claim to be authentic law. If the earlier, admittedly implicit, view of law reflects a common law view, then this explicit and formal view pronounced by Oakeshott may best be understood in the framework of positive law theory.

Might these two conflicting views be reconciled? Oakeshott seldom associates his views on any matter with a school of thought or intellectual forebears, although he is often willing to distance himself from such. Yet he does offer a clue to just such an association. In discussing the idea of a state organized according to his understanding of the rule of law, he suggests that such a "vision . . . was pioneered by Bodin and by Hobbes. In spite of some unnecessary nods in other directions, its character and presuppositions were fully explored by Hegel" (*OH*, 161).

While Oakeshott writes comparably little of Bodin, both Hobbes and Hegel share twin billing as the philosophers with the largest presence in his thought, and in some ways they represent the two sides of the contrast. Hobbes especially reflects the formal character of law emphasized in the discussions from *On Human Conduct* and "The Rule of Law." Among his many

encomia to Hobbes, Oakeshott writes, "The n account [of *societas*] is that of Hobbes; *Levia* integrity" (*OHC*, 252). One need not explor interpretation of Hobbes to see that the latter entirely dependent on a sovereign legislative no other source of law.

Hegel, however, reflects the emphasis on t *lich* foundations of civic order. In this Hegeli an external expression of the internal moral li suggests that for Hegel, *das Recht* may set tions or the satisfying of wants but not this a another mode of association . . . in which a ments of one another's satisfactions but *voll* 261). This expression of moral association th ciation that Oakeshott identifies with *societas* life of a community. In this mode, Oakeshott system of known, positive, self-authenticatin (*Gesetze*) enacted by human beings, accordin the system of law" (261). While there is no g this reading of Hegel's understanding of law may seem in conflict actually reinforce each

When the formal approach to law is contra important differences become apparent. Th rate and exclusive character of the office fo of law that comes from it; the latter has no r although it also need not exclude them. Yet the recognition that laws are human artifac authority and creation—each approach also God's law as what gives law its provenance o

Furthermore, while I have emphasized th and adjudication cannot be the foundation o ate law, Oakeshott clearly recognizes a place ancient usage as part of the deliberation co law. Here politics returns as an important el while political deliberation does not attend of law, it is what connects that form to the the various and sometimes conflicting ideal community.

Oakeshott offers some more hints for between the formalist and traditionalist acco

who hav
has prop
"it appea
over the
A some
with lun
develops
attention

As D
state. Fir
individu
sions fr
that also
writings
because
sided" a
formal c
lar com
the subs

Oake
aspects
in Polit
cal com
explores
more fc
Human
in ident
characte
unity of
there r
generic
two per
harmon

The
able co
politics.
practice
of diffe
role in
these de

particular laws to authoritative practices. Oakeshott still has some difficulty in resolving tensions, for instance, insisting in some places that there is no role for laws made by judges, while praising in others a judicial posture even in legislative activity. That these tensions remain, Oakeshott himself might not be surprised, for he himself offers a caution regarding the difficulty of understanding law: "The most difficult feature of the civil condition to identify and get into place has been law" (*OHC*, 181).

NOTES

1. Timothy Fuller writes, "The work was elaborated after World War II and completed probably in 1952" (*PFPS*, ix).

2. Richard Flathman suggests that "Oakeshott's is the best developed and most uncompromising version of a type of authority that insists on interpreting authority as an attribute of rules, procedures and offices." *The Practice of Political Authority* (Chicago: University of Chicago Press, 1980), 5.

3. Oakeshott's insistence on the noninstrumental character of *lex* has caused consternation among even sympathetic readers. John Gray, for instance, argues "that the contrast between moral and other considerations of a more instrumental sort is far from being as clear-cut as Oakeshott's account requires. No such contrast is postulated in Aristotle, and even with respect to our own moral life, our moral judgments often have an instrumental or consequential aspect inasmuch as they encompass estimates of the likely implications of our actions for the interest and well-being of ourselves and others." "Oakeshott on Law, Liberty, and Civil Association," in *Liberalisms: Essays in Political Philosophy* (New York: Routledge, 1989), 211–12.

4. Richard Friedman extends this stand by Oakeshott to the general issue of obligation, commenting that "Oakeshott, then, denies that the authority of law can be 'justified' by an appeal to something independent; it must float on itself; there is no 'solution' to the so-called problem of political obligation." "On the Authority of Law," *Ratio Juris* 2 (1989): 39.

5. Acknowledging that courts have no legislative duty, Charles Covell sees a different task for courts in Oakeshott than merely judging particular cases: "For Oakeshott, then, the courts were bound to preserve the systematic unity of law, not only by being bound to decide cases with reference to existing rules of law, but also because they were bound to justify their decisions through the amplification of the meanings ascribed to these rules in earlier cases." *The Defence of Natural Law: A Study of the Ideas of Law and Justice in the Writings of Lon L. Fuller, Michael Oakeshott, F. A. Hayek, Ronald Dworkin, and John Finnis* (London: St. Martin's Press, 1992), 84.

6. Duncan Kelly, "Revisiting the Rights of Man: Georg Jellinek on Rights and the State," *Law and History Review* 22, no. 3 (2004): para. 56, accessed December 14, 2009, http://www.history coopeative.org/journals/lhr/22.3/kelly.html.

COREY ABEL is an independent scholar who has taught at the University of Colorado, Colorado College, and the U.S. Air Force Academy. He is the co-editor of *The Intellectual Legacy of Michael Oakeshott* (Imprint Academic, 2005) and the editor of *The Meanings of Michael Oakeshott's Conservatism* (Imprint Academic, 2010).

DAVID BOUCHER is a professor of political philosophy and international relations, head of the School of European Studies, deputy pro vice-chancellor, and director of the Collingwood and British Idealism Centre at Cardiff University. His books include *The Social and Political Thought of R. G. Collingwood* (Cambridge University Press, 1989); *Political Theories of International Relations* (Oxford University Press, 1998); *British Idealism and Political Theory*, with Andrew Vincent (Edinburgh University Press, 2001); *The Limits of Ethics in International Relations* (Oxford University Press, 2009); and *British Idealism: A Guide for the Perplexed* (Continuum, 2011).

ELIZABETH COREY is an assistant professor of political science in the Honors College at Baylor University. Her major publication is *Michael Oakeshott on Religion, Aesthetics, and Politics* (University of Missouri Press, 2006).

ROBERT DEVIGNE is a professor of political science at Tufts University. He is the author of *Recasting Conservatism: Oakeshott, Strauss, and the Response to Postmodernism* (Yale University Press, 1994) and *Reforming Liberalism: J. S. Mill's Use of Ancient, Religious, Romantic, and Liberal Moralities* (Yale University Press, 2006), as well as numerous articles that have appeared in the *American Political Science Review, History of Political Thought, Political Studies, Political Theory*, and other journals and edited volumes.

PAUL FRANCO is a professor of government at Bowdoin College. His books include *The Political Philosophy of Michael Oakeshott* (Yale University Press, 1990); *Hegel's Philosophy of Freedom* (Yale University Press, 1999); *Michael Oakeshott: An Introduction* (Yale University Press, 2004); and *Nietzsche's Enlightenment: The Free-Spirit Trilogy of the Middle Period* (University of Chicago Press, 2011).

TIMOTHY FULLER is the Lloyd E. Worner Distinguished Service Professor at Colorado College, where he has also served as dean of faculty and acting president. He has published many essays and edited numerous books, including *Leading and Leadership* (University of Notre Dame Press, 2000); *The Voice of Liberal Learning: Michael Oakeshott on Education* (Yale University Press, 1989); *Michael Oakeshott on Religion, Politics, and the Moral Life* (Yale University Press, 1993); and *The Politics of Faith and the Politics of Scepticism* (Yale University Press, 1996).

STEVEN GERENCSER is an associate professor of political science at Indiana University, South Bend. He has published essays and book reviews on Michael Oakeshott and a monograph titled *The Skeptic's Oakeshott* (Palgrave, 2000). Besides his work on Oakeshott, Gerencser also writes about the legal status and public role of corporations in political life.

ROBERT GRANT is an emeritus professor of the history of ideas at the University of Glasgow. He is the author of *Oakeshott* (Claridge Press, 1990) and of two essay collections, *The Politics of Sex and Other Essays* (Macmillan, 2000) and *Imagining the Real* (Palgrave, 2003). His long-awaited biography of Michael Oakeshott is nearing completion.

NOEL MALCOLM is a senior research fellow of All Souls College, Oxford, and fellow of the British Academy. He is a general editor of the Clarendon edition of the Works of Thomas Hobbes (Oxford University Press) and has edited *Hobbes's Correspondence* (2 vols., 1994) and the English and Latin texts of *Leviathan* (3 vols., 2012) for that series. He is also the author of *Aspects of Hobbes* (Oxford University Press, 2002).

LESLIE MARSH is a research associate in the Dean's Office of the Medical School at the University of British Columbia. He is the founding editor of *EPISTEME* (Cambridge University Press) and the editor of *Hayek in Mind: Hayek's Philosophical Psychology* (Emerald, 2011).

KENNETH MCINTYRE is an assistant professor of political science at Sam Houston University. He is the author of *The Limits of Political Theory: Oakeshott's Philosophy of Civil Association* (Imprint Academic, 2004) and *Herbert Butterfield: History, Providence, and Skeptical Politics* (ISI Books, 2011).

KENNETH MINOGUE is an emeritus professor of political science at the London School of Economics. He has written extensively about liberalism and ideology; his latest book is *The Servile Mind: How Democracy Erodes the Moral Life* (Encounter Books, 2010).

NOËL O'SULLIVAN is a research professor of political philosophy at the University of Hull. He is author of *Conservatism* (Palgrave Macmillan, 1976); *Fascism* (Dent, 1984); *The Philosophy of Santayana* (Claridge Press, 1993); and *European Political Thought Since 1945* (Palgrave Macmillan, 2004). He has edited numerous books, most recently *The Concept of the Public Realm* (Routledge, 2010).

GEOFFREY THOMAS is a research fellow in the Department of Philosophy, Birkbeck College, University of London. He is the author of *The Moral Philosophy of T. H. Green* (Clarendon, 1987); *An Introduction to Ethics: Five Central Problems of Moral Judgement* (Duckworth, 1993); and *An Introduction to Political Philosophy* (Duckworth, 2000). His forthcoming book is on the philosophy of history (Duckworth).

MARTYN THOMPSON is an associate professor and chair of the Department of Political Science at Tulane University. He has published several articles on Michael Oakeshott and early modern political theory. He is currently finishing two books: *Logic and Method in the History of Political Thought* and *Johannes Althusius and the Origins of Political Science as a University Discipline*.

INDEX

Adorno, Theodor, 308
Aesop, 298
aesthetics, 4, 6, 9, 135, 151–72, 164–65. *See also* art, poetry
Althusius, Johannes, 201–5
Annan, Noel, 173
Anscombe, Elizabeth, 114
Aquinas, Saint Thomas, 105, 175, 177, 179, 207, 220
Arendt, Hannah, 147, 300
Aristotle, 3, 102, 103, 132, 151, 164, 168, 171n2, 198, 206, 207, 235, 287, 296, 299, 335n3
Arnold, Matthew, 9, 176, 178, 179, 182, 191, 192
art, 71, 78, 84, 118n15, 140, 153, 159, 161, 162–64, 165, 168, 170. *See also* aesthetics, poetry
Attlee, Clement, 3
Aubrey, John, 91n11
Augustine, Saint, 20, 23, 40n22, 96, 139, 145, 146, 148
Austin, J. L. 7, 66, 72, 80, 85, 90, 93n34
authority, 11, 218–19, 222, 225, 226, 228, 275–77, 279, 292, 295–300, 304, 306, 312, 318, 321, 323–34, 335n2, 335n4
Ayer, A. J., 50, 66

Bacon, Sir Francis, 220, 273, 284, 295
Bentham, Jeremy, 3, 66, 278, 317
Berkeley, George, 49, 53, 54, 236
Berlin, Isaiah, 44n58
Blackstone, William, 317
Blake, William, 145
Blanshard, Brand, 48, 49, 55, 56, 57, 62
Bloom, Allan, 193n7
Bodin, Jean, 202, 273, 332, 334
Bosanquet, Bernard, 72, 100, 115, 292
Boucher, David, 306
Boyd, Richard, 261
Boyle, Robert, 236
Bradley, F. H., 2, 48, 51–59, 62, 64, 65, 66, 72, 76, 97, 100, 101, 115, 271
Burgh, W. G. de, 103
Burke, Edmund, 3, 4, 11, 237, 244, 260, 271, 280, 281, 284, 285
    and Oakeshott, 268–71, 275, 278–79, 288
    Strauss's assessment of, 287–88

Burton, Kate (second wife of Michael Oakeshott), 30, 34, 42n43, 42n45, 43nn46–47, 43nn53–54, 44n59
Butler, Bishop Joseph, 262
Butterfield, Herbert, 116, 232

Caird, Edward, 48, 54
Calvin, John, 205, 294
Cambridge University, 15, 48, 51, 55
    and idealism, 50–53
    study of politics at, 291-92
Capitant, René, 224–25
Carritt, E.F, 50
Cervantes, Miguel de, 151, 158, 166, 170, 170n1
Christianity, 16, 17, 23, 24, 131, 132, 174
Churchill, Winston, 286
Cicero, 296
civil association, 5, 11, 128, 164, 170, 227, 290–311
    and authority, 324
    criticisms of, 305–7
    and enterprise association, 258, 275, 294–96
    future of, 307–10
    and Hobbes, 223, 227–30, 273
    and identity politics, 308–9
    and law, 274–75, 276
    and liberalism, 303–5
    and minimal state, 302–3
    as moral association, 323
    and respublica, 296–69
    rules in, 299–300
Coats, Wendell John, Jr., 48
cognitive science, 11, 248, 253
Coke, Sir Edward, 219, 317
Coleridge, Samuel, 145
collectivism, 242
Collingwood, R. G, 2, 10, 48, 49-50, 55, 64, 72, 76, 91n14, 92n23, 118n15, 224
    criticism of Oakeshott, 92n19
communism, 295
conservatism, 4, 11, 268–89
    and liberalism, 261, 278
    neo-, 269
constructivism, 249, 253, 254
contingency, 122, 125, 147

conversation, 4, 6, 9, 84, 137, 155, 172n19,
    182, 189
  analogy for university, 173, 178–79, 181
  and philosophy, 61–66
Cook Wilson, John, 66, 73
Copernicus, Nicolaus, 53
Corey, Elizabeth Campbell, 171n6
Covell, Charles, 335n5
Croce, Benedetto, 2, 72, 76, 91n15
Cromwell, Oliver, 236
culture, 175, 178, 183, 188–89, 191. *See also*
    conversation, education

Davidson, Donald, 115
death, 121, 122, 124, 125. *See also* mortality
democracy, 11, 85, 303, 307–8
Descartes, René, 11, 50, 53, 105, 220, 248,
    249, 250, 251, 252, 254
Dewey, John, 189
Dilthey, Wilhelm, 55, 64, 94n40, 103, 115,
    184, 248
Donatello, 158

education, 1, 6, 9, 137, 138, 173–94
  fragmentation of, 173, 177, 179, 192
  and specialization, 173, 174, 183, 192
  vocational versus university, 198
Eliot, George (Mary Anne Evans), 108
Eliot, T. S., 158, 171n14, 174, 178, 179, 191, 192
Enlightenment, 132, 268, 284, 285
Epicurus, 206, 207
epistemology, 6, 47, 49, 54, 53, 55, 58, 59, 72,
    80, 81, 97, 101, 104, 249, 251, 273. *See
    also* knowledge
  analytic, 250
  idealist, 8
  and sociology, 251
Eucken, Rudolph, 52
Evremond, Saint Charles de, 236
existentialism, 90
experience, 2, 3, 4, 6, 7, 8, 9, 49, 52–66,
    70–94, 85, 86, 98, 99–102, 107, 116. *See
    also* modality

Filmer, Robert, 207
Flathman, Richard, 335n1
Fontenelle, Bernard le Bovier de, 236
Foster, Michael, 168
Franco, Paul, 1, 61, 63, 90n3, 164, 172n24
Frankfurt School, 308
Frayn, Michael, 160, 172n27
freedom, 64, 123, 126, 129, 227, 24–22,
    255–61, 263, 265n37, 273, 283, 285, 287
  and authority, 11, 291, 306
  and civil association, 293, 295, 296, 291,
    299, 302, 304, 306, 308, 309

inherent in agency, 53, 121
French Revolution, 287, 288
Fricker, Joyce (first wife of Michael
    Oakeshott), 17, 18, 20, 21–25, 28, 30, 34,
    39n11, 44n62
Friedman, Milton, 11, 303
Fuller, Timothy, 235, 246

Gadamer, Hans-Georg, 9, 72, 90, 91n13, 152,
    164
Gale, Patricia, 33
Galileo, 206
Gasset, José Ortega y, 175, 179, 191, 309
Gerencser, Steven, 58, 59, 61, 63, 93n33
Gibson, W. R. Boyce, 52
gnosticism, 147
Godolphin, Sydney, 297
Goethe, Johann Wolfgang von, 182
government, 129, 131, 147, 222, 223, 232–33,
    235, 237, 240, 244, 268, 274, 277–81,
    313, 329
  limited, 4, 5, 273, 307
Grant, Robert, 1, 61, 172n22
Gray, John, 254, 335n3
Green, T. H., 48, 72, 292
Greenleaf, W. H., 48, 90n3, 171n17
Griffith, Guy, 3, 26, 30, 42n45

Habermas, Jürgen, 290
Haegler, Céline (Mrs. Romilly Jenkins),
    21–30, 37, 39n12, 40n26, 41n33, 42n39,
    44n62
Haldane, R. B., 48
Halifax, first Marquess of (George Savile),
    36, 236
Hart, Jenifer (Mrs. H. L. A.), 31, 34
Havel, Václav, 11, 290, 302
Hayek, Friedrich, 3, 11, 72, 90, 290, 303
  and civil association, 257
  and conservatism, 261, 266n55
  and Oakeshott, 248–67
  and planning, 258–59
Hegel, G. W. F., 2, 39n7, 52–56, 64–66, 72,
    76, 91n12, 92n23, 93n29, 96, 103, 115,
    118n15, 123, 164, 165, 182, 188, 200,
    208–9, 216n46, 222, 234, 237, 271, 273,
    278, 280, 284, 292, 307, 310, 312
  and law, 332–34
Heidegger, Martin, 72, 90, 152, 164, 252, 285,
    308
Hippocrates, 140
historicism, 185, 188, 283, 285, 288
history, 1, 2, 6, 7, 8, 9, 11, 51, 54, 59, 61, 64,
    65, 71, 74, 78, 79, 89, 93n35, 129, 130,
    131, 135, 143, 197–216
  and art or poetry, 151, 152, 160, 163–64, 168

as construction, 95, 98, 101–10, 116
of philosophy, 64
philosophy of, 95–119, 197, 198, 199, 200, 204, 205
of political thought, 197–216
Hobbes, Thomas, 3, 5, 6, 8,11, 38, 40n20, 52–53, 91n11, 120, 122, 126, 128, 129, 131, 144, 164, 197, 200, 201, 205–8, 209, 210–11, 216n46, 273, 278, 281, 283, 287, 296, 297, 305, 307, 312, 314, 334
  and civil association, 223, 227-30, 273
  and individualism, 218, 224–26
  and law, 332–34
  and liberalism, 224–26
  Leviathan, 3, 10, 40n25, 54, 127
  nominalism of, 221
  Oakeshott's reading of, 217–31
  and politics of skepticism, 237
  and rationalism, 223, 227-30
  views on reason, 220–21
Hobhouse, L. T., 292
Hooker, Richard, 207, 220
Horkheimer, Max, 308
Huizinga, Johan, 309
Humboldt, Wilhelm von, 182
Hume, David, 8, 100, 115, 128, 226, 236, 237, 254, 260, 278

idealism, 2, 7, 11, 47–69, 72, 76, 78, 91n6, 91n8, 92n26, 93n33, 99, 115, 100, 118n15, 153
  and art, 162
  British, 2, 7, 48, 50–58, 65, 91n8, 222, 292–93, 312
  and political philosophy, 292–93
  See also philosophy
ideology, 3, 10, 134, 137
individualism, individuality, 4, 51, 52, 53, 249, 250, 255, 263. *See also* Hobbes
Ireton, Henry, 236

James, William, 98
Jaspers, Karl, 193n8
Jellinek, Georg, 11, 334
Joachim, Harold, 48, 49, 56, 57, 58, 104
Jones, Henry, 48, 49, 54, 64

Kane, Sarah, 160
Kant, Immanuel, 8, 53, 76, 101, 105, 128–31, 254
Keats, John, 160
Kelly, Duncan, 334
Kelsen, Hans, 300
Keynes, John Maynard, 262
Kirk, Russell, 4
knowledge, 2, 6, 248, 250, 252, 262

absolute, 47, 50, 58, 59
practical, 80, 81, 93n30
theory of, 2, 7
See also epistemology, truth
Kronman, Anthony, 193n7

Labor Government, 3
Lamont, William Dawson, 48
Laslett, Peter, 207
law, 4, 5, 6, 11, 228, 235–39, 276–78, 312–35
  and civil association, 297–98, 319, 323, 325–26
  common, 331, 332
  and custom, 325–26, 331–32
  natural, 55
  and politics, 334–35
  and rationalism, 315
  rule of, 277
Lawrence, D. H., 20, 21, 37, 40n23
Leavis, F. R., 9, 175–76, 178, 179, 190, 191, 192
Letwin, Shirley, 44n60
Lewis, C. S., 158
liberalism, 129, 228, 249, 256, 261
  and civil association, 298, 303–5
  and conservatism, 261, 278
  and Oakeshott, 275–76
Lieb, Irwin C., 98
Lobel, Arnold, 134
Locke, John, 3, 8, 66, 128, 200, 205–6, 207, 216n46, 236, 237, 254, 276, 284, 285, 297
LSE (London School of Economics and Political Science), 16, 32
  History of Political Thought Seminar, 4–5, 60, 199, 214n10

Machiavelli, Niccolò, 129, 200, 283, 284, 285, 287
Maitland, F. W., 116, 237
Mandeville, Bernard de, 236
Manet, Édouard, 163
Mannheim, Karl, 174, 254
Marx, Karl, 131, 234, 244, 254, 273, 294
McTaggart, J. M. E., 48, 51, 53, 55, 56, 65, 97
metaphysics, 4, 6, 47, 48, 51, 54, 55, 62, 76, 80, 93n36, 97, 101, 104, 114
Metz, Rudolph, 91n8
Mill, J. S., 128, 297, 300, 304
Milton, John, 207
mind
  philosophy of, 248–55
  situated theory of, 249–50, 253
  social nature of, 248, 262
Mink, Louis O., 93n35
Mitchell, William, 48

Moberly, Sir Walter, 174–81, 191, 192, 193n7
modality, 7, 9, 53, 58, 60, 61, 62, 65, 66, 69, 70–94, 103, 104, 115, 116, 134, 135, 156, 170. *See also* experience
modernity, 11, 54, 120–33, 136, 137, 146, 233, 236, 239, 240, 241, 283, 286–87
critique of, 147
Montaigne, Michel de, 124, 144, 237, 278
Montesquieu, Baron de (Charles de Secondat), 237, 273, 285, 296
Moore, G. E., 49, 50, 56, 66, 72, 73, 106
Moore, Henry, 85
Moot, the, 174
morality, 9, 11, 126–33, 134, 135, 136, 137, 139, 143, 145, 147, 291
of individual, 5, 272–74, 278
and law, 6
and religion, 51
Morrison, Ashley, 261
mortality, 124, 140. *See also* death
Mouffe, Chantal, 304, 305, 306
Muirhead, John Henry, 48
Murdoch, Iris, 31, 33–34
Mure, G. R. G., 57

Nardin, Terry, 58, 90n3
Nazism, 295
Needham, Joseph, 18
Nettleship, R. L., 48
Newman, John Henry, 9, 173, 174, 175, 178, 179, 180, 182, 191, 192, 193n14
Nietzsche, Friedrich, 6, 9, 21, 24, 36, 191–92, 280, 285, 308
nihilism, 288
Nijinsky, Vaslav, 159
Nimrod, 137
Nozick, Robert, 11, 290, 302

Oakeshott, Sebastian, 31
Oakeshott, Simon, 16, 24, 25, 31, 34, 39n11, 43n48
Oakeshott, Michael
biography of, 1–6
love life of, 6, 15–44
Works:
"The Activity of Being an Historian," 60, 96, 93n31, 111, 153, 155, 162, 166
"Authority of the State," 222
"On Being Conservative," 4, 277, 314, 318
"On the Civil Condition," 319
"The Concept of a Philosophical Jurisprudence," 120, 293, 312
The Concept of a Philosophical Jurisprudence, 2, 11, 41n35, 55, 60, 92n24, 93n28, 141, 145, 206, 207, 292–93, 313

"The Definition of a University," 173, 181, 184, 186
"Education: the Engagement and Its Frustration," 173, 187, 189
"An Essay on the Relations of Philosophy, Poetry, and Reality," 141, 165
Experience and Its Modes, 2, 7, 8, 20, 47, 50, 52–63, 70-79, 80–83, 85–86, 90, 91n8, 91n16, 92n19, 92nn24–25, 93n31, 94n41, 96–99, 101–4, 108, 115–16, 120–21, 124–26, 135, 141, 144, 152–55, 165–67, 171n3, 171n18, 264n5, 312–13
A Guide to the Classics, 3
On History and Other Essays, 5, 7, 60, 89, 96, 98, 108–10, 112, 137, 167, 199–204, 228, 275, 276, 282, 293, 308–9, 321–30, 334
Hobbes on Civil Association, 5, 54–56, 60, 217, 222–23
On Human Conduct, 5, 7, 11, 40n22, 44n60, 55, 59–60, 62–63, 70–72, 85–90, 91n5, 92n17, 93n36, 94n39, 94n41, 96, 109, 115–16, 120, 136, 141–48, 151, 164, 167, 173, 187–88, 240, 252, 262, 264n5, 273–82, 293–97, 301, 303–5, 313, 319–24, 327–35
"The Idea of a University," 173, 174, 178
"Introduction to *Leviathan*," 3, 120, 220, 225, 229
"Learning and Teaching," 173, 181, 184–86
Lectures in the History of Political Thought, 136, 197–99, 206, 250, 295
"A Place of Learning," 89, 173, 187-90
"The Masses in Representative Democracy," 5
"The Moral Life in the Writings of Thomas Hobbes," 217
Morality and the Politics in Modern Europe, 5, 278
"Political Education," 3, 314, 316, 318
The Politics of Faith and the Politics of Scepticism, 10, 120, 131, 197, 223, 232–47, 278, 281–82, 284, 318–19
"Rational Conduct," 80
"Rationalism in Politics," 80, 134, 136, 147, 218, 220, 223, 227, 233, 314, 318
Rationalism and Politics and Other Essays, 3–4, 63, 83–85, 92nn24–25, 93nn30–32, 97, 103, 106, 113–14, 116, 120, 128, 132, 136, 137, 139, 145–46, 149, 152–70, 171n17, 172n19, 172n21, 182–84, 217–20, 233–34, 250–63, 264n5, 270–72, 278, 281–82, 284, 286, 314–18, 331, 334
Religion, Politics, and the Moral Life, 135, 138, 140, 144, 212, 222, 262, 282, 286

"Religion and the Moral Life," 51
"Religion and the World," 139
"The Rule of Law," 6, 11, 313, 319–20, 325,
    329, 331, 332, 334
*The Social and Political Doctrines of
    Contemporary Europe*, 226
"The Study of 'Politics' in a University,"
    165, 173, 181–86
"Talking Politics," 261
"The Tower of Babel," 8, 308, 309
"The Universities," 173, 174, 179, 187
The Vocabulary of a Modern European State,
    103, 93n29, 94n40, 203, 206, 212, 294
"The Voice of Liberal Learning," 6
The Voice of Liberal Learning, 128, 132, 139,
    145, 173–94, 251, 259, 262
"The Voice of Poetry in the Conversation
    of Mankind," 4, 9, 58, 61–62, 70–71,
    79–86, 90, 93n31, 132, 151–55, 162, 166,
    170, 171n3, 171n15, 171n18, 172n20, 181
What is History? And Other Essays, 62, 96,
    116, 142, 187, 232, 261, 291–92
"Work and Play," 166, 259
O'Sullivan, Luke, 164, 166

Pascal, Blaise, 165, 168, 237, 278
Pelagius, 136, 139, 142
philosophy, 2–3, 7, 8, 10, 11, 70–94, 103, 95,
    118n15, 137, 141
    analytic, 90, 91n4, 92n26
    Anglo-American, 114
    Hobbes's views of, 210–11
    and idealism, 47–69
    and ideology, 213
    and practice, 70–94, 141
    and religion, 141
    See also idealism
Picasso, Pablo, 157
Pieper, Joseph, 148
Plaat, June (née Hooper), 33, 34, 35, 43n51,
    43nn53–54, 44n62
planning, 3, 258–59
Plato, 110, 132, 144, 148, 154, 158, 167, 168,
    171n10, 171n15, 172n19, 198, 206, 250,
    279, 280, 286
    Strauss's reading of, 283–84
Pocock, John, 213
Podoksik, Efraim, 48
poetry, 8, 9, 54, 61, 80, 82, 93nn31–32,
    134–36, 142, 145–72
    and contemplation, 146, 153–54
    and delight, 149, 157, 159, 162–64, 168–69
    and history, 151, 152, 160, 163–64, 168
    play, 166, 167
    and politics, 169

and practice, 168–69
    voice of, 8, 132, 133
    See also aesthetics, art
Polanyi, Michael, 72, 80, 90, 92–93n26,
    93n29
political philosophy, 1–2, 6, 9,11, 56, 70
    history of 3, 9, 54, 197–216
    See also philosophy
political science, 290, 291–93
politics, 3, 6, 70, 132, 149, 268, 281, 283–88,
    299
    English tradition of, 269, 272
    of faith and skepticism, 8, 10, 130, 131,
        232–47
    and history, 282, 288
    study of at university, 198
Popper, Sir Karl, 102, 223, 261, 290
positivism, 1, 57, 72, 90
    logical, 50, 55, 57, 92–93n26
    See also scientism
postmodernism, 132
Pound, Ezra, 85
practical experience, 2, 8, 9, 53, 70–74,
    78–82, 85, 88–90, 91n12, 92n23, 93n28,
    94nn40–41, 95, 96, 102, 103, 111, 113,
    116, 121–26, 135, 138, 154, 155, 168–69
    and philosophy, 65
    and religion, 143–45
pragmatism, 72, 90, 104, 123
Prichard, Harold Arthur, 73
Pringle-Pattinson, Andrew Seth, 48, 51, 52
progressivism, 123, 132
Pufendorf, Samuel von, 207
Putnam, Hilary, 50

Quine, W. V. O, 50

Ranke, Leopold von, 201
Rashdall, Hastings, 52
rationalism, 3, 10–11, 80, 92n21, 104, 105,
    116, 144, 146–49, 220, 223, 227 232–47,
    249, 252, 253–55, 269–72, 284, 288
    and Hobbes, 217–31
    and love, 20, 37
    and religion, 136, 140, 143–45
rationality, 105, 109, 105, 115
Rawls, John, 85, 91n4, 295, 300, 305
Raz, Joseph, 258
religion, 1–2, 4, 6, 8, 51, 54, 103, 118n15,
    134–50. *See also* Christianity
Rescher, Nicholas, 104
respublica, 293–99, 324, 327–29. *See also*
    civil association
Ricoeur, Paul, 9, 152, 157, 162, 164, 166
Ritchie, David George, 48

Rorty, Richard, 110
Rothko, Mark, 85, 157
Rousseau, Jean-Jacques, 55, 285, 305, 309
Royce, Josiah, 48
Ruhnken, David, 263
Russell, Bertrand, 49, 50, 66, 72, 73, 106
Ryle, Gilbert, 7, 50, 72, 80, 90, 91n10, 92n21,
    92–93n26, 93n28, 93n30, 114, 252

Schama, Simon, 157
Schiller, Friedrich, 182
Schleiermacher, Friedrich, 182
Schmitt, Carl, 10, 225–27, 285, 306
Schneider, Christel (third wife of Oakeshott),
    37, 44n64
science, 2, 8, 10, 51, 54, 56, 61, 62, 64, 71, 74,
    78, 79, 80, 85, 89, 92–93n26, 95, 96,
    102, 103, 111, 116, 118n15, 130, 132, 138,
    143, 155, 165, 172n21. See also positivism,
    scientism
scientism, 152, 92n26. See also positivism
self-interest, 127–30
Sertillanges, A. G., 143
Shaftesbury, Third Earl of (Anthony Ashley
    Cooper), 236
Shakespeare, William, 157, 163, 164
Shelley, Percy-Bysshe, 145
Sidney, Algernon, 207
Simons, Henry, 256
skepticism, 71, 73, 92–93n26, 93n33, 166,
    247n3
  and idealism, 58, 59
  politics of, 3, 8, 10, 130, 131, 232–47
Skinner, Quentin, 10, 197, 201, 205, 207–13,
    214n11
Smith, Adam, 8, 128, 260, 265n37
Smith, J. A., 48
Snow, C. P., 190
societas, 5, 11, 239–40
  and universitas, 273–75, 278, 280–83
Socrates, 110, 133, 148, 198
Sophocles, 160
Sorley, William Ritchie, 48, 50, 51, 67
Spengler, Oswald, 96
Spinoza, Baruch, 95, 102, 142, 220, 273,
    287
Spragens, Thomas, 217
Sprigge, Timothy, 100
St. George's School, 16, 39n7
Stebbing, L. Susan, 55, 91n9, 97
Stoicism, 220
Stoppard, Tom, 160, 163, 172n27
Strauss, Leo, 10, 11, 54, 147, 148, 217, 225–26,
    269, 279, 282–87

compared with Oakeshott, 269, 282–87
  on Burke, 287–88
Sullivan, Andrew, 4
Syme, Sir Ronald, 116

Tacitus, 263
Tarski, Alfred, 106
Taylor, Charles, 126
temporality, 120–26, 131, 133
theology, 140. See also religion
Thompson, Martyn, 171n11
Titian, 163
Tocqueville, Alexis de, 234, 303, 307
Tolstoy, Lee, 161
totalitarianism, 295
Tower of Babel, 135–39, 308, 309
tradition, 10, 51, 251–52, 260, 262, 270
  political, 3, 11
  and practical reasoning, 248
Trevor-Roper, Hugh, 110
truth, 64, 66, 76, 78, 92n25, 104, 106
  coherence theory of, 57–58, 60, 76, 104,
    108, 109

understanding, 54, 59, 60, 62, 63, 65, 71, 73,
    75, 77, 81–83, 86–89, 92n17, 94n39. See
    also knowledge
utilitarianism, 123

Valéry, Paul, 145
Varela, Francisco, 252
Vellacott, Elisabeth, 30
Vialatoux, Joseph, 224
Voegelin, Eric, 147, 148

Walsh, Mary (mother of Sebastian Oakeshott),
    31, 42n39, 44n57
Ward, Seth, 216n44
Watson, John, 48
Webb, Beatrice, 273
Webb, Sidney, 273
Weber, Max, 113, 308
Weldon, T. D., 66
will, 54, 55
Wilson, E. O., 85
Wittgenstein, Ludwig, 7, 66, 72, 80, 85, 90,
    91nn10–11, 93n34, 92–93n26, 106, 208,
    209, 210, 213
Wordsworth, William, 145
World War II, 3, 26, 31, 47, 58, 293

Xenophon, 286

Zeno, 206

to each individual case on its own and not to any other case in the past or future. Earlier decisions may provide insight to a given case because of "the analogical force of the distinctions they invoked," but a court must not see earlier decisions as binding: "it will not recognize them as precedents to be followed" (146–47).

If a court were to recognize the judgment of an earlier court as an authoritative and binding restriction, then something other than lex would be creating obligations, and this, again, is a category error. "In respect of the rule of law," Oakeshott holds, "the expression 'case law' is a solecism" (*OH*, 147). Only a "'sovereign' legislative office" can create an authentic obligation; the decisions of a court can create no such general obligation.[5] Oakeshott's strictly defined conception of such a legislative office then limits adjudication as well and does so in a way that clarifies how different the idea of law in *On Human Conduct* and "The Rule of Law" are from the speculative view of his ideas about law that stem from the essays in *Rationalism in Politics*.

OAKESHOTT, COMMON LAW, AND LEGAL POSITIVISM

In the preceding pages I have highlighted a contrast. First, I reviewed an Oakeshott whose works advocate the importance of traditional practices and customs in politics; his approach there is wary of abstract approaches to politics, those disconnected from or dismissive of a community's traditions and customs, approaches that see law as something that can be rationally developed on the engineer's chalkboard or applied as if from an architect's blueprint. From this view, recognizable to anyone familiar with some of Oakeshott's most famous works, I suggested a related understanding of law that would reflect this traditional approach. This traditionalist view of law would be less concerned with rationally distinguishing the various functions or departments that inhere in the very idea of law and would rather be open to the sometimes ramshackle ways in which particular peoples and communities develop institutions and laws to provide some stability and regularity to their community's life. These laws would possess authority only to the extent that they reflect customary beliefs and sentiments and only when those subject to the law experience it as reflecting those beliefs and sentiments. The constable, the judge, the magistrate, or the member of a county council or even Parliament or Congress, among many others, may each potentially play a role as custodian of law.

While some may have the formal duty of creating law, the action of each authoritative agent contributes to its ongoing re-creation. In a healthy polity, law could then be adjusted to new conditions and changing customs and beliefs based on knowledge of what has been achieved; in an unhealthy or unlucky polity, much law may fall into desuetude when it is not amended to reflect new conditions or when legislators reject custom and tradition and try to create law anew. While nothing here mandates a role for judges, it would be easy to see them as uniquely positioned on an almost daily basis to assess how well the law and its subjects relate, to gain knowledge of how a particular case reflects previous cases and how previous decisions did or did not reflect settled understandings of justice, and to be aware of how their ruling contributes to ongoing expectations of what the law is. This is a roundabout way to suggest that the Oakeshott of his famous essays of the 1950s seems especially amenable to an understanding of the law deeply sympathetic to the common law. And it should be clear how far away this vision is from his formal writings on law.

When Oakeshott takes up the discussion of law in an essay such as "The Rule of Law" or in *On Human Conduct*, he explicitly rejects most of what I suggested was implicit in the earlier works. What gives law its authority? Neither its age nor its reflection of custom or common belief grants it authority, only that it is created in a formal legislative procedure. What makes such a formal procedure authentic? It takes place exclusively in an office of legislation explicitly authorized to make law—and nothing else. A law might be seen as just if it coheres with sentiments and beliefs about what the law should be, but this does not increase its authority; nor would a negative assessment of a law's justice undermine its claim to be authentic law. If the earlier, admittedly implicit, view of law reflects a common law view, then this explicit and formal view pronounced by Oakeshott may best be understood in the framework of positive law theory.

Might these two conflicting views be reconciled? Oakeshott seldom associates his views on any matter with a school of thought or intellectual forebears, although he is often willing to distance himself from such. Yet he does offer a clue to just such an association. In discussing the idea of a state organized according to his understanding of the rule of law, he suggests that such a "vision . . . was pioneered by Bodin and by Hobbes. In spite of some unnecessary nods in other directions, its character and presuppositions were fully explored by Hegel" (*OH*, 161).

While Oakeshott writes comparably little of Bodin, both Hobbes and Hegel share twin billing as the philosophers with the largest presence in his thought, and in some ways they represent the two sides of the contrast. Hobbes especially reflects the formal character of law emphasized in the discussions from *On Human Conduct* and "The Rule of Law." Among his many encomia to Hobbes, Oakeshott writes, "The most intrepid and least equivocal account [of societas] is that of Hobbes; *Leviathan* is a work of art of superb integrity" (*OHC*, 252). One need not explore the subtleties of Oakeshott's interpretation of Hobbes to see that the latter holds an account of law that is entirely dependent on a sovereign legislative authority and for which there is no other source of law.

Hegel, however, reflects the emphasis on tradition and the customary, *sittlich* foundations of civic order. In this Hegelian view, the rule of law reflects an external expression of the internal moral life of the community. Oakeshott suggests that for Hegel, das Recht may set the terms of transactional relations or the satisfying of wants but not this alone; das Recht also "postulates another mode of association . . . in which associates are not merely instruments of one another's satisfactions but *vollendeten sittlichen Willen*" (*OHC*, 261). This expression of moral association then ties together the type of association that Oakeshott identifies with societas and it also expresses the ethical life of a community. In this mode, Oakeshott claims, "*Das Recht* here . . . is a system of known, positive, self-authenticating, non-instrumental rules of law (*Gesetze*) enacted by human beings, according to a procedure authorized in the system of law" (261). While there is no giving ground to common law, in this reading of Hegel's understanding of law, the two approaches to law that may seem in conflict actually reinforce each other.

When the formal approach to law is contrasted to the customary approach, important differences become apparent. The former focuses on the separate and exclusive character of the office for making law and the authority of law that comes from it; the latter has no need for such sharp distinctions, although it also need not exclude them. Yet together these approaches share the recognition that laws are human artifacts, relying on humans for their authority and creation—each approach also rejecting either natural law or God's law as what gives law its provenance or its authority.

Furthermore, while I have emphasized that in his later work common law and adjudication cannot be the foundation of law's authority and cannot create law, Oakeshott clearly recognizes a place for custom, tradition, and even ancient usage as part of the deliberation concerning what ought to be the law. Here politics returns as an important element in understanding law, for while political deliberation does not attend to the form and thus authority of law, it is what connects that form to the substantive content reflective of the various and sometimes conflicting ideals, beliefs, and desires of a given community.

Oakeshott offers some more hints for resolving the seeming tension between the formalist and traditionalist accounts of law. In discussing those who have previously identified an understanding of the rule of law such as he has propounded, Oakeshott suggests not only Hobbes and Hegel but also that "it appears in a slimmed-down version in the jurist Georg Jellinek. It hovers over the reflections of many so-called 'positivist' modern jurists" (*OH*, 162). A somewhat obscure German legal scholar might seem an odd choice to list with luminaries like Bodin, Hobbes, and Hegel, yet Jellinek, like Oakeshott, develops a conception of law that integrates a formal "positivist" view with an attention to the traditional character of a particular society.

As Duncan Kelly suggests, Jellinek "developed a two-sided theory of the state. First, he accepted . . . that positive law is a closed system and that private, individual rights are essentially negative, self-limiting offerings or conces- sions from the state. Second, however, Jellinek attempted to offer an account that also accepted the importance of real-world individuals and groups. In his writings, the state is a ruling legal entity, as well as political and associational, because the individuals under its reach are also its 'members.'"[6] This "two- sided" account at least attempts to reconcile these approaches, accepting a formal character and set of constraints to law but acknowledging that particu- lar communities with unique individuals, with their given histories, provide the substance of those associations.

Oakeshott's writings on law, while not mimicking Jellinek, reflect some aspects of this two-sided account. In the essays from the era of *Rationalism in Politics* Oakeshott emphasizes the customary, traditional sides of politi- cal communities; in *On Human Conduct* and "The Rule of Law" Oakeshott explores the implications of ideal characters such as lex and he produces a more formal account that reflects "'positivist' modern jurists." Early in *On Human Conduct*, Oakeshott suggests that theoretical understanding is based in identification, and "to identify . . . is to specify a *this* in terms of an ideal character composed of characteristics; it is to understand a 'going-on' as a unity of particularity and genericity. . . . And in every 'going-on' identified there remains an imperfectly resolved tension between particularity and genericity" (*OHC*, 5). The themes regarding the "going-on" of law from the two periods evince this "imperfectly resolved tension," reflecting two sides harmonized, as in Jellinek, if not unified.

The tension in Oakeshott's discussion of law could have been an irresolv- able conflict, yet Oakeshott rescues it from this fate with his discussion of politics. The local traditions of particular communities, the variations in legal practices of different courts, the arguments about what substantive elements of different policies need legislative and executive pronouncements all have a role in politics and the deliberations of what ought to be the law; meanwhile, these do not create or undermine the authority of law, even while they suture